TRUST US, WE'RE EXPERTS!

ALSO BY SHELDON RAMPTON AND JOHN STAUBER

Toxic Sludge Is Good for You!
Mad Cow U.S.A.

TRUST US,

How Industry Manipulates Science and Gambles with Your Future

WE'RE EXPERTS!

Sheldon Rampton and John Stauber

JEREMY P. TARCHER / PUTNAM *a member of*
Penguin Putnam Inc. *New York*

Most Tarcher/Putnam books are available at special quantity discounts for bulk purchases for sales promotions, premiums, fund-raising, and educational needs. Special books or book excerpts also can be created to fit specific needs. For details, write Putnam Special Markets, 375 Hudson Street, New York, NY 10014.

Jeremy P. Tarcher/Putnam
a member of
Penguin Putnam Inc.
375 Hudson Street
New York, NY 10014
www.penguinputnam.com

First trade paperback edition 2002

The Library of Congress catalogued the hardcover edition as follows:

Rampton, Sheldon, date.
    Trust us, we're experts!: how industry manipulates science and gambles with your
future / by Sheldon Rampton and John Stauber.
        p.   cm.
Includes index.
ISBN 1-58542-059-X
    1. Industrial publicity—Corrupt practices—United States.
2. Corporations—Public relations—Corrupt practices—
United States.   3. Public relations consultants—Corrupt
practices—United States.   4. Public relations firms—
Corrupt practices—United States.   5. Expertise—Corrupt
practices—United States.   6. Endorsements in
advertising—Corrupt practices—United States.
7. Deceptive advertising—United States.   8. Risk
perception—United States.   9. Consumer protection—
United States.   10. Business ethics—United States.
I. Stauber, John.   II. Title.
HD59.6.U6 R35   2001   00-062920
659.2—dc21

ISBN 1-58542-139-1 (paperback)

Printed in the United States of America

10   9

This book is printed on acid-free paper. ♾

Book design by Lee Fukui
Cover art by Dan Perkins

ACKNOWLEDGMENTS

Thanks to the Center for Media and Democracy, for whom we wrote this book and love working, and thanks to our CM & D colleagues Margo Robb and Laura Miller. The Center extends its appreciation to the staff and board members of the following nonprofit foundations whose financial support helped make this work possible: The Jenifer Altman Foundation, The Bydale Foundation, Carolyn Foundation, Changing Horizons Charitable Trust, Deer Creek Foundation, DJB Foundation, Foundation for Deep Ecology, Richard & Rhoda Goldman Fund, Grodzins Fund, HKH Foundation, The Litowitz Foundation, Jessie Smith Noyes Foundation, Inc., Rockwood Fund, Inc., The Stern Family Fund, The Florence and John Schumann Foundation, Turner Foundation, and The Winslow Foundation.

Many individuals provided us with friendship, support, ideas, criticisms, and inspiration over the years spent discussing, researching, and writing *Trust Us, We're Experts*. In particular we thank Grant Abert, Dan Barry, Sharon Beder, Ellen and Eddy Bikales, Charlie Cray, Chris Crosby, Harriett M. Crosby, Ronnie Cummins, Carol Bernstein Ferry, Sharon Holland Force, Michele Gale-Sinex, Jonathan Frieman, Ross Gelbspan, Wade Greene, Wendy Gordon, Michael Hansen, Emily Headen, Linda Jameson, David King, Eric Koli, Sheldon Krimsky, Donna Balkan Litowitz, Sue and Art Lloyd, Chris Manthey, Gerald Markowitz, Camy Matthay, Kevin McCauley, Bob McChesney, Joe Mendelson, Dave Merritt, Alida Messinger, Margaret Mellon, Peter Montague, Tim Nelson, Dan Perkins, Tom Pringle, Arpad Pustzai, Carolyn Raffensperger, Scott Robbe, Abby Rockefeller, David Rosner, Debra Schwarze, Judith Siers, Louis Slesin, Paul Alan Smith, Sandra Steingraber, Virginia Waddick, Nancy Ward, Denise Wilson, John Woodmansee, and Winifred Woodmansee.

We especially welcome the contributions of three gifted investigative journalists who allowed us to incorporate into the text some of their research and writing that originally appeared in the quarterly journal *PR Watch*: Joel Bleifuss for parts of Chapter 3, "Deciding What You'll Swallow"; Bob Burton for parts of Chapter 5, "Packaging The Beast," as well as Chapter 10, "Global Warming Is Good for You"; and Karen Charman for parts of Chapter 7, "Attack of the Killer Potatoes."

John extends special appreciation to his parents, John H. and Jean M. Stauber, and to his wife, Laura—thanks for your endless faith, love, and patience. Sheldon thanks Dr. Carol Bernstein Levy and family members Renee Rampton, Debi Blanco, and Kenny Rampton for providing inspiration and examples.

Finally, we give our deep appreciation to some people without whom this book would not be: our insightful and patient editor, "Hurricane" Mitch Horowitz; our agent and sage adviser, Tom Grady; our trusting publisher, Joel Fotinos; Ken J. Siman and Allison Sobel of Jeremy P. Tarcher; and John's longtime friend and mentor, Jeremy Rifkin.

CONTENTS

The Smell Test

> This world is run by people who know how
> to do things. They know how things work.
> They are equipped. Up there, there's a layer
> of people who run everything. But we—
> we're just peasants. We don't understand
> what's going on, and we can't do anything.
>
> —Doris Lessing, in *The Good Terrorist*

This book really began while we were researching our first book together, *Toxic Sludge Is Good for You!* In the course of that research, we came across a striking passage in a public relations strategy document, published by the U.S. Environmental Protection Agency, for marketing sewage sludge as farm fertilizer. The document noted that there was a "major public acceptance barrier" to this practice—namely, "the widely held perception of sewage sludge as malodorous, disease causing or otherwise repulsive. . . . There is an irrational component to public attitudes about sludge which means that public education will not be entirely successful."

In other words, people are irrational because they think sewage stinks.

We found a strikingly similar passage while writing our next book, *Mad Cow U.S.A.*, as we researched some of the unsavory practices used by the meat industry to dispose of *its* waste. One practice, called "rendering," involves grinding up and cooking inedible animal parts and the corpses of diseased animals, which often arrive at the rendering plant in advanced stages of decomposition. It's a smelly process, as bad as or worse than what goes on in sewage treatment plants. Once again, we were struck by the way the industry dealt with odor complaints. Renderers had gone so far as to devise an instrument called a "scentometer"—a "small rectangular chamber that contains two sniffing tubes for insertion into the nostrils."

Using the tubes, a rendering plant manager could inhale filtered, theoretically odor-free air to get a sense of how it compared with "ambient air odors." Based on this pseudoscientific testing system, the industry had managed to convince itself that its odors were nonexistent or negligible. One industry consultant termed neighbors' odor complaints a "form of Parkinsonian madness."

Once again, it seemed, the public was crazy if it detected any unpleasant odors. The evidence of neighbors' noses couldn't be trusted. Their complaints were "anecdotal," as compared to the reliable, scientific data produced by the "scentometer."

The amazing thing about these passages was the serious, authoritative tone in which they were written. It would be one thing if these people were joking, but they were *serious*. They didn't just think that they were pulling off a good scam. They literally believed that their "analysis" was rational, objective, and reasonable, while their critics were deluded, prejudiced, and even emotionally unbalanced. They were the experts, and the public merely needed to be "educated."

In the popular image, scientists are dispassionate, objective searchers after truth. A scientist, this model assumes, is someone whose pursuit of the truth begins with independent discovery, proceeds to criticism by peers, and then to publication and use for the common good. In recent years, however, this idealized image has come under challenge from a variety of critics. Most academic critics of science focus on structural and economic factors that create unconscious bias, whereas the activist camps—environmental activists as well as the pro-corporate activists who campaign against "junk science"—focus on deliberately deceptive manipulations by "corporate whores" or "environmentalist fearmongers." Unconscious biases do undoubtedly exist, as do deliberate deceptions. Yet neither of these explanations is adequate. In order to understand the manipulations that are practiced today in the name of science, it is necessary also to understand the particular habits and practices of a particular class of experts who specialize in the management of perception itself—namely, the public relations industry.

"Perceptions are real," proclaims the website of Burson-Marsteller, the world's largest PR firm. "They color what we see . . . what we believe . . . how we behave. They can be managed . . . to motivate behavior . . . to create positive business results" (ellipses in the original).[1]

This credo does not necessarily tell you much else about what Burson-Marsteller believes. Just as attorneys are hired to advocate the point of view of their clients, Burson-Marsteller's job is not to hold opinions of its own but to promote those of its clients. And yet companies like Burson-Marsteller have become important arbiters in determining which experts appear on the public stage. Burson's clients have included the Philip Morris tobacco company, for which it created the National Smokers'Alliance, and Union Carbide, whose reputation it helped repair in the wake of the Bhopal disaster. Like the experts that Burson-Marsteller helps cultivate and train to perform in the public arena, B-M's own experts in perception management believe that the public *needs* to be manipulated for its own good. James Lindheim, B-M's worldwide director of public affairs, offered an example of his reasoning in a speech to the British Society of Chemical Industry. The key, he said, lay in "some very interesting psychological and sociological research on risk perception," which "suggests that the obvious, rational approach is not likely to succeed. . . . In fact, the research tells us that people's perceptions of the sizes of various risks and the acceptability of these risks are based on emotional, and not rational, factors. . . . All of this research is helpful in figuring out a strategy for the chemical industry and for its products. It suggests, for example, that a strategy based on logic and information is probably not going to succeed. We are in the realm of the illogical, the emotional, and we must respond with the tools that we have for managing the emotional aspects of the human psyche. . . . The industry must be like the psychiatrist: rationally figuring out how it can help the public put things in perspective, but knowing that dialogue can only begin with the trust on the public's side that says these people are taking my concerns seriously."[2]

How does Lindheim propose to serve as the public's "psychiatrist"? How does he reconcile his role as a professional perception manager with his desire for "trust on the public's side"? These are interesting questions, but it is even more interesting to ask *why* he believes the public is emotional and incapable of rational discourse. This assumption underlies the thinking not only of the PR industry's own experts, but also the thinking of the experts whom it promotes for public consumption.

While this assumption is somewhat amazing, it is not necessarily insincere. It reflects a set of elitist values that have become all too common in modern society. Functioning at a philosophical and psychological level, it amounts to a kind of anti–popular prejudice that is dangerously corrosive of democratic values. We have written this book both to expose the PR strategies used to create many of the so-called experts whose faces appear on TV news shows and scientific panels, and to examine the underlying assumptions that make these manipulations possible.

PART I

THE AGE OF ILLUSION

1

The Third Man

A third party endorsement can position a new brand so that it's poised for great success or, conversely, can blunt a serious problem before it gets out of hand and proves disastrous for a particular product or for a company overall.

—Daniel Edelman
founder of Edelman PR Worldwide

Suppose we told you that this book holds the key to wealth beyond your dreams—and that it can make you stronger, healthier, more intelligent, and in every way a better person. More love in your life. Freedom from worry and want, and knowledge that will protect you from illness of all kinds.

As a discerning reader, you would probably greet these claims with skepticism. "These guys are obviously snake oil salesmen," you might think. "They would probably dress up in chicken suits if they thought it might get me to buy their book. There's no way I'm falling for this."

Yet suppose we could supply testimonials from important-sounding people—from people whose names you've heard and respect, or who carry impressive titles and credentials. You'll see that the publisher has placed a few testimonials on the back cover. We hope you'll take a moment to read them and ponder their significance.

Better yet, suppose the testimonials came from people with no apparent connection to us. If that were the case, you might be less skeptical. And suppose we had some way of contriving things so that these other people were actually speaking on our behalf, while merely *appearing* to be independent. If we could put words of praise in the mouths of seemingly disinterested, knowledgeable third parties—if we could get a buzz going even among your friends and neighbors—and if we could do all that while keeping you completely in the dark about our behind-the-scenes scheming—then, ironically, you might start to believe us.

Of course, it's highly unlikely that we could ever pull this off. Neither we nor our publisher could ever afford a scheme this grandiose. We're doing the best that we can, but we're no Microsoft.

Trust Us, We're Anti-antitrust

In April 1998, as the Justice Department's antitrust investigation of the Microsoft corporation began to evolve from a background nuisance into a serious challenge to the company's future, a large binder of confidential company documents found its way into the hands of the *Los Angeles Times*. Leaked by an anonymous whistle-blower, the documents detailed a multimillion-dollar media campaign designed for Microsoft by Edelman Public Relations Worldwide, one of the world's largest PR firms. The plan aimed to head off new antitrust investigations being considered by attorney generals in eleven U.S. states. The *Times* described the Edelman plan as "a massive media campaign designed to influence state investigators by creating the appearance of a groundswell of public support for the company." It proposed to hire local PR firms as subcontractors in Arizona, California, Florida, Michigan, New York, North Carolina, Ohio, Pennsylvania, Texas, Virginia, and Wisconsin. Freelance writers would be hired to write opinion pieces, which the local PR firms would then submit to local newspapers. "The elaborate plan . . . hinges on a number of unusual—and some say unethical—tactics," noted *L.A. Times* writers Greg Miller and Leslie Helm, "including the planting of articles, letters to the editor and opinion pieces to be commissioned by Microsoft's top media handlers but presented by local firms as spontaneous testimonials." In the words of the leaked documents, the goal was to generate "leveragable tools for the company's state-based lobbyists," positive press clippings that "state political consultants can use to bolster the case" for Microsoft.[1]

With documents in hand, the reporters played a cat-and-mouse game with Microsoft spokesman Greg Shaw, who denied knowing about the plan until they informed him of the internal memos in their possession, in which Shaw's own name figured prominently. Presented with this reality, he smoothly adjusted his story, admitting that the Edelman plan existed but describing it as merely a proposal. "The idea that we'd hire people who wouldn't identify themselves as representing Microsoft is totally false," Shaw said. "Actually, the proposal we received is quite mundane."[2]

After a few days of embarrassing editorials in the computer trade press, the Edelman plan was largely forgotten. A year later, it went unmentioned when several news stories discussed an "Open Letter to President Clinton from 240 Economists" that appeared in the form of full-page advertisements in the *Washington Post* and *New York Times*. The ads were paid for by a California-based, nonprofit think tank named the Independent Institute, a conservative organization that had been a leading defender of Microsoft since it first came under fire from federal prosecutors. "Consumers did not ask for these antitrust actions—rival business firms did," the Open Letter stated. "Many of the proposed interventions will weaken successful U.S. firms and impede their competitiveness abroad. . . . We urge antitrust authorities to abandon antitrust protectionism," stated the economists, who came from institutions as far apart and as prestigious as the University of California, Johns Hopkins, the University of Miami, American University, Loyola, Ohio State, Dartmouth, Northwestern, Columbia University, Stanford, and Cornell.[3]

Underneath the letter itself, a paragraph at the bottom of the newspaper ads advised readers that for more information they should read a new book titled *Winners, Losers and Microsoft: Competition and Antitrust in High Technology,* published by the Independent Institute and authored by two of its research fellows, economists Stan Liebowitz and Stephen Margolis. The book was attracting favorable reviews from publications such as *The Economist* of London and *Wired* magazine. "Henceforth, any judges, economists, pundits or journalists who discuss Microsoft . . . without first dealing with the Liebowitz-Margolis critique should have their wrists soundly slapped," stated the *Wall Street Journal.*

Newsbytes magazine, a computer industry news service, noted that the Independent Institute's position "sounds like a brazenly partisan argument for Microsoft," but checked with a spokesman for the Independent Institute who said that Microsoft did not pay for either the Open Letter advertisements or the publication of *Winners, Losers and Microsoft.* The spokesman acknowledged that Microsoft was a member of the Institute, and "said membership dues for corporations start at approximately $1,000, but he would not comment on how much Microsoft has contributed to the institute over time," *Newsbytes* reported.[4]

In September 1999, however, a second group of leaked internal documents found its way into the hands of another reporter, this time Joel Brinkley of the *New York Times*, who reported that Microsoft was the largest single outside donor to the Independent Institute. During the 1999 fiscal year, Brinkley wrote, Microsoft had provided 20 percent of the institute's operating budget. In addition to helping pay for publication of *Winners, Losers and Microsoft,* the software company had paid for the newspaper ads in which the Open Letter appeared. Brinkley's documents included a bill from Independent Institute President David Theroux to Microsoft attorney John Kelly, in the amount of $153,868.67—the full price of running the full-page ads, plus $5,966 in airfares and expenses for Theroux and a colleague to appear at a press conference timed to coincide with the ads' release.

"Theroux has long acknowledged Microsoft is a dues-paying member of his institute," Brinkley reported. "But he has insisted all along that Microsoft is 'just one of 2,000 members' and as such pays . . . an inconsequential part of the organization's overall budget that gives the company no special standing. All Microsoft gets for that, he said, is 'free copies of our publications, discounted tickets to our events.' He has also maintained Microsoft had nothing to do with the newspaper advertisements. The ads, he said in the interview, 'were paid for out of our general funds.' "[5]

The documents leaked to the *New York Times* put the lie to these claims, but Theroux was unfazed, attacking Brinkley's story as a "smear campaign" based on "purloined" documents. "It appears that some people in the computer industry may now be stooping to any and all tactics that might be used to discredit the Independent Institute and our powerful new book," he responded. "Mr. Brinkley credits as his source, 'a Microsoft adversary associated with the computer industry who refused to be identified.' . . . Bottom line: Do Brinkley's charges make our book and the Open Letter any less credible or accurate? Absolutely not."[6]

The Independent Institute calls itself a "non-partisan, scholarly, public policy research and educational organization . . . that sponsors peer-reviewed, scientific studies on a wide range of economic and social issues." That its defense of Microsoft was company-financed is irrelevant, Theroux claimed, because "the academic process we use is independent of sources of revenue." There is some truth to these claims. It would be a little too facile to portray the Independent Institute as a mere mouthpiece for the company. As Theroux pointed out when its funding sources were uncovered, the institute was on record opposing antitrust laws since 1990, long before Microsoft came under federal scrutiny. And while professors Liebowitz and Margolis have worked on occasion as paid consultants to Microsoft, the positions they espouse in *Winners, Losers and Microsoft* were likewise developed years before the company became a target of government investigations.

Yet it is also ridiculous to pretend that the Independent Institute is truly independent. Microsoft had an obvious motive for helping the institute amplify its voice through major advertising, and it is precisely for this reason that the amount of its funding remained confidential until it was leaked to a newspaper reporter. David Callahan, a writer who has researched the relationship between corporate funders and conservative think tanks, notes that Microsoft's relationship with the Independent Institute is "perfectly legal given current tax laws," but adds, "At the same time, something is clearly wrong with this situation. . . . It is naïve to imagine that conservative think tanks aren't extremely beholden to their funders in the business world or to the corporate leaders on their boards. This is simply the way that the power of the purse works. Just as politicians can't ignore the demands of major donors if they want to survive, neither can institutions ignore their benefactors."[7]

Potemkin Pundits

During the reign of Catherine the Great in Russia, one of her closest advisers was field marshal Grigori Potemkin, who used numerous wiles on her behalf. When Catherine toured the countryside with foreign dignitaries, Potemkin arranged to have fake villages built in advance of her visits so as to create an illusion of prosperity. Since that time, the term "Potemkin village" has become a metaphor for things that look elaborate and impressive but in actual fact lack substance.

Microsoft's financing of the Independent Institute is a modern-day public relations strategy that amounts to Potemkin punditry—the manipulation of public opinion by financing and publicizing views congenial to the public policy goals of their sponsors. When the Edelman plan was first exposed in the *Los Angeles Times*, PR industry trade publications interviewed public relations practitioners around the country who saw nothing remarkable or particularly disturbing about the campaign. "Based on what I've seen it's a fairly typical PR plan. It's what we do," the manager of a major PR firm said to *Inside PR.*

One leading PR practitioner—Robert Dilenschneider of the Dilenschneider Group—did criticize the Microsoft plan, calling it "a synthetic campaign." The strategy was ethically wrong, he said, and dangerous to Microsoft's own interests besides. "The media got wind of it, and they made the story the sleaze alley of the computer industry," Dilenschneider said. "It has made Bill Gates, the richest, mightiest person in the world, look a little bit like the Wizard of Oz; a little bit of smoke and mirrors, no substance."[8] But Dilenschneider's critique was in the minority.

"Media plans are routine in PR although they don't sound too good when they hit print," said *Jack O'Dwyer's Newsletter,* another leading PR trade publication, which went on to offer some advice that Microsoft might want to use to avoid getting caught in the future: "PR pros we asked about this said: 'Don't put anything in writing you don't want to be on page one of your newspaper.' . . . 'Talking points' on the subject matter should have been distributed but no media relations methodology. Then, if the points became public, the press could only report on the length and breadth of Microsoft's arguments."[9]

As Microsoft and its defenders pointed out, in fact, its corporate rivals were also aggressively spinning the public debate, using a similar "media relations methodology." Netscape, Oracle, and Sun Microsystems pushed their side of the antitrust case by launching the "Project to Promote Competition and Innovation in the Digital Age" (ProComp). Netscape hired former U.S. Supreme Court nominee Robert Bork as a spokesman, a casting decision that Hollywood might term "playing against type." Bork is the author of *The Antitrust Paradox,* a 1978 book sharply critical of government antitrust rules. "Bork cannot easily be dismissed as a knee-jerk critic of big, successful companies," noted the *National Journal.* "His reputation as Mr. Anti-antitrust goes back a long time; when he was a Yale law professor, his students nicknamed his course on the topic 'Pro-trust.' "[10] Once in the employ of Netscape, however, Bork issued a 7,000-word position paper and opinion pieces for major newspapers, explaining that federal prosecutors were "simply stopping Microsoft from using its operating system as a club to bludgeon competition into the dust."[11] The anti-Microsoft coalition also hired former presidential candidate Bob Dole, now with the high-powered Washington lobbying firm of Verner, Liipfert, Bernhard, McPherson & Hand. Senator Orrin G. Hatch (R-Utah), a recipient of $17,500 in campaign contributions from Netscape, Sun, and America Online, added further conservative firepower to the anti-Microsoft armada, as did the Progress and Freedom Foundation (PFF), a think tank with links to former House Speaker Newt Gingrich. PFF's major financial donors included Netscape, Oracle, and Sun, along with other Microsoft adversaries, including Gateway 2000, IBM, Hewlett Packard, America Online, and CompuServe.

Even the exposé of the Independent Institute that appeared in the *New York Times* turns out to have been orchestrated by the Oracle company. In order to get the goods on Microsoft's funding of the institute, Oracle had hired a detective firm to go "dumpster diving" through Microsoft's garbage, and had used the Washington PR firm of Chlopak, Leonard, Schechter & Associates to circulate the incriminating documents.[12]

None of these tactics are in any way unique to the computer industry. "This kind of plan is . . . part of the standard arsenal of companies in the cable and TV industry, and in other industries where there's government regulation," one source told *PC Week* magazine after reviewing the Edelman PR proposal.[13] Computer industry columnist David Coursey went further. "If you think Microsoft is political bad news, compare computing/software generally to the telecommunications, broadcast and cable industries," he wrote. "Their political efforts make Microsoft look like the proverbial 98-pound weakling."[14]

Grigori Potemkin, if he were alive today, would probably be amazed at the number and sophistication of the political facades that have been erected in today's media landscape. Here are a few other examples of the process at work:

- After Nigeria's military dictatorship executed playwright Ken Saro-Wiwa in 1995, the dictatorship and Shell Oil Company faced international condemnation. Nigeria's security forces had massacred villages and terrorized the indigenous Ogoni tribespeople in order to quell protests against the company's natural gas drilling operations. Saro-Wiwa, an Ogoni leader, had denounced Shell for waging an "ecological war" against his people. Nigeria responded by ordering multipage, glossy color advertisements in black-owned U.S. newspapers and inviting newspaper editors on expense-paid "fact-finding tours" of Ogoniland. Minority newspapers in the United States are chronically strapped for cash, and the combination of windfall revenue and guided tours succeeded in blunting criticisms. In fact, several newspapers editorialized that it was "racist" to criticize Nigeria's dismal track record on human rights.

- In the fall of 1997, Georgetown University's Credit Research Center issued a study which concluded that many debtors are using bankruptcy as an excuse to wriggle out of their obligations to creditors. Lobbyists for banks and credit card companies seized on the study as they lobbied Congress for changes in federal law that would make it harder for consumers to file for bankruptcy relief. Former U.S. Treasury Secretary Lloyd Bentsen cited the study in a *Washington Times* opinion column, offering Georgetown's academic imprimatur as evidence of the need for "bankruptcy reform." What Bentsen failed to mention was that the Credit Research Center is funded in its entirety by credit card companies, banks, retailers, and others in the credit industry. The study itself was produced with a $100,000 grant from Visa USA and MasterCard International, Inc. Bentsen also failed to mention that he himself had been hired to work as a credit-industry lobbyist.[15]

- In Oxford, England, the Social Issues Research Centre (SIRC) calls itself an "independent, non-profit organization founded to conduct research on social issues." It has issued a call to establish a British "code of practice" governing what reporters should be allowed to write about issues of science and public safety. Designed to put a stop to "irresponsible health scares," the code stipulates that "scientific stories should be factually accurate. Breaches of the Code of Practice should be referred to the Press Complaints Commission." Such a code is necessary, SIRC suggests, because of the public's "riskfactorphobia," a term it has coined to describe a condition of excessive sensitivity to health concerns related to genetically engineered foods and foodborne illnesses. SIRC has also published popular reports in the British press about the pleasures of pub-hopping. When the *British Medical Journal* took a close look at the organization, however, it found that SIRC shares the same offices, directors, and leading personnel as a PR firm called MCM Research that claims to apply "social science" to solving the problems of its clients, who include prominent names in the liquor and restaurant industries. "Do your PR initiatives sometimes look too much like PR initiatives?" asked MCM's website in a straightforward boast of its ability to deceive the public. "MCM conducts social/psychological research on the positive aspects of your business," the website continued. "The results do not read like PR literature, or like market research data. Our reports are credible, interesting and entertaining in their own right. This is why they capture the imagination of the media and your customers."[16]

- Corporate sponsors have formed "partnerships" with a number of leading nonprofit organizations in which they pay for the right to use the organizations' names and logos in advertisements. Bristol-Myers Squibb, for example, paid $600,000 to the American Heart Association for the right to display the AHA's name and logo in ads for its cholesterol-lowering drug Pravachol. The American Cancer Society reeled in $1 million from SmithKline Beecham for the right to use *its logo in ads for Beecham's* NicoDerm CQ and Nicorette anti-smoking aids. A Johnson & Johnson subsidiary countered by shelling out $2.5 million for similar rights from the American Lung Association in its ads for Nicotrol, a rival nicotine patch. In 1999 manufacturers spent $630 million on these and similar kinds of sponsorship deals, some unseemly, such as a deal between the Eskimo Pie Corporation and the American Diabetes Association, which was designed to create the impression that Eskimo's "Sugar Freedom" line of frozen desserts was endorsed by the American Diabetes Association, when in fact the desserts contain high levels of both total and saturated fat—a risky dietary choice for diabetics, who have a propensity for obesity and heart disease. Although the nonprofit organizations involved in these deals deny that the use of their names and logos constitutes an endorsement, the corporate sponsors have no such illusions. "PR pros view those third-party endorsements as invaluable ways to build goodwill among consumers for a client's product line," notes *O'Dwyer's PR Services Report*. For propriety's sake, however, a bit of discretion is necessary. "Don't use the word 'endorse' when speaking to executives from non-profits about their relationships with the private sector," *O'Dwyer's* advised. "The preferred non-profit vernacular is: recommended, sponsorship, approved, or partnership."[17]

- An organization called "Consumer Alert" frequently pops up in news stories about product safety issues. What the reporters almost never mention is that Consumer Alert is funded by corporations and that its positions are usually diametrically opposed to the positions taken by independent consumer groups such as Consumers Union. For example, Consumer Alert opposes flame-resistance standards for clothing fabrics issued by the Consumer Product Safety Commission, and defends products such as the diet drug dexfenfluramine (Redux), which was taken off the market because of its association with heart valve damage. In contrast with Consumers Union, which is funded primarily by member subscriptions, Consumer Alert is funded by the industries whose products it defends—companies including Anheuser-Busch, Pfizer Pharmaceuticals, Philip Morris, Allstate Insurance Fund, American Cyanamid, Elanco, Eli Lilly, Exxon, Monsanto, Upjohn, Chemical Manufacturers Association, Ciba-Geigy, the Beer Institute, Coors, and Chevron USA.[18]

- In late 1993, a group called Mothers Opposing Pollution (MOP) appeared, calling itself "the largest women's environmental group in Australia with thousands of supporters across the country. . . . The group comprises mainly mothers and other women concerned with the welfare and rights of Australian women." MOP's cause: a campaign against plastic milk bottles, centering on the issues of waste disposal, the carcinogenic risks of milk in contact with plastic, and reduction in the quality of milk as a result of exposure to light. "The message to the consumer is never buy milk in plastic containers," said spokesperson Alana Maloney. Membership in MOP was free, which prompted some people to wonder how the group could afford to carry out expensive publicity in support of its cause. Although MOP claimed branches across Australia, Alana Maloney seemed to be its only spokesperson. Searches of basic public records, such as voting rolls, could find no such person. MOP's letterhead listed three addresses in different cities, each of which turned out to be a post office box. Finally, in February 1995, an Australian newspaper discovered that "Mrs. Alana Maloney" was in fact Janet Rundle, who heads a public relations company called J. R. and Associates. Rundle is also a business partner of Trevor Munnery, who owns his own PR firm called Unlimited Public Relations, which works for the Association of Liquidpaperboard Carton Manufacturers (ALC)— the makers of *paper* milk cartons. In the wake of these public revelations, MOP sank from public view and has since disappeared.[19]

Someone Else's Mouth

These examples share a common reliance upon a public relations strategy known within the PR industry as the "third party technique." Merrill Rose, executive vice president of the Porter/Novelli PR firm, explains the technique succinctly: "Put your words in someone else's mouth."[20] How effective is this strategy? According to a survey commissioned by Porter/Novelli, 89 percent of respondents consider "independent experts" a "very or somewhat believable source of information during a corporate crisis." Sometimes the technique is used to hype or exaggerate the benefits of a product. Other times it is used to create doubt about a product's hazards, or about criticisms that have been made of a company's business practices. The "someone elses" become Potemkin authorities, faithfully spouting the opinions of their benefactors while making it appear that their views are "independent." You used to see this technique in its most obvious and crude form in the television commercials that featured actors in physicians' lab coats announcing that "nine out of ten doctors prefer" their brand of aspirin. But advertisements are *obvious* propaganda, and the third party technique in its more subtle forms is designed to prevent audiences from even realizing what they are experiencing. "The best PR ends up looking like news," brags one public relations executive. "You never know when a PR agency is being effective; you'll just find your views slowly shifting."[21]

It is hard to say exactly when or where the third party technique originated as a conscious tactic for manipulating public opinion. Since antiquity, debates on important issues have frequently turned on appeals to the reverence that most people feel for a famous name. During the medieval period, the authority of priests and kings was considered a transcendent standard of truth, even when their doctrines clashed with the evidence of people's actual experience and scientific experiments. People who questioned officially accepted religious views were labeled heretics and could be arrested and killed on the grounds that he or she must have made a pact with the devil.

"It was only in the late nineteenth and early twentieth centuries that argument from authority commonly came to be treated as a fallacy," notes University of Toronto philosophy professor Douglas Walton in his book, *Appeal to Expert Opinion: Arguments from Authority.* "The rise of science brought with it a kind of positivist way of thinking, to the effect that knowledge should be based on scientific experiment and mathematical calculation and that all else is 'subjective.' "[22]

The rise of science accompanied a communications revolution, beginning with the printing press and continuing into the modern age of electronic media, and as Umberto Eco has observed, every new means of communication carries within itself a means of deception. Just as the invention of language made lying possible, the invention of mass media created newer, more sophisticated, subtle, and elaborate techniques of propaganda. Just as the anonymity of the Internet would eventually enable 14-year-old boys to pretend to be 24-year-old lingerie models, the mass media made it possible for the first time to conceal the identity of the voices that appeared within it, to deliver messages while hiding the identity of the messenger. It became possible to accomplish this act of concealment without ever committing an act of overt deception. Edward Bernays, the legendary "father of public relations" whose career we examine in Chapter 2, demonstrated an inkling of this potential during one of his early assignments as adviser to the Waldorf-Astoria hotel, which was plagued by rumors that it was about to close. Bernays knew that denying the rumors directly would only give them more credence. Instead, he advised his client to prominently announce the signing of a ten-year contract with its world-famous chef. The mere identity of the celebrated chef became a symbolic statement of the message that the hotel wanted to deliver.

"How can the persuader reach these groups that make up the large public?" Bernays asked in one of the early formulations of the third party technique. "He can do so through their leaders, for the individual looks for guidance to the leaders of the groups to which he belongs. . . . They play a vital part in the molding of public opinion, and they offer the propagandist a means of reaching vast numbers of individuals, for with so many confusing and conflicting ideas competing for the individual's attention, he is forced to look to others for authority. No man, in today's complicated world, can base his judgments and acts entirely on his own examination and weighing of the evidence. . . . The group leader thus becomes a key figure in the molding of public opinion, and his acceptance of a given idea carries with it the acceptance of many of his followers."[23]

For Jack O'Dwyer, the third party technique is what distinguishes public relations from advertising. "Your firm may want to deal directly with the public or with your employees, customers, suppliers, etc.," he says, "but this is not the best use of a PR firm. The most leverage will be when the firm supplies useful information to influential reporters and analysts who have large audiences. You get third-party endorsement and wide readership or viewership at comparatively low cost. . . . Look for third-party endorsements, not booklets, sales promotion and ads."[24]

From a PR point of view, the third party technique offers several advantages:

- *It offers camouflage,* helping to hide the vested interest that lurks behind a message. If Philip Morris were to come out itself and declare that "attorneys need to be stopped from suing tobacco companies," the message would be laughed into oblivion. Similar skepticism is bound to greet Bill Gates when he writes an editorial on his own behalf, or a polluting company when it claims that pollution doesn't cause illness. Putting the same message in someone else's mouth gives it a credibility that it would not otherwise enjoy.

- *It encourages conformity to a vested interest, while pretending to encourage independence.* Sometimes, in fact, the message is designed to look like the very epitome of rebellion. Take, for example, a legendary publicity stunt orchestrated by Edward Bernays, which used suffragettes as third party proxies for the tobacco industry. In 1929, Bernays was hired by the American Tobacco Company and charged with the task of persuading women to smoke—an activity that was then considered "unfeminine" and socially unacceptable. Bernays set out to turn this liability into an advantage by establishing cigarettes as symbols of women's liberation. At his instigation, ten New York debutantes marched in the city's 1929 Easter Sunday parade, defiantly smoking cigarettes as a protest against women's inequality. Bernays dubbed it the "torches of liberty" brigade. "Front page stories in newspapers reported the freedom march in words and pictures," Bernays would recall later. "For weeks after the event, editorials praised or condemned the young women who had paraded against the smoking taboo." Women began lighting up in droves, and a few weeks later a Broadway theater let women inside its heretofore men's-only smoking room.[25]

- *It replaces factual discourse with emotion-laden symbolism.* Sometimes the identity of the messenger becomes symbolically more important than the content of the message itself. Timber industry consultant Ron Arnold, who founded the "Wise Use" movement as a pseudo-grassroots campaign against environmentalism, explains the rationale behind his use of the third party technique: "The public is completely convinced that when you speak as an industry, you are speaking out of nothing but self-interest. The pro-industry citizen activist group is the answer to these problems. It can be an effective and convincing advocate for your industry. It can utilize powerful archetypes such as the sanctity of the family, the virtue of the close-knit community, the natural wisdom of the rural dweller. . . . And it can turn the public against your enemies. . . . I think you'll find it one of your wisest investments over time."[26]

Serving the Self-Serving

When they talk among themselves, PR professionals can be remarkably candid about their reasons for using the third party technique. During the Clinton/Lewinsky drama, *O'Dwyer's* noted that "what the Clinton Administration needs are credible third parties—both in quantity and quality—rising to its defense. In a word, it needs PR." Why? Because "third parties can say things that participants in a debate cannot."[27]

In 1994 Neal Cohen, of the Washington-based PR and lobby firm APCO & Associates, used similar reasoning at a conference organized by the Public Affairs Council, a trade association for some of the nation's top lobbyists. APCO was among the principal PR firms orchestrating the "tort reform" movement, which campaigns against "excessive" consumer liability lawsuits and is heavily financed by the insurance and tobacco industries. On the face of it, Cohen observed, tort reform is difficult to sell to the public. "It's not a very sexy issue," he said. " 'Tort' to the average person is dessert, it isn't a legal principle." The whole purpose of tort reform, moreover, is to make it harder for everyday citizens to sue corporations. This is hardly the sort of cause that brings masses into the streets. In fact, he said, people would reject the tort reform movement out of hand if they knew that the insurance and tobacco companies were behind it. "We want to pass a bill in Mississippi," he said by way of example, "and we've got a problem: Our industry can't pass the bill. If the legislators know we're the only industry that wants this bill, it's an automatic killer. And just to make it a little more difficult, we've joined up with one other industry to fund this effort, and they are worse than us. People dislike them more intensely, and in fact they don't even have any facilities in the state of Mississippi, not to mention the product they manufacture. . . . In a tort reform battle, if State Farm is the leader of the coalition, you're not going to pass the bill, it's not credible. OK? Because it's so self-serving."

In order to give tort reform any credibility at all, APCO had to figure out a way to reframe the issue, which they did by tapping into the public's distaste for attorneys. "We built a coalition around the concept of 'lawsuit abuse,' " Cohen explained, "and we enlarged the scope of the concept so that people understood how it would affect their pocket book, how it would address their fear, how it would deal with their anger at the legal profession. . . . Rule number one for me is stay away from substance. Don't talk about the details of legislation," he advised. "Talk about . . . 'lawsuit abuse,' 'trial lawyer greed,' 'increasing jobs.' "

When building a coalition, Cohen advised, "you'd better have a committed leader, a spokesperson, and you'd better train that spokesperson, and it should only be one person. . . . And if you can, find somebody who has stature and is not perceived as somebody who is typical. Somebody who . . . has the stature with the legislators." If possible, the public should be brought in as well, but as props, not as participants. "We made sure that it was typical people mixed in with large employers and political contributors," he said. "We had 1,500 Mississippians mixed in with who our clients were. . . . We had broadened the issue so it was identified . . . with a much broader group, and it was focused in as a constituent grassroots issue." But appearances are one thing, reality another. "The problem with broad-based membership is—don't confuse that with broad-based leadership," Cohen advised. "Broad-based membership is 'What does the public see?' 'What do the legislators see?' Decision-making is, you need a core group, three or so people, who have similar interests and are going to get the job done and not veer off." Other adornments, such as advertising and research-for-hire, help decorate the coalition tree. "We used every tactic we could think of to get a message out there," Cohen said. "We also used polls to get the media's attention. . . . We did a research study using a local professor, we spent $5,000 on a study. . . . It was to get the media's attention. . . . We used television [ads] in part to get the media's attention. . . . We also did billboards."[28]

Making News

The news media is a natural target for the third party technique, both because of its ability to reach millions of people and because the public expects journalists to serve as neutral sifters of the truth. The PR industry has mastered the art of putting its words into journalists' mouths, relying on the fact that most reporters are spread too thin to engage in time-consuming investigative journalism and therefore rely heavily on information from corporate- and government-sourced news releases. The news release as we know it today was invented in the 1920s by early PR practitioner Ivy Lee, a former journalist himself who realized that the more information his clients provided to reporters, the less likely the reporters would be to go out and investigate for themselves. Early news releases were simple typed statements. Today, PR firms produce regular syndicated columns and have their own wire services, such as PR Newswire, that deliver the news releases instantly via the Internet to both print and electronic journalists. Jennifer Sereno, the business editor for a major daily paper in Wisconsin, says she prefers electronic news releases because "the stories come up on our screens, as other wire stories do. We see them more quickly than we see faxes. . . . It's very convenient. We can send it electronically right to the reporter working on the story. Oftentimes it saves them some typing as well."[29]

There is nothing inherently deceptive about issuing a news release, but this sort of practice has changed the modern information environment in subtle yet important ways. A comparison of PR Newswire releases to actual newspaper stories shows that they are frequently repeated, verbatim or nearly verbatim, usually with no disclosure to tell readers that what appears on the page as a journalist's independent report is actually a PR news release. A study by Scott Cutlip found that 40 percent of the news content in a typical U.S. newspaper originated with public relations press releases, story memos, or suggestions. In 1980 the *Columbia Journalism Review* scrutinized a typical issue of the *Wall Street Journal* and found that more than half of its news stories "were based solely on press releases." Often the releases were reprinted "almost verbatim or in para-phrase," with little additional reporting, and many articles carried the slug "By a *Wall Street Journal* Staff Reporter."[30] There is no reason to think that the situation has improved since or that it is much different at other pa-pers. "Most of what you see on TV is, in effect, a canned PR product. Most of what you read in the paper and see on television is not news," says the senior vice president of a leading public relations firm.[31]

This tendency is especially pronounced in the electronic media. Some PR firms specialize in the production of prerecorded public service an-nouncements and "video news releases" (VNRs)—entire news stories, written, filmed, and produced by PR firms and transmitted by satellite feed or the Internet to thousands of TV stations around the world. "In the early 1980s, as news staffs were cut and airtime for news programming was ex-panded with cable television, we entered the golden age of VNR produc-tion and placement," noted Kevin Foley of KEF Media Associates in Chicago. By 1991, ten VNRs a day were being produced—4,000 per year.[32] Today the number is much higher, although no one has an exact count. VNRs are used heavily by the pharmaceuticals and food industries in particular, which provide a steady stream of stories touting new medical breakthroughs and previously unknown health benefits that researchers at-tribute to oat bran, garlic bread, walnuts, orange juice, or whatever prod-uct the sponsoring client happens to be selling. A subtle touch is needed to make sure that the VNR looks exactly like real news. PR consultant Debra Hauss advises VNR producers against seeming "too commercial. Don't try to sneak in too many product mentions."[33] Sometimes VNRs will use narrators who have previously worked as on-air reporters. That these scripted stories are actually cleverly disguised advertisements is well understood by the people who work at TV stations and networks, but is rarely mentioned within earshot or eyeshot of the news-watching public. On the evening news every night you see—but probably don't recognize—VNR footage mixed in with stories that reporters have gone out and gath-ered themselves. Sometimes VNRs are used as story segments without any editing whatsoever, let alone a disclaimer to inform audiences that what they are watching was produced by a PR firm on behalf of a specific client with a specific propaganda interest.

Kenneth Feather, director of the FDA's Division of Drug Advertising and Labeling, noted that medical VNRs manipulate the public when they promote drugs for unapproved uses or imply that the VNR sponsor's product is superior to other products. A major problem, he said, is that virtually none of them state that they came from the drug company but rather imply a third party. They use on-screen testimony from well-spoken doctors who have been coached so that their delivery perfectly fits the format of a news program, and the VNRs rarely mention that the doctors have been hired by the drug suppliers to test and promote their products. Often, in fact, pharmaceutical companies use VNRs to make claims for their products that would not be permitted under the FDA's rules for paid advertising. They can be used to promote unapproved uses of a drug, for example, or to create public pressure for the government to approve a drug that is still undergoing regulatory scrutiny. "Until recently, the drug companies have been largely discouraged from using TV commercials targeted at the public," said Eugene Secunda, a professor of marketing at Baruch College in New York. "However, they have been less constrained in their use of new media techniques like the VNR, for which the FDA has not yet established formal guidelines."[34]

Virtual Surrealities

The extent to which today's media can manufacture false realities was satirized in the 1998 movie *Wag the Dog*, in which government advisers created a fictional war on a Hollywood sound stage to distract public attention from a presidential sex scandal. When *Wag the Dog* first appeared, critics praised its humor but thought its plot seemed implausible. Then President Clinton's affair with Monica Lewinsky became public knowledge. When Clinton announced a bombing strike against "Arab terrorists" on the eve of his own impeachment hearings, more than a few people began to wonder if the movie was really so far-fetched. The question lingers: How far will people in power go to manipulate and control our perceptions of reality?

The notion that we live in an elaborate, technologically manufactured illusion has become a recurring theme in modern cinema. In *Total Recall*, Arnold Schwarzenegger discovers that his own memories are government-manufactured implants. In *The Net*, Sandra Bullock's identity is erased by a corporation that controls the world's information databases. In *The Truman Show*, Jim Carrey lives in a giant Potemkin village, unaware that his entire life is a made-for-TV fabrication. Virtual reality also figures prominently in later episodes of *Star Trek*, which feature a "holodeck" where people go to experience synthetic adventures in a room that can be programmed to realistically simulate a Parisian café, a lush rain forest, or any other pseudo-environment that the programmer requests. In *The X-Files,* agents Scully and Mulder spend their days exploring a vast, labyrinthine conspiracy, convinced that "the truth is out there" but never quite able to discover it or even identify the conspirators. "This, it seems, is a proliferating notion in today's world of film—blending theology and technology into a weird, low-level paranoia about existence," observes film critic Ted Anthony.[35]

This paranoia reflects a growing public awareness of what journalist Walter Lippmann described in 1921 as "the insertion between man and his environment of a pseudo-environment. . . . What is called the adjustment of man to his environment takes place through the medium of fictions."[36]

Lippmann served as a confidential assistant to the U.S. Secretary of War during the First World War and participated in drawing up the terms of the armistice. The experience left him disillusioned about the future prospects for democracy, and in a book titled *Public Opinion* he readily acknowledged that all sides in the war, his own included, had lied to their own citizens about matters ranging from battlefield losses to the real postwar objectives of the warring governments. "We have learned to call this propaganda," he wrote. "A group of men, who can prevent independent access to the event, arrange the news of it to suit their purpose."[37]

The "pseudo-environment" of fictions was inevitable and necessary, Lippmann argued, in part because of limitations in the speed with which information could be transmitted to the public at large. Even a skilled telegraph operator, he observed, could transmit no more than 1,500 words per day. As a result, foreign correspondents were forced to compress their firsthand accounts into a "few words," which "must often stand for a whole succession of acts, thoughts, feelings and consequences. . . . It is doubtful whether a supreme master of style could pack all the elements of truth that complete justice would demand into a hundred word account of what had happened."[38] Rather than informed consensus, therefore, public opinion was bound to be a hodgepodge of half-baked notions and stereotypes based on incomplete information and the personal biases of individuals.

Given the impossibility of educating the public about the full complexities of the world, Lippmann argued that democracy was unworkable "unless there is an independent, expert organization for making the unseen facts intelligible to those who have to make the decisions."[39] The expert, he argued, would "exercise more power in the future than ever he did before, because increasingly the relevant facts will elude the voter and the administrator. All governing agencies will tend to organize bodies of research and information, which will throw out tentacles and expand, as have the intelligence departments of all the armies in the world."[40] Lippmann thought this development would be a good thing and even recommended creating government-subsidized "bureaus of experts," whose members would enjoy lifetime tenure.[41] "The purpose," he said, "is not to burden every citizen with expert opinions on all questions, but to push that burden away from him towards the responsible administrator."[42]

Complementing the rise of the expert, Lippmann also foresaw the rise of a specialized *type* of expert whose job would be to control and discipline the thinking of the masses. "As a result of psychological research, coupled with the modern means of communication, the practice of democracy has turned a corner," he stated. "Persuasion has become a self-conscious art and a regular organ of popular government. None of us begins to understand the consequences, but it is no daring prophecy to say that the knowledge of how to create consent will alter every political calculation and modify every political premise."[43]

The world we live in today differs from Lippmann's in ways that he could never have foreseen. His argument about the difficulties involved in transmitting information from place to place not only seems irrelevant but absurd in today's world of the Internet, camcorders, cell phones, fiber-optic cables, and satellite dishes. The information bottleneck no longer exists. To the contrary, we are bombarded daily with more information than we can possibly absorb, and yet the modern information media have not eliminated the "pseudo-environment" of which Lippmann spoke. In fact, media noise has contributed greatly to its growth.

The Disinfotainment Industry

The creation of a media pseudo-environment is no easy task. It takes time, money, and advanced technology. No one knows exactly how much money is spent each year in the United States on corporate public relations, but $10 billion would be a conservative estimate. The PR industry has turned to the social sciences for help in developing techniques equal to the task. Psychologists, sociologists and opinion pollsters work in tandem with computer programmers to develop complex databases so refined that they can pinpoint the prevailing "psychographics" of individual city neighborhoods. Press agents used to rely on publicity stunts to attract attention for their clients. In today's electronic age, the PR industry uses 800 numbers and telemarketing, interactive websites and simultaneous multilocation fax transmission. Today's public relations industry has become so pervasive that part of its invisibility stems from the fact that it is, indeed, everywhere—from T-shirts bearing product brand names to movie product placements to various behind-the-scenes efforts at "issue management," "perception management," or "crisis management" (to use just a few of the currently fashionable buzzwords).

Some companies, with names like Capital Speakers, Inc., or Celebrity Focus, specialize in recruiting celebrity and expert spokespersons for the PR industry. Capital Speakers boasts that it can provide "access to virtually any speaker or entertainer on earth." Celebrity Focus says it allows clients "to focus on public relations, while entrusting the hiring of celebrities to seasoned professionals."[44] Other PR consultants specialize in coaching would-be experts and nervous corporate executives in how to present themselves before Congress or on television: what clothes to wear, what color tie, how to sit or stand (spread your feet so your head won't seem to rock on camera), what words to use and how to pronounce them, and—when asked a question you don't want to answer—how to say nothing while avoiding awkward phrases like "no comment." The larger PR companies offer all of these services and more under a single roof—one-stop shopping for advertising, public relations, traditional lobbying, research, polling, direct-mail canvassing, and creating "grassroots" support for issues.

The federal government is forbidden by law from spending money on public relations, but this has proved to be no barrier in practice, since the same activities go on under the rubric of "public affairs" and other euphemisms. In 1986, Senator William Proxmire asked the General Accounting Office how much money federal agencies spend on public affairs, and received an estimate of $2.3 billion—a figure that did not include the PR activities of Congress or the White House. This number has surely grown since, although there are no government statistics or even standards with which to track and measure its growth. During the Reagan administration's military interventions in Central America in the 1980s, its Office of Public Diplomacy for Latin America and the Caribbean used the third party technique to orchestrate media coverage of the war. On March 11, 1985, for example, Professor John Guilmarten wrote an op-ed piece for the *Wall Street Journal* alleging a dangerous arms buildup by the Nicaraguan government. "Professor Guilmarten has been a consultant to our office and collaborated with our staff in the writing of this piece. . . . Officially, this office had no role in its preparation," noted an internal White House memo that was uncovered during the Iran/Contra hearings. The memo also mentioned op-ed pieces that its consultants had drafted to be signed by contra leaders and submitted to the *Washington Post* and *New York Times,* and spoke of using a "cutout" (CIA-speak for "third party") to set up interviews between the contras and various Washington news media. In its first year of operations alone, the program claimed credit for 1,500 speaking engagements and for sending material to 239 editorial writers in 150 cities—all the while concealing the fact that the White House was the source of the propaganda.

Some PR campaigns are entertaining, some are merely frivolous, and some are undoubtedly beneficial to the public. The cumulative human cost of these experiments in thought control has nevertheless been profound. On repeated occasions in the twentieth century, experts in manipulating public opinion have led the United States and other nations into war. Washington, D.C., is home to prominent PR firms whose clients include dictatorships that murder and torture their own citizens and even spy on the United States, while simultaneously lobbying for foreign financial aid and special trade favors. The private health care industry has launched massive PR and lobby campaigns on repeated occasions to block health care reform, with the result that the United States remains the only major industrial power on earth with a large population of uninsured—ranking near the bottom in terms of the actual health of its citizens despite spending more per capita on health care than any other nation.[45]

There is nothing wrong with many of the techniques used by the PR industry—lobbying, grassroots organizing, using the news media to put ideas before the public. As individuals, we not only have the right to engage in these activities, we have a responsibility to participate in the decisions that shape our society and our lives. Ordinary citizens have the right to organize for social change. But ordinary citizens cannot afford the multimillion-dollar campaigns that PR firms undertake on behalf of their special interest clients, usually large corporations, business associations, and governments. Raw money enables the PR industry to mobilize attorneys, broadcast faxes, satellite feeds, sophisticated information systems, and other expensive, high-tech resources to outmaneuver, overpower, and outlast true citizen reformers.

That we live in a world of media manipulations is understood almost instinctively by the public. Whether we see through a particular propaganda campaign or not, we all know that we live in an age of half-truths, weasel words, and slick image campaigns. When someone says, "That's a bunch of PR," they rarely mean it in a positive sense. "PR has become a catchall phrase for what the public doesn't trust," observes Betty Keepin, the president of a trade association for women PR executives. In 1994, the Public Relations Society of America and the Rockefeller Foundation began a five-year survey aimed at determining which types of public figures were most trusted by the general public. Forty-five different types of public figures were assessed, using a "National Credibility Index" devised by the PRSA to measure "the degree to which an individual trusts the person advocating or espousing a position on an issue." To the PRSA's dismay, public relations professionals came almost at the bottom—number 43, just below "famous athletes" and barely squeaking past "famous entertainers" and "TV or radio talk show hosts."[46]

The PRSA's study was completed in 1999 and released with little fanfare on Friday, June 18—"just before the Fourth of July vacation period and a favorite 'burying ground' for those trying to minimize publicity," noted the PR trade publication *O'Dwyer's*. The survey prompted a few expressions of concern from industry practitioners, some of whom suggested that perhaps they should launch a "PR for PR" campaign. Others resignedly admitted that any such campaign would probably be doomed to failure. But for Dave Siefert, president of the International Association of Business Communicators, the results were neither surprising nor particularly bad news. PR pros work "in the background," he said, and people "see the results of our work, not our personal involvement." The public relations industry itself may lack credibility, but PRSA's survey showed that "national experts" were the third most trusted type of public figure in America (after Supreme Court justices and schoolteachers). And after all, Siefert said, "the national experts are often delivering messages developed by PR pros."[47]

The media stage on which much of modern public life is conducted has created two kinds of experts—the spin doctors behind the scenes, and the visible experts that they select, cultivate, and offer up for public consumption. The experts who work behind the scenes prefer to stay there, because invisibility is necessary to achieve their illusions. "Guys in my business hate becoming public figures . . . when we don't control it," says former Reagan aide Edward Rollins, now a vice president at Edelman.[48] Today's wizards of spin are rather like the Wizard of Oz. They have perfected the craft of speaking in a booming, magisterial voice that inspires admiration and awe, but they fear being unmasked for what they really are—showmen who have learned to use hidden wires, smoke, and mirrors to make little men and little ideas seem grand and convincing. There is a reason that the Wizard begged Dorothy to "pay no attention to that man behind the curtain." But she had to look, and understand the contrivance behind his magic, before she could find her way back home.

2

The Birth of Spin

*Few developments from the Civil War to the
present stand out so vividly or account for so
much of the shape of modern America as the
growth of the professions and the steady
retreat of the layman before the ever-
expanding claims of professional expertise.*
—Thomas L. Haskell[1]

Sitting atop a raised platform canopied in white, philan-
thropist Charles T. Yerkes sat blushing as eight hundred dignitaries greeted him with a standing ovation. William Rainey Harper, the
president of the University of Chicago, praised his "sincerity and simplicity." The head of the university board of trustees said that Yerkes had
helped build a monument to spiritual values in a materialistic age, contributing "to the uplifting of men and upbuilding of character."

The occasion was the dedication of Chicago's new astronomical observatory on October 21, 1897, to which Yerkes had made a substantial financial contribution. When Yerkes himself rose to speak, his modestly
phrased remarks hinted discreetly at the altruistic nature of his gift. "One
reason why the science of astronomy has not more helpers," he said, "is on
account of its being entirely uncommercial. There is nothing of moneyed
value to be gained by the devotee of astronomy; there is nothing that he
can sell."[2]

Nothing to sell, perhaps, but Yerkes was definitely trying to *buy* something—specifically, perfume for a bad reputation. Current flattery aside,
he was one of the most hated men in the city, a robber baron who had
spent time in prison for misappropriation of funds before developing a
winning business strategy that he described as "buy old junk, fix it up a lit-

tle, and unload it upon other fellows." Yerkes had built an empire by controlling the city's lucrative new electric streetcars, whose poorly strung power lines had killed or injured 382 people in 1895 alone. His crude attempts to bribe Illinois legislators had sparked a civic reform movement called the Citizens Independent Anti-Boodle League. The university officials and astronomers who courted his contribution understood full well, as did the rest of the city, that his investment in the observatory was a thinly disguised attempt to buy a new image. In retrospect, it is hard to say who was playing whom for a fool that day. After the day's pageantry, the Chicago newspapers and the Anti-Boodle League returned to their attack. Yerkes was eventually driven from the city in disgrace and died a few years later in poverty and obscurity.

From the perspective of today, the most striking thing about Yerkes and his charitable gesture was its almost quaint ineffectuality. He may have been a scoundrel, but he was no PR man. In 1897, in fact, the term "public relations" had not yet been invented.

Contrary to Yerkes's comment about its lack of helpers, astronomy was actually the most popular object of scientific philanthropy in nineteenth-century America. Civic groups went door-to-door collecting subscriptions to finance the construction of telescopes, with different cities vying for the honor of owning the instrument with the largest lens. As Yerkes observed during his brief moment of public approval, astronomy was an "entirely uncommercial" subject of study—literally, stargazing—and its noncommercial nature was precisely what explained its appeal. People turned to it the way they turned to art museums or great literature. They gazed into the heavens, pondered the mysteries of creation, and philosophized about the nature of the universe. Science and technology in those days were still seen as two very different things. The electric motors that drove Yerkes's streetcars were technology in action—machines of brute force, the ultimate expressions of industrial power and Yankee ingenuity. "Science" was something else, something both finer and less practical—the work of eccentric scholars who scribbled notes in makeshift labs, dug up dinosaur bones and rock samples in remote lands, hatched new theories and tested them with whatever scant resources they could scrape together. Their quaint explorations were appreciated but not particularly revered, nor were they particularly well-funded. "American indifference to science and scientists was . . . the perfectly natural consequence of the fact that neither science nor science-oriented technology was a particularly conspicuous feature of nineteenth-century American life," observes historian Howard Miller. "Not until the twentieth century would industrial, agricultural, and military technology force public recognition that research was a national resource. Until then scientists would in general remain, as one of them termed it, 'inoffensive but curious and useless members of the social order.' "[3]

Thomas Alva Edison, the "wizard of Menlo Park," was an inventor and tinkerer—a technological innovator, not a scientific researcher. His "invention factory" at Menlo Park, New Jersey, turned out literally hundreds of world-transforming gadgets—the typewriter, the phonograph, the lightbulb, the telegraph, storage batteries, electric meters and motors, moving pictures—yet in his entire career Edison made only one discovery that could be called "pure science": the observation that heated metals in a vacuum emit electrons. Because this phenomenon had no utility for his purposes, he simply wrote it down in a notebook and forgot about it. His success as an inventor and businessman, however, made him a prototype for scientists to come. Automaker Henry Ford, a close friend and admirer, observed that Edison "definitely ended the distinction between the theoretical man of science and the practical man of science, so that today we think of scientific discoveries in connection with their possible present or future application to the needs of man. He took the old rule-of-thumb methods out of industry and substituted exact scientific knowledge, while on the other hand, he directed scientific research into useful channels."[4]

"Useful channels," in Edison's eyes and certainly in Ford's, were virtually synonymous with commercial viability. Their concept of science fit perfectly within the American pragmatic tradition, and it was a concept that certainly had its virtues. Its flaws were less immediately obvious.

Galileo vs. the Guardians

Historically, science has often allied itself with the political philosophy of democracy. To function freely, science depends upon the democratic values of free speech, thought, and association, and in fact the ancient Greek democracies were the first Western societies to produce a substantial scientific literature. The Dark Ages brought both a return to authoritarian governments and a suppression of scientific inquiry, which threatened the absolute dogmas handed down from King and Church. The Italian mathematician and astronomer Galileo Galilei has come to symbolize both scientific genius and the importance of intellectual freedom for his persistent efforts to prove that the earth travels around the sun. Condemned in 1633 as a heretic by the Roman Inquisition, Galileo spent the last eight years of his life under house arrest. Eventually, of course, his astronomical conclusions won unanimous acceptance, and today he is frequently cited as an example of steadfast scientific dissent in the face of repressive orthodoxy.

The philosophy of democracy has as its core doctrine the belief that "the people" are better qualified to make decisions that affect their lives than anyone else. It follows from this assumption that governments should be elected by the people and serve their interests. Other institutions, such as corporations, are permitted to pursue their private goal of making money, but their activities may be restricted if the public deems them harmful.

Throughout history, the alternatives to this democratic worldview have been variations on the theme of "guardianship"—the notion that people are not really able to make wise decisions and therefore need to be governed by someone who is smarter, better informed, more rational, or somehow better fit to rule. Plato thought that society should be governed by "philosopher-kings"—men who understood the "science of ruling" and possessed the ability to see beyond appearances and grasp the essential "forms" of true justice. Since this ability is assumed to be rare, it follows that letting "the people" govern will lead to chaos, anarchy, and bad policies. The notion that people need a guardian to govern on their behalf has been used as a rationale by authoritarian governments of all stripes, from the monarchies of Europe to the Marxist-Leninist states in China and Russia to the military regimes that have ruled by terror in places like Argentina, Brazil, Chile, Paraguay, and Nigeria.

In reality, Plato's "royal science" of governance is a chimera. Politics is more of an art than a science. It depends on moral propositions that cannot be reduced to mathematical or physical "scientific laws." Should abortion be legal? Is it moral to build nuclear weapons? Should poor people have access to free medical care? These are only a few of the important questions that do not have scientific or technical answers.

In the struggle between democracy and guardianship, science has acquired a unique and often contradictory role. Heretic stargazers such as

Galileo have led scientific rebellions against society's guardians, but others have eagerly served the royal courts, sometimes even imagining that their specialized knowledge entitles them to become rulers themselves.

Sir Francis Bacon, who is widely regarded as the philosopher responsible for first codifying the modern scientific method, served as Lord Chancellor of England under King James the First. He was hardly an enemy of guardianship, but he recognized that the doctrines of his day, based on royal authority and religious tradition, had become stagnant. "The many surrender themselves to the leadership of one . . . and become incapable of adding anything new," he wrote. "For when philosophy is severed from its roots in experience, whence it first sprouted and grew, it becomes a dead thing." By contrast, he observed, the scientific method had shown its ability to "acquire new strength and capacities" by drawing upon "the talents of many individuals."[5] As an alternative to the concept of rule by philosopher-kings, he envisioned a utopian society run by a technical elite, which would draw upon the knowledge generated by science in order to govern in the interests of efficiency, order, and progress.

The Royal Society for the Improvement of Natural Knowledge, founded in 1660 as England's official scientific society, drew much of its inspiration from Bacon's belief that scientific knowledge should come from all quarters and walks of life. At the time of the society's charter, two-thirds of its members were interested amateurs rather than full-time scientists. Rather than narrow specialists, scientists of the period were wide-ranging intellectuals interested in all of the ideas of the day, from physics to theology. They combined passion for knowledge with practical interests in commerce, agriculture, and industry. "We find noble rarities to be every day given in," wrote Bishop Sprat, the first historian of the Society, "not only by the hands of the learned, but from the shops of mechanics, voyages of merchants, ploughs of husbandmen, gardens of gentlemen."

Simultaneously, however, an unmistakable thread of elitism ran through the thinking of the scientific utopians. Bacon openly disdained the "innate depravity and malignant disposition of the common people" and viewed science as a way to teach "the peoples [to] take upon them the yoke of laws and submit to authority, and forget their ungovernable attitudes."[6] Likewise, Sprat of the Royal Society saw particular value in the participation of its noble-born, amateur members—"gentlemen, free and unconfined . . . who by the freedom of their education, the plenty of their estates and the usual generosity of noble blood, may be well supposed to be most averse from sordid considerations."[7]

In France the *philosophes*, whose thinking helped inspire the French Revolution, dreamed of doing to government what Sir Isaac Newton had done to the human understanding of mathematics and physics. They believed that once men grasped the underlying "fundamental laws" of human society, they would be able to operate the "world-machine" smoothly and efficiently for the betterment of all.[8] This belief found realization in the Jacobin movement, whose goal, notes historian Lewis Coser, was "to make France over in the image of pure reason." And yet it was precisely the intensity of the Jacobin commitment to "pure reason" and "obedience to the law of nature, which intends every man to be just," that led to the French Terror and rule by guillotine. "As long as the demands of nature were violated, as long as there were corruption and rascals and lukewarm concern with public virtue, the purge must continue," Coser observes. "In the pursuit of so exalted an aim, men invested with high purpose and morally invulnerable need feel no pity. Their opponents were not in error; they were in sin. They could therefore be exterminated in good conscience."[9]

A great gulf obviously separated reality from revolutionary ideals, and yet the utopian vision of a world made perfect by reason proved too captivating to abandon. As the French Revolution gave way to disillusionment, philosopher Claude-Henri Saint-Simon became one of the most popular thinkers of the nineteenth century and has had a profound influence on later generations of thinkers. E. H. Carr has aptly described him as "the precursor of socialism, the precursor of the technocrats, and the precursor of totalitarianism."[10] Like Sir Francis Bacon, Saint-Simon believed that science and technology would "solve major social as well as technical problems." In order for technical experts to run society, however, the "unenlightened masses" had to be controlled. This in turn implied a "need to abandon mass democracy and, in turn, politics."[11] In their place, he proposed establishing a new science that would guide all of the others, which he called the "science of organization."[12]

Saint-Simon's ideas were promulgated further by his primary disciple, August Comte, who believed that politics should eventually become a form of "applied physics." Their thinking was similar in many respects to the ideas of the Jacobins. The main difference was that the terrors and trials of revolution had taught Saint-Simon and Comte a certain hostility to politics and even to democracy itself, leading to a "deep-seated conviction that politicians should be replaced by scientific and technical elites. These ideas," writes sociologist Frank Fischer, "occur again and again throughout technocratic writings. Only the historical circumstances change; the ideas themselves remain remarkably constant."[13]

Science, far from being merely a way to study the physical world, had undergone a dramatic transformation. The hard science of physics, with its precise measurements and exact mechanical laws, had become a metaphor, a model of rationality and discipline that people attempted to imitate as they studied softer subjects such as biology, language, human behavior and even the behavior of entire societies. Somehow it didn't seem to matter that none of these subjects lent themselves to precise measurements and predictions. Science had ceased to be merely a methodology and had become an ideology as well.

As an ideology, it lent itself to diverse and conflicting political uses. In England, the Utilitarians adopted an air of scientific rigor as they set out to collect data in support of abolishing the British Poor Law, the welfare system of the day. In its place, they imposed the more "efficient" (i.e., cheaper) workhouse system, whose vicious exploitation of the poor would later be depicted with heartrending detail in the novels of Charles Dickens. Somewhat later, the Fabian Socialists would pave the way for the British welfare state with similar assiduous compilations of meticulous, statistics-laden reports, through which they aimed to establish themselves as "unofficial expert 'clerks' to any decision-maker hampered by lack of expert advice."[14] The Utilitarian obsession with data collection also led to the compilation of the famous Victorian Blue Books, the densest collection of social statistics in human history, which in turn became the source from which Karl Marx drew all of the information he needed for his damning indictment of capitalism. The Marxist "science" of history and class struggle inspired the Bolshevik revolution in Russia, with its own belief in completely rational state power wielded by militant intellectuals. Like the Jacobins, the Bolsheviks believed that they were scientifically manipulating "objective laws of history" in order to create an ideal society. Once again, these ideals degenerated in practice into a new system of bureaucratic tyranny and repressive terror.

The "Science of Ruling" Comes to America

In the United States, the technocratic agenda found prominent expression in the Progressive movement that emerged in the last quarter of the nineteenth century. Herbert Croly, the founder of *The New Republic* magazine, was deeply influenced by the philosophy of August Comte, as was Walter Lippmann. Meanwhile, on the conservative side of the political ledger, Frederick Taylor was developing his theories of "scientific management." Using time and motion studies of workers, he sought to design factories and the work process in ways that would maximize productivity. His approach appealed not only to capitalists but to Russian revolutionary leader V. I. Lenin, who urged Soviet factories to "organize the study and teaching of the Taylor system," which he called one of the "greatest scientific achievements in the field of analyzing mechanical motions during work, the elimination of superfluous and awkward motions, the elaboration of correct methods of work, the introduction of the best system of accounting and control."[15]

"The functions of scientific management were twofold," observes Fischer. "First, they were to enter the workplace to learn (through time and motion studies) what the *workers* already knew: how to plan and direct the details of the work process. Second, through managerial planning and analysis, Taylorites were to employ this newly gained knowledge to 'efficiently' redesign the production process under *management* control. . . . On the shop floor, the division of labor was increased by giving workers more specialized, less complex tasks. As a cost-saving device, it permitted the substitution of cheaper, less skilled workers for skilled workers. Work was less interesting and more repetitive for the worker, but it was more profitable for management. To foil resistance, Taylor's strategy also introduced a number of technical changes. For example, work was designed to make the production process *incomprehensible* to workers. . . . As Taylor put it, 'all possible brain work should be removed from the shop and centered in the planning or layout department.' "[16]

Not only were workers denied control over their own work processes, they were declared psychologically unfit for rational thought. Here, the impetus came from the much-cited "Hawthorne Studies," which probably remain the most widely analyzed and discussed experiments in the history of the social sciences. Named after a Western Electric plant where the studies were conducted, the Hawthorne Studies were led by Harvard University professor Elton Mayo, who studied groups of women workers in an effort to determine what factors made them more productive. The Hawthorne Studies became influential not because of what they "proved," but because Mayo's conclusions found a ready audience in the business community. He claimed that there was a fundamental psychological difference between workers and management. Whereas management acts on the basis of logic and rationality, he said, workers are motivated by emotions.[17]

The period between World Wars I and II came to be known as the "Age of the Machine." It was during this period that mechanical technologies diffused throughout society. The automobile came into fashion. Machines became symbols of rationality, order, efficiency, power, and progress.[18] A fledgling "technocracy movement" arose in the United States that saw "science banishing waste, unemployment, hunger, and insecurity of income forever . . . we see science replacing an economy of scarcity with an era of abundance . . . we see functional competence displacing grotesque and wasteful incompetence, facts displacing disorder, industrial planning displacing industrial chaos."[19] Sometimes calling itself "Technocracy, Inc.," the movement exhibited protofascistic tendencies: "Organized around a rigid hierarchical structure, the members of technocracy featured gray uniforms with special insignias, drove a fleet of gray automobiles, and greeted one another with a special salute," Fischer notes.[20]

In the wake of the First World War, observed contemporary historian Frederick Lewis Allen, science was "the one great intellectual force which had not suffered disrepute. . . . The prestige of science was colossal. The man in the street and the woman in the kitchen, confronted on every hand with new machines and devices which they owed to the laboratory, were ready to believe that science could accomplish almost anything; and they were being deluged with scientific information and theory. The newspapers were giving columns of space to inform (or misinform) them of the latest discoveries; a new dictum from Albert Einstein was now front-page stuff even though practically nobody could understand it. Outlines of knowledge poured from the presses to tell people about the planetesimal hypothesis and the constitution of the atom, to describe for them in unwarranted detail the daily life of the cave-man, and to acquaint them with the electron, endocrines, hormones, vitamins, reflexes and psychoses."[21]

The 1920s was also the period when the psychosexual theories of Sigmund Freud found a mass audience. "Psychology was king," Allen observes. "Freud, Adler, Jung and Watson had their tens of thousands of votaries; intelligence-testers invaded the schools in quest of I.Q.'s; psychiatrists were installed in business houses to hire and fire employees and determine advertising policies."

The Wizard of Spin

Freud exerted particular influence on Edward L. Bernays, the man who has come to be known as the "father of public relations." For him, Freud was not just a towering intellect but a family member and personal mentor. Bernays was the son of Eli Bernays and Anna Freud Bernays, Sigmund's sister. In fact, the Freuds and Bernayses got along so well that Sigmund himself ended up marrying Martha Bernays, Eli's sister. What this meant for Edward Bernays is that he was not only Sigmund Freud's nephew but a nephew twice over. Through Bernays, Freud's influence on the fledgling public relations industry was enormous, and that legacy continues today in the most direct familial sense at Freud Communications, a high-powered British PR firm owned by Matthew Freud, Sigmund's great-grandson. In addition to handling celebrities such as Arnold Schwarzenegger, Sylvester Stallone, Bruce Willis, Hugh Grant, and Pamela Anderson, Freud Communications has worked for companies such as Volvo and Pizza Hut, and also handled the PR for the 1995 launch of Pepsi's redesigned soda pop cans.

It would not be any exaggeration to say that Edward Bernays viewed his famous uncle Sigmund as a father figure. He visited him in Europe whenever he got the chance, showered him with gifts of cigars, and helped arrange for and publicize the translation of Freud's *Introductory Lectures in Psychoanalysis* in the United States. From Freud's perspective, these efforts came as welcome assistance at a time when postwar inflation had wiped him out financially, although the relationship was strained somewhat by young Edward's eagerness to sacrifice intellectual rigor to the lowbrow demands of the publicity trade. When Bernays approached him with an offer from *Cosmopolitan* magazine to write an article titled "The Wife's Mental Place in the Home," Freud rebelled with a stinging letter of refusal. "The absolute submission of your editors to the rotten taste of an uncultivated public is the cause of the low level of American literature," he wrote.

Occasional tensions notwithstanding, Bernays saw his association with Freud as a way to establish his own reputation as a thinker and theorist—a reputation that was further enhanced when Bernays authored several landmark books of his own, most notably *Crystallizing Public Opinion, The Engineering of Consent,* and *Propaganda.* "When a person would first meet Bernays," notes PR industry historian Scott Cutlip, "it would not be long before Uncle Sigmund would be brought into the conversation. His relationship with Freud was always in the forefront of his thinking and his counseling."[22] In a profile written in 1958, author Irwin Ross observed that Bernays epitomized the PR industry's "wistful yearnings for scholarly distinction" and "likes to think of himself as a kind of psychoanalyst to troubled corporations. He talks, of course, far more than a psychoanalyst. . . . The words tumble forth in an endless cascade, the polysyllables lulling the auditor's critical faculties, the clods of jargon dropping like huge pillows which cushion the mind against anxiety. At times one only has a dim view of what Bernays is saying, but it sounds great. 'I got so I could write the stuff myself,' says Morris M. Lee, Jr. [a former Bernays employee], 'but I could never understand it.' "[23]

People who knew Bernays are unanimous in describing him as a man with a huge ego and an incessant habit of self-promotion. His writings include a lengthy bibliography of his own work and public utterances, in which Ross notes that "even editorial notes accompanying his articles are immortalized. . . . Books which merely listed Bernays in *their* bibliographies are reciprocally listed in *his;* an author who included Bernays in her acknowledgments in turn finds her own work acknowledged; a book which 'indirectly' quoted Bernays is duly rescued from obscurity, as are novels in which Bernays is mentioned in passing."[24] Bernays also authored an 850-page book of memoirs, titled *Biography of an Idea,* and after reaching the age of 100, he began work on a second memoir, titled *The First Hundred Years.* Sometimes his ego interfered with his professional success. Many of his contemporaneous peers in the PR industry disliked him intensely, regarding him as a pushy braggart who was hurting the industry's reputation with his frank talk about "propaganda" and "controlling and regimenting the masses."

Bernays used Freudianism's scientific claims as a sort of marketing hook with which to sell his services to anxious corporate executives. "The counsel on public relations," he explained, "is what sociologists call a societal technician who is fitted by training and experience to evaluate the maladjustments and adjustments between his client and the publics upon whom the client is dependent for his socially sound activity."[25] In *Propaganda*, his most important book, he argued that the scientific manipulation of public opinion was necessary to overcome chaos and conflict in society. "The conscious and intelligent manipulation of the organized habits and opinions of the masses is an important element in democratic society. Those who manipulate this unseen mechanism of society constitute an invisible government which is the true ruling power of our country," he wrote. "We are governed, our minds molded, our tastes formed, our ideas suggested, largely by men we have never heard of. This is a logical result of the way in which our democratic society is organized. Vast numbers of human beings must cooperate in this manner if they are to live together as a smoothly functioning society. . . . In almost every act of our lives, whether in the sphere of politics or business, in our social conduct or our ethical thinking, we are dominated by the relatively small number of persons . . . who understand the mental processes and social patterns of the masses. It is they who pull the wires which control the public mind."[26]

There was a striking paradox, however, in the way that Bernays went about trying to follow in the footsteps of Uncle Sigmund. Freud's "talking cure" was designed to unearth his patients' unconscious drives and hidden motives, in the belief that bringing them into conscious discourse would help people lead healthier lives. Bernays, by contrast, used psychological techniques to *mask* the motives of his clients, as part of a deliberate strategy aimed at keeping the public *un*conscious of the forces that were working to mold their minds.

Science and the "Intelligent Few"

It is no accident that Bernays developed his "science" of public relations in the 1920s—a decade that also saw the beginnings of mass production, mass communications, mass consumerism, and a belief in technological progress as a quasireligion. All of these trends shared a faith in the notion that society's problems can be engineered away, that democracy is dangerous, and that important decisions should be left in the hands of experts. In addition to psychoanalytic theory, Bernays drew heavily from the ideas of nineteenth-century French social philosopher Gustave Le Bon, a vocal critic of democracy who fretted that "the divine right of the masses is about to replace the divine right of kings." Stuart Ewen, a historian and author of *PR: A Social History of Spin,* notes that Le Bon feared "that the mob at any moment could seize society and destroy all he held sacred. Le Bon starts to examine the social psychology of the crowd. For him the crowd is not driven by rational argument, but by its spinal cord. It responds solely to emotional appeals and is incapable of thought or reason. Somebody interested in leading the crowd needs to appeal not to logic but to unconscious motivation." For Bernays in particular, Ewen notes, Le Bon's ideas "are applied to virtually everybody. Almost no one is seen as capable of rational thought. The most efficient way to win hearts and minds is through emotional appeals. By the 1920s, Le Bonian social psychology is used to design organizations that constantly take the temperature of public feelings. Survey research, polling and focus groups are all built around the science of how to lead the public mind."[27]

Ewen interviewed Bernays near the end of his life and was struck by his "unabashedly hierarchical view of society. Repeatedly, he maintained that, while most people respond to their world instinctively, without thought, there exist an 'intelligent few' who have been charged with the responsibility of contemplating and influencing the tide of history. . . . He expressed little respect for the average person's ability to think out, understand, or act upon the world in which they live. . . . Throughout our conversation, Bernays conveyed his hallucination of democracy: a highly educated class of opinion-molding tacticians are continuously at work, analyzing the social terrain and adjusting the mental scenery from which the public mind, with its limited intellect, derives its opinions."[28]

Expanding on Freud's theories about the unconscious motives for human behavior, Bernays believed that people are not merely unconscious but herdlike in their thinking, "subject to the passions of the pack in [their] mob violence and the passions of the herd in [their] panics. . . . The average citizen is the world's most efficient censor. His own mind is the greatest barrier between him and the facts. His own 'logic-proof compartments,' his own absolutism, are the obstacles which prevent him from seeing in terms of experience and thought rather than in terms of group reaction."[29]

Fortunately, Bernays added, being herdlike also made people "remarkably susceptible to leadership."[30] He saw public relations as an applied science, like engineering, through which society's leaders could bring order out of chaos and muddle. "If we understand the mechanism and motives of the group mind," he argued, it would be possible to "control and regiment the masses according to our will without their knowing it. . . . Theory and practice have combined with sufficient success to permit us to know that in certain cases we can effect some change in public opinion with a fair degree of accuracy by operating a certain mechanism, just as the motorist can regulate the speed of his car by manipulating the flow of gasoline."[31]

To exercise this type of control was not just an option, it was a duty: "It is certain that the power of public opinion is constantly increasing and will keep on increasing. It is equally certain that it is more and more being influenced, changed, stirred by impulses from below. . . . The duty of the higher strata of society—the cultivated, the learned, the expert, the intellectual—is therefore clear. They must inject moral and spiritual motives into public opinion."[32] A public relations counselor could accomplish this, Bernays said, because his special training and insight into human nature "permits him to step out of his own group to look at a particular problem with the eyes of an impartial observer and to utilize his knowledge of the individual and the group mind to project his clients' point of view."[33]

Of course, the mind of Edward Bernays had its own share of "logic-proof compartments." To begin with, there is the obvious contradiction in his notion that a public relations consultant can simultaneously be both an "impartial observer" and a special pleader for his client.

The First Front Group

Bernays stumbled into public relations almost by accident. In 1913, while working as editor of the *Medical Review of Reviews,* a monthly magazine owned by a college acquaintance, he discovered that the then-famous actor Richard Bennett was interested in producing a play titled "Damaged Goods," which Bernays described as "a propaganda play that fought for sex education." It discussed sexual topics, such as prostitution, that were considered unusually frank for their day. Bennett was afraid that the play would be raided by police, and he hired Bernays to prevent this from happening. Rather than arguing for the play on its merits, Bernays cleverly organized a group that he called the *"Medical Review of Reviews* Sociological Fund," inviting prominent doctors and members of the social elite to join.

The organization's avowed mission was to fight venereal disease through education. Its real purpose was to endorse "Damaged Goods," and apparently the plan worked. The show went on as scheduled, with no interference from police.

"This was a pioneering move that is common today in the promotion of public causes—a prestigious sponsoring committee," notes PR industry historian Scott Cutlip. "In retrospect, given the history of public relations, it might be termed the first effort to use the front or third party technique." It was a technique that Bernays would return to time and again, calling it "the most useful method in a multiple society like ours to indicate the support of an idea of the many varied elements that make up our society. Opinion leaders and group leaders have an effect in a democracy and stand as symbols to their constituency."[34] He helped jump-start sales of bacon, a breakfast rarity until the 1920s, by enlisting a prominent doctor to solicit fellow doctors' opinions on the salutary benefits of a hearty breakfast and by arranging to have famous figures photographed eating breakfasts of bacon and eggs. To sell bananas on behalf of the United Fruit Company, he launched the "celiac project," republishing and disseminating a 20-year-old medical paper which found that eating bananas cured children with celiac disease, a disorder of the digestive system.[35]

"Mr. Bernays has . . . created more institutes, funds, institutions, and foundations than Rockefeller, Carnegie, and Filene together," observed the Institute for Propaganda Analysis, a nonprofit educational organization that flourished in the years following World War I. "Typical of them was the Temperature Research Foundation. Its stated purpose was 'to disseminate impartial, scientific information concerning the latest developments in temperature control as they affect the health, leisure, happiness, and economy of the American people.' A minor purpose—so minor that rarely did Mr. Bernays remember even to mention it—was to boost the sales of Kelvinator refrigerators, air-condition units, and electric stoves."[36]

The tobacco industry, another early Bernays client, also relied heavily on expert testimonials to tout its products, recruiting opera singers and doctors to claim that cigarettes soothed the throat and aided digestion. Advertisements of this type became so ubiquitous that Bernays spoofed one of his industry rivals by creating a front group called the "Tobacco Society for Voice Culture" which mockingly claimed that its mission was to "establish a home for singers and actors whose voices have cracked under the strain of their cigarette testimonials."[37]

Light's Golden Jubilee

Bernays sectioned his autobiography into five parts and gave the title "Fulfillment" to the third section, which covered the years from 1923 to 1929. Those were the years that marked the emergence of the fledgling public relations industry, as Bernays rose from obscurity to wealth and influence. By January of 1929, his clients included the New Jersey Bell Telephone Company, Procter & Gamble, Knox Gelatin, and the American Tobacco Company. "In a typical month, January, our clients paid us gross fees of $16,524.43, with profits of $11,868.78," he said. "That was not considered bad for a 38-year-old, adventuring into an untried, unknown field." In fact, it would not be considered a bad monthly income today, even without adjusting for inflation. "I was doing well," he recalled, "but the profession of counsel on public relations lacked the respect that I felt it deserved. Our clients knew what we could do for them and respected our methods, but to many we were still sensation mongers and ballyhoo artists—a menace to the integrity of press and business alike."[38]

The 1928 publication of his book *Propaganda* helped drum up new corporate clients but also prompted a flurry of criticism. *Editor & Publisher* magazine described Bernays as "the young Machiavelli of our times." Another writer commented that "publicity agents for special and selfish causes inimical to the general interest and disturbing to the Commonwealth use just as much ingenuity and invention plus at least a fair measure of corruption."[39] Chafing at these criticisms, Bernays longed for the opportunity to stage "a dramatic event that would make others see us as we saw ourselves."[40]

The opportunity he was looking for arrived in February 1929 with a visit from Napoleon Boynton, an executive with the General Electric company. Like Bernays, General Electric was having a few image problems and wanted his help. Long under congressional attack for monopolistic practices in lamp manufacture, GE wanted to stage a massive publicity stunt that would showcase the benefits that lightbulbs had brought to humanity. As it happened, the fiftieth anniversary of Thomas Edison's invention of the lightbulb was fast approaching. What better way to polish the industry's image than to honor Edison with an event that they would call "Light's Golden Jubilee"? The Westinghouse Corporation, GE's main competition in the electric light market, was also eager to jump on the promotional bandwagon.

"I recognized the potential professional significance of the assignment and plunged into the given task eagerly," Bernays said. "The United States—and, for that matter, the world—was ripe for a new hero, and here was the 50th anniversary of one of the most significant and beneficial inventions of the age, and the inventor was still living."[41]

Aged 82, enfeebled and recovering from a bout of pneumonia, Edison had retreated from his business activities and was devoting his final years to a quixotic and ultimately unsuccessful effort to develop a process that would derive rubber from milkweeds. Moreover, Edison's feelings toward GE and Westinghouse were decidedly negative. In his own heyday as a businessman, he had viewed George Westinghouse as his archrival, calling him a "shyster" and "the enemy." As for GE, it had once *been* Edison's. Christened "the Edison General Electric Company," it slipped from his control in an 1891 power grab by J. Pierpont Morgan, who drove home the insult by stripping Edison's name from the company as soon as he took possession. There was more than a little irony in the idea that these robber barons should now want to honor him in his old age.

The glue that held the plan together was Henry Ford, whose admiration and affection for Edison knew no bounds. Ford, moreover, had propaganda aspirations of his own. A few years earlier, his offhand remark that "history is more or less bunk" had won him a reputation as a scholarly cretin, a rich but crude mechanic with no understanding of tradition or culture. Ford's response to his critics was to create some history of his own—not a written *book* of history, but history as inscribed in *things*—the gadgets and artifacts that he saw as the fundamental expressions of humanity's progress. At his birthplace in Dearborn, Michigan, Ford was building an eight-acre industrial museum and stuffing it with plows, furniture, milk pails, butter churns, china sets, flintlock rifles, grandfather clocks, music boxes, steam engines, threshers, fire engines, a Model T—anything and everything that might preserve the memory of America's mechanics, blacksmiths, and craftsmen. Once Ford learned of the plans to honor Edison, he realized that it would make a perfect capstone to his own monumental plans. Renaming his museum the Edison Institute of Technology, he created as its centerpiece a reverently reconstructed replica of the Menlo Park complex where Edison had done most of his inventing. He bought up every drill press, lathe, rusted machine, and empty chemical bottle that he could acquire from the now-decaying original Edison laboratory, disassembling whole buildings board by board and brick by brick and shipping them to Dearborn by rail for reassembly. He even transplanted some of the original trees and shrubbery. No expense was spared as he rebuilt Menlo Park right down to Edison's old outhouse. To celebrate Light's Golden Jubilee, he invited Edison to participate in a reenactment of the moment of creation of the electric light. The ceremony would be held in the rebuilt laboratory on October 21, 1929, exactly fifty years to the day from the date of Edison's successful experiment.

Bernays was now in a PR man's hog heaven. His clients were competing with Henry Ford to see who could do the most to honor the old inventor's legacy. Money was not an issue as he set out to put on a show unlike anything that Charles T. Yerkes could have imagined for his pathetic little telescope. It was a frenzy of activity that a Yale social psychologist would later call "one of the most astonishing pieces of propaganda ever engineered in this country during peacetime." In the months leading up to the reenactment, plans went out to public utility companies, giving instructions for local tie-in activities. Luncheons were held for newspaper editors and movie newsreel executives. *Scientific American,* the *Saturday Evening Post,* and other magazines planned special issues celebrating Edison and his achievements. Talks were given to Lions, Kiwanis, and Rotary Clubs, to Boy and Girl Scouts, chambers of commerce, women's clubs. Written tributes to Edison were collected from Albert Einstein, General John J. Pershing, Jane Addams, and Admiral Byrd. Bernays persuaded the postmaster general of the United States to issue a commemorative two-cent stamp in honor of the lightbulb. Songwriter George M. Cohan wrote a musical tribute. Costume competitions, fireworks, and pageants were held. "Light's Golden Jubilee no longer depended on a press bureau," Bernays recalled with jubilation of his own. "Everybody was joining the procession. From the grass roots to Broadway the spirit of ballyhoo took over. Mayors and Governors issued proclamations to celebrate Light's Golden Jubilee. Universities offered lectures on Edison and the implications of his discovery. Education groups conducted essay contests. Librarians displayed books about Edison. Museum heads arranged exhibits that would illustrate the history of light."[42]

Even Bernays was astonished at the scale of the campaign and its success at captivating the country's imagination. Of all the episodes in his career, he recounted this one most frequently in his later years. "I tried to look at it objectively," he said. "Someone has an idea—Light's Golden Jubilee—honoring a fine old man who has made significant contributions to American life. You realize that he can be made a myth, so you start myth-building. Perhaps it would be more accurate to say you help the myth to grow. The public, expressing its own unfulfilled aspirations, builds the myth until it becomes an overwhelming, meaningful reality. . . . Whether you accept the Freudian thesis or not, people want a father substitute. That is myth-building. Edison was an ideal subject—a great inventor symbolizing the scientific era of electronics to come."[43]

The timing helped as well to feed a spirit of enthusiasm. America was riding on an economic high as the stock market soared and everyone from elevator operators to the wealthiest families joined in the speculative mania. Everyone seemed to be rich and getting richer, with no end in sight. As the months ticked down toward October, the gains were especially phenomenal. The stock ticker (one of Edison's first successful inventions) showed steady gains with no downturns at all, not even a lull or temporary setback. The Dow Jones Industrials went from 299.13 on April 9 to 381.17 on September 3. The price for a share of Westinghouse went from 151 to 286. General Electric went from 268 to 391.

The challenge as October 21 approached was deciding which dignitaries had to be *excluded* from the day's events. Hundreds of notables attended, including President Herbert Hoover, Orville Wright, John D. Rockefeller, Jr., Will Rogers, and Madame Curie. The honored guests arrived in Dearborn and were taken to the festivities aboard a replica of the Grand Trunk Railway train, on which Edison had worked in his boyhood as a "news butch," selling sandwiches, newspapers, and other amenities to passengers. As part of the ceremony, a boy handed Edison a basket of similar merchandise that he was supposed to offer to President Hoover. But for Bernays, at least, the actual ritual was less satisfactory than its planners had imagined. "Edison, 82, enfeebled with age and sickness, took the basket, and offered his merchandise to President Hoover, crying, 'Candy, apples, sandwiches and newspapers!' in a valiant effort to reenact his boyhood sales pitch. It was embarrassing to all of us—a pathetic evocation of the past," Bernays recalled.

There was in fact something a little sad and contradictory about the day's festivities. "It became just a publicity thing, and we didn't care for it," Edison's daughter Madeleine said later. His wife Mina also had "mixed feelings," according to biographer Neil Baldwin. She "saw keenly the irony that corporate cosponsor General Electric was now making such a tremendous fuss over Edison, co-opting his presence as a symbol, especially considering the inauspicious circumstances under which her husband had long since parted with the company."[44]

Although Bernays doesn't speak of it in his memoirs, he himself became the object of Ford's animosity that day. An unabashed anti-Semite, Ford had disliked Bernays from the beginning and had only reluctantly allowed him to participate in arranging the Dearborn event. Ford took further offense at Bernays's ceaseless efforts at self-promotion. According to another chronicler of Light's Golden Jubilee, Bernays "as a matter of fact incurred Ford's wrath after the dedicatory party arrived in Dearborn because he tried repeatedly to inject himself into the group picture with Hoover, Edison and the host. Ford took Fred Black aside and told him to 'get Bernays the hell out of here or I'll have Harry Bennett's men throw him over the fence.' Black told Bernays of the threat and he moved out of camera range."[45]

The capstone of the day was scheduled for 6:15 that evening. Following a candlelight dinner, "Edison, looking like a benevolent old wreck, walked with Ford and President Hoover to the transplanted Menlo Park laboratory and re-enacted the invention of the electric lamp," Bernays recalled. The aging inventor demonstrated how he had made a carbonized thread and a vacuum globe, as radio announcer Graham McNamee dramatized each gesture for his listeners: "The lamp is now ready, as it was a half century ago! Will it light? Will it burn? Edison touches the wire . . . Ladies and gentlemen—it lights! Light's Golden Jubilee has come to a triumphant climax!" The entire laboratory building was bathed in searchlights. A Ford-commissioned replica of the Liberty Bell pealed, sirens and whistles blew through the city of Detroit, and planes flew overhead.

Overcome by emotion, Edison faltered, sat down, and wept. His wife calmed him and gave him warm milk, which seemed to revive him. He was assisted to his seat of honor and listened as President Hoover gave yet another tributory speech. Edison managed to say a few words himself before turning white and slumping in his chair in an exhausted faint. His wife and Hoover's physician helped him out of the room, laid him on a sofa, and administered drugs. It would take several days of recuperation at Ford's home before he was well enough to travel home. It was the old man's last public hurrah, and everyone knew it.[46]

What they *didn't* know was that the day's festivities were in many ways Hoover's last hurrah as well. Light's Golden Jubilee was held on Monday, October 21, but three days later, darkness rather than light would prevail. The celebration of Edison and his creations has left a mark on the American imagination, but October 24, 1929, is by far the better-remembered date: Black Thursday—the day the stock market crashed.

The Experts Speak

One of the striking historical facts about the Great Depression is the complete failure of society's economic and political experts to see it coming, or to deal with it sensibly once it arrived. Fourteen days before the crash, Irving Fisher had predicted, "In a few months I expect to see the stock market much higher than today." Fisher, America's most distinguished and famous professor of economics at Yale University, was so overconfident that he personally lost a fortune equivalent to $140 million in today's dol-lars when the market collapsed. John Maynard Keynes, the most famous British economist, lost the equivalent of £1 million. The headline in the *New York Journal* on the day after Black Thursday was "Experts Predict Rising Market." The Harvard Economic Society responded to the news by telling its subscribers, "A severe depression such as 1920–21 is outside the range of probability. We are not facing a protracted liquidation."

As it became apparent that the Depression was more than a tempo-rary downturn, President Hoover appointed Edward Bernays to his three-member Presidential Emergency Committee for Employment. "It was really a public relations committee," Bernays recalled in his memoirs. Hoover's refusal to countenance "socialist" ideas such as social security and public works programs left the committee with few options. "We en-couraged various ways of spreading employment: through reduced daily and weekly schedules, shorter shifts, alternating shifts and rotation of days off. . . . We urged employers to find personnel willing to go on fur-lough without pay; to disclose duplication of wage earners in the same family, as a measure of spreading wages; to maintain lists for preferential employment and to determine the adequacy of part-time wages." In the end, however, Bernays realized, "these efforts were all ineffective. Partic-ularly unsound was the share-the-work idea, which put the onus of sacri-fice on the shoulders of the wage earner instead of the employer." Advertisers and businesses offered empty slogans such as "Be patriotic and spend money," "Spend ten cents more each day and help drive hard times away," or "Help the jobless by doing your Christmas shopping now." As the economy careened into deeper and deeper trouble, newspapers resorted to desperate cheerleading. "Optimism Gains as U.S. Speeds Jobless Relief," read one headline. "Hoover's Drive to Aid Jobless Shows Results," read another. "President Declares Voluntary Cooperation of Industry Will Solve Problem."[47]

In 1932, Bernays joined Hoover's doomed campaign for reelection. He helped line up experts to sing Hoover's praises, including a pair of Yale economists who predicted that the economy was now on a "sound foundation" and "the run of the dollar had been stopped."[48] He formed a "Non-Partisan Fact-Finding Committee," which issued a poll showing Hoover trouncing his opponent, Franklin Delano Roosevelt. Outside the circle of businessmen and their sycophants, however, no one believed a word of it. The election of Roosevelt brought new experts into power, with new and grandiose ideas about what could and should be done to secure the general welfare. For Hoover and the old guard, it was the end of an era and everything that they believed in, but for Bernays and the propaganda industry, business was booming like never before.

3

Deciding What
You'll Swallow

Everything is possible but nothing is real.

—song lyric by Living Colour

In 1992, the food industry's International Food Information Council (IFIC) retained Dr. G. Clotaire Rapaille, "an international market research expert," to research "how Americans relate to food biotechnology and genetic engineering." IFIC, a PR lobby for the use of biotechnology in agriculture, wanted to know how it could overcome consumer apprehensions about the new technology. A "core team" was assembled to aid in the research, consisting of representatives from the Monsanto Agricultural Company, NutraSweet, Kraft General Foods, Ajinomoto, DuPont, and Calgene. Other research sponsors included Frito-Lay, Coca-Cola, Nestlé, Procter & Gamble, and the M&M/Mars candy company. The goal of the research team was to "develop actionable strategies, messages, and language that will express information positively about the process and products—without stirring fears or negative connotations."[1]

Dr. Rapaille is a Jungian psychologist who uses a technique he calls "Archetype Studies," which claims to delve into the "primordial cause for . . . opinions, attitudes or motivations." As his report to IFIC explained, "For each element in the world, there is a first meaningful experience called the Imprinting Moment. The Archetype is the pattern which underlies this Imprinting Moment. The Archetype is completely preordained by the culture, and it is common to everyone in a given culture. . . . The Archetype is the Logic of Emotion that forms the Collective Unconscious." Discover these Archetypes, Rapaille's theory promised, and "you can 'read' the consumers like a book, and you can understand their unconscious 'logic.' "[2]

Rapaille's process for uncovering Archetypes was similar in most respects to what another advertising or PR person might term a "focus group," but Dr. Rapaille liked to refer to them as "Imprinting Groups." Each group consisted of 20 to 30 everyday Americans, which Rapaille's team of "Archetypologists" led through a series of "relaxation exercises and visualization" aimed at eliciting their innermost feelings about biotechnology.[3]

The result of these exercises, the team concluded, was that the biotech industry stood at a crossroads. "In one case, we have tremendous public support—we can be viewed as farmers bringing new varieties and improved foods to consumers. But if we do not position ourselves and our products correctly, we can just as easily be viewed in the same class as Hitler and Frankenstein." The difference depended on which "imprint" provided the Archetype for public perception of the new foods. And the public would choose its Archetype based largely on the food industry's choice of words.[4]

"In communicating about food biotechnology and genetic engineering, we now know a variety of 'trigger' words that will help consumers view these products in the same vein as farming, hybrids, and the natural order, rather than as Frankenfoods," the study concluded. In the category of "words to use," Rapaille suggested terms such as beauty, bounty, children, choices, cross-breeding, diversity, earth, farmer, flowers, fruits, future generations, hard work, heritage, improved, organic, purity, quality, soil, tradition, and wholesome. "Words to lose" included: biotechnology, chemical, DNA, economic, experiments, industry, laboratory, machines, manipulate, money, pesticides, profit, radiation, safety, and scientists.[5]

In a memo accompanying the completed study, IFIC's Libby Mikesell and Tom Stenzel summarized the lessons learned. "The technology in bio*technology* has 'scary' overtones in connection with life in any form. . . . Biotechnology may not be the optimal term to use in our discussions," they wrote. "Clotaire recommends that we 'sandwich' the word genetic between other words that create an association with tradition and nature. Some possible terms he suggested were 'biogenetic gardening,' 'natural genetics' or 'natural genetic gardening.' He composed this sentence as an example of how to use the terms: *New genetic discoveries allow us to be successful gardeners of the 21st century and to accomplish cross-breeding at* *a highly sophisticated level, fulfilling a vision of the gardeners of the 19th century.*"[6]

It is worth noting that many of the terms in Rapaille's list of "words to lose" are straightforward characterizations of the actual scientific process used in developing genetically engineered foods, while many of the "words to use" are vague, pleasant-sounding euphemisms designed to obscure the details about everything that is new and unique about the process. Dr. Rapaille has a Ph.D. from the Sorbonne, but his analytical method does not necessarily require one. William Lutz, a professor at Rutgers University and author of the book *Doublespeak,* has catalogued numerous similar examples of industry and government linguistic coinage, many of which originated with people who lacked any background what-soever in Jungian Archetypology. The Reagan administration, for example, invented the phrase "revenue enhancements" as a substitute for "taxes." Gambling casinos prefer to call themselves the "gaming industry." Corporations refer to failed business ventures as "nonperforming assets." The military refers to civilian deaths as "collateral damage," bombs as "vertically deployed antipersonnel devices," and killing the enemy as "servicing the target."

It is also worth noting the irony in IFIC's choice of someone like Rapaille to help design its strategy for defending biotechnology. Whatever dangers biotechnology may or may not present to the public, it is undeniably an example of modern science in action. When talking among themselves, biotech's promoters frequently invoke the name of science, characterizing their opponents as irrational, fear-driven technophobes. "We all are frustrated by the public's emotional response to scientific, factual issues," stated the IFIC report. Yet Rapaille's advice to IFIC was not only calculated to *evoke* an emotional response and to avoid any mention of science, his very methodology for arriving at his analysis is at best a parody of the scientific method. In its relentless effort to probe the supposedly irrational mind of the public, it is a modern-day example of the legacy of Edward Bernays and his famous uncle, Sigmund Freud.

Hard Science and Liquid Truth

The power that science wields in modern society is a reflection of its ability to create knowledge that is as close to infallible as any product of human endeavor. Reasonable people may disagree in their opinions about

Shakespeare or religion, but they do not disagree with the laws of thermodynamics. This is because the theories of science, especially the hard sciences, have been developed through methodologies that require verification by multiple, independent researchers using clearly defined, replicable experiments. If the experiments do not bear out a hypothesis, the hypothesis must be rejected or modified.

The very prestige that science enjoys, however, has also given rise to a variety of scientific pretenders—disciplines such as phrenology or eugenics that merely *claim* to be scientific. The renowned philosopher of science Karl Popper gave a great deal of consideration to this problem and coined the term "pseudoscience" to help separate the wheat from the chaff. The difference between science and pseudoscience, he concluded, is that genuinely scientific theories are "falsifiable"—that is, they are formulated in such a way that if they are wrong, they can be proven false through experiments. By contrast, pseudosciences are formulated so vaguely that they can never be proven or disproven. "The difference between a science and a pseudoscience is that scientific statements can be proved wrong and pseudoscientific statements cannot," says Robert Youngson in his book *Scientific Blunders: A Brief History of How Wrong Scientists Can Sometimes Be.* "By this criterion you will find that a surprising number of seemingly scientific assertions—perhaps even many in which you devoutly believe—are complete nonsense. Rather surprisingly this is not to assert that all pseudoscientific claims are untrue. Some of them may be true, but you can never know this, so they are not entitled to claim the cast-iron assurance and reliance that you can have, and place, in scientific facts."[7]

Judged by this standard, many of the "social sciences"—including the psychoanalytic theories of Freud, Jung, and others—are actually pseudosciences rather than the real thing. This does not mean that Freud and Jung were charlatans or fools. Both were creative thinkers with fascinating insights into the human psyche, but a research methodology that derives its data from the dreams of mentally ill patients is a far cry from the orderly system of measurements that we associate with hard sciences like physics and chemistry.[8]

Regardless of their scientific limitations, theories of human psychology figure prominently in the thinking of the public relations industry. What is more important than their actual effectiveness is the seemingly authoritative justification that they provide for the PR worldview—a belief that people are fundamentally irrational and that therefore a class of behind-the-scenes manipulators is necessary to shape opinion for the public's own good. But this belief is at odds not only with the ideals of democracy but also with the fundamental and necessary ideological underpinnings of the scientific method itself. Before scientists can reach any conclusions whatsoever about the elements in the periodic table or the space-time continuum, they have to first believe that "the truth is out there" and that their investigations will take them closer to it. The public relations worldview, however, envisions truth as an infinitely malleable, spinnable thing. For consultants like Clotaire Rapaille, the truth is not a thing to be *discovered* but a thing to be *created,* through artful word choices and careful arrangement of appearances.

"Given a choice, do you serve your client or the truth?" a reporter asked John Scanlon, one of today's leading spinmeisters, during a 1991 interview.

"You always try—you always serve the truth," Scanlon replied. "But again—but the truth is often, you know, is often not necessarily a solid. It can be a liquid. . . . What seems to be true is not necessarily the case when we look at it and we dissect it and take it apart, and we turn it around and we look at it from a different perspective. . . . Whose truth are we talking about, your truth or my truth?"[9]

John Scanlon specializes in representing high-profile clients, especially clients embroiled in controversy. In 1997, the trade publication *Inside PR* ranked him as the number-two expert in the world at "crisis management"—the PR field that specializes in helping clients fend off scandals and repair bad reputations. In 1999, for example, he represented famed fellatrix and self-proclaimed liar Monica Lewinsky as she embarked on a media tour to promote her book, *Monica's Story.* Lewinsky too, it seems, had a version of the truth to tell, as did the president whose sexual relationship with her depended on what your definition of "is" is. Scanlon's other assignments have included PR for CBS when it was sued for libel by Vietnam-era general William Westmoreland. Later, he squared off against *60 Minutes* when he went to work for the Brown & Williamson tobacco company in its effort to discredit tobacco-industry whistle-blower Jeffrey Wigand, whose story was dramatized in the movie *The Insider.* In both cases, Scanlon's methodology was similar: disseminate as much dirt as you can about the opposing camp in order to distract the media from the substance of the story. In the case of Wigand, Scanlon compiled a lengthy catalogue of allegations—Wigand was a shoplifter, a wife-beater, a drunk—and circulated them in the form of a detailed dossier to print and TV journalists. The *Wall Street Journal* eventually set out to verify Scanlon's dossier and found that it was an amalgam of half-truths and unsubstantiated rumors, but for a time at least tobacco's version of the truth prevailed, and a potent message was sent not only to Wigand but to other would-be whistle-blowers that they had better not come forward. Scanlon also represented Ivana Trump during her divorce from The Donald. "What we did was quite scientific," he said. By "scientific," however, he meant something quite different from what a particle physicist would mean. "I mean we sat down with Mrs. Trump, with Ivana early on with her attorneys and talked about what was the specific critical message that she wanted to communicate. I mean, we had a very, very clear position."[10] But having a "very, very clear position" is an entirely different thing than seeking the truth, which is what an actual scientist would be doing.

It would be nice to imagine that Scanlon's fluid attitude toward the truth is some kind of aberration, but it is not. Richard Edelman, his onetime boss at Edelman Worldwide, goes even further. Not only are there different versions of the truth "in this era of exploding media technologies," Edelman says, "there is no truth except the truth you create for yourself."[11]

"Marketing is a battle of perception, not products. Truth has no bearing on the issue," says advertising executive Jack Trout. The role of public relations, he adds, "is to deliver the exact same thing as advertising," while using PR's unique ability to provide "third party credibility and reinforce the product's positioning in multiple media appearances."[12]

One of the rules of PR is that spin cannot be a *demonstrable* lie, a point that is driven home in every PR textbook. "Never lie to a reporter" has become an industry mantra. Fortunately, there is a loophole. Spin is the art of appearances, not substance. When there is no truth except what you create for yourself, lies become unnecessary, even irrelevant. To lie is to respect reality enough to falsify it. The practitioners of public relations do not falsify the truth, because they do not believe that it even exists. This worldview, conceived in spin and dedicated to the proposition that all spin is created equal, is spreading like a virus beyond the mediaspindustrial complex that was its original host and has begun to infect the rest of society. "We live in a world where everyone is always battling for the public mind and public approval," says PR historian Stuart Ewen. "I think the public believes there is no truth, only spin—in part because much of the educated middle class spins for a living."[13]

You're Stupid and You Smell Bad

The age of spin has also cheapened the practice of democracy, as Scott Cutlip ruefully admits. A dean emeritus of journalism at the University of Georgia, Cutlip was a longtime PR industry practitioner and one of its leading historians. His own "baptism in PR," as he put it, began in 1936 when he served as press secretary for a Democratic candidate in the West Virginia gubernatorial primary. "Political PR was startingly simple in those days of small campaign budgets: no TV, no opinion polls, no handlers, no campaign consultants," he recalls. "Statewide candidates had to rely on speeches in county courthouses or rural schools; handshaking up and down Main Street, and what publicity could be squeezed out of 'The Speech' for the local newspapers and possibly an interview on the local radio station. This brought the candidate face to face with voters; he heard their complaints, their needs, their aspirations. In contrast, today the major candidates—President to Governor to Senator—are carefully shielded from contact with the voters save for the customary pressing of flesh along the airport fence or at $1,000 receptions." Today's multimillion-dollar campaigns, he notes, are "themed to the latest opinion polls, powered by glitzy TV commercials that convey shadows, not substance, and managed by carpetbagger consultants. . . . Is this progress? Does it serve our democratic process? My answer is no."[14]

The result of all this sophisticated PR is that although Americans still give ritual lip-service to democracy, the concept has lost much of its meaning. In fact, it has become boring and irrelevant in most people's lives. Our political process functions formally the way we think it should—campaigns happen, votes are cast, someone ends up taking an oath of office—but the ugly truth, as we all know, is that the campaign promises are empty rhetoric, based not on what the candidates believe but on what their expert pollsters have told them we want to hear. If you ask the managers of these ever-more-expensive propaganda campaigns why they have vulgarized the democratic process, they will frequently tell you that the problem is not with them but with the voters, who are too "irrational," "ig-norant," or "apathetic" to respond to any other kind of appeal. Like Clotaire Rapaille, they have come to the conclusion that there are words they must not use, concepts they dare not utter. Apparently people today are less hungry for serious talk and less capable of comprehending it than the half-literate voters a century and a half ago who turned out in multitudes and sat for hours listening to the debates between Abraham Lincoln and William Douglas.

"The minute you begin to view the public as something that doesn't operate rationally, your job as a publicist or journalist changes," Ewen observes. "The pivotal moment was when those who provided the public with its intelligence no longer believed the public had any intelligence."[15] It is disturbing to see how frequently this ideology, which corrodes democratic values in an acid bath of cynicism, surfaces today among the political insiders who claim to govern in the name of democracy and popular sovereignty. "On issue after issue, the public is belittled as self-indulgent or misinformed, incapable of grasping the larger complexities known to the policymakers and the circles of experts surrounding them," observed author William Greider in *Who Will Tell the People,* his 1992 study of the Washington political establishment. "The public's side of the argument is said to be 'emotional' whereas those who govern are said to be making 'rational' or 'responsible' choices. In the masculine culture of management, 'emotion' is assigned a position of weakness whereas 'facts' are hard and potent. The reality, of course, is that the ability to define what is or isn't 'rational' is itself loaded with political self-interest. . . . For elites, the politics of governing is seen as a continuing struggle to manage public 'emotions' so that they do not overwhelm sound public policy."[16]

Not only are we the people too dim-witted to understand the world, some advisers believe that we are mentally ill, suffering from "chemophobia," "technophobia," or some sort of "infantile regression," to choose just a few of the pseudoscientific terms that have been coined to diagnose our condition. James Cox, a consultant to rendering plants that dispose of the spoiled leftovers from slaughterhouses, came up with the phrase "hypermotivated complainant" (HMC, for short) to characterize people who object to the odors that emanate from his clients' factories. An HMC, he explained, is "reacting abnormally," suffering from "a form of Parkinsonian madness." The U.S. Environmental Protection Agency reached similar conclusions as it worked to overcome "public acceptance barriers" to its disposal plans for sewage sludge. The main problem, it concluded, was "the widely held perception of sewage sludge as malodorous, disease causing or otherwise repulsive. . . . There is an irrational component to public attitudes about sludge which means that public education will not be entirely successful." Unlike the manic masses, the EPA in its expert wisdom knows better than to trust people's noses: "It is difficult to say to what extent odors emanating from sludge may be imagined," it concluded.

"My child is currently enrolled in Watauga Elementary School," says Tamara Rich of Ridgetop, Tennessee. "Both his school and our home are approximately 1,000 yards from a sludge dump called 'Show Me Farms.' Although the experts will tell you there is no danger, they will also tell you there is no smell. For the past year, more often than not, people gag when they walk out the door. Our school has not been able to open windows or let the children play outside on most days. Of course, my house is now on the market, with little to no hope of selling. Ridgetop citizens seem to be having a high level of strokes, defined as due to unknown toxins by Vanderbilt Hospital. There's also been a lung malfunction for one child that was also labeled by Vanderbilt as unknown toxins."

From the point of view of the technocrats and spin doctors, the Tamara Riches of the world are just "hypermotivated complainants," and their stories of illness, inconvenience, and injury are merely "unfounded anecdotes" that should not be taken seriously. Given the public's evident inability to smell the difference between sludge and shinola, someone has to do our thinking for us, and that's where the experts come in.

Spinning the Moral Compass

It would be a mistake to think that the practitioners of public relations are blind to the ethical dilemmas posed by their profession. They talk about them, even joke about them. At a two-day industry trade seminar in 1998 called "Media Management '98," PR industry consultant Jim Lukaszewski delivered two workshops, leading off each with slide presentations of cartoons that provided a PR version of gallows humor. "I admire your honesty and integrity, Mr. Wilson, but there's no room for them in this firm," went one punch line. In another, a CEO informed his flack that "we're laying off half our staff and raising executives' salaries. Announce it to the media and put a good spin on it."

After the chuckling subsided, Lukaszewski introduced himself as "a specialist in managing other people's bad news. If there's a million gallons of toluene under your parking lot, I'm the guy you want to call."[17] A consultant to Fortune 500 companies, he has worked with senior executives on issues such as product recalls, plant closings, chemical spills, and hazardous-substance exposures. In advertisements in PR industry trade publications, he describes himself as an "expert's expert." He helps clients prepare themselves to be interviewed on *60 Minutes* or *Nightline,* or to give testimony in front of congressional hearings. He also teaches communications at New York University and has written numerous articles for publications such as *Public Relations Quarterly, PR Reporter,* and *PR Tactics.*

On his website (www.e911.com), Lukaszewski gives examples of some of his recent work. As the following excerpts show, his clients are typically major corporations that have been targeted for criticism by environmental, human rights, labor, and other citizen groups:

- "Provided . . . counsel to a large state-owned petrochemical company in South America related to its efforts to relocate neighboring villages now too close to its growing manufacturing facilities. The strategies developed addressed issues related to litigation, activist intervention by nongovernmental organizations and advocacy groups from other areas of the world, anti-government action, the damage caused by cultural intervention, and long-term community-company relationship building."

- "For senior environmental officer of Canadian natural resource company, provided strategic response recommendations for managing aggressive campaign by U.S. environmental groups against the company and its largest U.S. customer."

- "Helped prepare executives of major U.S. defense contractor for annual meeting disruptions by anti-nuclear activists."

- "Prepared directors, senior managers, and locally based executives of national financial cooperative for public demonstrations against farm foreclosures."

- "Guided Fortune 500 toy manufacturer through attack by largest U.S. animal rights organization over the issue of animal testing."

- "Developed specific, targeted, pro-active face-to-face communications response to noise, odor, and quality-of-life complaints by neighbors of a mid-size manufacturing facility."

- "Counseled senior executives of major U.S. retailer/merchandiser facing very public action by a national and international labor organizations protesting manufacturing practices in Central and South America."

In person Jim Lukaszewski is amiable, unflappable, and seemingly sincere. A member of the Public Relations Society of America Board of Ethics, he comes across as something of a moralizer within the industry, arguing that ethical behavior is the only way to avoid bad publicity in today's world. Where does the "ethical" part come in? At Media Relations '98, Lukaszewski explained that he advises clients "to resolve the situation with the activist. It's unavoidable. We're eventually going to have to sit down with them. Let's do it today. We're probably not going to make them happy, but we can probably resolve it down to where they don't have a case. . . . Honorable action, on the ground, is the crucial ingredient, not media coverage. . . . If you're a crook, if you're a slimeball, then the media strategies I recommend will not work."

These comments came during a provocatively titled panel discussion on the subject "When the Press Attacks: Should You Stonewall or Cooperate?" Debating Larry Kamer of Kamer/Singer Associates, Lukaszewski took the side in favor of stonewalling. "Respond to the media only when your message goals are served," he said. "There is nothing in the U.S. Constitution that says you have to call the press back." In order to communicate effectively in crisis situations, he advised that people should stick to scripted messages or shut up altogether. To keep friends and relatives quiet as well, he joked, "duct tape is very handy."[18]

The following day, Lukaszewski's message seemed at first to be diametrically reversed. Speaking at a workshop titled "Face the Press," he argued that PR strategy should be based on four principles: (1) "openness and accessibility"; (2) "truthfulness . . . unconditional honesty is the only policy"; (3) "responsiveness . . . recognition that any constituent concern is by definition legitimate"; and (4) "no secrets. Our behavior, our attitudes, our plans, even our strategic discusions must be unchallengeable, unassailable, and positive."[19]

How do you achieve openness and accessibility while stonewalling? Lukaszewski's recipe consists of first making a list of the ten or so questions that a client most dreads answering, plus another list of questions that the client wishes someone would ask. Then he writes out and rehearses scripted answers to each question.

During actual interviews, he advises clients to use "bridging language" so that their answers actually respond to their preferred rather than the feared list of questions. He has developed a number of specific phrases that can accomplish this bridging function:

- "I have heard that too, but the real focus should be . . ."

- "Opinions can differ, but I believe . . ."

- "Here's an even tougher question . . ."

(The question you *wish* they'd ask is "tougher"? This must be some strange new definition of "unconditional honesty" that isn't in the dictionary.)

Lukaszewski also puts a tight time limit on interviews, allowing reporters at most half an hour to interview his clients. Otherwise, he fears, reporters will start to ask "off-the-wall questions" that don't fit the script. He advises clients to repeat all of their messages three times during the course of an interview, so that in reality reporters get only about 10 minutes' worth of quotable material. To limit things still further, he has a standing rule that interviews should end as soon as a reporter hesitates for more than (literally) seven seconds between questions. To emphasize this point to the audience at Media Relations '98, he counted deliberately from one to seven. "See? That's plenty of time," he said. "If they pause any longer than that, you shake their hand and say, 'Thank you for coming.' Here too, you want to use positive language."[20]

Lukaszewski even advises his clients who are being interviewed to give reporters printed versions of their scripted answers, which he calls "communications objectives." "It's amazing how accurate the reporters become when you give it to them," he said. "The communications objectives become the core of the story, generally."[21]

Sweetspeak

Pat Farrell, a PR executive at Ralcorp Holding, the human-feed company spin-off from Ralston Purina, understands and shares Lukaszewski's passion to eradicate candor. Farrell's résumé includes more than two decades "managing issues" like "restructuring, reengineering, downsizing, rightsizing, capital expansion, product improvement, technological advances, synergy, long-term plans, short-term outlook, new product introductions, cost-reduction initiatives, strategic alternatives, and renewed focus." He has helped employers weather food tamperings, firings, and two fatal shootings in the workplace—"not at the same time," he notes.

Speaking at a November 1996 PR trade conference, Farrell described his experience managing the image of chemical giant Monsanto's artificial sweetener, aspartame (trade name Nutrasweet). The product was having a hard time winning public acceptance, he said, because of "emotional and seemingly illogical responses" from the public. "This was important to our company because we were seeking to grow our franchise outside the accepted context of diet," he explained. In order to understand the public's resistance, Monsanto hired a psychologist. Farrell did not mention the psychologist's name, but his advice was remarkably similar to Clotaire Rapaille's suggestions for genetically engineered foods.

For years, Farrell said, the company had described Nutrasweet as "an artificial sweetener." But the word "artificial," it realized, "conjures up cancer, headaches, rat studies, laboratories, dueling scientists, allergies, epilepsy, you name it, none of which are very appetizing." Referring to Nutrasweet as a "sugar substitute" was also a mistake. "People don't like it when you claim to be like sugar," Farrell said, because "memories of sugar take them back to their childhood, a simpler time when there was less to worry about and sugar was a sweet treat, a reward. . . . Our own words were defining our product in a manner that created thoughts of being unnatural, unsafe, unsweet and led people to conclude that we believed Nutrasweet was better than the most beloved food product in history." The psychologist also advised them that "the American public admires and takes great pride in discoveries and innovations gained through hard work."

Armed with this knowledge, Nutrasweet created "sweetspeak." According to Farrell, "Words such as 'substitute,' 'artificial,' 'chemical,' 'laboratory,' 'scientist' were removed forever from our lexicon and replaced with words such as 'discovered,' 'choice,' 'variety,' 'unique,' 'different,' 'new taste.' "

Using sweetspeak, Farrell gave an example of how Nutrasweet now responds to the question: How do you know aspartame is safe? The answer: "Aspartame was discovered nearly 30 years ago. Since that time, hundreds of people in our company and elsewhere around the world—people with families like yours and mine—have devoted themselves to making sure consumers can be confident of their choice when they choose the taste of Nutrasweet. People have looked at our ingredient in every which way possible, and we encourage that because we want consumers to be comfortable when they choose Nutrasweet. That has been our commitment for nearly three decades, and it will always be our commitment. You can feel confident choosing products that contain our ingredient, but if you don't, you have other choices."

Euphemisms are not always enough, however. Sometimes, says Washington-based PR professional Jeff Prince, a public relations expert needs to speak sweetly and carry a big stick. A veteran of food wars fought by the National Restaurant Association, Prince spoke at the same 1996 trade conference as Farrell and described his years battling the Center for Science in the Public Interest (CSPI), a media-savvy nonprofit organization that warns consumers about risks from sugar- and fat-laden foods. CSPI is the organization that documented the high fat content in movie theater popcorn and once garnered headlines by calling fettuccine Alfredo "a heart attack on a plate." In recent years, it has campaigned heavily to inform the public about bowel discomfort and other health problems associated with Olestra, the "nonfattening fat" developed by Procter & Gamble and used in Wow brand potato chips.

Prince described CSPI as "the megabeast of science hype." He pointed with particular alarm to a CSPI study which found that a mushroom cheeseburger with fried onion rings at TGI Friday's contains about 1,800 calories and the same amount of fat as five strips of bacon, four chocolate frosted donuts, three slices of pepperoni pizza, two banana splits, and a Big Mac combined.[22] "The restaurant industry needs to be concerned," Prince said, because eventually CSPI's nutritional information will lead to "a decline in consumer confidence, a growing sense of guilt about eating out."

The National Restaurant Association has developed three different themes to counteract the CSPI message. First and foremost, it has stressed "variety and choice—arguing that studies show that only 31 percent of restaurant-goers are not concerned about nutrition when they eat out, and restaurants cater to customers by offering low fat items. The second thing the restaurants have pushed, of course, is the 'food police' line, and they push that as far as possible," Prince said. "The idea is simply that people . . . don't need a third party interfering and making those choices for them especially when this third party seems inhuman, inflexible, puritanical, rigid." The third tactic employed by the restaurant industry is to raise questions about CSPI's science, its accuracy, and its procedures. So far this has been underutilized, Prince said, urging "a concerted effort to make the case against CSPI's science and to raise the whole question of how and when and where you report scientific studies. . . . Raise the question of proper use of science and you begin to chip away, as you do that, at CPSI's credibility."

Rather than attacking CSPI directly, however, he recommended that interested companies employ the third party technique. "If it is the National Restaurant Association and Procter & Gamble out there making the case, nobody is going to believe them. Their ox has been gored. . . . What I am talking about is doing briefings behind the scenes to educate the media, and you would have to distance it from interested companies . . . and you would have to get the scientific community involved," he said. "The whole project would, I think, require considerable scientific expertise, it would require considerable skill in media management and almost infinite tact, but through a concerted effort I think it could be done, because the press no longer wants to believe CSPI. They would like to find an excuse not to carry those stories, but we haven't given it to them yet. It may well be a job for some currently underfunded organization, or perhaps for some new organization, but it seems to me the food industry ought to get together and get this job done soon. . . . We would need well written objective backgrounders. We would need expert testimony, perhaps even a panel. We would need to win the support of media critics such as Howard Kurtz of the *Washington Post*. . . . We'd need their support and I think we could get it."

In the months immediately following Prince's remarks, CSPI indeed came under intensified attack from conservative think tanks, several of which receive heavy funding from Procter & Gamble. There is no paper trail to prove that this was a coordinated campaign, but to CSPI head Michael Jacobson at least, it seemed like more than mere coincidence.

"The whole operation reeks of behind-the-scenes manipulation," he said. Henry Miller of the Hoover Institution wrote a blistering op-ed, defending Olestra and attacking CSPI, that ran in the *Wall Street Journal* and was subsequently republished by the *Washington Times* and the *Cincinnati Inquirer*. Norman Ornstein of the American Enterprise Institute, which received about $125,000 from Procter & Gamble's foundation, wrote a column for *USA Today* that accused the CSPI of attempting to intimidate the FDA into blocking Olestra and called the Center a "national nanny." The *Detroit News* published a column by two writers affiliated with the industry-funded organization Consumer Alert, who characterized the CSPI as "food police" offering "the uninvited opinion of nutrition activists." Another article, titled "Attack of the Food Police," ran in *Reader's Digest*, which counts Procter & Gamble as its third-largest advertiser. In the *New Republic*, CSPI was accused of "using sloppy data" and "misleading" the public by Stephen Glass, a *New Republic* assistant editor who had previously worked for *Policy Review*, the journal of the right-wing Heritage Foundation. (When it comes to misleading the public, Glass turned out to be in a class by himself. His later firing from *The New Republic* became one of journalism's most embarrassing scandals, after it was discovered that he had habitually fabricated information and that some of his stories were in fact completely fictional.)*

Perhaps the most interesting attack on CSPI came from an industry-funded group calling itself The Advancement of Sound Science Coalition (TASSC). After CSPI released a study about high levels of fat and cholesterol in breakfast foods, TASSC issued a news release via PR Newswire titled "Much Ado About Nothing—Sound Science Group Responds to the

---

*Prior to his firing, Glass was considered a rising journalistic star, writing for *Rolling Stone*, *Harper's* and *George* magazines in addition to the *The New Republic*. His unraveling came in June 1998 when a reporter for another publication discovered that a company mentioned in one of his stories did not exist. A subsequent investigation found that 6 of the 41 articles Glass wrote for *The New Republic* were entirely fictional, while another 21 were blends of fact and fiction containing nonexistent organizations, events and people, such as the "Cops & Justice Foundation," "Donny Tyes, a former California police officer," "Daniel, a young professor at an Illinois college," "James, a television news producer," "a small skydiving industry newsletter" called *Jump Now*, and the "Church of George Herbert Walker Christ," which supposedly believed that former President Bush was a reincarnated Jesus. The magazine's apology appeared in "To Our Readers: A Report," *The New Republic*, June 29, 1998. For further details of the fraud, see Ann Reilly Dowd, "The Great Pretender," *Columbia Journalism Review*, July/August 1998.

Latest CSPI Scare." Rather than disputing CSPI for being *wrong,* however, the news release attacked the study on the grounds that its conclusions were too obviously *correct* to deserve mention. "The CSPI Sherlocks have discovered that eggs, sausage and butter contain fat and can push up cholesterol. So what?" the news release scoffed.

"This is just another example of how CSPI cloaks common sense with a mantle of 'science' for no purpose other than garnering free publicity from the all-too-willing news media," complained TASSC director Garrey Carruthers. "It's time for everyone to say no to this junk science."[23]

What is interesting about this line of attack is the way it recasts the definition of science itself. For TASSC, the distinction between "sound science" and "junk science" hinged not on the empirical question of whether facts are true, but on the PR question of how the facts might *appear.* In the empiricist tradition, scientists do not attack their colleagues for repeating widely accepted facts. If a physicist says that gravity exists, you would not expect other physicists to accuse him of "junk science." TASSC's rejoinder, however, was not intended to raise factual questions about the CSPI study but rather to persuade journalists that the study was not newsworthy. People already know how much fat is in the food they eat, the argument went, so why make a big deal out of it? "There's no news," said Michael W. Pariza, a food industry–funded researcher at the University of Wisconsin and TASSC adviser who was quoted in their news release.[24]

The following year, CSPI released another study. This one surveyed 203 registered dietitians to assess their ability to estimate the nutritional content of restaurant meals. "Trained dietitians underestimated the calorie content of five restaurant meals by an average of 37 percent and the fat content by 49 percent," the study reported. "The survey revealed that not even one of the 203 dietitians surveyed estimated the calorie or fat content of all meals within 20 percent of the correct values."

"The survey proves that even nutrition professionals can't estimate accurately the calorie and fat content of restaurant meals," said Dr. Marion Nestle, who chairs New York University's Department of Nutrition and Food Studies and participated with CSPI in conducting the study. "If nutritionists can't tell what's in restaurant meals, consumers certainly can't," Nestle added. "Huge restaurant meals are one of the reasons why so many Americans are gaining weight."

Indeed, a June 1999 study by the U.S. Department of Health and

Human Services found that more than half of U.S. adults and more than 20 percent of children are overweight. "We are facing a real epidemic of obesity," said Dr. Jeffrey Koplan, director of the U.S. Centers for Disease Control and Prevention. "All segments of the population are getting fatter, but the highest increase is among the youngest ages. . . . There is no worse harbinger of what's to come."

"It's so subtle," said Dr. Robert Kushner, a clinical nutrition researcher. "People aren't even aware of what's happening to them. Tongue in cheek, I say it's an alien plot to fatten up Americans. . . . I believe you can liken the restaurant industry to the tobacco industry in the 1960s. The industry's attitude is, we are responding to what the public wants. . . . Most Americans struggle with estimating how much food they consume. You would get 100 different guesses from 100 people if you put a plate of food in front of them."[25]

But so what? Apparently it's our choice. And besides, it's not news. Have you tried those Wow brand potato chips?

PART II
RISKY BUSINESS

n Peter Bernstein's book *Against the Gods,* he notes that a few hundred years ago, risk as we understand it today did not exist. Death and disease certainly existed alongside myriad other miseries, but people regarded them as the inevitable consequences of divinely appointed destiny over which they had little control. Rather than risk, they thought of fate. People did not weigh the consequences of different career choices, technologies, and social policies, because for most people those options did not exist. Risk-taking was the province of gamblers with dice and cards   the first people to seriously study ways of measuring, quantifying, and managing risk, thereby pioneering many of the systems and assumptions that rule the world today.[1]

The emergence of global capitalism, in tandem with science and technology, has created benefits that few people would be willing to forgo, but it has also transformed us into gamblers on an unprecedented scale. As we enter the twenty-first century, we face a mind-blowing array of technological possibilities: cloning, genetically engineered babies, replacement of food with "nutraceuticals," surgically implanted cyborg enhancements of the human body. Technological change continues to accelerate, and with it come unintended consequences and risks that no one can predict in advance. The globalization of economics and politics means that events in remote locations affect us more rapidly and more intensely than ever before. In a world this complicated, it is hardly surprising that experts have become our guides, shaping our buying habits, health decisions, and public policy debates. But the experts who have created these technologies and the experts who encourage us to use them can be appallingly blind to the problems that they pose.

The downside to progress during the twentieth century included technological advances that enabled wars and government-sponsored atrocities to kill some 180 million people—a far larger total than for any other century in human history.[2] And that's just the number of people whose deaths were *deliberately* engineered by government planners. The list of other problems, accidents, and mayhem linked to technological advance would include, for starters, train wrecks, toxic chemical releases, and emerging antibiotic-resistant diseases. Progress has given us air pollution, groundwater contamination, burgeoning landfills, extinctions of living species, deforestation, risks from transport of nuclear material, explosions, dietary exposure to chemicals, and nerve gas attacks by Saddam Hussein in the Middle East and terrorists in Japan. The worst disasters, such as global thermonuclear war, have not yet occurred but remain real possibilities.

Clearly, there are some gambles that we dare not take, yet as technological change accelerates, the economic interests that stand to benefit from those changes have become increasingly skillful at imposing their view of the respective risks and benefits upon society at large. The chapters in this section examine how industry experts think about the issue of risk and their strategies for discussing it with the public.

4

Dying for a Living

*They shrug at the pleas of workers whose
health they destroy in order to save money.
They hire experts—physicians and
researchers—who purposely misdiagnose
industrial diseases as the ordinary diseases of
life, write biased reports, and divert research
from vital questions. They fight against
regulation as unnecessary and cry that it
will bring ruination. They ravage the people
as they have the land, causing millions to
suffer needlessly and hundreds of thousands
to die.*

—Rachel Scott, *Muscle and Blood*[1]

No one knows how many people died in the Hawk's Nest
tragedy of the early 1930s, and no one ever will. The number of deaths is probably greater than the number who perished with the
sinking of the *Titanic*, but there is no ship's register or other list of names
that can be used to tabulate the casualties, many of whom were buried in
unmarked graves. Nor are you likely to read about Hawk's Nest in history
books, even though it is generally recognized by industrial health researchers as the worst industrial disaster in U.S. history. For a long time
it was dangerous to talk about it in West Virginia, where the disaster occurred. In 1939, the governor of West Virginia refused to sanction a Federal Writer's Guide to his state until the writers toned down their lengthy
and graphic discussion of Hawk's Nest. Even in the 1960s, a West Virginia
university professor received more than a dozen death threats when he set
out to interview some of the survivors. In 1986, physician Martin Cher-

niack wrote a meticulously documented account of the disaster, titled *The Hawk's Nest Incident,* but although Cherniack's book was praised by reviewers, it too has gone out of print and into obscurity.

The passengers on the *Titanic* included scions of wealthy families people whose passing was deemed important enough to memorialize in books and movies. By contrast, the five thousand workers at Hawk's Nest were poor, predominantly black, and considered expendable in the early years of the Great Depression. Drawn by promises of better pay and steady work, they left the coal mines and were put to work drilling a three-mile-long tunnel to divert water for a hydroelectric plant being constructed by the Union Carbide Company to provide power to its nearby petrochemical plant. They had no way of knowing that the dusty air in the tunnel would send as many as half of them to an early death. The tunnel still stands today, behind a commemorative plaque that describes it as an engineering marvel. In 1986, the state of West Virginia finally agreed to place a second marker at the site, a three-foot-square sign with a mere eleven lines of text dedicated to the memory of the men who died there.

The mountain through which the workers bored was made of almost pure silica, the hard glassy mineral from which sand and quartz derive. Inhalation of silica dust had been identified 15 years earlier as the cause of an often fatal disease that slowly suffocates its victims by destroying the ability of their lungs to absorb oxygen. Before the scientists labeled it "silicosis," the disease was called "miners' phthisis," "potters' consumption," or "grinders' rot"—names associated with the professions that brought workers into contact with the dust. At Hawk's Nest, Union Carbide's management and engineers were mindful of the dangers associated with silica dust, and they wore face masks or respirators for self-protection when they entered the tunnel for periodic inspections. The workers themselves, who spent eight to ten hours a day breathing the dust, were not told about the hazard, nor were they given face masks. Wetting the job site would have reduced the amount of dust in the air, but this was not done either. "The company doctors were not allowed to tell the men what their trouble was," one of the doctors would testify later. If a worker complained of difficulty breathing, he would be told that his condition was pneumonia or "tunnelitis."[2] For treatment, the doctors prescribed what came to be called "little black devils"—worthless pills made from sugar and baking soda.

In moderately dusty conditions, workers would be expected to contract silicosis after 20 or 30 years. For jobs such as sandblasting, accelerated silicosis might strike in 10 years. At Hawk's Nest, conditions were so bad that workers were dying from acute silicosis within a single year. The road that led from the workers' homes to the work site became known as the "death march." On their way home, the workers would be covered in white rock dust, giving them a deathlike appearance. Many were disturbingly thin, sick, coughing and bleeding.[3] "I can remember seeing the men, and you couldn't tell a black man from a white man. They were just covered in white dust," recalled a woman who lived near the Hawk's Nest tunnel.

George Robison, a tunnel worker, said people were forced to live in company houses until they were too sick to work, at which time the sheriff would evict them. "Many of the men died in the tunnel camps," Robison said. "They died in hospitals, under rocks, and every place else. A man named Finch, who was known to me, died under a rock from silicosis."[4] A local undertaker, paid by the company, buried 169 of the men in a mass grave in a nearby field.[5] The widow of one worker had her husband's body exhumed only to find that the man, buried by the company barely hours after his death, had three other men stacked on top of him.[6] Some family members never found out what had happened to their loved ones. When they inquired, the company would just say that the worker had moved on.

It took a militant labor movement and Franklin Delano Roosevelt's New Deal to bring the Hawk's Nest scandal to national attention. Congressional hearings were held in 1935 to probe what one senator described as "American industry's Black Hole of Calcutta." At the hearings, a Union Carbide contractor admitted, "I knew I was going to kill those niggers, but I didn't know it was going to be this soon."[7] The estimated number of deaths among the workers who labored in the tunnel ranged from a few hundred to two thousand. Worse yet, the Hawk's Nest disaster was not an isolated incident. Thousands of other workers throughout the country were developing silicosis through occupational exposures in foundries, mines, potteries, and construction sites. With public interest aroused, popular and scientific magazines began to write about conditions in the "dusty trades." Frances Perkins, Roosevelt's secretary of labor, declared "war" on silicosis.

The response from industry set a pattern that would be repeated countless times in subsequent years when corporate interests faced similar crises. As science writer James Weeks observes, "Surprisingly similar

stories—concerning the meaning of 'scientific' terms and attribution of responsibility—could be and have been told about asbestos-related dis-
cases, 'black lung,' byssinosis [brown lung disease], cancers caused by
occupational exposures, lead poisoning, and others."[8] In each case, the exposures that cause disease were only the symptoms of a deeper problem—corporate denial regarding the deadly risks associated with growing
industrialization. The company doctors who lied to dying workers at
Hawk's Nest were following a new version of the Hippocratic Oath: "First,
do no harm to the boss." This willingness to subordinate health to profits
was common and notorious among physicians who worked for industry. As
physician and public health reformer Alice Hamilton observed, a doctor
who left private practice to take such employment thereby earned "the
contempt of his colleagues." Company doctors were known as the least
competent and least ethical members of their profession.

Hygiene Hijinks

Less than a week after the 1935 Hawk's Nest hearings adjourned in Congress, a group of industrialists met privately at the Mellon Institute, a
foundation that had been established by financiers Andrew and Richard
Mellon in 1913 to "benefit American manufacturers through the practical cooperation of science and industry." The meeting led to the formation
of a new organization, headquartered at Mellon, called the Air Hygiene
Foundation (AHF). "Because of recent misleading publicity about silicosis and the appointment of a Congressional committee to hold public
hearings," noted a confidential Mellon report, "the attention of much of
the entire country has been focused on silicosis. It is more than probable
that this publicity will result in a flood of claims, whether justified or unjustified, and will tend toward improperly considered proposals for legislation." In order to fend off these feared laws and lawsuits, the Air Hygiene
Foundation planned a public relations campaign that purported to "give
everyone concerned an undistorted picture of the subject."[9]

Leading scientists and public officials were appointed to serve as
members and trustees of the foundation. Its spokesmen began to be
widely quoted in popular trade publications. "Silicotics are rare compared
with men driven from their jobs by shyster lawyers," commented AHF representative Alfred C. Hirth. The AHF's own "shyster lawyer," Theodore C.
Waters, accused doctors of fabricating claims of silicosis. "In many in-

stances," he stated, "employees have been advised by physicians, untrained and inexperienced in the diagnosis and effect of silicosis, that they have the disease and thereby have sustained liability. Acting on this advice, the employee, now concerned about his condition, leaves his employment, even though that trade may be the only one in which he is able to earn a living."[10]

Companies did finally begin to limit the worst abuses, improving ventilation, wetting down the dust, offering respiratory masks, and using other methods to reduce silica exposures. Gross slaughters like Hawk's Nest were easily preventable, and they generated headlines that were bad for business. Businesses were also aware of their increasing financial liability due to lawsuits. At the beginning of the twentieth century, the legal system was heavily biased to prevent workers from successfully suing their employers. By the 1930s, however, courts had become increasingly willing to hold employers liable for both actual and punitive damages. Driven by rising jury awards and insurance awards, the "dusty trades" took their problem out of the courts by convincing state governments to incorporate silicosis into state workers' compensation schedules.

With the Air Hygiene Foundation, industry had found an effective propaganda formula: a combination of partial reforms with reassuring "scientific" rhetoric, under the aegis of an organization with a benevolent, independent-sounding name. Even though the AHF was governed by and for the dusty trades, it had successfully become a vehicle for deployment of the "third party" technique. "A survey report from an outside, independent agency carries more weight in court or before a compensation commission than does a report prepared by your own people," explained AHF membership committee chairman C. E. Ralston at the foundation's fifth annual meeting. By 1940, the AHF had 225 member companies, representing such major polluters of the day as American Smelting and Refining, Johns-Manville, United States Steel, Union Carbide, and PPG Industries. In 1941, it changed its name to the Industrial Hygiene Foundation (and later still to the Industrial Health Foundation), broadening its agenda beyond dust-related diseases to encompass other industrial health issues. By the 1970s, it had more than 400 corporate sponsors, including Gulf Oil, Ford Motor Company, General Motors, Standard Oil of New Jersey, Kawecki Berylco Industries, Brush Beryllium, Consolidated Coal, Boeing, General Electric, General Mills, Goodyear, Western Electric, Owens-Corning Fiberglass, Mobil Oil, and Dow Chemical.[11]

In the mid-1930s, silicosis was regarded as the "king of occupational diseases," as well known and notorious as asbestos would become in the 1990s. Thanks in large measure to the work of the AHF, however, it began to fade from the headlines by the end of the decade. The history of silicosis is documented in a book titled *Deadly Dust* by professors Gerald Markowitz and David Rosner, who study the history of occupational and public health policies. By the 1940s, they note, industry health analysts declared silicosis a "disease of the past," and by the 1950s, it was "officially declared unimportant, and those who spoke about it found it necessary to apologize for 'bringing up such a shopworn, dusty topic.' " Its disappearance from the headlines is arguably an even bigger scandal than the cover-up at Hawk's Nest, because the disease itself has not been eliminated, even though its cause is well understood and avoidable. In England and other parts of Europe, a ban on sandblasting has been in place since 1949. In the United States, however, the National Institute for Occupational Safety and Health (NIOSH) currently estimates that a million U.S. workers are at risk of developing silicosis, of whom 100,000 are in high-risk occupations—such as miners, sandblasters, rock drillers, pottery and mason workers, roof bolters, and foundry workers. NIOSH estimates that 59,000 of these workers will develop adverse health effects from silica exposure.

"Despite years of assurance that silicosis was a disease of the past and that workers could be adequately protected through proper ventilation, substitution of non-silica abrasives such as steel shot or garnite, and protective equipment, the reality is that during the postwar years workers continued to be exposed to excess amounts of silica and that silicosis never really vanished," write Rosner and Markowitz. "However, it is virtually impossible to develop reliable statistics concerning its prevalence in the decades following World War II given the general complacency of industry and the industrial hygiene and medical communities regarding this disease and the fact that silicosis was often not listed on death certificates as a cause of death or contributing factor. In general, doctors were neither trained to diagnose this disease nor given reason to suspect its prevalence among industrial workers."[12]

Recent cases that we do know about, culled from news stories and the Centers for Disease Control and Prevention,[13] include the following:

- A 39-year-old man was diagnosed with silicosis and tuberculosis in April 1993 after working 22 years as a sandblaster, during which he typically spent six hours a day sandblasting. He had worn a charcoal filter respirator, but it failed to protect him.

- A male nonsmoker was diagnosed with advanced silicosis, emphysema, and asthma at age 49 after working 23 years as a tile installer. His work included polishing and drilling tile, and he was exposed to grout dust and sandblasting. He did not use a respirator, because information about dust control had not been made available to workers.

- A brick mason was diagnosed with silicosis, emphysema, and lung cancer at age 70 after 41 years on the job. He had worn a respirator while working in dusty conditions, but again it wasn't enough protection.

- A 47-year-old man was diagnosed with severe silicosis in 1992 after working 22 years as a rock driller. He lingered for two years before dying in 1994. The drills he had used were equipped with dust controls, which were usually inoperable.

- Leslie Blevins, a 41-year-old coal miner, spent three months cutting through sandstone to get to a coal seam. On orders from the company, he helped conceal his sandstone mining from federal inspectors. "There's a lot of things that wasn't supposed to be done, but you either do it or you go home," he explained. The mining machine that he worked on was an old machine. Its water sprays—used to suppress dust—were constantly breaking. The dust was suffocating. "Sometimes I'd have to shut the miner down and go back in the fresh air and puke," he said. "My boss would come back and tell me to go back in." A year later, he was diagnosed with severe silicosis. A doctor gave him two years to live, but he managed to hang on for three.[14]

Not everyone dies from silicosis. Some are permanently disabled and turn for help to the worker's compensation system that industry helped put in place in the wake of the Hawk's Nest scandal. Often, however, they must fight insurance companies to obtain benefits. "Even if they win, the payments they receive rarely equal their previous earnings and may end after a period of years," notes *Houston Chronicle* reporter Jim Morris. "The maximum benefit for a 'permanent, total' disability in Texas, for example, is $438 per week for 401 weeks, or a little more than 7½ years. That's hardly comforting to an incapacitated, 40-year-old silicosis victim who had expected to work another 25 years."[15]

Rediscovering the Obvious

Even today, most states and the federal government make no serious attempt to track silicosis, which is not classified as a reportable disease. "If you look at the whole surveillance system, it's been a joke," says Dr. Kenneth Rosenman, an associate professor of medicine at Michigan State University, noting that government health officials "can't even keep track of how many people actually die from falls and other trauma in the workplace. The Bureau of Labor Statistics probably has a 75 percent undercount of silicosis."[16] The workers of today, in other words, are not that much different from the workers at Hawk's Nest. No one knows how many are dying from exposure to deadly dust, and perhaps no one ever will. Aside from the workers themselves and a few academics and isolated government officials, no one really seems to care.

The story of silicosis since Hawk's Nest has unfolded as a series of episodes in which, every decade or so, the disease gets "discovered" all over again, followed by efforts at regulatory reform. Each time, these efforts to defeat the disease have been thwarted by industry campaigns modeled after the pattern set by the Air Hygiene Foundation. In the 1960s, for example, university researchers documented an epidemic of silicosis among shipyard workers in Louisiana. When similar reports in the 1970s prompted the National Institute for Occupational Safety and Health (NIOSH) to propose more stringent standards for worker silica exposure, the affected industries established a group called the Silica Safety Association (SSA). Like the AHF, it professed concern for worker safety, stating that its mission was to "investigate and report on possible health hazards involved in [the] use of silica products and to recommend adequate protective measures considered economically feasible."[17] The key phrase here, of course, is "economically feasible." In reality, the SSA regarded *any* new policy measures to restrict silica exposure as unfeasible. After successfully lobbying to prevent the Occupational Safety and Health Administration (OSHA) from adopting the proposed new NIOSH standard, the SSA disbanded in 1982, its true mission accomplished. At about the same time, a new epidemic of silicosis emerged, this time among Texas oil workers who contracted the disease while sandblasting pipes and storage tanks. A six-month investigation by the *Houston Chronicle* in 1992 found that "silicosis is often misdiagnosed by doctors, disdained by industry officials and unknown to the very workers who stand the greatest chance of getting it. . . . Old warnings and medical studies have been ignored, products falsely advertised and government rules flouted—especially with regard to sandblasting, an activity so hazardous that NIOSH recommended its banning in 1974." As late as 1996, the National Institute for Occupational Safety and Health estimated that more than a million workers continue to be exposed to silica.[18] A study by the Centers for Disease Control found 14,824 cases of silicosis-associated deaths between the years of 1968 and 1994.

These disclosures prompted a National Conference to Eliminate Silicosis in 1997, which attracted more than 600 federal employees, industry representatives, union officials, and public health workers. New evidence has emerged suggesting that silica exposure may cause lung cancer in addition to silicosis. In May 1998, the official publication of the American Society of Safety Engineers dubbed crystalline silica "the new asbestos." Once again, the dangers of silica exposure have been rediscovered. Nearly seven decades after Hawk's Nest, silicosis has become a "new" disease all over again.

In response, industry has mobilized again. "Silica Scare Beginning to Hit Home," complained the *Aggman*, a trade publication of the aggregates industry, which produces crushed stone, sand, and gravel. Writing in the same publication, Mark Savit, the industry's lobbyist at the well-connected Washington law firm of Patton Boggs, accused "regulatory agencies, such as OSHA, the Mine Safety and Health Administration (MSHA) and the Environmental Protection Agency (EPA)" of going to "great lengths to whip up emotions regarding this issue," which "could have a profound effect on the way in which our industry does business in the future." He added, however, that industry would have "multiple opportunities to challenge the regulations that the agencies are trying to impose, and to expose the flawed science upon which they are based. . . . As a first step, my law firm, Patton Boggs, will sponsor 'Silica in the Next Century—The Need for Sound Public Policy, Research and Liability Prevention' on March 24, 1997, the day before the OSHA/MSHA meeting.

Top scientists, industry and association executives, and attorneys will provide participants with the ammunition they need to defend themselves from the coming attack."[19]

As a second step, the "dusty trades" created yet another group, this time called the Silica Coalition. "While the organization is ostensibly aimed at providing 'sound science' and legal resources to companies potentially affected by any change in government regulation of silica, it is also clear that increased awareness of the dangers of silica and the resulting threat of litigation hang over the heads of industry executives," note Rosner and Markowitz.[20]

Different Disease, Same Story

We have chosen to detail the history of silicosis because it serves as an archetype for the way that government, industry, and public health authorities have reacted to countless similar health threats. Each year, more than 800,000 people develop new cases of occupational illness that, combined with on-the-job injuries, kill as many as 80,000. "The medical costs of occupational injuries and illnesses appear to be much larger than those of AIDS," concluded a 1997 report in the *Archives of Internal Medicine*. "The total costs appear to be larger than those for Alzheimer's disease and are of the same magnitude as those of cancer, of all circulatory disease and of all musculoskeletal conditions."[21] In 1991, former *New York Times* labor correspondent William Serrin noted that some 200,000 U.S. workers had been killed on the job since the passage of the Occupational Safety and Health Act of 1970, and as many as two million more had died from diseases caused by the conditions where they worked. "That's 300 dead men, women and children a day. In fact, work kills more people each year than die from AIDS, drugs, or drunken driving and all other motor vehicle accidents," he observed. "Moreover, another 1.4 million people have been permanently disabled in workplace accidents since the act became law. Yet in those twenty years, only fourteen people have been prosecuted by the Justice Department for workplace safety violations, and only one person, a South Dakota construction contractor who was convicted in the deaths of two workers in a trench cave-in, has gone to jail—for forty-five days."[22]

In many cases, corporate and public officials have known for decades about life-threatening chemical hazards while failing to protect workers and publicly proclaiming their safety. The solvent benzene, for example, was considered dangerous as early as the 1920s and was linked to leukemia and other cancers in a 1948 toxicological review prepared for the American Petroleum Institute which stated that "the only absolutely safe concentration for benzene is zero." Yet benzene continues to be widely used and manufactured in refineries and chemical plants and is still present in the workplace today.

As early as 1918, asbestos was considered so hazardous that a medical statistician for Prudential Insurance Company advised against offering coverage to asbestos workers, "on account of the assumed health-injurious conditions of the injury." The Metropolitan Life Insurance Company reached similar conclusions in 1922, linking asbestos to fibrosis of the lungs. Numerous articles about asbestosis and "industrial cancer" among asbestos workers appear in the 1930s files of the Industrial Hygiene Foundation. All of these industry sources were talking among themselves about the link between asbestos and cancer long before the *Journal of the American Medical Association* first reported in 1944 that asbestos was among "agents known to cause occupational cancer." In 1948, the American Petroleum Institute's Medical Advisory Committee spoke of the need to "aim at the complete elimination" of worker exposures to both asbestos and benzene. For public consumption, however, industry churned out one misleading study after another, such as a massive 1958 study funded by the Quebec Asbestos Mining Association that was widely cited as the largest epidemiological study done on asbestosis, involving some 6,000 asbestos miners. Performed by the Industrial Hygiene Foundation, the report looked impressive unless you happened to pay attention to its method. "Among numerous errors in method was one central, scientifically inexcusable flaw," notes David Kotelchuck, director of the Center for Occupational and Environmental Health at Hunter College in New York:

> The investigators, Daniel Braun and T. Truan, virtually ignored the 20-year time lag between exposure to an agent known to cause lung cancer and the first visible signs of disease (the so-called latent period). They studied a relatively young group of workers, two-thirds of whom were between 20 and 44 years of age. Only 30 percent of the workers had been employed for 20 or more years, the estimated latent period for lung cancer. With so many young people in the study, too young to have the disease although they might well be destined

to develop it, Braun and Truan of course did not find a statistically significant increase in lung cancer among the miners. As became obvious later, they had drowned out a clear danger in a sea of misleading data.[23]

By 1960, 63 scientific papers on the subject of asbestosis had been done, 11 of which were sponsored by the asbestos industry, the other 52 coming from hospitals and medical schools. The 11 industry studies were unanimous in denying that asbestos caused lung cancer and minimizing the seriousness of asbestosis—a position diametrically opposite to the conclusions reached in the nonindustry studies. In 1962, the Gulf Oil Company's advice to workers, in a training manual for insulators, was that "the fibers of asbestos . . . are not injurious to the respiratory organs. Working with this material does not subject one to this hazard to one's health."[24] As we all know today, this advice was not only a lie but a murderous lie. The history of industry denials was neatly summarized by David Ozonoff from Boston University, who served as a witness in asbestos litigation and described the series of defenses used by the asbestos industry:

> Asbestos doesn't hurt your health. OK, it does hurt your health but it doesn't cause cancer. OK, asbestos can cause cancer but not our kind of asbestos. OK, our kind of asbestos can cause cancer, but not the kind this person got. OK, our kind of abestos can cause cancer, but not at the doses to which this person was exposed. OK, asbestos does cause cancer, and at this dosage, but this person got his disease from something else, like smoking. OK, he was exposed to our asbestos and it did cause his cancer, but we did not know about the danger when we exposed him. OK, we knew about the danger when we exposed him, but the statute of limitations has run out. OK, the statute of limitations hasn't run out, but if we're guilty we'll go out of business and everyone will be worse off. OK, we'll agree to go out of business, but only if you let us keep part of our company intact, and only if you limit our liability for the harms we have caused.

Much the same story can be told with respect to brown lung disease, an affliction of cotton mill workers that was first observed in the early

1900s but, following the standard pattern, was barely studied for half a century after its discovery. In 1945, a report by the U.S. Department of Labor said brown lung disease was not a problem in American cotton mills. The extent of the problem came to light when a Yale researcher began studying the health of prison inmates who were found to suffer a high experience of the disease at cotton mills operated by inmates of the Federal Penitentiary in Atlanta.[25] Similar histories of official neglect have been written about worker deaths from exposure to the metal beryllium; exposures to heavy metals such as lead, mercury, or cadmium; lung hazards such as fiberglass and coal dust; or chemicals such as chlordane and dioxin.

Without Propaganda, Pollution Would Be Impossible

As evidence began to mount in the 1970s about the harmful effects of chemicals such as DDT, PCBs, vinyl chloride and benzene, companies—including Mobil Oil, Monsanto, and Union Carbide—launched multiple massive advertising and public relations campaigns, using slogans like Monsanto's "without chemicals, life itself would be impossible." Union Carbide's propaganda efforts alone involved some 200 company managers, coordinated by the company's communications department as they pumped out speeches, tapes, canned editorials, educational films for public schools, and articles for newspapers and magazines.[26]

The propaganda effort relied heavily on questionable statistics designed to create the impression that excessive regulation was stifling American creativity and prosperity. Faced with proof that vinyl chloride caused a rare form of liver cancer, chemical manufacturers announced that a proposed federal standard for vinyl chloride exposure would cost two million jobs and $65 billion. "The standard is simply beyond compliance capability of the industry," declared their trade association. After the screaming was over, the standard was adopted and the industry continued to flourish, without job losses and at 5 percent of the industry's estimated cost.[27]

Information on occupational health hazards is rarely collected and even more rarely reported in the news. In the early part of this century, the concept of industrial safety was a novelty in the United States when Alice Hamilton, the country's first industrial physician, began to investigate what she came to call "the dangerous trades." In her autobiography, Hamilton described how she became aware of the problem: "It was also my experience at Hull House that aroused my interest in industrial diseases. Living in a working-class quarter, coming in contact with laborers and their wives, I could not fail to hear talk of the dangers that working men face, of cases of carbon-monoxide gassing in the great steel mills, of painters disabled by lead palsy, of pneumonia and rheumatism among the men in the stockyards." Hamilton went to the library "to read everything I could find on the dangers to industrial workers, and what could be done to protect them. But it was all German, or British, Austrian, Dutch, Swiss, even Italian or Spanish—everything but American. In those countries, industrial medicine was a recognized branch of the medical sciences, in my own country it did not exist."[28]

Decades later, Rachel Scott found the situation had not changed much when she set out to research her 1974 book, *Muscle and Blood*, which examined conditions affecting workers in steel foundries and other industrial settings. "At the library I had hoped to find some explanation of hazards to foundry workers—mortality studies, perhaps, which would shed some light on whether foundry employees showed higher incidences of diseases commonly associated with dusts and fumes, such as heart disease, respiratory disease, or lung cancer. I found French studies, Italian studies, German studies, and a few British studies, but in the American literature, nothing. . . . In spite of my failure at the library, I could not believe there were no studies of present-day American foundries. But calls to federal and state officials confirmed that, indeed, no one knew how foundry workers may be reacting to their often hazardous environment."[29]

Even today, the situation is not much better. "We have better data on cattle slaughter in the United States than we do on work-related deaths and injuries," says Joseph Kinney of the National Safe Workplace Institute in Chicago, which he founded in 1987 after his brother died in a workplace accident for which the employer was fined only $800.[30]

Industry-financed propaganda campaigns like the Air Hygiene Foundation have helped create this vacuum of information, along with the notion that other people's problems are not our own and that the benefits of modern society outweigh the dangers. There is a cost, however, attached to this disregard for what happens to workers in their places of employment. Like coal-mine canaries, workers are often the first to encounter and recognize hazards in the broader environment that affects us all. Exposures to harmful chemicals are typically more severe and frequent in the workplace than elsewhere, and workers who fall sick often serve as early warnings that the solvent, metal, or pesticide with which they are working may be a threat to the broader community. Often, in fact, it has been workers themselves—not doctors, scientists, scholars, or government officials—who have discovered and raised the first alarm about a new health risk.

Lead and the "House of the Butterflies"

Given the long history of worker poisonings from exposure to lead, simple common sense should have been enough to avert the massive lead contamination that the United States and other industrial nations experienced during the twentieth century. After all, lead has been a known poison since antiquity. During the first century A.D., lead miners strapped animal bladders over their mouths as a way to avoid inhaling it. Benjamin Franklin wrote about the "mischievous effect from lead," which he experienced firsthand in his work as a printer. "You will observe with concern," he wrote, "how long a useful truth may be known, and exist, before it is generally received and practis'd on." If he had lived on into modern times, Franklin would no doubt be amazed at the "scientific" arguments that corporate propagandists have mustered to prevent the "useful truth" of lead's dangers from being "received and practis'd on."

"Why had it taken so long to confirm that environmental lead was a legitimate hazard?" asks William Graebner, a professor of history at the State University of New York at Fredonia. "The single most important answer to that question is that the lead industries did not want to see the triumph of an environmental perspective; and the lead industries exercised enormous influence over the production and dissemination of knowledge about lead in the four decades after 1925. This influence might best be described as a kind of hegemony over scientific research and over perceptions of lead-related problems."[31]

Lead exposure can cause anemia, kidney cancer, brain damage, abdominal pain, weight loss, weakness, reproductive system impairment, and miscarriage. Its effect on the brain can be severe and permanent, causing hallucinations, tremors, outright insanity, and even death. These effects were detailed in 1861 by novelist Charles Dickens, who exposed the horrors visited upon women who went mad working in lead factories. By the late nineteenth century, England was regulating workplace exposure to lead, and by the 1920s Australia and a number of European countries were regulating lead in paint, which was affecting painters and was becoming a common cause of poisoning among children. In the United States, however, the regulatory mechanisms moved in the opposite direction, thanks largely to America's infatuation with the automobile and the discovery of "no-knock gasoline."

In 1922, researchers for General Motors discovered that adding tetraethyl lead to gasoline could raise the compression and power of internal combustion engines. By the end of the decade, this discovery helped GM displace Ford as the country's number-one automaker. The downside, however, was instantly recognized by industrial hygienists. Lead in paint is bad enough, but dried paint at least fixes most of the lead in a solid form that requires some effort to ingest. Tetraethyl lead, however, is an oily liquid that is easily absorbed through the skin or inhaled as it evaporates. This makes it more "bioavailable" than lead in solid form, as a series of tragedies quickly demonstrated. The first to reach the attention of the public occurred at a tetraethyl lead processing plant owned by Standard Oil in Elizabeth, New Jersey. Within a five-day period beginning on October 24, 1924, five of the plant's 49 workers died and 35 developed severe dementia and other neurological symptoms of lead poisoning. Several would spend the rest of their lives confined to insane asylums.

Following the all-too-familiar protocol in such cases, the company's spokesmen responded to these poisonings by attempting to blame the workers for their own fate. The *New York Times,* which reported on the disaster, noted that a company doctor had suggested that "nothing ought to be said about this matter in the public interest." The workers' supervisors opined that "these men probably went insane because they worked too hard."[32] Reports soon emerged, however, of other cases in which workers had died while handling tetraethyl lead. A General Motors research site in Dayton, Ohio, saw worker deaths, as did a DuPont chemical plant at Deepwater, New Jersey. During a two-year time span, the Deepwater plant saw more than 300 cases of lead poisoning. Eighty percent of the workers at DuPont who handled tetraethyl lead during that period were poisoned, some repeatedly. Other employees took to calling the tetraethyl lead unit the "house of the butterflies," a grim joke about the nonexistent insects that the exposed workers were seeing as part of their hallucinatory dementia.[33]

The political struggle over the introduction of leaded gasoline marked a historical watershed, a moment that would help define the future direction of technological development and corporate power in American society. The automobile was fast becoming the mechanical "chicken in every pot" that each American family craved as a symbol of personal financial success. Simultaneously it was coming to symbolize the idea that technological innovation marked the way forward for human freedom and progress. "No-knock" gasoline meant that automobile engines would have more power, more efficiency, more speed—in short, everything that modern society has come to see as desirable indicators of progress. The worker poisonings at several different locations suggested, however, that this progress might come at a great price. No one knew or could even imagine yet the sheer number of automobiles that would be racing down public highways 50 years hence, but it was clear that the lead going into gas tanks would exit through the tailpipe—not as a liquid but as an aerosol, making it almost entirely bioavailable from the moment it left the engine. It would float in the air, then gradually settle to the ground, contaminating streets and soil.

A proper, precautionary response to the lesson learned from worker exposures would have been to ban leaded gasoline. Instead, automakers and government officials preferred to assume that the amount of lead in leaded gasoline was so small as to present no danger. In a letter to the U.S. Surgeon General, DuPont's chairman stated that this question "had been given very serious consideration . . . although no actual experimental data has been taken." Even without data, he was confident that "the average street will probably be so free from lead that it will be impossible to detect it or its absorption." In order to minimize public concern about the product's potential hazard, leaded gasoline was given the brand name Ethyl, with the word "lead" deliberately omitted.

For help in generating a scientific rationale for the introduction of leaded gasoline, General Motors turned to the U.S. Bureau of Mines. As an official arm of the U.S. government, the Bureau of Mines purported to offer an "independent" and hence reliable assessment of the safety risks involved with leaded gas, but in fact its independence was compromised at multiple levels. Its history with respect to the safety of mineworkers had shown it to be a pliable tool of industry. In reality it was an institution that existed to promote and support the mining industry, and tetraethyl lead promised to create a huge new market for mined lead. Worst of all, GM was *paying* the Bureau to conduct its study on the safety of leaded gas—creating an obvious conflict of interest, as several prominent public health specialists pointed out to little avail. "It seems to me extremely unfortunate that the experts of the United States Government should be carrying out this investigation on a grant from General Motors," wrote Dr. Yandell Henderson, a leading public health physiologist at Yale University, pointing to the "urgent need for an absolutely unbiased investigation."[34]

Just as the Ethyl Gasoline Corporation had taken the word "lead" out of its own name, the Bureau of Mines went out of its way to omit references to lead in its internal correspondence regarding the GM-funded study. Questioned about this omission, a Bureau of Mines official replied that it was deliberate. "If it should happen to get some publicity accidentally, it would not be so bad if the word 'lead' were omitted as this term is apt to prejudice somewhat against its use," he stated. Censoring the word "lead" out of research into lead toxicity strays considerably, of course, from what might be considered strict scientific rigor. Not surprisingly, the Bureau of Mines study produced a scientific whitewash, which was promptly released as "proof" that "there is no danger of acquiring lead poisoning through even prolonged exposure to exhaust gases of cars using Ethyl Gas."

In addition to the Bureau of Mines, industry turned for scientific backing to the Charles F. Kettering Foundation and the Kettering Laboratory of Applied Physiology. Forerunners of today's Sloan-Kettering Institute for Cancer Research, both the foundation and the laboratory were founded by Charles Kettering, a General Motors executive who had been directly involved in the company's efforts to develop tetraethyl lead as a gasoline additive. The laboratory's first director, Robert Kehoe, was the Ethyl Gasoline Corporation's medical director. He quickly became the most vocal scientist in the United States on the subject of lead hazards. His writings, which remained influential well into the 1960s, claimed that lead occurs "naturally" in human beings and that the body "naturally" eliminates low-level lead exposures. At "natural" low levels, it was safe. The only exposures that mattered, he said, were acute exposures like the worker poisonings that had occurred at the "house of butterflies." This formulation of the facts, which has since been conclusively refuted, provided the scientific weapon that industry needed to fight off the threat that lead poisoning might be environmentally defined and that tetraethyl lead might be banned.

God, Gas, and Civilization

On May 20, 1925, the U.S. Surgeon General convened a national conference that brought together representatives from labor, business, and the public health community to discuss the future of tetraethyl lead. "At this conference the ideologies of the different participants were clearly and repeatedly laid out and provide an important forum in which we can evaluate the scientific, political, economic, and intellectual issues surrounding this controversy," Rosner and Markowitz observe. "In the words of one participant, the conference gathered together in one room 'two diametrically opposed conceptions. The men engaged in industry, chemists, and engineers, take it as a matter of course that a little thing like industrial poisoning should not be allowed to stand in the way of a great industrial advance. On the other hand, the sanitary experts take it as a matter of course that the first consideration is the health of the people.' "[35]

Frank Howard of the Ethyl Gasoline Corporation provided industry's viewpoint. "Our continued development of motor fuels is essential in our civilization," he told the conference, describing the discovery of leaded gasoline as a "gift of God. . . . Because some animals die and some do not die in some experiments, shall we give this thing up entirely?" he asked. "I think it would be an unheard-of blunder if we should abandon a thing of this kind merely because of our fears."[36]

Not everyone shared this faith, however. Yandell Henderson, the Yale physiologist who had criticized the Bureau of Mines study, warned presciently that as the automobile industry expanded, hundreds of thousands of pounds of lead would be deposited in the streets of every major city of America. "The conditions would grow worse so gradually and the development of lead poisoning will come on so insidiously . . . that leaded gasoline will be in nearly universal use and large numbers of cars will have been sold . . . before the public and the government awaken to the situation," Henderson said.[37]

In fact, even Henderson's warning turns out to be a gross underestimate. By the mid-1970s, 90 percent of the gasoline used for automobiles in the United States was formulated with ethyl. During the 60 years that leaded gasoline was used in the United States, some 30 million *tons* of lead was released from automobile exhausts. "When many cars were getting just ten miles to a gallon in stop-and-go traffic, a busy intersection might have gotten as much as four or five tons of lead dumped on it in a year," notes Howard Mielke, an environmental toxicologist and lead expert at the College of Pharmacy at Xavier University of Louisiana, in New Orleans. "That's roughly equal to having a lead smelter at every major intersection in the United States. As a result, there is a very, very large reservoir of lead in soil."[38]

Industry trade associations, in particular the Lead Industry Association, vigilantly responded to research that might have alerted the public to lead's environmental risks. In 1939, Dr. Randolph Byers, a pediatrician at Boston Children's Hospital, tracked the development of 20 children who had been treated successfully for lead poisoning. He found that even though they had been cured of their acute symptoms, many were experiencing profound learning disabilities and showed evidence of personality disorders. The lead industry responded by threatening Byers with a million-dollar lawsuit. In 1955, a study of Philadelphia tenements revealed that the city's children were becoming ill and dying from eating chips of lead-based paint. This, too, failed to have any appreciable impact on public perceptions or public policy. In the 1960s, the lead industry tried to have a scientist fired from the California Institute of Technology after his research indicated that leaded gasoline posed a risk to public health. "It really is a sorry track record of dirty tricks and dirty science to promote the broader use of lead," says Don Ryan of the Alliance to End Childhood Lead Poisoning.[39]

The Industrial Hygiene Foundation, which had previously risen to the defense of the "dusty trades" in the matter of silicosis, also helped to disseminate the pro-lead writings of the Kettering Foundation's Robert Kehoe. It argued against the need for government regulations on lead, and railed against those who "exaggerate and dramatize accidental occurrences and alleged injurious effects which have not been established."[40] IHF's complaint reflected a common industry approach to environmental as opposed to occupational health risks. High-level, occupational exposures like the "house of butterflies" poisonings create obvious, acute responses. The effect of lower-level environmental exposures, however, is typically less obvious and harder to establish scientifically beyond all reasonable doubt. A commonsense precautionary approach would have aimed at preventing even low-level exposures, but in the absence of absolute proof of harm, industry preferred to characterize such precautions as extreme, unscientific, and unnecessary. Thanks to this industry campaign, the first U.S. government regulations on gasoline lead emissions were not issued until 1973. For children, whose developing bodies are much more sensitive to lead than are adults', even those regulations would prove inadequate.

Faster Cars, Slower Kids

The dangers of lead exposure first came to the attention of Herbert Needleman in the 1950s, while he was still a student in medical school. To help cover his tuition, Needleman took a summer job as a day laborer at DuPont's chemical plant in Deepwater, New Jersey. He noticed that one group of older workers kept to themselves, moving and speaking slowly and awkwardly, spending their breaks staring into space. His coworkers told him that they were the survivors of the "house of butterflies"—deeply damaged, but still able to work.

Needleman began reading the available literature on lead poisoning and was struck in particular by the work that Byers had done decades earlier showing long-term effects of lead on children. In 1974, he undertook his own study of 2,500 first- and second-graders. Lead tends to accumulate in bones and teeth, and by testing children's "baby teeth," he was able to determine which kids had experienced higher-than-average lead exposures. The results, published in the *New England Journal of Medicine* in 1979, were explosive, showing impaired mental development even at levels of exposure that had previously been considered safe. In addition to having lower intelligence, lead-exposed children are more likely to be hyperactive, suffer from attention deficits, or engage in violent behavior and delinquency.

"The paper was devastating to the lead industry and came at a critical time," observes writer Thomas A. Lewis. "A federal ban on lead in household paint had taken effect in 1977. Exposure to lead in the workplace had come under strict monitoring and remediation requirements under the 1978 Occupational Safety and Health Act (OSHA). . . . Needleman's work suggested that far more stringent regulations were needed."

Industry's experts, of course, disagreed—in particular, Dr. Claire Ernhart, a developmental psychologist at Case Western University who has received substantial grants from the industry-funded International Lead Zinc Research Organization. Ernhart also serves periodically as a courtroom "expert witness" for defendants in cases involving lead contamination and cleanup. In 1982, for, example, she testified in favor of the lead industry before an EPA panel that was contemplating phasing out all leaded gasoline. More recently, she served as an expert witness for a landlord who was sued after a young girl developed severe brain damage as a result of ingesting lead paint.

In 1981, Ernhart formally accused Needleman of flawed research, leading to a two-year EPA investigation by a panel of six outside experts. After reviewing and reanalyzing his data, the panel found some inconsequential statistical errors and concluded that his data was insufficient to support the hypothesis that low levels of lead impaired children. The panel also concluded that Ernhart's data was insufficient to *refute* Needleman's hypothesis, but Ernhart had the benefit of a coordinated PR campaign on her side. The firm of Hill & Knowlton—then the world's largest PR firm—"papered the world" with a draft copy of the EPA panel's report, in the words of EPA senior scientist Joel Schwartz. Copies were sent to journalists throughout the United States, accompanied by a cover letter claiming that the EPA advisory panel had rejected Needleman's findings. In fact, Needleman's point-by-point response to the EPA panel's criticisms was so persuasive that the agency ended up reversing its position and adopting his findings as part of the basis for restricting lead in gasoline. Hill & Knowlton stood their course. "To this day they are circulating the draft report," Schwartz noted in 1992.[41]

In 1991, Needleman was scheduled to testify against a lead smelter in a Superfund case involving the cleanup of lead tailings. Ernhart and another psychologist, Sandra Scarr, were hired as expert witnesses for the defense. The case was settled out of court but sparked a renewed attack on Needleman's credibility. In a letter to the National Institutes of Health, Ernhart and Scarr charged him with scientific misconduct and threw in a new claim that Needleman had "failed to cooperate" with the earlier investigation. His university convened a new inquiry, and although it found "no evidence of fraud, falsification or plagiarism," it added that it could not "exclude the possibility of research misconduct" and recommended further investigation. The process dragged into 1992, when Needleman requested and obtained an open hearing so that he could publicly confront his accusers. During two days of testimony, Needleman brought forth other scientists to testify on his behalf, including Joel Schwartz from the EPA.

The charges by Ernhart and Scarr were based on arcane statistical details. Essentially, they were claiming that he had manipulated variables in his data to produce a biased, anti-lead result. Needleman's scientific defenders, however, showed that even when those variables were taken out of the analysis, the result would be essentially identical to the conclusion that Needleman had published in 1979—namely, that for every 10 parts per million increase of lead in a child's tooth there was a two-point drop in IQ. After two months of deliberation, the full hearing board concluded that no evidence suggested scientific misconduct, although it added that Needleman's research methods had been "sub-standard." Outraged, Needleman filed a lawsuit to force the university to retract this finding.

The matter was referred to the federal Office of Research Integrity for yet another hearing. Nearly two years later, ORI found him innocent of intentional scientific misconduct, again noting that he had made "numerous errors and misstatements," mostly of a statistical nature that did not affect his conclusions—the same result, in other words, as that of the previous 1981 investigation. After 13 years of harassment, he had managed, more or less, to clear his name. Nevertheless, he said in 1995, "The misrepresentation is still being used by people in the lead industry to try to discredit my work."[42]

"When U.S. callers dial an (800) lead industry hotline, they are sent a thick packet of information, including a quasi-scientific paper that questions the work of [lead researcher] Ellen Silbergeld and others, and a *Wall Street Journal* story about the integrity charges brought against Needleman; a more recent *Journal* article by the same reporter, describing Needleman's vindication before NIH, is not included," noted *Common Cause* magazine in 1992. "The packets are issued by Edelman Public Relations Worldwide, which is under contract to the Lead Industries Association."[43]

Winners and Losers

Herbert Needleman's work is a success story, relatively speaking. His research has been confirmed by dozens of separate scientific studies conducted by other researchers and has become generally accepted. Thanks to federal regulations that followed from this research, the amount of lead in gasoline in the United States has dropped 99.8 percent from pre-1970s levels. The amount of lead found in the blood of Americans has also dropped dramatically.

Even today, however, the average North American carries between 100 and 500 times as much lead in his or her blood as our preindustrial ancestors. In cities where there has been a high density of automobile traffic, adults have blood-lead levels of about 20 to 25 micrograms per deciliter—roughly half the level at which lead exposure leads to impairment of peripheral nerves. No other toxic chemical has accumulated in humans to average levels that are this close to the threshold for overt chemical poisoning. How has this affected us? Has it made us less intelligent, less rational? As the lead industry will be the first to tell you, it is difficult if not impossible to answer these questions with any degree of scientific precision.

What we do know is that the lead industry continues to lobby, even today, against measures such as an excise tax on lead that would discourage its use and generate funds to help clean up its toxic legacy. Cleanup is needed because some three million tons of lead remain on the walls of homes that were built and painted prior to 1970. Another five million tons is found in the soil near busy roadways. Lead from batteries ends up in waste dumps and incinerators and enters people's drinking water through the lead in plumbing fixtures. Opposition to a cleanup comes from a diverse array of economic forces: the National Association of Water Companies, which doesn't want to replace lead pipes; the National Association of Realtors and the National Association of Home Builders, which want to avoid the costs of cleaning up lead-painted homes; the electronics, plumbing, and ceramics industries, all of which use lead in their products. "The war over lead, like so many consumer and environmental problems, is largely waged out of public view, in the bureaucratic and congressional trenches," observes *Common Cause*. "It is at this unglamorous level that industry goes head to head with government rule makers, wearing down their resistance and often winning through brute persistence."[44] It is a war, in other words, in which advocates for public health are perpetually outnumbered and outmaneuvered by expert hired guns whose mission, it seems, is literally to pump the public full of lead.

5

Packaging the Beast

> *"All is not right in the kingdom,"* King
> Corporate *sighed as he sat upon his royal
> throne in the Great Hall of Commerce. . . .
> "I need someone who will make the town
> criers stop gossiping and saying those awful
> things. We need to improve the Queen's
> image and get the townspeople to sing her
> praises. I need someone who will prove that
> the moat water is harmless and that these old
> people are getting sick because they are old."*
>
> —"A Fable," from the website of the
> Karwoski & Courage PR firm[1]

You are widely seen as being a bad actor. . . . How do you
move from being a bad actor to being seen as a good actor,
as a good guy?" Peter Sandman asked, pacing as he addressed the audience of 400 public relations and mine managers from Australia, the Philippines, South Africa, Papua New Guinea, and the United States.

Billed as the star attraction for the Minerals Council of Australia's
1998 Annual Environmental Workshop, Sandman was posing a question
that the Australian mining industry had been asking itself with increasing
urgency. The industry had spent millions of dollars on failed PR and advertising campaigns to improve its reputation. Now Sandman, an affable
"risk communication" consultant, was delivering his recipe for success.

Sandman began by ticking off the reasons for the industry's falling
public image: debate over the role that the Rio Tinto mine played in spark-
ing civil war on Bougainville Island in Papua New Guinea; the dumping
of mine tailings in a Papua New Guinea river; the collapse of a tailings

dam at another mine; and the push by one company to build a uranium mine in a national park against the wishes of the traditional Aboriginal owners. "There is a growing sense that you screw up a lot, and as a net result it becomes harder to get permission to mine," Sandman said. The solution, he advised, lay in finding an appropriate "persona" for the industry.

One option, he said, was to present the industry as a "romantic hero . . . which basically says, 'Well, the critics are wrong. I am not a bad actor. I'm terrific. The mining and minerals industry is what made the world the wonderful place that it is.'" He noted, however, that this approach had already failed when it was used as a basis for the mining industry's TV advertisements.

The next option, he suggested, would be to portray industry as a "misunderstood victim. . . . You feel you are David and [environmentalists] are Goliath." But this approach was equally unlikely to succeed. "No one thinks you are David," he said. "You look like Goliath, especially in Australia. 'Misunderstood victim' doesn't play very well."

A third option would be to present the industry as a "team player." However, Sandman told the miners, "You can't get from 'bad actor' to 'team player' without pausing at some other image. As a characteristic of human nature, I don't think people can go from thinking you are bad guys to thinking you are good guys, without pausing somewhere in the middle."

One intermediate position, he suggested, is the role of "reformed sinner," which "works quite well if you can sell it. . . . 'Reformed sinner,' by the way, is what John Brown [of British Petroleum] has successfully done for his organization. It is arguably what Shell has done with respect to Brent Spar. Those are two huge oil companies that have done a very good job of saying to themselves, 'Everyone thinks we are bad guys. . . . We can't just start out announcing we are good guys, so what we have to announce is we have finally realized we were bad guys and we are going to be better.' . . . It makes it much easier for critics and the public to buy into the image of the industry as good guys after you have spent awhile in purgatory."

For the Australian mining industry, however, Sandman thought that even "reformed sinner" would be a "tough sell," because "the public is rather skeptical when companies say they have reformed."

Fortunately, there was one more "middle" role that the industry could adopt on its path to salvation. "There is a fifth image that I think works by far the best," he said, "and that is the 'caged beast.' What is the persona of this 'caged beast'? Useful, perhaps even indispensable, but dangerous. This is the image I would recommend to you. If you want to come back from 'bad actor' to 'team player,' the easiest path back is to make a case that you would continue to be a bad actor if you could, but you can't, because the cage works."

Why should the industry portray itself so negatively? Because, Sandman explained, the "caged beast" was a marketable image that at least would convey the idea that the industry was no longer harmful. "You are behaving much better, not because you want to, not because you have become the Mother Teresa of the mining companies, but because nongovernmental organizations have been successful, regulators have been successful, your neighbors have been successful, the entire society has been successful in persuading you at least that you will make more dollars if you reform.

"You have two basic postures," Sandman advised. "Either you are free to rape and pillage as you want to, but fortunately you don't have the taste for it. Or you have a taste for it and you might continue to rape and pillage if you could, but fortunately you can't get away with it anymore," he said. "I believe the second is true, and I am certain the second is salable. I can't imagine why you keep claiming the first except that it nurtures your self-esteem, it reduces your outrage. Once again, whose outrage do you want to mitigate? The critics' or yours? Do you want to get even or get rich?"

Environmentalism in Moderation

Sandman's candid advice may seem unusual, but some of the largest companies in the world view him as a risk communications expert and pay big bucks—between $650 and $1,200 per hour—for his analysis. His clients have included the Chemical Manufacturers Association, Ciba-Geigy, Dow Chemical, DuPont, Exxon, the U.S. Department of Energy in connection with the proposed high-level nuclear waste dump in Yucca Mountain, Nevada, and the U.S. Environmental Protection Agency on radon testing in houses and home testing for lead. What kind of clients would he turn away? "I wouldn't work to develop risk communication strategies to keep tobacco sales high," he says. "I have never been asked to work for the handgun industry, but if asked I suspect I'd say no. Now that I think about it, I might even work for the tobacco industry if they were prepared to come clean. There are a few specific companies that I believe have behaved so dishonorably—killing Karen Silkwood comes to mind—that I doubt I would work for them unless they were prepared to come clean."[2]

In style and even in substance, Sandman defies many PR industry stereotypes. Formerly a professor of human ecology at Rutgers University, he works from a small office in Newton, Massachusetts. In an industry dominated by big companies, he adamantly refuses to let his one-person company get any bigger. He is a prolific writer, describes himself as a "moderate" environmentalist, and works on retainer to the Environmental Defense Fund. He is scathingly critical of manipulative PR techniques and, unlike many PR people, talks candidly about his strategies and tactics. Ask a straight question, and more often than not you'll get a frank answer.

Scratch the surface, however, and you can find attitudes that are remarkably similar to the rationalizations of conventional spin doctors. Take, for example, the case of Shell's collaboration with the military dictatorship in Nigeria, where military repression aimed at the indigenous Ogoni people has helped facilitate Shell's extraction of natural gas from Ogoni lands. When playwright Ken Saro-Wiwa became a leader for the Ogoni people, he was arrested by the country's military dictatorship. Following a trial before a military tribunal, Saro-Wiwa and seven other Ogoni activists were executed by hanging in 1995.

Sandman sighs when asked if Shell deserved the international condemnation it received followed the killings. "Oh boy, is that hard," he says. "I think the outrage was absolutely legitimate. I also think that Shell had nothing it could have done." While acknowledging the Ogoni grievances as "largely justified," Sandman characterizes Saro-Wiwa as the "Tom Paine" of the Ogoni and describes their campaign as an armed rebellion. "Though Saro-Wiwa was not armed . . . he was their pamphleteer," he says. "Some of the people with whom he was executed were soldiers in this rebellion."

Setting aside the question of whether people like Thomas Paine deserve to be killed, the facts themselves in Sandman's rationalization are strongly disputed by Andy Rowell, a Britain-based freelance writer who has monitored Shell's activities since 1992. "Sandman's views are typical of a corporate spin doctor relying on information from a client. They bear no relation to the truth about the events which actually occurred in Nigeria," says Rowell, who is the author of numerous articles on the subject as well as the book *Green Backlash.* "Sandman's story is not what happened, but what Shell wants us to believe happened," Rowell says. "It is a virtual reality, which has been worked out in PR offices in Europe. . . . The Ogoni struggle was a non-violent struggle for ecological and social justice. It was not an armed rebellion. All they were demanding was an end to the double standards of the oil industry that had devastated their environment, and a greater share of the oil wealth that was drilled from under their land. The Ogoni suffered a brutal backlash. Over 2,000 were killed, 30,000 made homeless, and countless others were raped and tortured by the Nigerian military, which received logistical and financial support from Shell."[3]

Shell is Nigeria's largest foreign investor, earning an estimated $312 million a year in profits from its oil operations there. Its high-pressure pipelines crisscross the Niger Delta where the Ogoni live, emitting air and noise pollution as well as bright flames of light, sometimes as close as 100 meters from Ogoni houses. Massive oil spills and unlined waste pits from company operations have also contributed to the devastation of the region.

Sandman's claim that Shell was powerless to prevent the execution of Ken Saro-Wiwa also repeats the official company line. "Some campaigning groups say we should intervene in the political process," Shell stated around the time of the execution. "But even if we could, we should never do so. Politics is the business of governments and politicians. The world where companies use their economic influence to prop up or bring down governments would be a frightening and bleak one indeed."[4]

Rowell and other observers familiar with Shell's massive presence in Nigeria say that reality belies the talk about nonintervention. When local Ogoni communities began organizing in 1990, Shell in fact sent a letter asking the Nigerian government to "urgently provide us with security protection." The government sent in its notorious Mobile Police Force, whose actions included the massacre of 80 people in the village of Umuechem in 1991. In 1993, the growing opposition to Shell culminated in a 300,000-person mass rally, and Shell was forced to suspend its operations in the Niger Delta. That same year, General Sani Abacha took control of the country and began a vigorous persecution of the protesters, killing more than 2,000 people. Internal memos from Nigerian security forces document Shell's support of the Nigerian military, including payments to soldiers engaged in what one memo described as "ruthless military operations . . . undertaken for smooth economic activities to commence." Mil-

itary tactics included "wasting operations" (killings) coupled with "psychological tactics" and the "restriction of unauthorized visitors, especially
those from Europe to the Ogoni."[5]

"Shell is involved in Nigerian politics up to their neck," said Ken
Saro-Wiwa's younger brother, Dr. Owens Wiwa. "If they had threatened to
withdraw from Nigeria unless Ken was released, he would have been alive
today." Wiwa recounted his own personal meetings with Brian Anderson,
the head of Shell in Nigeria, on three separate occasions during the
months leading up to the executions. "Each time I asked him to help get
my brother and others out," Wiwa said. "He said he would be able to
get Ken and the others freed if we stopped the protest campaign abroad.
I was very shocked. Even if I had wanted to, I didn't have the power to
control the international environmental protests."[6]

Calculating Outrage

As the Nigeria example suggests, Sandman tends to accommodate himself to his clients' views, but this does not mean that he merely tells them
what they want to hear. As a specialist in what he calls "outrage management," he tells companies that they have to change their behavior, at least
on the surface, if they want to win public acceptance.

Sandman's theories have been programmed into Outrage, a software
package designed to assist companies in predicting and managing the
anger of "stakeholders" affected by corporate actions. The Outrage software sells for $3,000 a copy or $48,000 for a worldwide license. A demonstration version is also available, which provides a revealing look at the
limits of Sandman's approach to corporate enlightenment. The demo offers a hypothetical sample "situation definition" that lays out the following scenario: "Our factory in the South Side neighborhood has long had
visible air emissions, sometimes very thick. The poor, minority residents,
with whom we have very little relationship, recently began organizing to
do something about the problem, maybe even shut us down." The demo
then leads users through the steps needed to track and categorize people
as allies, neutrals, or opponents. Among the sample "opponents," it lists
names including "S.S. Latino Assn.," "Mrs. Charles," "City Air Quality
Board," "Sierra Club," "Greenpeace," "South Side Elementary School,"
and "nearest neighbors."

"For obvious reasons, we are also interested in how much power each important stakeholder can bring to bear," the demo explains. It invites users to use a fairly crude but effective formula that maps the overlap between "passion" and "power" among stakeholders. Depending on how they rank in these two areas, the company can choose one of four strategies: "deflect, defer, dismiss, or defeat." Stakeholders with power but no passion should be "deflected." Distract them, change the subject, or just wait them out until their attention wanders elsewhere. People with passion but no power, on the other hand, can be "defeated." Sure they care, but can they do anything about it? And people with neither passion nor power are easier still. Just "dismiss" them. The one occasion when real reform is necessary, Sandman says, is when dealing with people who have both high passion and high power. Those people are "a force to reckon with," and the company will eventually have to "defer" to their demands—"one way or another, to one extent or another."

In most cases, Sandman believes that the public inaccurately perceives the level of hazard and risk associated with a company's activities. Where the public and the experts disagree, he thinks the experts are usually right. "The most usual situation," he says, is that "the company isn't doing a lot of damage, but is acting like a jerk: unresponsive, contemptuous, even dishonest. The company thinks that because it isn't doing a lot of damage, it is entitled to act like a jerk. The public thinks that because the company is acting like a jerk, it must be doing a lot of damage."

This analysis suggests that rather than focusing on real hazards or harm to the public, companies should focus their public relations attention on *perceptions of process*. Does the public think the company is "responsive" or "unresponsive"? Is it "honest" or "lying"? Do decisions that affect the community seem "voluntary" or "coerced"? Is the company seen as doing something "natural" or "industrial"? "Familiar" vs. "exotic"? "Fair" vs. "unfair"? Answer these questions, Sandman says, and you are well on your way to managing public outrage. In order to stop seeming like jerks, companies should adopt a posture of apologetic humility in their public communications. "Acknowledge your prior misbehavior," he advises—within certain limits. "I don't chiefly mean things you have done that nobody knows you have done and when we find out you will go to jail," he adds. "If there are any of these, I urge you to seek legal counsel before you seek communication counsel. I'm talking about negative things on the public record. . . . Should you keep talking about them or is it enough that you have revealed them once? The argument I want to make is that you should keep talking about them incessantly. You should wallow in them."

The reasoning behind this strategy of public humility is encapsulated in a formula that Sandman has invented and which is now widely quoted within the public relations industry. Humility helps reduce public outrage, he explains, and public outrage can be as big a threat to corporate profits as any actual hazard. "Risk," he says, "equals hazard plus outrage."

This deceptively simple formula has become a staple in PR industry discussions of risk communications. It has been adopted as gospel by leading practitioners such as James Lindheim at Burson-Marsteller and Thomas Buckmaster, chairman and general manager of the PR firm of Hill & Knowlton. By understanding that risk equals hazard plus outrage, Buckmaster says, risk communicators can overcome the fear and hostility of "grassroots members, stakeholders and the public at large." The "irrational" factor of outrage, he says, "makes it impossible to teach anyone anything—when they are afraid. . . . Once people are outraged, they don't listen to hazard statistics . . . don't use numerical risk comparisons." In fact, he says, "managing the outrage is more important than managing the risk."[7]

Rolling the Dice

For most people, "risk" and "hazard" are virtual synonyms, although conventional risk analysts assign them somewhat different meanings. A sharp knife blade, they will tell you, is an example of a hazard, while risk is the probability that the knife will actually hurt someone. Sandman's formula, however, is concerned with a different kind of risk—namely, the probability that a given hazard will hurt a company's bottom line. His formula recognizes that beyond the direct liabilities associated with a hazard, a company's reputation and profitability are affected by the way the public reacts to it.

Businesses are accustomed to thinking of risk as an economic reality. They take a serious approach to dealing with it and have evolved rigorous and elaborate systems for managing it, with their own specialized vocabulary: country risk, currency exchange risk, inflation and price risk, credit risk, insurance, cost of residual uncertainty, risk pooling, probability, variation, standard deviation, diversification. "Every financial firm of any substance has a formal risk management department," says Daniel Geer, an e-commerce security expert. "The financial world in its entirety is about packaging risk so that it can be bought and sold, i.e., so that risk can be securitized and finely enough graded to be managed at a profit. Everything from the lowly car loan to the most exotic derivative security is a risk-reward trade-off. Don't for a minute underestimate the amount of money to be made on Wall Street, London and/or Tokyo when you can invent a new way to package risk. . . . You don't have to understand forward swaptions, collateralized mortgage obligations, yield burning, or anything else to understand that risk management is where the money is. In a capitalist world, if something is where the money is, that something rules. Risk is that something."[8]

Businesspeople gamble with money, and a bad gamble simply means that someone loses some cash. "Risk analysis" of chemicals and other potential environmental and health risks is derived from "cost-benefit analysis," which in turn derives from simple profit-and-loss accounting used by private companies. Arbitrary and indefensible assumptions enter the equation, however, when this methodology is used to gamble on things as important as human lives or the natural environment in which people live. What is the dollar value, after all, of a human life? What is the value of the air we breathe, the fertility of our soil, or our continued health and ability to have children? A price can be put on the cost of hospital care for cancer patients, but what price can we put on the suffering that the patients and their families endure? These questions have been asked by government regulators and in product-liability lawsuits, with widely varying answers.

A growing number of hard decisions facing modern societies involve the question: "How safe is safe enough?" Nuclear waste, recombinant DNA, food additives, and chemical plant explosions are just a few of the effects of technological progress that raise this question. The answers are difficult, because they involve multiple uncertainties: uncertainty about the magnitude of the risk at hand, contradictory data and theories, business trade secrets, conflicting social values, disagreements between technical experts and the public at large. What makes these problems even more intractable is that politics and sophistry are frequently used to shift the blame away from those who cause the harm to those who suffer the consequences. "Risk analysis is a subtle discipline," observes Ian Stewart, a mathematics professor at Warwick University in England. "It is an elaborate and rather naive procedure that can be abused in several ways. One abuse is to exaggerate benefits and tone down risks. A particularly nasty kind occurs when one group takes the risk but a different group reaps the benefit."[9] Risk management is not merely a technical discipline. Psychology, economics, politics, and the power of vested interests all lurk beneath the seemingly objective language of "balancing risks against benefits."

The question of which risks are acceptable depends ultimately on where the person passing judgment stands in relation to those risks. Under our current regulatory system, the risk of chemical exposures is usually passed on to the people who suffer those exposures. If 10 or 20 years later they come down with cancer or their children suffer health problems, identifying the cause—let alone proving it in a court of law—is virtually impossible. Companies find this arrangement profitable, and it certainly encourages technological innovation, but the cost to others can be considerable, as the tobacco industry and the makers of leaded gasoline have tragically proven.

"Risk assessment is a decision-making technique that first came into use during the presidency of Jimmy Carter, who was trained as a nuclear engineer," says Peter Montague, the editor of *Rachel's Environment and Health Weekly,* a newsletter that offers weekly investigative reporting and opinion on issues of ecology and public health. "At its best, risk assessment is an honest attempt to find a rational basis for decisions, by analyzing the available scientific evidence. In theory it is still an attractive ideal," Montague says. "However, 20 years of actual practice have badly tarnished the ideal of risk assessment and have sullied the reputation of many a risk assessor." It arose, he says, in response to the growing realization that "many modern technologies had far surpassed human understanding, giving rise to by-products that were dangerous, long-lived, and completely unanticipated." The same technologies that have created unparalleled wealth have also created unparalleled problems with municipal and industrial wastes, agricultural chemicals, auto exhausts, smokestack emissions, and greenhouse gases.

As government regulators and pollution-producing industries came under pressure in the 1970s to address these problems, they began devising quantitative measurements to assess impacts, to weigh risks against benefits, and to establish numerical thresholds that would distinguish between dangerous and safe exposure levels. The effort to develop these quantitative standards, however, is fraught with difficulties. The natural environment is quite different from a laboratory, and laboratory studies cannot hope to duplicate the myriad conditions and environments into which chemical compounds are being released. Financial realities also limit the quality of the information that can be generated through laboratory research. To determine whether a chemical causes cancer, for example, researchers typically take a relatively small number of mice and pump them with large quantities of the chemical in question, because the alternative approach—using tens of thousands of mice and subjecting them to lower exposures—would cost a fortune. The effect of low-dose exposures is estimated by statistical extrapolation from the high-dose exposures. When one set of researchers set out to assess the accuracy of high-dose to low-dose extrapolation models, however, they found that the predicted low-dose results vary by a factor of a million. This, they note, "is like not knowing whether you have enough money to buy a cup of coffee or pay off the national debt."[10]

In 1995, three well-known and respected risk assessors—Anna Fan, Robert Howd, and Brian Davis—published a detailed summary of the status of risk assessment, in which they pointed out that there is no scientific agreement on which tests to use to determine whether someone has suffered immune system, nervous system, or genetic damage. In other words, the best available science lacks the tools with which to provide definite, quantitative answers to the questions that are at the heart of risk assessment. "There are other problems with risk assessments," Montague observes. "Science has no way to analyze the effects of multiple exposures, and almost all modern humans are routinely subjected to multiple exposures: pesticides, automobile exhaust, dioxins in meat, fish and dairy products; prescription drugs; tobacco smoke; food additives; ultraviolet sunlight passing through the earth's damaged ozone shield; and so on. Determining the cumulative effect of these insults is a scientific impossibility, so most risk assessors simply exclude these inconvenient realities. But the resulting risk assessment is bogus. . . . Risk assessment, it is now clear, promises what it cannot deliver, and so is misleading at best and fraudulent at worst. It pretends to provide a rational assessment of 'risk' or 'safety,' but it can do no such thing because the required data are simply not available, nor are standardized methods of interpretation."[11]

Publicly, industry and government remain committed to risk assessment, but defectors are increasingly willing to admit that it is an art rather than a science. Different risk assessors, using the same evidence, can easily come up with radically opposed conclusions as to the costs and benefits of a course of action. Where uncertainty reigns, spin doctors rush in to fill the information vacuum. Notwithstanding its limitations, the methodology of risk assessment offers important advantages to the corporate spin doctor. "These methods are especially valuable politically in that their use tends to obscure the basic policy questions of government regulation of business in a technocratic haze of numbers (numbers readily manipulated), focusing attention upon the statistics rather than the issues," observes science historian David Noble. "The methods offer other advantages as well, not least of which is the seeming monopoly on rationality itself. All qualitative or subjective decision-making is relegated to the realm of irrationality and dismissed without a hearing. By invalidating experience and intuition, they thereby disqualify all but the technically initiated from taking part in the debate, which becomes enshrouded in an impenetrable cloak of mystery. People are encouraged to suspend their own judgment and abandon responsibility to the experts (who have already surrendered their responsibility to their paymasters)."[12]

Risk analysis comes in a variety of flavors. One approach seeks to quantify everything in the analysis, assigning dollar values to such unquantifiable, qualitative things as human lives and environmental beauty, along with genuinely quantifiable factors such as corporate profits and wealth created. The analyst then totals up the sum of various alternatives, and whichever one costs the least is deemed the most "acceptable" risk. Another approach relies heavily on comparisons between different types of risks. If the risk to health posed by the use of a technology or chemical is questioned, the analyst calculates the likelihood of someone dying from exposure to that chemical and shows that it is less likely than the risk of dying from other events such as a car crash or drowning in a flood. Since people choose to drive cars and live downstream from dams, those risks must be acceptable to the public, the analyst concludes, and therefore this chemical must be acceptable too.

"If a person is horrified by the consequences of a carcinogenic pollutant, he is reminded that every day he takes greater risks driving to work, so what's all the fuss: Be consistent," Noble observes. "The appealing thing about such methods for the analyst aside from the fact that they reinforce his prerogatives is that they so often yield counter-intuitive results; the answers come out in ways one would not have anticipated (unless, of course, one were the analyst). The happy consequence of this, for the promoters of the techniques, is that the naïveté of the non-specialist is forever being revealed; the public is thus further cautioned about relying upon their experience and intuition and encouraged instead to rely upon the wisdom of the expert who alone can put things in perspective."[13]

H. W. Lewis, a professor of physics at the University of California–Santa Barbara who has chaired numerous government risk-assessment committees on defense, nuclear power, and other matters, exemplifies the attitudes of the modern risk assessor. He has written a book, *Technological Risk,* which promises to reveal the real dangers, "if any, of toxic chemicals, the greenhouse effect, microwave radiation, nuclear power, air travel, automobile travel, carcinogens of all kinds, and other threats to our peace of mind." It offers mortality tables and a lesson in the statistical techniques used to measure risk and is in many ways a useful and thoughtful guide. Lewis believes that the problem of overpopulation is more serious and pressing than technological risk, a judgment with which many reasonable people would certainly agree. He points out that some of the largest risks confronting individuals today stem from activities such as smoking and automobile use, facts that are indisputable. He notes furthermore that it is impossible to eliminate all risk from life, which is also indisputable. Why, then, he asks, do people worry about little things like nuclear waste and pesticides, which he regards as trivial risks? The answer, he concludes, is that the public is irrational and poorly educated. "The fraction of our population that believes in UFOs and reincarnation is mind-boggling, less than half of us know that the earth goes around the sun once a year, and it is an unending struggle to keep the teaching of evolution legal in the schools," he writes. "Our very literacy as a nation is in danger."[14]

The ignorance of the masses is such a serious problem, Lewis believes, that democracy itself is a dangerous proposition. "We are a participatory democracy and it is everyone's country, not just the educated," he writes. "The common good is ill served by the democratic process. The problem is exacerbated by the emergence of groups of persuasive people who specialize in technology-bashing and exploitation of fear, make their livings thereby, and have been embraced by large segments of the media as experts."[15]

Paradoxically, however, Lewis also believes that "the core of the anti-technology movement today" is composed not of society's least-educated members, but of the wealthiest and therefore the best-educated. "It seems to be an upper-middle-class phenomenon," he writes. "We in the affluent societies are preoccupied with safety, while risk is recognized as a normal condition of existence by the less affluent. . . . Such people are genuinely concerned that technology may be destroying the environment, and have presumably never seen the environment in other, less technically advanced, countries."[16]

Following this logic to its conclusion would seem to suggest that we should be taking our cues on matters pertaining to risk from impoverished sweatshop laborers in Central America, but since many of them are indeed genuinely illiterate and in any case rarely receive invitations to write books or serve on risk-assessment committees, the burden falls upon Lewis himself—a member of the educated upper middle class—to speak on their behalf.

When Risk Turns to Crisis

One problem with efforts to assess risk is that many factors—notoriously, the human factor—can never be quantified. Take, for example, the case of the 1984 poison leak in Bhopal, India, which is widely recognized as the world's worst industrial accident. The Bhopal disaster killed more than 2,000 people and seriously injured an estimated 200,000, many of whom suffered permanent blindness and damage to their respiratory systems. The disaster occurred when a pesticide plant owned by Union Carbide released methyl isocyanate gas, creating what *Time* magazine called "a vast, dense fog of death" that wiped out whole neighborhoods. "Even more horrifying than the number of dead," wrote *Fortune* magazine, "was the appalling nature of their dying—crowds of men, women and children scurrying madly in the dark, twitching and writhing like the insects for whom the poison was intended."[17]

Peter Sandman, who helped advise Union Carbide in the aftermath of the disaster, believes that the accident was triggered by deliberate employee sabotage. "Union Carbide has persuasive evidence," he claims. "The guilty party probably didn't intend to kill and maim thousands of people; he just wanted to get even for some real or imagined mistreatment by ruining a batch of methyl isocyanate."[18] In making this claim, he is repeating a theory that Union Carbide has repeatedly floated over the years.

However, the company has never provided enough specifics to enable independent verification of whether this was indeed what happened.[19] Even if this version of events is true, of course, it in no way mitigates the company's responsibility for the disaster. A whole cascade of failed safety measures went into the Bhopal tragedy. At the time of its occurrence, a refrigeration unit designed to prevent just such a catastrophe was shut down and had been inoperative for five months. Other fail-safe devices were also out of commission. The plant was understaffed, and employees were inadequately trained due to budget cutbacks. The plant lacked a computerized monitoring system for detecting toxic releases. Instead, workers were in the habit of recognizing leaks when their noses would burn and their eyes would water. No alarm system existed for warning the surrounding community, and no effort had been made to develop evacuation procedures and other emergency plans that could have saved many lives. As the *New York Times* concluded in its report, Bhopal was "the result of operating errors, design flaws, maintenance failures, and training deficiencies," all of which reflected corporate management decisions— human factors, in other words, not technical ones.[20]

"There are two kinds of uncertainty," Montague notes. "First, there is risk, which is an event with a known probability (such as the risk of losing your life in a car this year—the accident and death rates are known). Then there is true uncertainty, which is an event with unknown probability." The human factor, and many of the risks associated with environmental problems, involve true uncertainty. Since these risks cannot be quantified, they tend to be treated as ghosts within the machine of risk assessment—minimized, or subjected to arbitrary estimates based on guesswork rather than hard knowledge.

In the wake of most major accidents it is usually easy to find embarrassing examples of experts who predicted beforehand that such an event could never, ever occur. "I cannot imagine any condition which would cause a ship to founder. . . . Modern shipbuilding has gone beyond that," said Edward J. Smith, captain of the *Titanic*.[21] A year before the nuclear meltdown at Chernobyl, a Soviet deputy minister of the power industry announced that Soviet engineers were confident that you'd have to wait 100,000 years before the Chernobyl reactor had a serious accident.[22] Shortly before the explosion of the *Challenger* space shuttle, Bryan O'Connor, NASA's Washington-based director of the shuttle program, recalls that he "asked someone what the probability risk assessment was for the loss of a shuttle. I was told it was one in ten thousand."[23]

When actual disaster strikes, risk communications gives way to another PR specialty known as "crisis management." Emerging in the aftermath of the 1979 nuclear near-meltdown at Three Mile Island, crisis management is now taught by highly paid consultants in industry seminars and conferences. Crisis managers help companies cope with bad publicity in the wake of everything from sexual harassment cases and embezzlement scandals to plant explosions, strikes, employee shootings, toxic leaks, product tamperings, and food poisonings. Examples include the *Exxon Valdez* oil spill, *E. coli*–contaminated hamburgers at the Jack in the Box restaurant chain, the crash of TWA Flight 800, and the Pan Am Lockerbie disaster.

Unlike risk communicators, whose job is usually to tell the public that hazards are slight and risk is remote, crisis managers warn their clients that danger is everywhere and disasters are bound to happen. "There are two kinds of companies: those that have had crises, and those that will," proclaimed *PR Week* in May 1999. "It is a matter of timing and prescience but sooner or later most companies will probably need a crisis expert to help them." The Pittsburgh managing director for the Ketchum PR firm estimated in 1999 that 35 to 40 percent of the income for his unit came from crisis counseling. In the near future, *PR Week* predicted, "crisis consulting could mean hundreds of millions of dollars to the PR industry."[24]

"All corporations are living closer to the edge, increasing the potential of crises. Things are being done faster with fewer people, which is adding more risk," explained Robert Wilkerson of the Corporate Response Group, a PR firm whose crisis résumé includes a major fraud case and labor dispute in Europe, a food embargo, a plane crash, oil spills, product recalls, and two hostile corporate takeovers.[25]

As the range of these examples indicates, crisis management is not limited to health and safety issues. Spin doctors repair the reputations of politicians, celebrities, and corporations alike—anyone, in fact, who is rich enough to afford the service. Rubenstein Associates, owned by attorney Howard Rubenstein, is considered one of the top crisis managers in the business. The firm's clients have included George Steinbrenner, Rupert Murdoch, Donald Trump, "Queen of Mean" Leona Helmsley, and sportscaster Marv Albert. Rubenstein came to the aid of billionaire Adnan Khashoggi when he was accused of helping Imelda Marcos defraud the

Philippines, saw both Murdoch and Trump through high-profile divorces, and soothed Kathie Lee Gifford's embarrassment during husband Frank's extramarital fling and also when it was discovered that child labor was being used in sweatshops to manufacture clothing that bore her name.

"For me, it's fascinating to be able to deal with a Kathy Lee Gifford problem or a Leona Helmsley case. It's the kind of thing that pushes your intellectual skills," says Rubenstein vice president Gary Lewi. Speaking at a PR seminar titled "How to Polish a Tarnished Reputation," Lewi stressed the moral as well as mental rigor of his craft. "There was nothing unethical in our dealings with Kathie Lee Gifford," he said. As for Leona Helmsley, "I think that while she may be a tough SOB, it's not the kind of thing you go to jail for. . . . At the end of the day, you only have your ethics. No client is going to be in a situation where they dictate to you your morality and your ethics. If I find myself lying to the press or stonewalling to the press, and the press is no longer taking my phone calls because they regard me as a lying heathen, I might as well open up a deli." Asked for an example of a client that Rubenstein has turned away, he answered, "There was a fellow who was trafficking kiddie porn on the Internet. The company canned him and wanted to rebuild its image, and we declined. It was clearly something that had gone on for a while, where the corporate culture had allowed it. We didn't want to go anywhere near it."[26]

Sometimes, however, the PR industry seems to take perverse pleasure in exploring the "intellectual" challenge of rehabilitating clients who are appallingly beyond the pale. In the July 1997 issue of *Public Relations Tactics,* a monthly tabloid published by the Public Relations Society of America, writer Steve Crescenzo examined the case of Swiss authorities who were being sued by Jewish Holocaust survivors seeking to reclaim the assets of their murdered family members. "Would you accept as a client someone who knowingly purchased gold that had been pulled from the teeth of people murdered by the Nazis?" Crescenzo asked, and then went on to praise the work of PR firms that indeed accepted just those sorts of clients.[27] Following the rape conviction of Mike Tyson and the controversial acquittal of O. J. Simpson on murder charges, *Public Relations Tactics* devoted its cover story and several accompanying articles to another challenging PR problem: "What do you prescribe for a public relations client who's a world-class athlete, charged with a vicious crime, and forced to endure a protracted incarceration?" It surveyed a variety of PR professionals, whose free advice for Tyson and Simpson included the following:

- "Tyson's handlers need to 'reinvent' him, similar to the way Richard Nixon was reinvented."

- Tyson "ought to think seriously about cultivating a handful of journalists he can trust and then build on those few relationships."

- Simpson "has a lot of rebuilding to do," observed one PR director. But Run Fuhs, a PR manager for the Whirlpool Corporation, opined that "through some sort of public atonement process he could probably serve as a celebrity spokesman in a limited situation."

- For now, Simpson's best strategy is to "retreat for a time, say little, speak humbly, and become a nice guy," suggested another PR pro. "He'll have to feed himself back slowly. Public service would be a good start."[28]

The PR formula for Simpson or Tyson, in other words, would be basically similar to the advice that Peter Sandman offers the Australian mining industry and other companies faced with bad publicity. Speak softly. Show humility. Create a process of "public atonement" for your sins. *Crisis Communications,* a PR textbook, offers the following observation in a case-study analysis of the *Exxon Valdez* oil spill: "If the media had captured, on video and film, the CEO on the site at Prince William Sound holding an oil-covered bird in his hand and looking as if he were crying, the entire story would be told differently today."[29] There may be no point crying over spilt oil, but there is certainly a point to *looking* like you're crying.

Dress Rehearsals for Disaster

When PR firms are not fending off a real crisis, they help their clients practice for the ones that haven't happened yet. In April 1999, the Hill & Knowlton PR firm unveiled The Virtual Crisis, an interactive CD-ROM that simulates a crisis exercise. Don't look for it in stores, though. "The Virtual Crisis is not available as a stand-alone CD-ROM," reported *PR Week.* "Two H&K facilitators, specially trained to conduct the simulation, must be present to lead as many as 20 corporate team leaders through the exercise. Following the simulation (usually six hours in length), the H&K staff provides a comprehensive oral critique of the participants' decisions and responses. Pricing for the entire exercise is $10,000. . . . It is designed for top-level executives . . . who, in the case of a real crisis, would be called upon to act and to communicate the appropriate response." Developed by H&K managing director Richard Hyde, who was part of the PR firm's crisis management team at Three Mile Island, the exercise lets "participants attempt to ward off the media" while simultaneously coping with "a whole set of other distractions."[30]

Some crisis management experts specialize in "war games" that go beyond computer simulations and create actual on-the-ground situations to give corporate executives a more realistic role-playing experience. In one such drill, held after the *Exxon Valdez* oil spill, the PR firm of Kamer-Singer & Associates used popcorn and orange peels in place of actual oil to simulate a 10,000-barrel spill during a two-day "megadrill" that involved some 600 Chevron employees. As employees pretend-battled to contain the fake oil spill, Chevron's executives practiced handling a barrage of questions and complaints from Kamer-Singer's staff and the company's own internal PR people, who played the role of various outsiders: environmental activists, grandstanding politicians, aggrieved area residents, skeptical reporters, and so forth.

Crisis drills are more than mere exercises in PR symbolism. Kamer-Singer's Larry Kamer notes that in a real crisis, people face stress, high emotions and other pressures that can exacerbate the original problem. Practicing for a crisis beforehand enables managers to test the vulnerabilities in a contingency plan, and may help save lives and property when a real crisis occurs. "Responding to a crisis or emergency without practice is highly risky," Kamer says. "More importantly, it's irresponsible. . . . A real crisis is no time to test plans or capabilities. You don't want to be in the middle of the corporate equivalent of germ warfare before you find out whether the plan works or not."[31]

Nevertheless, the symbolism and stagecraft associated with Kamer-Singer's disaster rehearsals make interesting reading. In 1997, PR industry writer Paul Holmes participated in one such exercise and wrote about it as the cover story for an issue of his publication, *Reputation Management*. During the drill, he stated, the PR team worked from "four separate 'scripts' that are essentially lists of telephone calls to be made by the media, residents, politicians, and ultimately people with claims against the company." Just as a conventional theatrical production tells us something about the worldview of its creators and audience, the scripts that Kamer-Singer prepared for Chevron provide an interesting peek at the PR/corporate worldview.

To begin with, Kamer-Singer's script carefully minimizes the possibility of actual corporate culpability. The oil spill that begins its fictional version of a crisis occurs when a privately piloted airplane inexplicably crashes into one of the company's oil tanks. As the drama unfolds, members of the general public appear in a succession of brief roles in which they are stereotyped as quaint troublemakers at best, dangerous fools at worst. "The community calls (by far the most entertaining, since they allow for almost infinite improvisation) range from a guy with a million-dollar view who was planning to sell his home this weekend to an irate commuter whose ferry was canceled to an elderly gentleman who broke his ankle falling out of bed after hearing the crash," Holmes writes. Reporters first accuse the company of cutting corners for deciding that its cleanup crew will not work through the night, and then accuse it of bowing to political pressure when it changes its mind. A governor, a congressman, and a senator each call, threatening investigations. The mayor also calls, demanding on short notice to tour the disaster with an entourage of reporters, then fails to show up at the agreed-upon time. The company's labor union uses the oil spill as a pretext to threaten a strike. An environmental activist group sets up a website, blasting the company for allowing the spill to occur. An area resident complains that one of the company's cleanup vehicles ran over her cat. Another resident calls, threatening to "buy myself an [expletive deleted] gun and I'm going to pay you guys a little visit." A producer calls from the "Bush Wambaugh show, one of this country's leading conservative commentators. . . . Mr. Wambaugh is very concerned that this country is being taken over by pencil-pushing bureaucrats, feminazis, and tree huggers, and he wants to know why a giant corporation like Chevron is sucking up to namby-pamby liberals instead of protecting the interests of its shareholders."[32]

Come again? The producer for "Mr. Wambaugh" goes on to explain: "Your company is engaged in rescuing oil-covered birds from the water and from the shore, correct? . . . Then they're cleaned up. And your company pays for the cleaning materials and the cost of the centers themselves, and pays people to supervise the cleanup? . . . Isn't it true that even after being cleaned up, more than 90 percent of these birds will die anyway?"

"I'm afraid I don't have that information. I'll have to look into it," the company's PR man diplomatically replies. Holmes notes that Wambaugh's observation "is, in fact, true. Almost all the birds 'rescued' after being covered in oil die anyway. The main advantage of cleaning them off is that it makes local volunteers feel as though they are doing something useful. It's also an effective way to convey the company's environmental sensitivity, even if it is largely a symbolic gesture."[33]

6

Preventing Precaution

When an activity raises threats of harm to human health or environment, precautionary measures should be taken even if some cause and effect relationships are not fully established scientifically.

—Wingspread Statement on the
Precautionary Principle

One crisis that PR firms rarely anticipate is the possibility that their own internal documents may be leaked to the public. This happened to the Ketchum PR firm in 1991 when one of its own employees, apparently offended by some of the techniques proposed in a "Draft Crisis Management Plan for the Clorox Company," faxed a copy of the plan to the Seattle office of Greenpeace USA.

The Ketchum plan, designed to counter situations in which environmentalists might launch a major campaign against Clorox household bleach, attempted to "provide a 'crystal ball' pinpointing some of the issues which could arise over the next year. For each scenario we have suggested different levels of attention and response." Examples included:

- *"Crisis Scenario #1: Chlorine Free by 93.* Greenpeace has announced a worldwide effort to rid the world of chlorine." In this Ketchum scenario, Greenpeace releases a study linking chlorine exposure to cancer; demonstrators hold a rally outside the Clorox corporate headquarters; and reporters "interview three unsuspecting Clorox employees, on their way to lunch, who agree that the safety of chlorine may be in question." In this sort of situation, Ketchum advised, the company's objective should be to "make sure this is a one-day media event with no follow-up stories." To achieve this, Clorox would announce that it "will seek an independent, third-party review of the Greenpeace study and promise to report back to the media. (While this last strategy may seem to be counter to the objective, the independent study will gain little media attention if it supports the company position; its primary value will be to cause reporters to question Greenpeace's integrity and scientific capabilities.)" Simultaneously, a PR crisis management team would begin "alerting key influentials, scientists, government environmental and health officials, and others previously identified as potential allies. . . . Names of independent scientists who will talk about chlorine are given to the media. (These names are assumed to be already on file as per Master Crisis Plan.)"

- *"Crisis Scenario #2: Back to Natural.* The movement back to more 'natural' household cleaning products is gaining momentum." In this scenario, a prominent newspaper columnist targets the environmental hazards of liquid chlorine bleach, and consumers begin turning to safer, natural cleaning products such as vinegar and borax. Anti-Clorox picketing campaigns occur in 10 major U.S. cities. Once again, the third party technique figures prominently in Ketchum's response plan: "An independent scientist is dispatched to meet with the columnist and discuss the issue. Teams of scientists, independent or from Clorox or both, are dispatched to the 10 cities to conduct media tours. . . . [Crisis management team] arranges for sympathetic media, local, state and national governmental leaders, and consumer experts to make statements in defense of the product. These statements are then widely distributed in the affected communities. . . . Industry association (Chlorine Institute?) advertising campaign: 'Stop Environmental Terrorism,' calling on Greenpeace and the columnist to be more responsible and less irrational in their approach. . . . Consider video and audio news release to affected markets. . . . Conduct research to determine if and how a slander lawsuit against the columnist and/or Greenpeace could be effective."

- *"Crisis Scenario #3: National Toxicology Program (NTP) Study."* In this scenario, an NTP study concludes that chlorine is an animal carcinogen, attracting "widespread national media coverage." In response, Ketchum proposes, "third-party scientific experts are brought to Washington to testify and advise both Congress and the EPA. . . . Third-party spokespeople are scheduled for major television and newspaper interviews. Industry generates grassroots letters to legislators calling on them to show restraint."

Each of these scenarios and strategies entailed the recruitment, prior to any specific crisis, of "ambassadors in the scientific community to gain third-party credibility for Clorox environmental messages. . . . In addition to the relatively small group of scientists and academicians the Clorox Company will tap as spokespersons, the Crisis Team also must educate a broad network of scientific, medical and academic organizations that may be called upon by the media to comment on any health or environmental concerns. These groups include the American Medical Association, the American Academy of Pediatrics, . . . the American Academy of Family Physicians, as well as key chapters of the American Public Health Association. Third-party scientists working with the Clorox Company will provide the peer credibility needed to dialogue with these groups."[1]

Public disclosure of the Ketchum plan prompted the usual corporate disavowals. "Clorox management was not involved in its preparation, and is not acting on its recommendations," said Clorox spokesperson Sandy Sullivan. Ketchum president David Drobis insisted that there was nothing unusual or inappropriate about the plan. "It shouldn't be surprising that any company has such a plan," he said. "In fact, it would be more surprising to find out that a major company didn't."[2]

In an interview with *Executive Report,* a business publication, Ketchum president Paul Alvarez explained further. "We routinely envision worst-case circumstances for our clients. That's our job," he said. "In the case of Clorox, we knew Greenpeace was very hot on the whole chlorine issue and we were concerned—as was the client—that Clorox, which doesn't use chlorine, might be a mistaken target."[3]

In fact, Clorox *does* use chlorine—specifically, sodium hypochlorite, a chlorine-based chemical that is widely used as a bleaching compound and disinfectant. What Alvarez probably meant to say is that sodium hypochlorite is generally regarded as safe for the environment. Even Greenpeace, which has campaigned heavily for a phase-out of all industrial uses of elemental chlorine, regards household bleach as a low-priority concern.[4]

Ketchum may indeed have been just doing its job. It is ironic, however, that many PR firms are willing to "envision worst-case circumstances for our clients" while working assiduously to prevent the public from envisioning worst-case scenarios that may affect human health and the environment. Nowhere is this more clear than in the high-stakes PR battle over organochlorines—the class of chlorine-based chemicals that Greenpeace *does* oppose. Environmentalists and public health advocates believe organochlorines threaten us with everything from cancer to sterility and birth defects. For more than a decade, however, the chemical industry—working through a variety of trade associations, including the Chemical Manufacturers Association, the Chlorine Institute, the Chlorine Chemistry Council, the Vinyl Institute, the National Association of Manufacturers, and the U.S. Chamber of Commerce—has been working to persuade the public and government policymakers that there is no threat at all.

The two sides in this debate both have access to the same scientific information, although they interpret it differently. Fundamentally, however, the difference between the two sides does not revolve around science. It revolves around a concept known as the "precautionary principle."

Looking Before Leaping

Most of us learned some version of the precautionary principle as children. Our parents taught us to look both ways before crossing the street and admonished us that we were "better safe than sorry." As a guideline for social and environmental policy, the precautionary principle has emerged in recent years as an expression of the growing realization that human technological advances have made it possible to do previously unimaginable damage to human health and the environment. With new power comes new responsibility, and the precautionary principle aims to anticipate and prevent potential disasters before they occur.

The principle has been formulated in various ways. "When there are threats of serious or irreversible damage, lack of full scientific certainty shall not be used as a reason for postponing cost-effective measures to prevent environmental degradation," stated the 1992 United Nations Earth Summit Conference in Rio de Janeiro. Versions of the precautionary principle have been incorporated into several international treaties, including the Kyoto Protocol on global warming, and it has been enacted into law on a Europe-wide basis in a treaty that states, "Community policy on the environment . . . shall be based on the precautionary principle and on principles that preventive action should be taken, that environmental damage should as a priority be rectified at source and that the polluter should pay." In January 1998, an international panel of scientists, grassroots environmental activists, government researchers, and labor representatives from the United States, Canada, and Europe formulated the "Wingspread Statement on the Precautionary Principle," which defined the principle as follows: "When an activity raises threats of harm to human health or the environment, precautionary measures should be taken even if some cause-and-effect relationships are not fully established scientifically."

"To foresee and forestall is the basis of the precautionary principle," explain Carolyn Raffensperger and Joel Tickner in their book, *Protecting Public Health and the Environment*. "It is the central theme for environmental and public health rooted in the elemental concepts of 'first do no harm' and 'an ounce of prevention is worth a pound of cure.' . . . Scientific uncertainty about harm is the fulcrum for this principle. Modern-day problems that cover vast expanses of time and space are difficult to assess with existing scientific tools. Accordingly, we can never know with certainty whether a particular activity will cause harm. But we can rely on observation and good sense to foresee and forestall damage."[5]

The reason that scientific uncertainty is the fulcrum for the precautionary principle is that the harm associated with technological innovations is often impossible to prove at the time the new technology is introduced. When DDT was discovered, for example, it was considered a safe alternative to toxic metallic compounds then in use. Chlorofluorocarbons (CFCs) were also considered extraordinarily safe when they were introduced for use as coolants in refrigerators, and remained in use for decades before scientists discovered their destructive effect on the earth's ozone layer. There was a scientific basis for concerns about leaded gasoline at the time of its introduction, but no irrefutable scientific proof. In each of these cases, waiting for proof to appear meant that action was not taken until serious damage to health and the environment had already occurred. Amassing unambiguous proof is a long and costly process, particularly after a product is in widespread use and industries have a vested interest in defending it. The idea behind the precautionary principle is that a lack of conclusive scientific evidence should not be used as an excuse for failing to take measures to protect human health and the environment.

Of course, like any guideline the precautionary principle can be abused. "One problem is that the precautionary principle could become a very convenient way to protect domestic industry and agriculture," observes Jean Halloran of Consumers Union. "Let's say for example that hothouse tomatoes grown in Holland are cutting significantly into U.S. hothouse tomato sales because the Dutch tomatoes are much more flavorful. The U.S. tomato industry searches around for a scientist-for-hire and finds one who will say that the tomato varieties that happen to do well in Dutch hothouses also have slightly higher levels of a toxic chemical that affected cell reproduction in one lab test done at the scientist-for-hire's lab. He is also willing to lay out a theory whereby in a worst-case scenario this could suggest reproductive difficulties in 20 percent of the people who eat the Dutch tomatoes for three years or more. U.S. tomato growers demand a ban on imports under the precautionary principle."

Obviously, some balance needs to be struck between hypothetical scenarios and actual plausible risks. "As a practical matter in these situations, one ends up weighing the scientific uncertainty against the benefits," Halloran says. "In the case of bovine growth hormone, with zero benefits to consumers, there's no reason to tolerate *any* risk, no matter how farfetched or small. With a new cancer drug, we'll tolerate a lot of risk. With beef hormones, we can imagine two different societies coming to different judgments, but we can also imagine the beef industry in one of those societies distorting science to exaggerate or underestimate a risk in order to influence how society ends up feeling."[6]

Most people probably think that the precautionary principle is already part of the process of evaluating and approving risky or unfamiliar chemicals, products, and industrial practices. To a casual observer, there might not seem to be a lot of difference between an industry lobbyist who talks of "assessing risks with sound science" versus an environmentalist who talks of "acting to mitigate potential risks before they appear." In the real world, however, the differences are much greater than mere linguistics. Today's regulatory system essentially allows anything to be released into nature unless it is proven unsafe by scientific data, which is defined to mean measurable harm. In practice, this means that preventive action is not taken until damage has already been done.

In 1998, for example, the U.S. Department of Agriculture attempted to promulgate standards for "organic agriculture" that would have defined any practice as "organic" provided it did not produce measurable degradation of soil quality. "One of the ways we could document 'degradation' to soil quality was measurable damage to earth worms," says North Dakota organic farmer Frederick Kirschenmann, a member of the National Organic Standards Board. "But every soil scientist working with earth worms and soil quality with whom I have conferred has told me that it sometimes takes years to establish cause-effect relationships between farming practices and earth worm populations. And even then it is almost impossible to document precisely which practice causes the degradation. That means that under this regulatory scheme (i.e., risk assessment) we might have to allow ecologically damaging practices for years because we can't say no before we can document degradation. This is especially true with respect to soil, since soil scientists are still debating how to measure soil quality, and since soil microbe communities are only now beginning to be understood. . . . It will be years before we will be able to determine which microbes cause which effects in soil and plant systems. And then some years more before we learn how to manage soil to take advantage of this miniature world of ecosystem services—critical to our understanding of organic agriculture. In the meantime, using the risk assessment model, certifiers would not be allowed to prohibit practices we suspect might be harmful to this microbial community, because we can't yet prove it by establishing the necessary cause-effect data."[7]

As Kirschenmann observes, this "risk management" approach runs contrary to the precautionary principle that has historically defined organic agriculture. "We have always operated on the assumption that we did not possess the cleverness to understand the intricate interrelationships of nature's biological and evolutionary systems," Kirschenmann says. "Consequently we have no choice but to act with caution. That is why we have always said 'no' to exogenous [foreign] materials, unless they were absolutely necessary, and the material had been proven safe, rather than merely not proven unsafe."[8]

Adopting the precautionary principle shifts the burden of proof in decisions about whether to adopt new technologies. It prioritizes safety over innovation, and this is precisely why conventional business interests prefer to use risk analysis, which makes it easier to spin rationales in favor of business-as-usual. "In the face of scientific uncertainty, decision-makers who are responsible for the welfare and safety of the public are more frequently choosing what has become known as the precautionary principle," complains Gregory Bond, corporate director of product responsibility at

Dow Chemical. "This approach is being demanded by consumers and the general public, particularly in Europe where the Bovine Spongiform Encephalopathy (Mad Cow Disease) epidemic caused widespread outrage. Application of the precautionary principle has many in industry very concerned, because it is viewed as starting down a 'slippery slope' that could result in public policies based on theories, fear, and innuendo rather than sound science."[9]

For the chemical industry, the precautionary principle is revolutionary because there are tens of thousands of chemicals that have already been introduced into common use without careful testing for long-term health effects. For the biotechnology industry, the principle is dangerous because thousands of products in development involve genetically modified foods, medical treatments, and other processes that they believe are safe but whose safety cannot be proven except in practice. For the automobile, fossil fuel, and mining industries, the precautionary principle is dangerous because growing evidence of global warming threatens to impose substantial changes on the way they do business. In their eyes, therefore, the slogan "better safe than sorry" means economic disruption, lost profits, and controversy—all because of risks that they are not convinced even exist.

The End of All We Hold Dear

"The precautionary principle holds that a manufacturer must prove that its product does no harm, before it can be marketed," complains Jack Mongoven, president of the Washington-based public affairs firm of Mongoven, Biscoe & Duchin (MBD). Writing in *eco.logic,* an anti-environmentalist newsletter, Mongoven warned that "activists want to use this weapon to control the behavior of other Americans . . . [to] revolutionize American thinking about regulation, constitutional law, and government's role in society. . . . If the type of thinking that underpins the precautionary principle prevails, future historians may refer to the last score of years of the twentieth century as the 'Death of the Linear Period' or the 'Birth of the Holistic Age' "—as the end, in other words, of "devotion to logic and the abstract purity, clarity and certainty of Euclid and Aristotle," which "provided Western civilizations with the basis for scientific learning and its tools for progress." He warned that corporations need to "take the precautionary principle seriously, and develop a strategy to deal with it. . . . If industry does not participate in the process and ensure that logic and sound science prevail, it will have to live with the consequences, including the kind of fuzzy thinking which brought us the likes of the precautionary principle."[10]

Like Gregory Bond, Jack Mongoven views the precautionary principle as a rhetorical ploy that appeals to the general public's inability to think rationally or grasp the principles of science. "The modern day 'common knowledge,' as understood by most Americans, stems not from examination of facts, but from analogy and individual or group intuition," he complains. Although Mongoven himself is not a scientist, he passes judgment on a variety of scientific issues, invariably reaching conclusions that match the interests of his clients. "Errors in common knowledge abound," he states, "such as the impact of a 10 percent decrease in the ozone layer, the potential impact of global warming, the impact of manmade as compared to natural toxins, and the impact of acid rain. The unconscionable establishment of public policy based on known error to serve the ends of an individual or group is compounded when the issue involves science, because the average American is ignorant of science and of scientific method."[11]

You have probably never heard of Mongoven, Biscoe & Duchin before. It is a company that deliberately maintains a low profile, in keeping with its mission as a sort of ongoing corporate spy operation, expert in providing what it calls "public policy intelligence." Its company literature describes it as "a public affairs firm specializing in issue management. It helps clients anticipate, cope with and respond to movements for change in public policy which would adversely affect them."[12] MBD is highly secretive about its activities and refuses to name its clients, but an internal company document says they "are almost all members of the Fortune 100, and six are members of the Fortune top 20."[13] Known clients have included Monsanto, DuPont, Philip Morris, Shell Oil, and the Chlorine Chemistry Council, an offshoot of the Chemical Manufacturers Association that was formed in 1993 to combat a growing body of evidence linking chlorine-based chemicals to a wide-ranging series of environmental and health problems.

MBD's services do not come cheap. Regular clients pay a retainer ranging from $3,500 to $9,000 per month. In addition, it produces special reports on specific organizations, which it sells to its corporate clients for upward of $1,000 per copy. According to MBD literature, the groups it routinely monitors are involved with issues including: "acid rain, animal rights, clean air, clean water, endangered species, environmental groups/movements, greenhouse effect, ozone layer, rainforest, global climate change, . . . superfund, hazardous and toxic wastes, environmental justice, drinking water, risk assessment/sound science, women's and children's health, . . . incineration, ocean waste, packaging, disposables, polystyrene, recycling, landfills, waste-to-energy conversion, . . . Eastern European developments, The Green Party (non-US), Greenpeace International, . . . indoor air pollution, dioxin, chlorine, organic farming/sustainable agriculture/[low impact sustainable agriculture], pesticides, . . . multiple chemical sensitivities, endocrine system disruption, . . . biotechnology—all phases, . . . vegetarianism/veganism, . . . oil spills, wetlands."[14]

MBD promotional literature boasts that it maintains "extensive files" on "forces for change," which "often include activist and public interest groups, churches, unions and/or academia."[15] A typical dossier includes an organization's historical background, biographical information on key personnel, funding sources, organizational structure and affiliations, publications, and a "characterization" of the organization aimed at identifying potential ways to co-opt or marginalize the organization's impact on public policy debates.[16]

To compile this information, MBD tries to get on the mailing list of nonprofit organizations, and its employees read activist newsletters and other publications to keep tabs on controversial issues that may affect its clients. Its field operatives telephone members of the groups they monitor, politely asking detailed questions while doing their best to sound sympathetic to the people they interrogate. They have on occasion misrepresented themselves, claiming falsely to be journalists, friends of friends, or supporters of the groups they monitor.[17] Most of the time, however, they simply give very limited information, identifying their company only by its initials and describing MBD euphemistically as a "research group" that works to "resolve contentious public policy issues in a balanced and socially responsible manner." During the heat of the Monsanto company's campaign to win FDA approval for genetically engineered recombinant bovine growth hormone (rBGH), for example, MBD operative Kara Ziegler placed information-gathering calls in a single day to rBGH opponents including U.S. senator Russ Feingold; Dr. Michael Hansen of Consumers Union (the publisher of *Consumer Reports* magazine); and Francis Goodman, a Wisconsin dairy farmer. In June of 1996 another MBD employee, Emily Frieze, phoned environmental activist Paul Orum to ask about activities regarding ethylene glycol, a highly toxic poison used in antifreeze. The call came at a time when ethylene glycol manufacturers were lobbying to have the chemical removed from the government's Toxic Release Inventory of right-to-know chemicals. In May of 1996, an MBD operative who identified herself as Tanya Calamoneri contacted Ann Hunt, executive director of the Citizens for Alternatives to Chemical Contamination (CACC), a Michigan group located near the headquarters of Dow Chemical, the nation's largest producer of chlorine. Calamoneri wanted information about an upcoming environmental conference that CACC was sponsoring. "I asked which group she represented," Hunt said. "Her response was 'MBD,' which she characterized as a public policy and research consulting group. I later learned that it was Mongoven, Biscoe and Duchin, chief consultants and dirt-diggers for the Chlorine Chemistry Council. . . . It amazes me that the forces of darkness are that interested in what a little grassroots group in central Michigan is doing."

Mongoven claims to be "outraged" by the charge that any of these information-gathering practices are unethical. "We always identify exactly who we are," he says. "In every case, we had identified ourselves as a Washington consulting firm. I don't think that makes you a spy."

The people his company snoops on, however, think differently. Australian writer and environmental activist Bob Burton took particular offense to a misleading MBD "survey" that he received in the mail. The accompanying cover letter, written by Jack Mongoven's son Bart, sought Burton's "assistance in a significant research undertaking" to "promote improved understanding and cooperation between major businesses and consumer- and environmentally-oriented interests throughout Asia and the world. . . . We would be very appreciative if you or a colleague could send us via phone, fax or mail some information about your organization. We obviously would welcome any materials that you believe would give us an accurate picture of your group—its basic structure, issue concerns, activities (past, present and future), alliances and goals. Perhaps you would be able to include samples of any newsletters or other publications your group publishes. In addition, we would be grateful for any thoughts you may have regarding the overall situation in your country and in Asia with respect to the issues you care about." This information would be used, Mongoven promised, to help "corporate decision makers . . . develop a better appreciation of the public interest movement."[18]

Whatever gratitude MBD claims to feel when activists cooperate by answering its questions, however, it doesn't express that appreciation in any meaningful way, such as sending them copies of the reports it writes about them. Those reports are stamped confidential and sold only to MBD's clients.

Defending the Free Enterprise System

Like many people in public relations, Jack Mongoven began his career as a journalist. He later moved into politics as a Republican party operative, serving as director of press relations for the Republican National Committee and in advisory roles to the Nixon, Ford, and Reagan presidencies. His work as an anti-activist began in 1981 when he was hired to help the Nestlé corporation cope with a massive protest against its infant-formula marketing practices in Third World countries. Nestlé was the world's largest seller of infant formula, which provided a profitable outlet for surplus milk produced in Europe and the United States. Using advertisements, brochures, and free product samples distributed in hospitals, Nestlé and other multinational corporations successfully persuaded many Third World mothers to switch from breast-feeding to formula. The advertisements argued that use of store-bought infant formula was supported by medical experts, that it was more scientific, that it was healthier for babies, and that mothers who cared about their children would use modern formula instead of the old-fashioned breast method.

What Nestlé's promotional materials failed to mention was that powdered infant formula could be fatal to children in the Third World, where people often lack the clean drinking water needed to dilute it, let alone facilities to sterilize feeding utensils. Cecily Williams, a pediatric physician in Africa, was one of the first to identify the problematic nature of the practice. After "seeing day after day this massacre of the infants by unsuitable feeding," she stated bluntly that "misguided propaganda on infant feeding should be punished as the most criminal form of sedition, and that these deaths should be regarded as murder."

Nestlé responded with a broadside accusing its critics of "an indirect attack on the free world's economic system." As vice president of the Nestlé Coordination Center for Nutrition (NCCN), Jack Mongoven began collecting files on the various churches, student groups, trade unions, women's organizations, and health workers who had joined a boycott of Nestlé products. The strategy behind this surveillance, according to NCCN president Rafael Pagan, was "to separate the fanatic activist leaders—people who deny that wealth-creating institutions have any legitimate role to play in helping the Third World to develop—from the overwhelming majority of their followers."

This notion that corporate critics are dupes of "fanatic activists" has served as the prototype for Mongoven, Biscoe & Duchin's subsequent work for other corporate clients.

- In 1987, Mongoven and Pagan developed a plan, code-named the "Neptune Strategy," to neutralize boycotts of Shell Oil related to its business activities in apartheid South Africa. The plan involved creation of a third-party group called the Coalition on Southern Africa, which countered calls for Shell to divest its South African holdings by talking of ambitious plans to promote education and training of South African blacks and develop black–black business links between South Africa and the United States. In reality, COSA was a deceptive paper front group with no resources to carry out these goals.[19]

- In the 1990s, MBD gathered intelligence for the Monsanto Company and Philip Morris's cheese division at Kraft General Foods aimed at identifying critics of Monsanto's genetically engineered bovine growth hormone.

- In the 1990s, it developed PR plans for chemical and meat-industry clients anxious to counter the work of consumer and environmental groups that were raising concerns about the harmful effects of dioxin and other chlorine-based chemicals.

- In 1997, MBD's work became the focus of a minor scandal when agricultural journalist Alan Guebert discovered that the National Pork Producers Council (NPPC) had paid MBD some $48,000 to investigate groups, including the National Farmers Union, the Iowa Citizens for Community Improvement, the Center for Rural Affairs, the Land Stewardship Project, and the Missouri Rural Crisis Center. NPPC is a quasigovernmental organization that gets most of its funding in "pork checkoff funds" that farmers are required to pay when they market their pigs, in return for which the NPPC is supposed to represent the interests of farmers by helping to promote pork. However, $24 million of the $45 million in checkoff funds comes from America's largest 40 producers, and it is the large producers who really call the shots within the organization. The larger corporate producers have been building massive factory farms that not only pollute the environment with noxious odors and manure runoffs, but also threaten the livelihood of many of the smaller, independent hog farmers among the NPPC's 80,000 members. MBD's report to the NPPC was aimed at advising it on how to counter "agricultural activist groups" that oppose construction of new corporate hog facilities. These activist groups were in fact defenders of small family farms, and their farmer-members were understandably unhappy to learn that their own trade organization had hired a PR firm to investigate them.[20]

What we know about MBD comes primarily through two sources: the company's literature, which it distributes sometimes at industry meetings, and leaked internal documents provided by whistle-blowers. The "Neptune Strategy," as well as MBD's work for Philip Morris and Monsanto on bovine growth hormone, its work on the chlorine issue, and its work for the National Pork Producers Council, are each examples of MBD activities that came to light when persons working for the company or one of its clients chose to provide copies of internal MBD documents to outside groups that were the target of its surveillance activities.

There are, of course, certain limitations to the conclusions that can be drawn from looking at leaked documents. MBD's internal memoranda provide snapshots into moments of time and pieces of advice provided by an influential adviser to major corporations, but they do not reveal which specific suggestion was followed and which was ignored. Nevertheless, consistent patterns and themes recur in MBD's advice to each client, themes which are also consistent with the advice that Ketchum provided to Clorox and with the crisis management strategies that PR firms have developed for other companies dealing with environmental and health issues. Taken together, the evidence suggests that MBD's advice is in keeping with the standard practices of PR crisis management.

In 1996, a whistle-blower leaked two documents produced by MBD to map out "the battlefield for chlorine" on behalf of the Chlorine Chemistry Council (CCC), a chemical industry trade association. The earliest of the two documents was titled "Activist Update: Chlorine" and was dated May 18, 1994. The second, titled "Re: Activist Report for August" and dated September 7, 1994, included "a list of all the recommendations we provided CCC in August as to how best to counter the activists. The main recommendation—to mobilize science against the precautionary principle—still applies and dovetails with the long-range objectives regarding sound risk assessment." These documents provide only a fragmentary picture of MBD's work for the Chlorine Chemistry Council. Nevertheless, they provide some indication of the scope of the chemical industry's enemy list, and the strategies that it is willing to pursue in order to defeat them.

Mongoven's correspondence with the CCC also reveals a corporate mind-set that is overtly hostile to the environmental, consumer, and women's health groups that it monitors. The groups mentioned in its 1994 reports to the CCC included the Sierra Club, Greenpeace, Ralph Nader's U.S. Public Interest Research Group (PIRG), the Clean Water Network of the Natural Resources Defense Council, a New York–based environmental research group called INFORM, a St. Louis environmental group called the Gateway Green Alliance, the Women's Economic and Development Organization (WEDO), and the National Wildlife Federation. In the May memorandum, Mongoven alerted the CCC about the Clean Water Network's warning that "chlorine causes birth defects, reproductive problems, cancer and other human- and animal-health problems." In response to these concerns, Mongoven stated, the Clean Water Network "is expected to expand its assault . . . to press attacks on other areas of chlorine chemistry—product-by-product, step-by-step, application-by-application."[21]

Mongoven expressed particular alarm at the 1994 publication of *Fertility on the Brink* by the National Wildlife Federation (NWF), a group that he described as "highly respected by mainstream environmentalists, conservationists, industry and government." Like the Clean Water Network, he noted, *Fertility on the Brink* "attributes fertility and reproductive problems to exposure to chlorine-based chemicals. The report depicts widespread and devastating effects on the reproductive, endocrine and immune systems of humans and animals as a result of exposure to an environment permeated with chlorine-based chemicals."[22]

Rather than express concern about these "complex and severe effects," however, MBD worried about the chlorine industry's image.

Mongoven accused the NWF of using "the issue of fertility as a vehicle to play on the emotions of the public and its concern for future generations." Moreover, he added, "anti-chlorine activists are also using children and their need for protection to compel stricter regulation of toxic substances. This tactic is very effective because children-based appeals touch the public's protective nature for a vulnerable group. . . . This tactic also is effective in appealing to an additional segment of the public which has yet to be activated in the debate, particularly parents. . . . The tone of the debate will focus on the needs of children and insist that *all* safeguards be taken to ensure their safety in development. For most substances, the tolerances of babies and children, which includes fetal development, are obviously much lower than in the general adult population. Thus, 'environmental policies based on health standards that address the special needs of children' would reduce all exposure standards to the lowest possible levels."[23]

Most people, of course, regard "concern for future generations" and "the special needs of children" as something more than mere emotionalism. For MBD, however, such concerns are not only irrational but a threat to science itself. "Anti-chlorine groups will probably devise tactics which promote the adoption of the 'precautionary principle,'" Mongoven warned, although "the principle, which shifts the burden of establishing a chemical's safety to industry, is unlikely to be adopted. The debate over the 'precautionary principle' will elevate the dioxin issue to a more conspicuous level. . . . This is a critical time for the future of risk assessment as a tool of analysis. The industry must identify the implications posed by the 'precautionary principle' and assist the public in understanding the damage it inflicts on the role of science in modern development and production."[24]

The Chlorine War

Jack Mongoven's preoccupation with the precautionary principle is a reaction to an emerging body of controversial science regarding a class of chlorine-based chemicals—including DDT, dioxin, PCBs, and many others—that have come to be labeled "hormone mimickers" or "endocrine disruptors." Prior to the 1990s, much of the debate over these chemicals was shaped by the legacy of science writer Rachel Carson and her 1962 environmental classic, *Silent Spring*. For years, concerns about these chemicals focused on whether they could cause cancer, and indeed there is a substantial body of scientific evidence suggesting that this is the case. The focus on cancer, however, has tended to obscure the fact that these chemicals also interfere with the hormonal messaging systems that control body development during fetal growth and infancy, thereby affecting growth, the reproductive and immune systems, and even personality, intelligence, and behavior. Although the science surrounding the "endocrine disruptor hypothesis" is still incomplete, leading researchers and scientific bodies have called for precautionary action now to avert the threat of serious harm to the environment and human health.

The role of DDT as a hormone mimic was observed as early as 1950, when researchers noticed that roosters exposed to DDT failed to develop male characteristics. DES was synthesized in 1938 by British scientist Edward Charles Dodds. At the time of its discovery, it was hailed by leading researchers and gynecologists as a synthetic form of estrogen, the female sex hormone. Doctors began prescribing DES for women with problem pregnancies, and eventually 4.8 million pregnant women worldwide would use the synthetic hormone—a massive and irresponsible experiment, as it turned out. In 1971, DES was linked to vaginal cancer in daughters whose mothers had taken the drug during the first three months of pregnancy. Subsequent research would also link DES with reproductive problems, including deformities of the genitals.

It was the hormonal effects of yet another chlorine-based chemical— dioxin—that served as the catalyst for the Chlorine Chemistry Council's concerns and its decision to hire Jack Mongoven. Dioxin has been a subject of fierce debate since the 1970s, when it earned a reputation as one of the most toxic substances known to humans.[25] Formed as an unintentional by-product of many industrial processes such as waste incineration, chemical manufacturing, and pulp and paper bleaching, dioxin tends to bioaccumulate in fatty tissue, which means that it can be found at elevated concentrations in foods such as meat and dairy products. Dioxin was a toxic component of the Vietnam war defoliant Agent Orange, was found at Love Canal in Niagara Falls, New York, and was the basis for evacuations at Times Beach, Missouri, and Seveso, Italy. In 1985, an EPA risk assessment found that dioxin causes cancer in animals and probably in humans as well.

In 1985 and again in 1988, the EPA conducted risk assessments of dioxin, concluding in both cases that it should be classified as a probable human carcinogen. However, scientific data regarding its effect on humans has been limited, in part because scientists have not been certain how much dioxin people are exposed to, and also because of the difficulty in separating dioxin's effects from the confounding effects of the many other chemicals to which people are routinely exposed. In 1990, a group of scientists representing both industry and the public health/environmental communities met at a conference, held at the Banbury Center of Cold Spring Harbor Laboratory in New York, which called for a new and more comprehensive EPA risk assessment. For industry, the hope was that a new risk assessment would conclude that the risks from dioxin were lower than previously estimated. The Chlorine Institute went so far as to have Edelman, its PR firm, issue a news release which falsely claimed that the Banbury Conference had reached a "consensus" to the effect that "dioxin is much less toxic to humans than originally believed."[26] Although this claim was later retracted following angry complaints by several conference participants, EPA administrator Bill Reilly stated publicly that dioxin seemed less dangerous than previously thought. With industry's blessing, he began a third EPA assessment of dioxin. Unfortunately for industry, the results of that reassessment ran contrary to expectations.

EPA's reassessment took almost four years and cost $4 million. In addition to dioxin, the agency also considered a range of "dioxin-like" chemicals such as PCBs that are known to produce similar effects. It commissioned separate scientists from both inside and outside the agency to draft each chapter of the study, which ultimately involved the participation of about 100 scientists, including non-EPA scientists who peer-reviewed each chapter. In 1994, a six-volume, 2,000-page draft report was released and opened to public comment. It concluded that in addition to promoting cancer, dioxin and a number of other similar chemicals can disrupt the endocrine, reproductive, and immune systems, and that they can do this to a developing fetus at extremely low levels of exposure. Owing to pressures from industry, however, the draft report has become such a hot potato that EPA staff has become reluctant to talk about it publicly. As of late 2000 (the date of this writing), the finalized risk assessment remains unpublished.

"EPA's study indicated that there is no safe level of dioxin exposure and that any dose no matter how low can result in health damage," admitted the 1994 MBD advisory to the Chlorine Chemistry Council. "New findings on the mechanism of dioxin toxicity show that tiny doses of dioxin disrupt the action of the body's natural hormones and other biochemicals, leading to complex and severe effects including cancer, feminization of males and reduced sperm counts, endometriosis and reproductive impairment in females, birth defects, impaired intellectual development in children, and impaired immune defense against infectious disease. . . . Further, dioxin is so persistent that even small releases build up over time in the environment and in the human body."[27]

Some of the strongest concerns about the effect of endocrine-disrupting chemicals have come from observations of their effect on wildlife. In California, ecologists have found an abnormally high ratio of female to male seagulls. In polluted parts of Florida, panthers have undescended testicles and endocrinologists have observed abnormally small or deformed penises in alligators near a former Superfund pollution cleanup site. In Great Britain, biochemists have noticed "hermaphroditic" fish with both male and female genitals breeding in wastewater effluent. Arctic seals and polar bears have shown declining fertility. In humans, a series of studies have shown an alarming decrease in male sperm counts in different parts of the world, which have plummeted to half the level found 60 years ago.

Researchers have been able to replicate many of these effects in laboratory experiments with captive animals. At the University of California at Davis, toxicologist Michael Fry found that injecting the eggs of seagulls with DDT would cause ferminization of the testes tissue in baby male gulls and result in sterile adults. In one study, 79 percent of monkeys exposed to dioxin developed endometriosis (the development of endometrial tissue in females in places where it is not normally present).

Chlorine Plus Carbon

What DDT, DES, dioxin, and PCBs all have in common, along with many other endocrine-disrupting solvents and pesticides, is that they belong to a class of chemicals called organochlorines—organic compounds containing chlorine bonded to carbon. In nature, chlorine makes up less than 0.2 percent of all chemicals, but some 15,000 organochlorines are now commercially manufactured and marketed, and approximately half of the endocrine disruptors identified to date have been organochlorines. "This doesn't mean that all chlorine compounds behave the same way, but virtually every organochlorine that's ever been tested has been found to cause at least one significant adverse effect," says biologist Joe Thornton, the author of *Pandora's Poison: Chlorine, Health and a New Environmental Strategy.*[28] Although organochlorines are rare in nature, they are produced in the manufacture of pesticides, herbicides, petrochemicals, plastics, and paper. They wind up in such common products as household cleaners, plastic wraps, food containers, children's toys, compact disks, car doors, tennis shoes, and TV sets. Chlorinated chemicals are also introduced into water as a result of pulp and paper bleaching and through the use of chlorine to treat sewage and disinfect drinking water.

Chlorine-based chemicals are valued in the commercial world because they retain their potency for long periods of time. This very durability, however, also means that they remain in the environment for a long time after they have been released. DDT, for example, continues to accumulate to alarming levels in the fatty tissues of Great Lakes fish nearly a generation after its use was banned in the United States. Likewise, PCBs are still ubiquitous in the environment despite having been banned in 1976 because of links to human cancer.

Given the expense and difficulty involved in individually testing each of the 15,000 organochlorines currently in use, many environmental groups believe that this is a case where the precautionary principle should apply. Rather than assuming that each chemical is safe until it is proven otherwise, they believe that industry should bear the burden of proving a chemical's safety or else find a safer alternative. Greenpeace has called for a 30-year phaseout of organochlorines. In addition to environmental groups, a number of governmental and other organizations have reached similar conclusions:

- The International Joint Commission on the Great Lakes (IJC) is an environmental policy group organized by the U.S. and Canadian governments that focuses on the Great Lakes region. In 1986, the IJC's science advisory board drew up a list of 362 toxic compounds found in the Great Lakes and noted that at least half of these were chlorinated chemicals. In 1992, it recommended phasing out the use of chlorine and chlorine-containing industrial feedstocks as part of an effort to restore and protect the Great Lakes ecosystem.

- In October 1993, the American Public Health Association (one of the groups targeted as a potential ally in Ketchum's PR plan for the

Clorox Company) called for the eventual elimination of chlorine-based bleaches in the paper and pulp industry. In March 1994, the APHA called on industry to reduce or eliminate chlorinated organic compounds and processes and to introduce lower-risk alternatives. "Virtually all chlorinated organic compounds that have been studied exhibit at least one of a wide range of serious toxic effects such as endocrine dysfunction, developmental impairment, birth defects, reproductive dysfunction and infertility, immunosuppression, and cancer, often at extremely low doses," it noted in a policy statement.[29]

- The Paris Commission on the North Atlantic, representing 15 European governments and the European Community, has recommended that emissions of chlorine-containing compounds be reduced and that European governments adopt programs to phase out their use.

Don't Say Maybe, Baby

The debate over endocrine disruptors was first introduced to a popular audience with the 1996 publication of *Our Stolen Future* by authors Theo Colborn, Dianne Dumanoski, and Pete Myers. *Our Stolen Future* acknowledged the difficulties and the limited knowledge that currently surrounds the theory of endocrine disruptors. "Because of our poor understanding of what causes breast cancer and significant uncertainties about exposure, it may take some time to satisfactorily test the hypothesis and discover whether synthetic chemicals are contributing to rising breast cancer rates," they stated, adding that "the magnitude of this threat to human health and well-being is as yet unclear."[30]

Given the unanswered questions that still exist and the serious potential harm that may be caused by endocrine disruptors, Colborn, Dumanoski, and Myers recommended further research, coupled with efforts to minimize unnecessary chemical exposures. Like Greenpeace, their position was based partly on emerging science and partly on the precautionary principle. "Shift the burden of proof to chemical manufacturers," they urged. "To a disturbing degree, the current system assumes that chemicals are innocent until proven guilty. This is wrong. The burden of proof should work the opposite way, because the current approach, a presumption of innocence, has time and again made people sick and damaged ecosystems. We are convinced that emerging evidence about hormonally active chemicals should be used to identify those posing the greatest risk and to force them off the market and out of our food and water until studies can prove their impact to be trivial."[31]

The attack on the book was instant and vicious. The *Wall Street Journal* called it an environmental "hype machine." The Competitive Enterprise Institute, an industry-funded Washington think tank, released two separate studies attacking the book, as did another libertarian outfit called Consumer Alert, which labeled *Our Stolen Future* "a scaremongering tract." The industry-funded Advancement of Sound Science Coalition called a press conference to introduce 10 scientific skeptics who described the book as "fiction." The American Council on Science and Health (ACSH), another long-standing, industry-funded defender of DDT, dioxin, and other chemicals, obtained a copy of the book in galley form months before publication and prepared an 11-page attack on it before it even hit bookstores. Toxicologist and ACSH member Stephen Safe called the book "paparazzi science." In a debate with authors Colborn and Myers, ACSH president Elizabeth Whelan even attacked the caution with which the book presented its analysis. *"Our Stolen Future* uses the word 'might' 30 times," she said. "The word 'may,' 35 times. We didn't bother counting all the 'could's."

Myers replied that he found it ironic to be "now criticized for using 'might' and 'may' and the caution with which we present some of the discussion. . . . When the book first came out, there were words put in our mouths that concluded we . . . had exaggerated the data. In fact, there were calls made to scientists who had not yet had the opportunity to read the book, and those claims were put in front of them, and of course they responded, 'That would be ridiculous. That would be unscientific.' But now that people have had the opportunity to read the book, and have discovered the care with which the arguments are presented, some folks are trying to find other ways to criticize the conclusions by ridiculing the care we take in stating them."[32]

The Cure for Prevention

In one of Jack Mongoven's memos to the Chlorine Chemical Council, he expressed particular alarm at the Clinton administration's appointment of Dr. Devra Lee Davis to assist in formulating government policy regarding breast cancer. "As a member of the Administration, Davis has unlimited access to the media while her position at the [Department of] Health and Human Services helps validate her 'junk science,'" he wrote. "Davis is scheduled to be a keynote speaker at each of the upcoming . . . breast cancer conferences . . . sponsored by Women's Economic and Development Organization (WEDO). Each conference is expected to emphasize a regional interest. . . . Topics include 'Environment and Breast Cancer,' 'Organochlorines, Pesticides and Breast Cancer' and 'Environmental Justice.'"

In response, MBD advised the Chlorine Chemistry Council to shadow and preempt the WEDO conferences. "It is important in all cases to stay ahead of the activists," he stated, "e.g., get to the New Orleans media and opinion leaders before the Chemical Week Chlorine Conference and the same in each of the cities where WEDO will hold conferences this fall. Let me know if you need more, e.g., we maintain calendars of anti-chlorine events and could include same if you would like."[33] Prior to the 1994 WEDO conference in Dayton, Ohio, Mongoven recommended that the CCC use another of its PR firms, Ketchum Public Relations, to schedule "editorial board meetings in Dayton prior to . . . Davis' speech," and "enlist legitimate scientists in the Dayton area who would be willing to ask pointed questions at the conference."[34]

Although Mongoven calls Devra Lee Davis a "junk scientist," she is in fact one of the world's leading researchers into environmental causes of cancer and chronic disease. The holder of advanced degrees in both physiology and epidemiology, she has taught at the Mt. Sinai Medical Center, Rockefeller University, and other prestigious schools. She is a member of both the American College of Toxicology and the American College of Epidemiology. She has advised leading health officials, including the Surgeon General and the Deputy Assistant Secretary for Women's Health, on a variety of cancer-related issues, and is the founder of the International Breast Cancer Prevention Collaborative Research Group, an organization dedicated to exploring the causes of breast cancer. An epidemiologist and former senior science adviser at the U.S. Department of Health and Human Services Department, she has authored more than 140 articles in publications ranging from *Scientific American* to the *Lancet* and the *Journal of the American Medical Association*. She has organized international meetings on the subject of cancer and, as a frequent speaker to women's groups, is not only a scientist but an activist in the cause of cancer prevention.

Davis's work is significant—and controversial—because it goes directly to the question of whether environmental factors other than smoking are causing an increase in cancer rates. In 1989, she compiled one of the few systematic comparisons of recent changes in deaths from cancer. Drawing information from millions of death certificates in six industrialized countries, she documented an increase since the 1960s in deaths from breast cancer, brain cancer, kidney cancer, myeloma, melanoma and non-Hodgkin's lymphoma. None of these types of cancer had been linked to cigarette smoking. Davis noted also that these increases have occurred during a period when deaths from heart disease—another major disease linked to tobacco—have fallen.[35] "Both heart disease and cancer share a number of common causes, including cigarette smoking, heavy alcohol drinking, and possibly diets high in fat and low in fiber and anti-oxidants," Davis notes. Nevertheless, "trends in these diseases are in opposite directions . . . with heart disease declining, while some forms of cancer are increasing."[36] The trend is not uniform across all age groups. Improvements in treatment have led to dramatic decreases in cancer deaths among children. Death rates have increased, however, in people aged 45 or older. "We're not talking about small increases here," Davis says. Since the early 1970s, "some of these cancers have increased 25 percent to more than 200 percent."[37]

Breast cancer, in which Davis has taken a particular interest, may be linked to the endocrine-disrupting effects of dioxin and other chemicals. Estrogen, the hormone that makes women feminine, is a well-known breast cancer risk factor. Early menstruation, late menopause, not bearing children, and alcohol use all raise the level of women's lifetime exposure to estrogen, and they have all been associated with higher-than-average rates of breast cancer. In recent years, research by Davis and other scientists has pointed to synthetic chemicals that Davis calls "xenoestrogens," meaning "foreign estrogens"—as another risk factor.[38] "It seems quite obvious, doesn't it?" Davis says. "There's only one common thread tying together all of the known risk factors: The more estrogen exposure in a woman's life, the greater her risk of breast cancer." She adds, "We have tended to assume that because estrogen is a hormonal thing, a woman's thing, there's nothing we can do about it. Why haven't we looked at these environmental chemicals that we now know can act like estrogens?"[39]

Some research into this possibility began in the 1990s. Various studies have found elevated breast cancer rates among women who work in chemical plants or near hazardous waste sites, or whose drinking water has been contaminated with organochlorines. In 1992, Frank Falck, an assistant clinical professor at the University of Connecticut School of Medicine, analyzed tissue samples from 40 women who had biopsies of suspicious breast lumps. Compared with lumps judged benign, those that were cancerous showed much higher levels of organochlorines.[40] In a larger study that was published in 1993, biochemist Mary Wolff studied 14,290 women in New York who visited a mammography clinic between 1985 and 1991. She found that breast tissues with cancerous malignancies contained higher concentrations of DDT and PCBs. Women with higher levels of DDE (a breakdown product of DDT) in their blood faced as much as a fourfold increase in their risk of developing breast cancer.[41]

These results are tentative and scientifically controversial. Most studies, including some in which Wolff also participated, have not found evidence to support the hypothesis that DDT and PCBs increase breast cancer risk.[42] What is clear, however, is that in the last 50 years, breast cancer rates have risen dramatically almost everywhere in the industrialized world. In 1960, one woman in 20 in the United States could expect to be diagnosed with breast cancer in her lifetime. Today the number is one in eight. In the United States alone, 1.6 million women currently have diagnosed cases of the disease. Each year, 182,000 new cases are detected, of which 46,000 will lead to death.[43]

There is no question that the reported rate of breast cancer has been rising. The question is how to interpret this increase. Opponents of the environmental thesis claim that the increase is a statistical artifact due to better medical screening procedures that detect cases of breast cancer which previously would have gone unreported. Davis, however, points to research which shows that even after factors like improved mammography are taken into account, "a sustained one percent annual increase in breast cancer mortality has occurred since the 1940s. Others have also documented increased mortality from breast cancer in a number of industrial countries."[44] And these are studies of *deaths* from breast cancer, not merely of detected cases. If improved screening saves lives, and if treatment methods are improving, better screening would be expected to cause a decline in the mortality rate.

Davis's research implies that curtailing pollution is important in order to prevent cancer. "With respect to breast cancer, most of the confirmed risk factors, which relate to reproductive behavior and dietary factors, are not easily changed by social policy," she observes. "Many of the proposed interventions to reduce breast cancer involve the lifelong use of pharmaceutical agents or the advocacy of radical changes in diet, lifestyle, or even reproductive behavior. As to the latter point, a generation of women that has struggled long for reproductive freedom is unlikely to embrace eagerly suggestions that place constraints on their reproductive choices."[45] Unlike lifestyle factors, however, environmental exposures to xenoestrogens can be changed through policies that place stricter limits on pollution. "We don't have to wait for conclusive proof," Davis says. "It took 100 years from the first warnings about tobacco until we finally got tough. We must not wait that long to act against the epidemic of breast cancer."[46]

Rather than efforts to identify environmental causes affecting cancer rates, however, much of the scientific research and public discussion has focused on treatments—the so-called "race for the cure." On paper, about a third of the U.S. National Cancer Institute's $2 billion annual budget is dedicated to prevention research, but those are "rubber numbers," according to longtime cancer researcher John C. Bailar III of McGill University. Most of what the institute calls "prevention" is actually basic research into the cellular mechanisms of cancer development rather than epidemiological studies and prevention trials. Research into cellular mechanisms and molecular biology has yet to accomplish much by way of saving lives, but it is politically safe research because it doesn't rock many boats. A researcher who studies cell biology doesn't have to risk getting hammered by the tobacco industry, agribusiness, or chemical manufacturers. "The prevention of cancer on a big scale is going to require that we change our habits, change our life styles, clean up the workplace, clean up the environment, change the consumer products that contain hazardous materials," says Bailar. "It's going to mean a whole new approach to everyday living."[47]

The story with breast cancer research is much the same as the story with research into other types of cancer. Instead of prevention, researchers focus on the basic cellular research or on various treatments for women who already have the disease. The major treatments are surgery, chemotherapy, and radiation—termed "slash, poison, and burn" techniques by Dr. Susan Love, a breast surgeon at the University of California at Los Angeles and author of *Dr. Susan Love's Breast Book*.[48] Prior to the 1980s, in fact, no major studies on preventing breast cancer had ever been approved by the National Institutes of Health, the clearinghouse that awards the bulk of U.S. government medical research grants. NIH officials note that funding for breast cancer research has increased consistently since that time, but even in recent years several promising studies have been rejected, postponed, or abandoned.

Women and Children First

"It is obvious that the battleground for chlorine will be women's issues—reproductive health and children," Jack Mongoven observed in his 1994 memorandum to the Chlorine Chemistry Council. To counter the recommendations of scientists like Devra Lee Davis, he advised the CCC to mobilize the third party technique behind a campaign to create the impression that the pro-industry status quo was essential to public health. "It is especially important to begin a program directed to pediatric groups throughout the country and to counter activist claims of chlorine-related health problems in children," he wrote. "Prevent medical associations from joining anti-chlorine movement. Create panel of eminent physicians and invite them to review data regarding chlorine as a health risk and as a key chemical in pharmaceuticals and medical devices. Publish panel's findings and distribute them widely to medical associations and publications. Stimulate peer-reviewed articles for publication in *JAMA* [the *Journal of the American Medical Association*] on the role of chlorine chemistry in treating disease. . . . Convince through carefully crafted meetings of industry representatives (in pharmaceuticals) with organizations devoted to specific illnesses, e.g., arthritis, cystic fibrosis, etc., that the cure for their specific disease may well come through chlorine chemistry and ask them to pass resolutions endorsing chlorine chemistry and communicate their resolutions to medical societies."

"I think of myself as jaded," said Charlotte Brody of the Center for Health, Environment and Justice after reviewing MBD's leaked documents, "but it still takes my breath away to see a professional, totally amoral directive that editorial visits be done because the scientific information that Devra Lee Davis has is too dangerous to go unfiltered." Brody was also struck by MBD's "recommendations that the chlorine industry should go to health groups and sign them up to defend the benefits of chlorine, without telling them what they are really signing up for, and before we can get to them and talk about how dioxins and other endocrine disrupters are harming their health. MBD doesn't suggest going out and talking about why dioxin isn't as dangerous as we say. Instead, it's a much more clever and insidious strategy, where they sign up people with cystic fibrosis to defend the benefits of chlorine chemistry by suggesting to them that without chlorine there will never be a cure for their disease. They don't even bring up dioxin, but they falsely suggest that we would bring an end to pharmaceutical research."

The CCC and other chemical-industry trade associations appear to be following Mongoven's advice. In December 1994—three months after Mongoven advised the CCC to "mobilize science against the precautionary principle"—the *National Journal* reported that the CCC "has increased its budget substantially. The council this year amassed a lobbying and public relations war chest of about $12 million—compared with about $2 million in 1993—from such members as Dow Chemical Co. and Occidental Chemical Co. The campaign to defend chlorine could expand to $15 million in 1995, according to a recent report in *Chemical and Engineering News*." About a third of that budget was being spent on research, such as financing a "scientific review panel" to challenge the conclusions of the EPA's dioxin reassessment. "In anticipation of the EPA report, the council hired Ketchum Public Relations to orchestrate a 30-city tour last summer in which scientists sympathetic with the industry's positions met with news media representatives and community leaders to play down fears about dioxin," the *National Journal* reported.[49]

"We identified a number of independent scientists and took them on the road," explained Mark Schannon, an associate director of Ketchum's Washington office. In this context, of course, "independent" means pro-industry, as Schannon tacitly admitted. "Basically what we're trying to do is assure that industry's voice is heard by people who make policy decisions," he said.[50]

"After a year and a half of fighting regulatory and legislative threats, the Chlorine Chemistry Council . . . says it is shifting to a longer range goal of building a science base from which to argue its case," reported the trade publication *Chemical Week,* quoting CCC operating committee chairman Leon Anziano, who said, "We want to move from firefighting to long-term advocacy of sound science."[51]

The CCC is only one of several industry groups that have mobilized to fight the chlorine war. Others include the Chlorine Institute, the Chemical Manufacturers Association, the Vinyl Institute, the National Association of Manufacturers, and the U.S. Chamber of Commerce. Each of these has a public relations budget, and staff to write newspaper op-ed pieces, testify before Congress or the EPA, appear on news shows as "experts," and speak to civic groups. In addition to Mongoven, Biscoe & Duchin, other PR firms that have been hired as footsoldiers include Goddard*Claussen/First Tuesday; the Jefferson Group; John Adams Associates; Keller & Heckman; Ketchum Communications; and Nichols Dezenhall.[52]

The pesticide, plastics, pulp and paper, household products, oil, and cosmetics industries have all mobilized to defend chlorine chemistry against its environmentalist critics. The food industry has also weighed in, mindful that dioxin accumulates in fatty tissue and is therefore omnipresent in meat and dairy products. Coordinated by the National Cattlemen's Beef Association, the food industry's "Dioxin Working Group" includes the National Milk Producers' Federation, American Society of Animal Science, National Broiler Council, National Turkey Federation, International Dairy Foods Association, American Sheep Industry Association, National Pork Producers Council, American Meat Institute, National Renderers Association, American Farm Bureau Federation, and the National Food Processors Association. In his report to the CCC, Mongoven noted that these groups "have a history of strong relations with the Agriculture Department, and it's certain they will use these solid ties to put pressure on EPA through Agriculture."[53]

I Love Danger

In addition to bringing pressure to bear on the chlorine issue itself, Mongoven advised the Chlorine Chemistry Council to take measures that would directly attack the precautionary principle. "Bring the state governors in on the issue of risk assessment by communicating the benefits to them from being able to rely on a national standard," he advised. "Establish third-party entities devoted to developing these standards in the near future. Take steps to discredit the precautionary principle within the more moderate environmental groups as well as within the scientific and medical communities."[54]

In 1999 alone, industry-allied groups mounted at least two forums aimed at attacking the precautionary principle. On June 3 and 4, 1999, the heavily industry-funded Harvard Center for Risk Analysis hosted a conference titled "The Precautionary Principle: Refine It or Replace It?" Funders of the conference included the CCC and the Chemical Manufacturers Association, along with the right-wing Koch Foundation, funded by Koch Industries, one of the largest oil pipeline operators in the United States and a notorious polluter.[55] In January 2000, Koch Industries agreed to pay a record $35 million in civil fines and restitution for hundreds of oil leaks in six states, the largest fine ever imposed on a single company for violations of the Clean Water Act.

Promotional material for the conference noted that the precautionary principle "is playing an increasingly influential role in public policy toward technologies that pose potential risks to public health, safety and natural resources. The principle is invoked frequently in Europe, and it is now beginning to enter policy discussions in North American and Asia. . . . Concerns have been raised that the precautionary principle may be too simplistic to guide decision-makers facing complex choices involving technologies with uncertain risks, benefits and costs to current and future generations. . . . We will . . . examine the role of the precautionary principle in the following regulatory case studies: biotechnology, synthetic chemicals, electric and magnetic fields, and global climate change."

Recognizing again the important role that women would play in the debate, Mongoven advised that "an ideal partnership to undertake such a national debate" on the precautionary principle "would be the League of Women Voters and the American Chemical Society. These two organizations could in turn attract other credible organizations—and even accept corporate donations for the project—without jeopardizing their credibility. Clearly, given the issue's importance to women's organizations and children's welfare organizations, these and reasonable environmental groups also should be encouraged to participate." Perhaps the League of Women Voters turned out to be unavailable. Instead, an antifeminist lobby group called the Independent Women's Forum, which receives 90 percent of its funding from the conservative Olin, Coors, Bradley, and Carthage Foundations, hosted a conference titled "Scared Sick" in February 1999 at the National Press Club in Washington, D.C. IWF's science adviser, psychiatrist Sally Satel, opened the event by commenting that "women, as a group, tend to be more risk-averse. That's why the IWF has chosen to explore the relationship between unjustified fears and health and science policy."[56]

The leadoff panel was an attack on the precautionary principle moderated by Neal B. Freeman, CEO of the Blackwell Corporation and producer of the PBS show "TechnoPolitics." Freeman echoed Mongoven's complaint about "holistic mind-sets" and the death of "linear thinking" before warming to the main theme of the day. The precautionary principle, he said, "jumped the ocean about ten years ago in the campaign to suppress the chlorine chemistry industry. Now it pervades policy debates. It informs—or misinforms—the global warming debate, the debate over the biotechnology industry, and . . . the whole cluster of women's health issues. We can be thankful that the precautionary principle does not yet govern our creative lives. If it did, Columbus would not have discovered this continent, Thomas Edison would not have illuminated it, and Philo T. Farnsworth would not have transmitted television pictures of it."

"If we must ensure that things are safe, how are we ever to cross streets?" fretted panelist David Murray of the Statistical Assessment Service (STATS), a conservative think tank that markets itself to journalists as an expert source for interpreting statistical and scientific news. "Must every pedestrian be so outfitted as to survive an encounter with the Metrobus?" Murray asked. "And how do we understand the potential benefits of certain things that are unforeseen? . . . The precautionary principle was mercifully never adopted by life on earth at its inception. After all, most mutations are deleterious. . . . What we have had to be most adapted for, as a species, is change itself."

"The precautionary principle itself is a hazard both to our health and our high standard of living," added panelist Elizabeth Whelan of the industry-funded American Council on Science and Health, arguing that efforts to fight pollution could lead to a collapse in the American standard of living, thereby creating "more poverty, more people without health insurance, and less access to health care generally. . . . Go back to what your mother said: 'When in doubt, throw the precautionary principle out.' " Apparently the mothers of Murray and Whelan gave different advice than most moms, who usually advise their kids to look both ways before crossing the street, and who use the phrase "when in doubt, throw it out" as a precautionary principle for avoiding questionable foods.

The hypocrisy in these attacks on "environmentalist scaremongering" is that the attackers themselves rely heavily on rhetorical appeals to exaggerated fears. Will the economy *really* collapse if we protect kids from air pollution? Does "holistic thinking" *really* mean an end to scientific progress and Western civilization?

Jack Mongoven's hostility to the precautionary principle is ironic because he himself is a practitioner of the precautionary principle with respect to the reputations and profits of his clients. MBD does not wait to be called before responding to the activist menace. Its ongoing surveillance of environmental, consumer, and church groups is designed to anticipate criticisms of his clients long before those criticisms are even aired in the news or other public forums. "It is important in all cases to stay ahead of the activists," he advised the Chlorine Chemistry Council.

In its campaigns against environmentalists and consumer groups, Mongoven, Biscoe & Duchin has helped create its own form of fearmongering in which industry appears as an innocent giant under attack from "radicals" who, in the words of MBD's Ronald Duchin, "want to change the system; have underlying socio/political motives," and see multinational corporations as "inherently evil. . . . These organizations do not trust the . . . federal, state and local governments to protect them and to safeguard the environment. They believe, rather, that individuals and local groups should have direct power over industry." In one memo to the chlorine industry, Mongoven argues that concerns about endocrine disruptors reflect "a grand strategy . . . to give Greenpeace a strong lead on the issues but to use various groups—some of which are more acceptable to the mainstream—to appear to lead specific issues, thus giving the overall campaign the appearance of a widespread, generally accepted grassroots uprising against chlorine chemistry."

7

Attack of the Killer Potatoes

*My guess is that for most people who have
concerns about this, their concerns are
based on the question of whether we are
going to use these technologies wisely,
whether we have the wisdom to keep
up with our scientific capabilities. And
there have been enough precedents when
humanity has at best muddled through
the application of new technology in ways
that are sometimes frightening, nuclear
technology being the most obvious example.*

—Robert Shapiro, former CEO of Monsanto[1]

For Dr. Arpad Pusztai, two and a half minutes was all it took
to end a 36-year career.

"It was timed. It was 150 seconds," Pusztai says of his August 1998
appearance on the British television program *World in Action*. "All I said
was that we had come across a bizarre surprise finding when we ran experiments to test what happened to animals who ate genetically modified
potatoes. Then the whole world caved in around me."[2]

Pusztai, a mild-mannered research biologist, is the son of a highly
decorated Hungarian war hero who led the resistance against Nazi occupation during World War II. "They put a high price on his head, but that
didn't stop him from doing what he knew was right," Pusztai recalls. His
father was equally outspoken against the communist regime that took
power at war's end, and when the Soviet army invaded Hungary in 1956
to crush a citizen uprising, young Arpad fled the country. By then he had

already established a name for himself as a scientist, and after several months of living in Austrian refugee camps, he accepted a scholarship from the Ford Foundation that enabled him to live and study where he wanted. He selected England, he recalls now with some irony, because he believed it was a tolerant country.

After completing his doctorate in London's Lister Institute of Preventative Medicine, Pusztai was recruited to work at the prestigious Rowett Research Institute in Aberdeen, Scotland, where he published more than 270 scientific papers and became known as the world's leading expert on lectins, a class of carbohydrate-binding proteins. Lectins are present in most plants, especially cereals, potatoes, and beans. Some lectins are toxic, but others are safe for humans and other mammals. During the late 1980s, Pusztai spent six years studying a particular type of lectin taken from snowdrop bulbs. The "snowdrop lectin," also known as GNA, killed insect pests but proved safe even when fed to test animals in high concentrations. Pusztai's research therefore attracted intense interest as a possible safe way to develop genetically modified food crops that would resist insects but remain safe for human consumption. Pusztai's ability to attract research funding was considered so valuable that he was asked to stay on at Rowett after retirement age. In 1995, his expertise helped the Rowett Institute beat out 27 contenders to win a government contract to "identify genes . . . which will be suitable for transfer into plants to enhance their resistance towards insect and nematode pests, but will have minimum impact on non-target, beneficial organisms, the environment, livestock fed on these plants, and which will present no health risks for humans."

"When we started the project in 1995, we ran a search for biological testing papers on genetically modified foods," Pusztai recalls. "There were none, so we did more searches from time to time." In 1996, he finally found a study published in the *Journal of Nutrition*. It was written by B. G. Hammond, a scientist with Monsanto, the company that leads the drive to develop genetically modified foods. After feeding Monsanto's genetically modified "Roundup Ready" soybeans to rats, catfish, chickens, and cows, Hammond concluded that the modified soya had the same nutritional value as conventional soybeans.[3] Methodologically, however, Pusztai thought Hammond's paper was weak. "The main problem is they were using mature animals which are not forming body tissues and organs," he said. "Adults only need a small amount of protein because their bodies are in equilibrium, in homeostasis. But a young growing animal needs a great deal more protein because it's laying down muscle and tissues and forming its organs. Moreover, there was only a small proportion of raw genetically-modified soya in their diet—about seven percent. It was obvious that the study had been designed to avoid finding any problems. Everybody in our consortium knew this. I thought that GNA—the snowdrop lectin—should be much better. If we could show that the snowdrop lectin was safe in genetically modified potatoes, we would be real heroes."

At the time Pusztai's own feeding experiments began, he considered himself a "very enthusiastic supporter" of gene technology. He fully expected to issue a clean bill of health to the genetically modified potatoes that he was testing. The longer the experiments continued, however, the more concerns arose.

Pusztai's experiments involved feeding potatoes to four different groups of rats. A control group was fed on regular, unmodified potatoes. Two other groups were fed on different strains of potatoes that had each been genetically engineered to produce the snowdrop lectin. The fourth group was fed potatoes that had not been genetically modified, but which had been spiked with the snowdrop lectin through conventional, nongenetic means. As expected, the rats that ate unmodified potatoes did well, as did the rats in the fourth group that ate lectin-spiked potatoes.

To Pusztai's surprise, however, the rats fed on genetically modified potatoes showed a variety of unexpected and troubling changes in the size and weight of their body organs, including smaller livers, hearts, and brains. Pusztai's research team also found evidence of weakened immune systems. "Feeding transgenic potatoes to rats induced major and in most instances highly significant changes in the weights of some or most of their vital organs," he concluded. "Particularly worrying was the partial liver atrophy . . . Immune organs, such as the spleen and thymus were also frequently affected."[4]

"I was totally taken aback; no doubt about it," Pusztai recalled. "I was absolutely confident that I would not find anything, but the longer I spent on the experiment the more uneasy I became. I believe in the technology. But it is too new for us to be absolutely sure that what we are doing is right."[5]

Unmodified potatoes were harmless by themselves. The snowdrop lectin was also harmless by itself, or when added directly to potatoes. In fact, Pusztai's previous research had shown that rats suffered no harmful effects even when fed 1,000 times the amount of snowdrop lectin that appeared in his genetically modified potatoes. It appeared, therefore, that something about the genetic engineering process had produced the unexpected result. It was a troubling observation that raised more questions than it answered, and Pusztai felt that more research was needed. As his concerns emerged, however, questions began to be raised about Pusztai's research methodology. A government immunologist was brought in to inspect his work. She found no flaws, but his requests for further government funding were turned down.

Initially, the Rowett Research Institute agreed with Pusztai that something should be done to drum up funding so that further research could be conducted into the safety of genetically modified (GM) foods. In June 1998, with the Rowett's approval, Pusztai agreed to the TV interview with *World in Action.* "My appearance was to highlight the need for a case-by-case program of biological testing of all GM foodstuffs," he said. The interview was recorded seven weeks prior to broadcast, with the Institute's public relations officer present as an observer. "If the Rowett had any qualms about the content of the TV program, they had seven weeks to stop it," Pusztai said. "I kept to our agreement and only talked about the necessity of biological testing of GM foodstuffs before they were accepted into the human food chain. No experimental details or even the identity of the gene used were mentioned by me in the program. It was thought at the time, and the Rowett agreed with me, that our short- and long-term nutritional and immunological work with our two distinct lines of GM potatoes could have been a good starting point for a biological testing program. In the TV program I said that GM science might bring benefits, but only if we got it right and made sure that the GM foodstuffs were safe by testing them thoroughly and handling everything transparently."

The interviewer posed a couple of difficult questions. Did Dr. Pusztai feel concerned about the lack of safety testing of GM foods? "I could answer but two things: either yes or no," Pusztai said. "I am afraid I have never learned to lie, so I said yes." Would he personally eat his own genetically modified potatoes? Pusztai answered in the negative, noting that it is "very, very unfair to use our fellow citizens as guinea pigs."

In the weeks immediately following the taping and even up until the time of the broadcast, the Rowett Research Institute seemed happy with the publicity. Its director, Professor Philip James, even called Pusztai's wife after the broadcast to express his congratulations on how well he had handled the interview. Then suddenly, two days after the broadcast, everything changed. Pusztai knew he was in trouble when he was called into the director's office. Professor James was sitting stern-faced, flanked by Rowett's personnel manager and an attorney. He handed Pusztai a news release, which stated that he had been suspended from work "and he will now retire from the Institute."[6]

"I was suspended for 12 days and then returned to the Rowett to finish off the rest of my year's contract," Pusztai said. "When I got to my laboratory I found the computers sealed, the desks locked and all my papers taken away. Worse, no one was speaking to me. All my former colleagues acted as though I didn't exist. When I went into the coffee room they would turn their backs on me."[7]

"Suspended," in other words, was a not-so-polite euphemism for being fired. And it wasn't just Pusztai who was getting the sack. His experiments were abruptly terminated, his data confiscated. His potatoes were seized, his 18-member scientific team was disbanded, and his research designed to shed light on the safety of genetically modified foods was stopped in its tracks.

Con A

A persistent error appeared in early news stories about Pusztai's research. In story after story, journalists claimed that Pusztai's genetically modified potatoes contained a lectin called Concanavalin A—Con A for short. Derived from the South American jackbean, Con A is completely different from the snowdrop lectin and is known to harm the immune systems of mammals. If he *had* used Con A, damage to the immune system would not be surprising, but that's not what he used.

"I am not sure how the Con A story came about, but I can assure you it did not originate with me," Pusztai says. "I have been doing experiments with lectins, including Con A, in a gut context for 25 years. I more or less created this field of study, and I do not take very kindly to the idea that I did not know whether I talked about Con A or GNA. I must say I was very surprised when the few reporters I spoke to questioned me about our Con A studies."[8]

One of the first mentions of the Con A lectin seems to have come from Dan Verakis, a spokesman for Monsanto. On the morning of August 10, just prior to the broadcast of the *World in Action* interview, Pusztai did a separate live interview in which Verakis also participated. "I was surprised when I heard him say that we should not have used the gene of the toxic protein from the South American jackbean," Pusztai recalls.

Later that morning, he returned to the Rowett Research Institute. "By that time all the phones were ringing, and secretaries were logging phone calls," he says. "I was tired and therefore Professor James kindly suggested that I was not to give more interviews." Although Pusztai did not realize it at the time, his interview on the morning of August 10 would be the last time he was allowed to speak publicly for six months.

Over the course of the next two days, the Rowett Institute's correspondence with journalists came from Professor James himself or from other staff members who inexplicably repeated the Con A confusion. A news release issued by the institute on August 10 stated that Pusztai's experiments used "the potent insecticidal lectin Concanavalin A." This official line became the basis for news stories titled "Scientist's Potato Alert Was False, Laboratory Admits," and "Doctor's Monster Mistake." The *Times* of London described the situation as follows:

> The data to which Dr. Pusztai had referred, first in an interview with World in Action and then with the *Times* and other media, did not involve genetically modified potatoes. Rather, it involved feeding trials in which a protein from the jack bean, a lectin, was added to a potato-based feed. Since this lectin is known to harm the immune system, the damage was not surprising.
>
> The institute does intend to carry out feeding trials with a potato modified by inserting the gene for this lectin, called Con A, but has yet to start. It said it "regrets the release of misleading information about issues of such importance to the public and the scientific community." Professor Philip James, the director, had suspended Dr. Pusztai from all responsibility for the studies, and put Dr. Andrew Chesson, head of research, in charge.
>
> Dr. Colin Merritt of Monsanto, the leading company involved in gene-modified crops, said: "It seems the researcher leading this programme was out of the country . . . Meanwhile, Dr. Pusztai had gone to the media. Basically he has picked up non-genetically mod-

ified potato data, in which the naturally occurring poison Con A has been added, and read that as the effect of transgenic modified potatoes. It is an awful mistake and these revelations are absolute dynamite."[9]

The only problem with this explanation is that every important fact in it was false. Pusztai's experiments *had* used genetically modified potatoes. The Con A lectin is indeed poisonous, but Pusztai was not experimenting with Con A. He had used the snowdrop lectin, GNA. If Professor James had only shown him the news release before sending it out, Pusztai says, he could have corrected the mistake. The Rowett Research Institute would eventually admit that its news release was wrong, but by then the damage had already been done. Its errors would continue to appear in some news stories for more than a year after they were publicly retracted.

"We have never done any experiments with GM-potatoes expressing the gene of Concanavalin A," Pusztai says. "I still do not know and cannot make up my mind whether the Director was telling the world about Con A in his Press Releases on August 10 to discredit me or just did this out of ignorance, but the effect was the same. When I had to say that there were no such experiments I was regarded as a bumbling idiot, a thief or a cheat. The strategy, if I can assume him to be clever enough, was to put something into my mouth that was manifestly wrong and then to shoot me down for it."[10]

The Con A misunderstanding reverberated for months afterward as the basis for all sorts of confused and misleading news stories. "Instead of rodents fed with genetically altered potatoes, Dr. Pusztai had used the results of tests carried out on rats treated with poison," reported the *Scottish Daily Record & Sunday Mail*.[11]

"Lectins are a known poison; of course if they were in the potatoes you would expect an effect," wrote Charles Arthur, technology editor of the London *Independent*.[12]

Sir Robert May, the British government's chief scientist, also echoed the Con A fallacy. "If you mix cyanide with vermouth in a cocktail and find that it is not good for you, I don't draw sweeping conclusions that you should ban all mixed drinks," he told a radio interviewer.[13]

In addition to misrepresenting Pusztai's research, Professor James spun out a series of subtle slurs on his competence and character, describing Pusztai as "an outstanding scientist who has done good work but who had got himself in a terrible fix." James hinted that Pusztai was suffering from senility, describing his thinking as "muddled" and saying that he was "on the verge of collapse," "gibbering," and "absolutely mortified. He is holding his hands up and is apologizing," James said, which was another falsehood. "I am desperate that dear old Arpad Pusztai maintains his scientific credibility," he would say at another point. "I am desperate to protect him."[14]

Publicly, Pusztai was unable to respond to any of these statements for the simple reason that the Rowett Research Institute had used restrictive clauses in his employment contract to impose a gag order preventing him from speaking out. Like tobacco industry whistle-blower Jeffrey Wigand, he risked forfeiting his pension if he spoke to reporters. Professor James would claim later that the restrictions on Pusztai were justified because "he was exhausted and not used to dealing with the media. He was naïve and overwhelmed and therefore I relieved him of any press relations. I was amazed when I was accused of gagging him."[15] Pusztai, however, has copies of letters from James threatening him with court action if he spoke to the press. His wife, Susan, who was also a scientist at Rowett, was forbidden from speaking with reporters or even being photographed. "All my life I have been afraid of people who said they were helping me. I grew up under a communist regime, and they told me they also had my best intentions at heart," Pusztai said. "I didn't believe them and escaped as a political refugee. Unfortunately I couldn't escape from Professor James. . . . For the first time in my life I was deprived of my right of self-defense. My restrictive contract prevented me saying the things necessary to defend myself."[16]

As public controversy continued to swirl, the Rowett Research Institute established a four-scientist "audit committee" to review Pusztai's work. Normally an audit of this type is performed only if there is reason to suspect actual scientific fraud. The Rowett's committee found no such evidence and confirmed that he had indeed been working with potatoes genetically modified to contain the snowdrop lectin. The committee disagreed, however, with the conclusions that Pusztai had drawn from his data. The Rowett gave Pusztai three days to write a reply to the audit committee, while continuing to deny him access to his own data. It then posted the text of its audit report on the Internet, along with Pusztai's reply, which it described as "unpublishable"—that is, insufficiently rigorous for publication in a peer-reviewed scientific journal. Pusztai agrees, pointing out that this is hardly surprising given the limitations under which he was forced to produce it.[17]

Prevented from speaking directly to the media, Pusztai sent a letter to a friend, which was then passed on to journalists. In the letter, he noted that the Rowett Research Institute, during testimony about his work before a government review committee, had provided the conclusions of its own audit report while neglecting to inform the committee of the existence of Pusztai's rebuttal. By then, two months had passed. Rowett had said it would "consider" his rebuttal, but had made no reply. When he pressed further, he was told to write up his data as scientific papers and submit them to Professor James, who would decide whether they could be submitted for publication in scientific journals. Even if James would give approval—obviously a big *if*—this process would have taken at least six to eight months. "But for someone like me, with my destroyed scientific reputation, it may take considerably longer. So, I am sure it is another delaying ploy," Pusztai stated in the letter to his friend.[18]

Since Pusztai's contract with the Rowett Research Institute prevented him from publishing his findings on his own, he passed some of his samples for evaluation on to Dr. Stanley Ewen, a pathologist at Aberdeen University. Ewen carried out his own measurements and agreed with Pusztai's findings. Finally, in February 1999, a 20-member international scientific panel went on record in support of Pusztai. Only then did the Rowett Institute lift the gag order so that he could begin to speak publicly on his own behalf. Without permission from the Institute, however, he was still unable to publish. As a sort of scientific end run around this restriction, Ewen wrote up his own appraisal, which was eventually published in October with Pusztai as coauthor in the *Lancet,* England's leading medical journal.

As someone who had built a good portion of his career laying the scientific groundwork for the development of genetically modified foods, Pusztai now found himself in a situation where his primary defenders were environmentalists, organic food advocates, and other stalwart opponents of biotech foods. "I have landed up in no-man's land. It is not a comfortable place to be," Pusztai stated. "I am in a situation I cannot get out of now. I feel responsible to keep going because I am the only one with data that shows there are problems. I have a choice: apologize for being incorrect or keep going, and I know I am correct."[19]

Big Stakes for Small Potatoes

The battle between environmentalists and the biotech food industry is shaping up to become one of the most contentious and important political struggles of the twenty-first century. Financially, the stakes are immense. Many of the world's largest chemical corporations—including Monsanto, Novartis, Hoechst of Germany, Pharmacia, Dow Chemical, and DuPont—have been shifting their investments out of industrial chemicals and into agribusiness, pharmaceuticals, and food. In 1998, the U.S. government gave the green light to genetically modified soybeans, cotton, corn, summer squash, potatoes, canola oil, radicchio, papayas, and tomatoes, opening the floodgates on what until then had been a trickle of biotech crops. In early 1999, the International Seed Trade Federation predicted that the world market for genetically engineered seed would reach $6 billion by the year 2005. "Almost 100 percent of our agricultural exports in the next five years will be genetically modified or combined with bulk commodities that are genetically modified," Deputy U.S. Treasury Secretary Stuart Eizenstat said in testimony before the U.S. Senate in June of 1999. These projections, however, are threatened by growing consumer unrest in Europe, Japan, and elsewhere raising questions about this altered harvest. In fact, Eizenstat added, "the European Union's fear of bioengineered foods . . . is the single greatest trade threat that we face."[20]

In Europe, the public's concerns in this regard are particularly acute as a consequence of the "mad cow disease" scandal in England, which erupted in 1996 when government ministers and scientists reversed more than a decade of denial by admitting that a fatal brain disease in cows had begun to infect humans.[21] Formally known as "bovine spongiform encephalopathy," or BSE, mad cow disease kills its victims by filling their brains with microscopic spongelike holes. Prior to the 1980s, BSE had never been identified in British cattle. It reached epidemic levels in the British cattle population due to an innovation in animal feeding practices—the widespread use of "rendered animal by-products" as feed supplements. Rendering consists of cooking the inedible remains of slaughtered animals. Some researchers believe mad cow disease originated when cows were fed the rendered remains of sheep that were infected with a BSE-like disease called scrapie. Whether this theory is correct or not, scientists who have studied the disease agree that the practice of feeding rendered cows back to other cows is what enabled mad cow disease to spread and multiply into an epidemic. In its eagerness to use every bit of protein from slaughtered animals, agribusiness had created a cannibalistic feeding loop. "It happened when, for economic reasons, herbivores were fed offals derived from other species, something they would never eat in nature," says developmental biologist Stuart Newman. "Basically, commercial interests forced the crossing of biological boundaries, leading to a new disease."

The practice of feeding rendered animal protein back to cattle is actually a fairly low-tech procedure. As innovations go, it is simplicity itself compared to the complexity and scope of changes being considered and introduced into our food as a result of new scientific discoveries such as chemical antibiotics and pesticides, fake fats, and fake sweeteners. Of all these innovations, genetic engineering is the most radical and innovative procedure, the most complex, and the least understood even by scientists. For European consumers, the mad cow outbreak marked a warning shot across the bow, an example of the unpredictable dangers inherent in scientific efforts to tamper with their foods. Arpad Pusztai's 150 seconds of fame came at a time when European opinion was turning sharply in favor of greater caution and greater safety, and his saga added further fuel to the fires of an already growing debate about the wisdom of introducing genetically modified organisms into the human food supply. Monsanto and the other commercial interests seeking to profit from biotech foods regard this debate as an example of unwarranted public hysteria, driven by fear-mongering activists and media sensationalism. "Everybody over here hates us," lamented Dan Verakis, Monsanto's chief European spokesman, in February 1999.[22]

The public's concern reflects the arrogance with which the biotech industry has attempted to manipulate public opinion and awareness. In July 1999, the journal *Science* published a comparison of news coverage in Europe versus the United States on the subject of biotechnology and concluded that while Europeans were more scientifically literate than their U.S. counterparts, they were "more likely than Americans to perceive GM foods as menacing or dangerous based on scientifically inaccurate assumptions."[23]

Many of the public's concerns in fact go beyond narrow issues of scientific interpretation or technical expertise. The Pusztai case, for example, raised questions about the political effect of the interlocking relationships between research institutions and their government and corporate sponsors. The Rowett Research Institute receives a small percentage of the funding for its research through contract arrangements with Monsanto. More important, 90 percent of its funding comes from the British government, which at the time of the Pusztai controversy was aggressively courting biotech investments. "We now have to recognize a new sort of scientist, and with it a new sort of science," observed one commentator at the time. "The scientists working for publicly funded institutions are . . . hired and fired by convenience, they are assigned tasks set by their bosses, and they have few rights, or none, to the intellectual property of their work. And their employers may be engaged in work that involves risks, small, great or unquantifiable. If the scientist-worker doesn't like it, he can, like Pusztai, choose to be a whistle-blowing martyr or he can search for another career. The difference in the situation of the 'independent' university-based scientists is only of degree, not of kind; they all need grants. And, as the GM affair shows so clearly, industry-based scientists have influence in high places—they move in the corridors of government. What then is the price of criticism?"[24]

Mutatis Monsanto

The world leader in the biotech industry has been Monsanto, whose 1997 sales of $10.7 billion and market capitalization of $22 billion easily dwarfs the many tiny start-up companies also clamoring for a share of the emerging biotech market. Although Monsanto today calls itself a "life sciences" company, most of its history has been devoted to chemical manufacturing. Founded in 1901 to manufacture saccharine, the first artificial sweetener, Monsanto quickly branched out into the production of industrial chemicals. During World War II, it participated in the development of plastics and synthetic fabrics and also played a significant role during the Manhattan Project in developing the atom bomb. In the decades following the war, it was one of the agrochemical companies that relentlessly promoted the use of chemical pesticides in agriculture. By the 1960s, it had become the primary producer of PCBs—the widely used chemical compound that causes cancer and birth defects. Monsanto was also the largest producer of dioxin-contaminated Agent Orange herbicide, used by U.S. troops to defoliate the rain forests of southeast Asia during the Vietnam War and a known cause of skin rashes, joint pains, muscle weakness, neurological disorders, and birth defects. By the late 1960s, the company's association with some of the world's worst poisons had begun to threaten not only its reputation but its future corporate viability. "We were despised by our customers," admitted former Monsanto vice president Will Carpenter.[25] Its interest in genetic engineering was driven as much by the need to escape this past as by an interest in the future. By the 1980s, it had begun to divest its chemical interests and invest in biotechnology with an eye to positioning itself as a savior and solution to many of the pressing environmental problems that it had created in the first place. As recently as 1996, Monsanto was still the fourth-largest chemical company in the United States, but in 1997 it spun off its industrial chemicals business as a separate company and devoted itself fully to biotech.

Many of the battle lines in the biotech food debate were drawn during Monsanto's PR and lobbying campaign to win approval for recombinant bovine growth hormone (rBGH), a controversial product that, when injected into dairy cows, can induce them to produce more milk. In 1986, Wisconsin dairy farmers led by fifth-generation milker John Kinsman formed an alliance with biotechnology critic Jeremy Rifkin to oppose rBGH, and by 1988, the anti-rBGH coalition had come to include family farm organizations, consumer groups, and animal welfare activists. One thing that these groups easily agreed upon was the need for safety testing and mandatory consumer labeling so that individual consumers could decide for themselves whether or not to purchase rBGH-treated milk. As early as 1986, however, industry surveys showed that labeling milk from cows treated with the drug would lead to consumer rejection. Not content with escaping from mandatory labeling, Monsanto tried to make it impossible for anyone to *voluntarily* put labels on milk from cows that had *not* been injected with rBGH. When some states and several dairies tried to label their products as rBGH-free, Monsanto threatened to take the dairies to court and backed up the threat by actually filing suit against two of them.

The Washington, D.C.–based PR and lobby firm of Capitoline/ MS&L brought together drug and dairy industry groups in an ad hoc network called the Dairy Coalition, comprising university researchers funded by Monsanto, as well as carefully selected "third party" experts. Participants included:

- The International Food Information Council, which calls itself "a non-profit organization that disseminates sound, scientific information on food safety and nutrition to journalists, health professionals, government officials and consumers." In reality, IFIC is a public relations arm of the food and beverage industries, which provide the bulk of its funding. Its staff members hail from industry groups such as the Sugar Association and the National Soft Drink Association, and it has repeatedly led the defense for controversial food additives including monosodium glutamate, aspartame (Nutrasweet), food dyes, and olestra.

- The National Association of State Departments of Agriculture, representing the top executive of every department of agriculture in all 50 states.

- The American Farm Bureau Federation, the powerful conservative lobby behind the movement to pass food disparagement laws like the one under which Oprah Winfrey was sued in Texas.

- The American Dietetic Association, a national association of registered dietitians that works closely with IFIC and hauls in large sums of money advocating for the food industry. Its stated mission is to "improve the health of the public," but with 15 percent of its budget—more than $3 million—coming from food companies and trade groups, it has learned not to bite the hand that feeds it. "They never criticize the food industry," says Joan Gussow, a former head of the nutrition education program at Teachers College at Columbia University. The ADA's website even contains a series of "fact sheets" about various food products, sponsored by the same corporations that make the products (Monsanto for biotechnology; Procter & Gamble for olestra; Ajinomoto for MSG; the National Association of Margarine Manufacturers for fats and oils).[26]

- The Grocery Manufacturers of America, the country's leading trade association for the food and beverage industries. Its member companies account for more than $460 billion in sales annually in the United States. GMA itself is a lobbying powerhouse in Washington, spending $1.4 million for that purpose in 1998.

- The Food Marketing Institute, a trade association of food retailers and wholesalers, whose grocery store members represent three-fourths of grocery sales in the United States.

In the campaign for rBGH approval, its proponents engaged in extensive media monitoring to detect and attack unsympathetic journalists. In 1989, the PR firm of Carma International was hired to conduct a computer analysis of every story filed on rBGH, ranking reporters as friends or enemies. This information was used to reward friendly reporters while complaining to editors about those who filed reports that were deemed unfriendly. Leaked internal documents from the Dairy Coalition reveal how journalists who failed to toe the line have been handled. On February 8, 1996, dairy officials wrote Mary Jane Wilkinson, assistant managing editor of the *Boston Globe,* to complain about an upcoming food column by freelance writer Linda Weltner. In her column, Weltner cited concerns about rBGH expressed by Dr. Samuel Epstein, a professor of occupational and environmental medicine at the University of Illinois and author of the prizewinning 1978 book *The Politics of Cancer,* as well nine other books and 280 scientific articles. Epstein has been a leading critic of rBGH and the use of growth hormones for fattening cattle in feedlots and has consulted on these topics for the European Community, on whose behalf he testified during hearings before the World Trade Organization.

"On [January] 23rd, [Dr.] Samuel Epstein . . . made unsupported allegations linking milk and cancer," the letter stated. "We're concerned that Ms. Weltner will give Epstein a forum in the *Boston Globe* to disseminate theories that have no basis in science." The letter smeared Epstein as a scaremonger with "no standing among his peers in the scientific community and no credibility with the leading health organizations in this country." It noted that "others in the news media who attended Epstein's press conference or reviewed his study—such as *The Wall Street Journal, The New York Times* and the *Washington Post*—chose not to run this 'story.' . . . *USA Today* was the only newspaper to print these allegations and we recently held a heated meeting with them."[27]

Another internal dairy industry document described the handling of *USA Today* health reporter Anita Manning, whose article on the subject offended rBGH lobbyists. "On Wednesday representatives of the Dairy Coalition met with reporter Anita Manning and her editor at *USA Today.* When Manning said that Epstein was a credible source, the Dairy Coalition's Dr. Wayne Callaway pointed out that Epstein has no standing among the scientific community. . . . When Manning insisted it was her responsibility to tell both sides of the story, Callaway said that was just a cop-out for not doing her homework. She was told that if she had attended the press conference, instead of writing the story from a press release, she would have learned that her peers from the *Washington Post, The New York Times, The Wall Street Journal* and the Associated Press chose not to do the story because of the source. At this point Manning left the meeting and her editor assured the Dairy Coalition that any future stories dealing with [rBGH] and health would be closely scrutinized."[28]

A February 1996 internal document of the Dairy Coalition notes that "the Coalition is convinced its work in educating reporters and editors at the *New York Times,* the *Wall Street Journal,* the *Washington Post* and the Associated Press led to those organizations' dismissal of Samuel Epstein's pronouncements that milk from [rBGH] supplemented cows causes breast and colon cancer. They did not run the story."[29]

The same document tells of knocking *New York Times* food reporter Marian Burros off the beat entirely. "As you may recall," it stated, "the Dairy Coalition worked hard with the *New York Times* last year to keep Marian Burros, a very anti-industry reporter, from 'breaking' Samuel Epstein's claim that milk from . . . supplemented cows causes breast and colon cancer. She did not do the story and now the NYT health reporters are the ones on the [rBGH] beat. They do not believe Epstein. Marian Burros is not happy about the situation."[30]

In Florida, Monsanto's attorneys intervened in 1997 when investigative reporters Steve Wilson and Jane Akre attempted to air a critical story about rBGH. Their investigation, conducted for Tampa Bay Fox network affiliate WTVT, made a series of disturbing claims about Monsanto and its product:

- Bovine growth hormone was never adequately tested before FDA allowed it on the market. A standard cancer test of a new human drug requires two years of testing with several hundred rats. But rBGH was tested for only 90 days on 30 rats. Worse, the study has never been published, and the U.S. Food and Drug Administration has refused to allow open scientific peer review of the study's raw data.

- Some Florida dairy herds grew sick shortly after starting rBGH treatment. One farmer, Charles Knight, reported losing 75 percent of his herd and said that Monsanto and Monsanto-funded researchers at University of Florida withheld from him the information that other dairy herds were suffering similar problems.

- Interviewed on camera, Florida dairy officials and scientists refuted Monsanto's claim that every truckload of milk from rBGH-treated cows is tested for excessive antibiotics.

- A visit by Akre to seven randomly selected Florida dairy farms found that all seven were injecting their cows with the hormone. Wilson and Akre also visited area supermarket chains, which two years previously had promised to ask their milk suppliers not to use rBGH in response to consumer concerns. In reality, store representatives admitted that they have taken no steps to assure compliance with this request.[31]

- Finally, the story dwelt heavily on concerns raised by scientists such as Epstein and Consumers Union researcher Michael Hansen about potential cancer risks associated with "insulin-like growth factor one" (IGF-1). Treatments of rBGH can lead to significantly increased levels of IGF-1 in milk, and recent studies suggest that IGF-1 is a powerful tumor growth promoter.

The resulting story, a four-part series, was cleared by management and scheduled to begin airing on Monday, February 24, 1997. As part of the buildup to network ratings sweeps, the story was already being heavily promoted in radio ads when an ominous letter arrived at the office of Fox News chairman Roger Ailes, the former Republican political operative who now heads Rupert Murdoch's Fox network news. The letter came from John J. Walsh, a powerful New York attorney with the firm of Cadwalader, Wickersham & Taft, who accused the reporters of bias and urged the network to delay the story to ensure "a more level playing field" for Monsanto's side. "There is a lot at stake in what is going on in Florida, not only for Monsanto but also for Fox News and its owner," Walsh wrote.[32]

"Monsanto hired one of the most renowned lawyers in America to use his power and influence," Wilson says. "Even though our stories had been scheduled to run, even though Fox had bought expensive radio ads to alert viewers to the story, it was abruptly cancelled on the eve of the broadcasts within hours of receiving the letter from Monsanto's lawyer."

Initially, the story was postponed for a week. Akre and Wilson offered to do a further interview with Monsanto and supplied a list of topics to be discussed. In response, Walsh fired back an even more threatening letter: "It simply defies credulity that an experienced journalist would expect a representative of any company to go on camera and respond to the vague, undetailed—and for the most part accusatory—points listed by Ms. Akre. Indeed, some of the points clearly contain the elements of defamatory statements which, if repeated in a broadcast, could lead to serious damage to Monsanto and dire consequences for Fox News."

What followed next, according to Wilson and Akre, was a grueling nightmare of perpetual delays and station-mandated rewrites—73 in all, none of which proved satisfactory to station management. "No fewer than six air dates were set and cancelled," Wilson recalls. "In all my years as a print and radio and local and national television reporter, I've never seen anything like it." When the reporters balked at some of the station's proposed changes—such as deleting Epstein's warning of cancer risks—they say the station's general manager notified them they would be fired for insubordination within 48 hours and another reporter would make the requested changes.

"When we said we'd file a formal complaint with the FCC if that happened," says Wilson, "we were not fired but were each offered very large cash settlements to go away and keep quiet about the story and how it was handled." The reporters refused the settlement, which amounted to nearly $200,000, and ultimately were fired in December 1997.

No Label? No Problem!

If industry's own polls were not enough to prove that labeling could be the marketing kiss of death for genetically modified foods, the launch of Calgene's "Flavr-Savr" tomato in 1994 helped drive this lesson home. The Flavr-Savr was the first genetically modified fruit approved for sale in American supermarkets, but it failed to catch on. Designed to last longer on store shelves than regular tomatoes, it was expensive, had a soft texture that made it bruise during packaging, and some consumers thought it had a strange, metallic taste.[33] Calgene's marketing efforts also suffered due to its brand name and the publicity surrounding the product launch. Consumers knew that the Flavr-Savr was genetically engineered, and many were wary.

In the early 1990s, biotech promoters lobbied intensely and successfully to prevent genetically modified foods from being labeled as such. In 1992, the U.S. Food and Drug Administration decreed that GM foods are substantially equivalent to conventional foods. Under FDA rules, a new food must be thoroughly tested unless it falls into a category of foods that FDA terms "generally regarded as safe" (GRAS). By declaring that biotech foods are equivalent to the conventional variety, FDA deemed them GRAS and therefore exempt from mandatory safety testing or special product labeling. Government regulators rely on biotech companies to do their own voluntary safety tests and also determine themselves if the product in question is GRAS.[34] One of the key decision-makers who helped draft FDA's policy was Michael Taylor, previously an attorney for Monsanto. After the policy was written, in fact, Taylor left the FDA and eventually went back to work for Monsanto.[35]

Rather than subject the merits of GM foods to open public debate, industry has tried to get the products quickly on the shelves and then deal with public opinion after the innovation has already become an accomplished fact. Until fairly recently, this strategy appeared to be succeeding. The first large-scale commercial plantings of transgenic crops went into the ground in 1996, and by 1998, they covered nearly 69 million acres in eight countries, not including China. In 1999, about a third of the U.S. corn crop and more than half of the soybeans planted were estimated to be genetically engineered varieties.[36] Gene-altered products allowed on the market include cottonseed oil, canola, potatoes, tomatoes, sweet peppers, squash, sunflowers, milk (from rBGH-treated cows), and chymosin, an enzyme commonly used in hard cheese. Corn and soy in particular are widely disseminated in processed foods as sweeteners, oils, texturizers, fillers, and extenders. As a result, American consumers have been eating increasing amounts of genetically engineered food—mostly without their knowledge or consent—because the food has not been labeled as such.

A 1999 industry-sponsored opinion poll found that 62 percent of Americans were still unaware that GM foods were already widely marketed. Tom Hoban, a sociology professor at North Carolina State University who has done extensive opinion polling for the biotech industry, likes to poke fun at the purported ignorance of the general public. "Lots of American consumers probably don't know seeds are involved in agriculture—they don't even know *farms* are involved in agriculture," he quipped at a June 1998 meeting of the Biotechnology Industry Organization. Hoban sees such public ignorance as a great opportunity for industry to "proactively educate" consumers. Ultimately, he says, industry will win as GM-free products become difficult to find on store shelves. "Everybody's going to be using biotech foods pretty soon, so there won't be a lot of alternatives," he said.

In Europe, however, this disdain for the consumer backfired badly. Genetically modified tomato puree was one of the first biotech foods to reach British supermarket shelves. As in the United States, its introduction was marked by little fanfare. By the time that Professor Pusztai appeared on *World in Action,* however, consumers in England and other parts of Europe were realizing that they were eating GM food, and they were starting to resent it. According to the *Wall Street Journal,* Monsanto shot itself in the foot in 1998 when it not only refused to label but "decided to make a point of not segregating genetically modified soybeans from regular soybeans for the European market. It wasn't Greenpeace but the supposedly responsible leaders of the supermarket industry who led the backlash. Malcolm Walker, head of the Iceland grocery chain, posing as the defender of 'consumer choice,' denounced Monsanto in ads and interviews. At Safeway, Chairman David Webster stormed a podium in 1999 to declare that his company was "fighting back against the tide of genetically modified foods and ingredients hitting UK shelves."[37]

By the fall of 1998, Monsanto's own research showed that it was losing the battle for public opinion in Europe. An internal report by opinion pollster Stan Greenberg showed that the company's pro biotech advertising campaign had been "overwhelmed" by the public backlash. Monsanto's refusal to label bioengineered products had even angered senior executives from leading British supermarket chains. "The latest survey shows an ongoing collapse of public support for biotechnology and GM foods," Greenberg wrote. "At each point in this project, we keep thinking that we have reached the low point and that public opinion will stabilize, but we apparently have not reached that point. The latest survey shows a steady decline over the year, which may have accelerated in the most recent period. . . . The number saying that these products are 'unacceptable' has skyrocketed: 35 percent last year, rising to 44 percent before the summer and to 51 percent now." The only positive indicators, Greenberg said, were poll results showing that politicians and government scientists continued to side with the company. Their support was key, he noted, since Monsanto's strategy was focused on winning over "a socio-economic elite" consisting of members of parliament and "upper-level civil servants."[38]

A newspaper opinion poll released that same month found that 68 percent of the respondents were worried about eating genetically modified foods. In March 1999 another poll found that "nine out of ten shoppers would switch supermarkets to avoid genetically modified food." The Church of Scotland issued a study condemning the "unethical" practices of transnational biotech corporations. "There is indignation from people that they are not being given a choice," said church spokesperson Donald Bruce. "It smacks of imperialism—but instead of a Boston Tea Party, this time we could have a Rotterdam Soya Bean Fest with soya and maize dumped into the North Sea."

As resistance grew, supermarket chains throughout Europe began bowing to consumer pressure by pulling genetically modified foods from their shelves. In April 1999, even Unilever, England's largest food manufacturer and itself an investor in biotech research, was driven by hard economics to announce that it would remove GM ingredients from its products. "The announcement started a week-long stampede by leading companies, all household names," stated the London *Independent*. The day after Unilever's capitulation, Nestlé followed suit, as did England's leading supermarket chains, including Tesco, Sainsbury, Safeway, Asda, and Somerfield. "When these phase-outs are complete, no major supermarket brands will continue to contain GM ingredients," the *Independent* noted. "It's an extraordinary reversal from the rapid, silent, expansion of GM foods—from nothing to 60 percent of the products on supermarket shelves in less than three years."[39]

An internal report by the Deutsche Bank, Europe's largest, recommended that investors sell their holdings of ag biotech stocks. "In the past month," the report noted, "a senior manager at a European-based chemical giant expressed serious reservations to us about the benignness of GMOs [genetically modified organisms] and said that given a choice, he would select non-GMOs any day. By the way, the company he works for is actively involved in ag-biotechnology."[40]

The Empire Strikes Back

As the tide of anti-biotech sentiment rose, industry strategists began to reconsider their hush-hush approach. In May 1998, Monsanto launched an aggressive publicity campaign, spending $5 million on advertisements in French and British newspapers touting genetic engineering as a miracle solution for hunger in the Third World. Headlined "Let the Harvest Begin," the ads used the rhetoric of environmentalism and social concern. "We all share the same planet—and the same needs," they proclaimed. "In agriculture, many of our needs have an ally in biotechnology and the promising advances it offers for our future. Healthier, more abundant food. Less expensive crops. Reduced reliance on pesticides and fossil fuels. A cleaner environment. With these advances, we prosper; without them, we cannot thrive. As we stand on the edge of a new millennium, we dream of a tomorrow without hunger. To achieve that dream, we must welcome the science that promises hope. . . . Biotechnology is one of tomorrow's tools today. Slowing its acceptance is a luxury our hungry world cannot afford."[41]

The campaign came under immediate attack, however, from international agencies that actually work on hunger issues. "This is a technology that's being developed for profit. It is not to any degree going to help with world poverty," said Isabel McCrea of Action Aid, one of England's largest overseas development agencies. "We are appalled by the cynical use of that argument by the industry to convince northern consumers that this is a technology that they should accept," she added.[42]

Biotech advocates claim that genetically engineered crops will be good for the environment by reducing the need to use environmentally toxic pesticides and fertilizers. So far, however, the opposite may be true. The vast majority of genetically modified crops currently on the market have been modified to either withstand herbicide (so that more can be sprayed) or produce their own insecticide. For Monsanto, of course, herbicide-tolerant crops create the perfect opportunity for marketing tie-ins. Not only do they get to charge farmers premium prices for their patented, genetically modified seeds, they also get to sell more weed-killing chemicals. In 1999, more than half of the U.S. soybean crop was "Roundup Ready"—genetically engineered to survive spraying with Monsanto's best-selling weedkiller, Roundup. However, an independent analysis of 8,200 university research trials by Dr. Charles Benbrook found that contrary to Monsanto's promised advantages, yields of herbicide-resistant GM soybeans were 5 to 10 percent *lower* than comparable conventional varieties. Benbrook, a former executive director of the National Academy of Sciences Council's Board on Agriculture who now works as an independent consultant, reported that lost production due to this yield drag amounted to an estimated 80 to 100 million bushels in 1999. Benbrook also noted that nobody is testing the crops for increased pesticide residues.

The EPA, moreover, has raised the allowable residue limits for Roundup on soybeans and cotton.[43]

Some genetically modified crops do require fewer chemical pesticides—at least in the short term. The most common way to accomplish this is through the insertion of a gene that causes the plant to produce *bacillus thuringiensis,* or Bt, which has been used for decades by organic farmers as a natural pesticide. Like Pusztai's snowdrop lectin, the Bt toxin has been tested and used for a long time with no reported harmful effects to humans, but it destroys the digestive tracts of certain very pesky insects. Biotech companies have successfully spliced the Bt gene into corn, cotton, canola, potatoes, and rice. Monsanto's New Leaf potato, for example, is legally registered as a pesticide with the U.S. Environmental Projection Agency because it contains the Bt gene, making it toxic to Colorado potato beetles. The Novartis company's Bt corn is similarly deadly to European and Southwestern corn borers, caterpillars that mine into cornstalks and cause up to $1 billion worth of crop losses annually.

Enabling a plant to make its own insecticide may seem like a good idea, but it poses problems of its own. Organic farmers have applied Bt sparingly to their crops as a natural pesticide of last resort, but insect exposure was short-lived, and far fewer acres were sprayed than currently are planted with Bt crops, which are now planted on about 20 million acres in the United States alone. Moreover, Bt crops typically express the toxin in every cell of the plant. The widespread use of conventional pesticides has led to the emergence of more than 500 types of pesticide-resistant insect since 1945, and biologists who study bugs expect that the widespread introduction of Bt into the environment will create similar selection pressures that speed the emergence of Bt-resistant pests. If Bt-resistant pests emerge, organic agriculture will lose one of its most effective, time-honored tools, making it harder and more expensive to control insects without the use of synthetic chemical sprays.[44]

Plant biologists also worry that pollen from genetically modified crops is spreading the genetically inserted traits to closely related weeds. Rice with the Bt gene, for example, might pollinate wild grasses that are close relatives. This could make the weeds pest-resistant and help them multiply. Similarly, the use of Roundup Ready crops might create herbicide-resistant "superweeds." Even commercial crops can become weeds if they turn up in unwanted places, which is what happened to Charles Boser, a Canadian farmer who found to his dismay that some of Monsanto's

Roundup Ready canola had drifted from a neighbor's farm into a field that he was trying to fallow. Boser, who was not trying to grow canola, tried unsuccessfully to kill the plants with two applications of herbicide before finally calling Monsanto in frustration. "Take your product and get it the hell off of my land is exactly what I told them," Boser said. "I don't want the stuff." Monsanto dutifully complied, hiring workers to pick the plants out of Boser's field by hand and compensating him for the additional costs of spraying that he had incurred.

The issue of allergenicity is another health concern with GM crops. In 1995, the Pioneer Hybrid seed company added a Brazil nut gene to soybeans in hopes of achieving a more nutritional balance of proteins. Pioneer Hybrid abandoned the project after tests on the transgenic soybeans revealed that they could induce potentially fatal allergies in people sensitive to Brazil nuts. We can feel thankful that Brazil nuts contain a known allergen, so researchers knew what to look for. However, many of the other foreign genes now being inserted into foods are taken from viruses, bacteria, and insects, and they produce proteins that have never before been part of the human food supply. Are they toxic? The only way to find out would be to test them rigorously, first on animals and then on volunteer human subjects. By deciding that GM foods are "substantially equivalent" to normal foods, the FDA has left it up to industry to decide when and if such testing will ever be done, an approach that "would appear to favor industry over consumer protection," according to the *New England Journal of Medicine*.[45]

The risk of introducing unpredictable hazards into foods is inherent in the use of recombinant DNA technology. Genetic manipulations are frequently described as "gene splicing," a term that obscures much of the uncertainty and imprecision of the process. It evokes the idea that gene manipulators are doing something akin to splicing a movie—an exacting process in which film is secured firmly on a cutting board, giving the editor complete control over which frames of the film are removed or added and in which order. By contrast, one common gene-splicing technique uses a patented "gene gun" that shoots little metal slivers that have been coated with DNA taken from one organism into the cell of another organism. If all goes well, the genes slip off the metal "transports" and are incorporated into the DNA in the cell of that organism, but no one can predict where the new gene is going to land within the genome of the targeted organism. It may attach to the site of any chromosome, or may attach in the middle of another gene and interfere with the normal functioning of the cell.

"These positioning effects are not simple to predict," Pusztai says. "Think of William Tell shooting an arrow at a target. Now put a blindfold on the man doing the shooting, and that's the reality of the genetic engineer when he's doing a gene insertion. He has no idea where the transgene will land in the recipient genome." In his experiments with transgenic potatoes, Pusztai observed the imprecision of the technique firsthand. "We had two transgenic lines of potato produced from the same gene insertion and the same growing conditions," he says. "We grew them together along with the parent plant. With our two lines of potato, which should have been substantially equivalent to each other, we found that one of the lines contained 20 percent less protein than the other. So the two lines were not substantially equivalent to each other. But we also found that these two lines were not substantially equivalent to their parent. This demonstrates that the unpredictability is inherent in the genetic manipulation process on a case by case basis—and also at the level of every single GM plant created."

Biotechnologists compare DNA to the digital codes that make up computer software, but computer programs are vastly simpler and better-understood than the genetic codes inscribed in DNA. According to Harvard geneticist Richard Lewontin, genetic codes are more like an interacting ecosystem than a linear computer program. "You can always intervene and change something in it, but there's no way of knowing what the downstream effects will be or how it might affect the environment," he told the *New York Times Magazine* in 1998. "We have such a miserably poor understanding of how the organism develops from its DNA that I would be surprised if we *don't* get one rude shock after another."[46]

The Hell in Health Food

Bea Stefani knows firsthand what it feels like to be a human guinea pig. She was just trying to lose a few pounds when, at the recommendation of her doctor, she started taking L-tryptophan in the summer of 1989. L-tryptophan is an essential amino acid that occurs naturally in meats, beans, brewer's yeast, and peanut butter. In the late 1980s, it enjoyed a reputation as a popular "all natural" food supplement, recommended not only as a diet aid but as a natural treatment for insomnia, premenstrual symptoms, and depression. For Stefani, at first it seemed to work like a miracle, helping her to lose 25 pounds in two months. Then the problems started, beginning with an itching sensation.

"I had a very severe itch around my head and then my ears," Stefani said. "Then it went all the way down my body. I thought I was allergic to some kind of soap. I changed all my laundry soap and all my bath soap but it didn't help. I itched so bad that in my sleep, I'd be digging in my ears and make my ears bleed."[47]

After the itching came aches and pains throughout her body. Stefani started losing her hair. Her skin felt hot to the touch. She began having severe muscle spasms and was admitted to a hospital. Doctors at first were baffled. She was one of thousands of people throughout the United States suffering from a previously unheard-of disease that eventually came to be called "eosinophilia-myalgia syndrome," or EMS. Of the 5,000 people affected by the disease, 37 died and 1,500 were left permanently disabled with symptoms including paralysis and neurological problems, painful swelling and cracking of the skin, memory and cognitive deficits, headaches, extreme light sensitivity, fatigue, and heart problems. Bea Stefani still suffers severe pain, is no longer able to golf or ride a bicycle, and will probably have to take medication for the rest of her life. As EMS victims go, however, she was relatively lucky. At least her heart was spared, and she can breathe without a respirator.[48]

What shocked victims the most was the discovery that the cause of their disease came from the health food store. Their L-tryptophan, it turned out, was not as "natural" as the label had led them to believe. It was in fact one of the first genetically engineered dietary products to reach consumers.

Several different companies manufacture L-tryptophan, but the people who developed EMS had been consuming one particular brand made by Showa Denko, Japan's third-largest chemical company. Showa Denko had safely manufactured L-tryptophan for many years previously using fermentation, which involves growing a large number of bacteria in a nutrient medium, similar to making a yogurt culture. To increase production, they introduced genetically modified bacteria that express higher quantities of tryptophan. Unfortunately, the modified process also apparently created a highly toxic tryptophan breakdown product. According to a study published in *Science,* Showa Denko's product was contaminated with a "novel amino acid" not present in conventional tryptophan.[49] The contaminant occurred in trace quantities and, because of its similarity to tryptophan itself, was difficult to detect or remove through filtration. Once ingested, however, it apparently overstimulated the body's immune system, causing it to attack nerves and other body tissues. This immune system attack was what caused one of the disease's most horrifying signatures: "ascending paralysis," in which a person loses nerve control of the feet, followed by the legs, then bowels and lungs, finally requiring a respirator in order to breathe.

The Food and Drug Administration responded to the EMS outbreak by banning over-the-counter sales of L-tryptophan—not just Showa Denko's brand, but all brands.[50] EMS victims sued the company for an estimated $2 billion dollars in damages, and Showa Denko has quietly settled these cases out of court. On several occasions, FDA officials have downplayed or denied evidence linking the disaster to genetic engineering. If pressed, they will usually stress that such a link has not been proven. It has also never been *dis*proven.[51]

Suppose for a moment that genetic engineering should introduce something like the L-tryptophan contaminant into your corn bread or the tomato that sits atop your salad. Were this to happen, standard food safety analyses will not detect it. They can detect the presence of known toxins based only on known properties of preexisting food. The "novel amino acid" in genetically engineered tryptophan was not a known toxin. By the standard that the FDA uses to regulate genetically modified foods, your killer tomato would be "substantially equivalent" to a safe one.

Moreover, industry's refusal to countenance labeling of genetically engineered foods creates an additional risk. The labeling and packaging of L-tryptophan made it possible for the Centers for Disease Control to trace the link between Showa Denko's contaminated product and eosinophilia-myalgia syndrome. In the absence of labeling for genetically modified products, however, it is impossible to determine who has been eating mutant soybeans and who has been eating natural ones. If something toxic enters the food supply, tracing it to its source will be difficult if not impossible.

The Terminator

By its very nature, the capital-intensive technology of genetic engineering both reflects and deepens a growing trend toward corporate monopolization of agriculture. "The past half century in American agriculture has witnessed not only the flow of people from farms to cities but also the flow of information—and with it economic and technological power—from farmers to agricultural corporations," observed Verlyn Klinkenborg of the *New York Times* in a 1997 op-ed piece. "The introduction of gene-altered crops, and the licensing used to protect them, is one of the final steps in the reduction of farmers to what one agricultural foundation calls 'bioserf-dom'—becoming mere suppliers of labor."[52] As gene engineers move in to dominate and monopolize the global market for seeds and medical products, they are turning the ancient craft of farming, which is still practiced successfully with stone-age tools in many parts of the world, into a high-tech "agribusiness" that must conform first to the coercions of the "free market" and second to the arcane precepts of Tomorrowland's neoscientific priesthood. Instead of producers of food and fiber, farmers in this new world order will become mere reproducers of Monsanto's intellectual property, like clerks at a biological Kinko's.

"One of the ironies of the development of this issue is the contrast between the enthusiasm of food producers to claim that their biologically engineered products are different and unique when they seek to patent them and their similar enthusiasm for claiming that they are just the same as other foods when asked to label them," notes Julian Edwards, the director general of Consumers International.[53] From the point of view of companies like DuPont, Novartis, and Monsanto, the ability to patent and therefore exert corporate control over life itself is the true magic that makes biotechnology worthwhile. Genetic engineering turns seeds themselves into "intellectual property," so the farmers using the seeds don't own the right to save seeds from their harvest for use in the next planting. Monsanto likes to use the analogy of renting a car—at the end of the rental period, the car is returned.[54] This new arrangement makes it illegal for farmers to engage in the time-honored practice of saving seeds, a practice that is especially common in the Third World. In the United States and Canada, Monsanto has pursued this concept to the point of hiring private investigators to swipe plants from farmers who didn't buy their seeds to see if they are planting Monsanto's transgenic varieties. Monsanto has also encouraged its farmers to snitch on neighbors they suspect of planting transgenics without paying for them. In Canada, Monsanto sued Percy Schmeiser, an elderly farmer, for intellectual property theft. He swears he never planted Monsanto's transgenic seed, yet it showed up in his field, quite possibly through genetic drift—that is, contamination of his crops by windblown, genetically engineered pollen.

To tighten the noose even further, in May 1998 Monsanto acquired a technology that anti-biotech activists quickly dubbed "the Terminator." Developed with your tax dollars by the U.S. Department of Agriculture, the Terminator (known formally as the "Technology Protection System") is a genetic construct that, once fully developed, can be spliced into any crop, rendering all of the plants infertile in the second generation. This makes it the ideal platform for companies to introduce patented genetic traits they don't want farmers to save from season to season, thus enabling Monsanto to enforce its "rights" without the use of strong-arm tactics. "The Terminator will allow companies like Monsanto to privatize one of the last great commons in nature—the genetics of the crop plants that civilization has developed over the past 10,000 years," observed the *New York Times*.

After the Terminator Technology became a lightning rod for public outrage, Monsanto announced in late 1999 that for the time being it would suspend plans to commercialize the technology—over the objections, it should be noted, of the U.S. Department of Agriculture. As co-owner of the Terminator patent, the USDA wants to see the technology move forward so it can recoup the money it invested to develop it. Now research is proceeding into an alternative that has been dubbed the "Traitor technology"—a sort of "Terminator II" that disrupts plant reproduction until sprayed with an activator chemical.

Terminator-like technologies pose a threat even to farmers who don't use the seeds. "Pollen from crops carrying the new trait will infect the fields of farmers who either reject or can't afford the technology," says Neth Dano, director of the Philippines-based SEARICE, an organization that works with farmers in Southeast Asia. "When farmers reach into their bins to sow seed the following season they could discover—too late—that some of their seed is infertile." Monica Opole of the Community Biodiversity Development and Conservation Program in Kenya agrees. "Farmers could find that their neighbor bought the technology and it cross-pollinated into their field, leaving them with dead seeds," she warns. "Who knows how this technology will interact with nature, especially as it spreads out over time and inevitably crosses with farmers' varieties?"[55]

Regulatory Underkill

Government regulatory agencies are supposed to provide an important check on otherwise unrestrained corporate power. With respect to the planting of genetically modified crops, however, the U.S. government has done just about everything except help drive the tractor. The biotech industry excels in the fine art of cultivating Washington politicians. "Monsanto, which makes large donations to both the Democratic and Republican parties and to congressional legislators on food-safety committees, has become a virtual retirement home for members of the Clinton Administration," observed the Toronto *Globe and Mail.* "Trade and environmental protection administrators and other Clinton appointees have left to take up lucrative positions on Monsanto's board, while Monsanto and other biotech executives pass through the same revolving door to take up positions in the administration and its regulatory bodies." Mickey Kantor, the chairman of Bill Clinton's 1992 presidential campaign and a former U.S. chief trade negotiator, now sits on Monsanto's board of directors.

"No foods in history have been subjected to as much scrutiny in advance by the federal government as those improved through biotechnology," claims Michael J. Phillips, who himself created controversy when he left his position as director of a National Academy of Sciences panel that was reviewing the safety of GM foods to become executive director of the industry's main lobby group, the Biotechnology Industry Organization. In reality, not only are biotech foods exempt from special health safety testing and labeling, testing for their environmental safety is equally lax. It is up to the USDA to ensure that genetically modified crops are ecologically safe. In 1999, however, the *New York Times* reported that the agency has not rejected a single application for a biotech crop and that many scientists say "the department has relied on unsupported claims and shoddy studies by the seed companies."[56]

Far from being antagonists, government agencies and the biotech companies they regulate often appear to be a club of elite insiders, accustomed to having their way and suspicious of "outsiders" (i.e., the general public) who try to influence or question their decisions. And they have good reason to be suspicious, because their own opinion research has told them that the public's opinion of biotech foods is sharply opposed to their own. In 1997, an opinion poll conducted by biotech giant Novartis found that 93 percent of Americans were in favor of labeling biotech foods. Other polls conducted in recent years by the USDA and *Time* magazine reached roughly similar conclusions. Scores of environmental, consumer, family farm, and animal welfare groups have been campaigning, litigating, protesting, publicizing, and writing letters about the issue. In 1998, when the USDA issued a proposal that would have allowed GM foods to be classified as "organic," 275,000 people sent the agency letters opposing the proposal.

Government and industry insiders rationalize the gulf that separates them from popular opinion by dismissing citizen concerns with the usual rhetoric about the public's ignorance. Terms such as "Luddite" and "loony" abound as the biotechnicians compete among themselves to see who can express the most contempt for the intelligence of the great unwashed masses. In the *Financial Post* of Canada, business columnist Terence Corcoran attacked critics of Monsanto and biotech foods as "radically slanted," "alarmist," "scaremongering" industry bashers. "They want to save the world from killer tomatoes," he complained. "Frankenstein Food is now part of the language in Britain. Genetic research has been compared with Nazi experiments in genetics. Intimidated by media hysterics and an alarmed public, supermarkets no longer carry genetically modified food."[57] Gene Grabowski, a spokesperson for the Grocery Manufacturers of America, complained about the "shrill statements and outrageous tactics by people who are attacking biotech foods."[58] Europe's rejection of biotech foods prompted Richard Morningstar, the U.S. ambassador to the European Union, to complain bitterly that "politics and demagoguery have completely taken over the regulatory process" and that "the outlook for the resolution of this issue is bleak." Europe's impertinence led the editorialists at the *Wall Street Journal* to write, "In Europe, across the whole food technology front, confusion and hysteria have displaced reason and economics," characterizing biotech critics as "zealots" and complaining that "on matters of trade and technology, the mob has been running the show for a while."[59]

New Scientist, one of England's leading science journals, offered similar reasoning in its coverage of the Arpad Pusztai affair. In retrospect, it concluded, the Rowett Research Institute's decision to fire Pusztai was a "blunder" because it had created a "martyr," thus giving "ammunition on a plate" to "conspiracy theorists" and environmental fanatics. "Nothing sets a nation's pulse racing like a food scare," it added. *New Scientist*'s coverage also provides a telling indicator of the consistency with which pro-biotech forces hold to their conclusions about the safety of biotech foods, regardless of new facts as they arise. When the Pusztai story first broke in August 1998, *New Scientist* joined the rest of the media chorus in repeating the "Con A" fallacy promulgated by the Rowett Institute: "Pusztai and his colleagues gave potatoes a gene from the South American jack bean," it stated. "But the product of the jack bean gene, concanavalin A, has long been known to be harmful. It is one of many toxic proteins called lectins with which plants defend themselves against insects. Other lectins include ricin, the poison used on an umbrella tip to kill Bulgarian dissident Georgi Markov in 1978. Iain Cubitt, chief executive of Axis Genetics in Cambridge, was alarmed by the publicity given to the findings. 'Everyone has known for years that concanavalin A is toxic, so if you put this in a potato and it ends up toxic, why is that such a surprise?' he says."[60]

By February 1999, however, everyone knew that Pusztai's potatoes had used the snowdrop lectin and not Con A. As the facts changed, therefore, so did *New Scientist*'s opinion about the safety of lectins. "What is still woefully unclear is what Pusztai's experiments really mean for the safety of GM foods," it wrote. "The lectin gene used in his potato could certainly be hugely important—and not just to the food industry. It may yet end up warding off insect pests from rice, a staple crop for millions. Pusztai's one indisputable result—that the lectin does not in itself harm rats—is therefore reassuring."[61]

Crisis Containment

"Although most U.S. consumers aren't aware of it, ingredients made from genetically modified crops are present in various products made by Coca-Cola Co., Kellogg Co., General Mills Inc., H.J. Heinz Co., Hershey Foods Corp., Quaker Oats Co., McDonald's Corp.—and on and on," the *Wall Street Journal* reported on October 7, 1999. "Nothing would please these companies more than for Americans to remain oblivious or indifferent to this fact. But that's hardly likely." Pointing to the situation in Europe, the *Journal* noted that "regulators in Australia, New Zealand, Japan and Canada are devising strategies for labeling such foods, and many other countries are considering similar actions. Increasing the likelihood that such concerns will spread to the U.S., the same organizations that incited the GMO consternation in Europe—among them Greenpeace and

Friends of the Earth—are considering ways to awaken Americans to the issue. . . . If pressure builds in the U.S. to label all genetically modified foods, the impact on sales could be chilling. . . . Such a backlash would also be a devastating blow to U.S. biotechnology pioneers Monsanto Co. and DuPont Co. The premium prices they are charging farmers for genetically modified seed is only now beginning to help them recoup the billions of dollars they invested in biotechnology research and acquisitions."[62]

U.S. farmers have already felt the consequences of the growing international rebellion against biotech crops. Between 1997 and 1998, European purchases of U.S. corn fell from nearly 70 million bushels to less than 3 million—a 96 percent drop in a single year.[63] In June 1998, U.S. Undersecretary of Agriculture Gus Schumacher said American farmers were losing $200 million a year from French refusal to import genetically modified corn and soybeans. Farmers who initially responded favorably to industry's intense pro-biotech sales pitch have begun rebelling. The American Corn Growers Association, a commodity group that represents thousands of corn growers in 28 states, is encouraging its members to plant non-GMO varieties. "American farmers planted [gene-altered crops] in good faith, with the belief that the product is safe and that they would be rewarded for their efforts," the American Corn Growers Association complained in a September 1999 statement. "Instead they find themselves misled by multinational seed and chemical companies and other commodity associations who only encouraged them to plant increased acres of [these crops] without any warning to farmers of the dangers associated with planting a crop that didn't have consumer acceptance."[64] Even the pro-biotech National Corn Growers Association (NCGA), the "official" corn commodity group that represents larger growers, can't argue with market reality. At a U.S. Senate Agricultural Committee hearing, NCGA board member Tim Hume called on biotech seed companies to make sure they offered their best hybrid varieties in conventional versions.[65]

As the biotech controversy grows, the food industry appears to be realizing the consequences of ramming through market approvals without full public debate. "Consumers' faith in the government and retailers as watchdogs over food safety could be broken, undermining one of the pillars upon which the modern supermarket was built," observed an October 1999 issue of the trade publication *Supermarket News.*[66]

Eyeing the wreckage in other countries, the biotech industry is now fighting against the consumer backlash emerging in the United States.

Stories questioning various aspects of the technology and reporting on the international consumer revolt have been appearing in publications such as the *New York Times,* the *Los Angeles Times,* the *Wall Street Journal, Time, Newsweek,* and *Consumer Reports.* In June 1999, the public relations industry trade publication *PR Week* reported that the Grocery Manufacturers of America (GMA)— representing 132 firms including Heinz, Kraft, and Procter & Gamble—was launching a multimillion-dollar PR campaign to provide what it called "balanced" (i.e., favorable) information to consumers about genetically modified foods. According to GMA's Gene Grabowski, the campaign reflected the food industry's determination to "act before a potential crisis."

In a July 5, 1999 story, "Field of Bad Dreams," *PR Week* writer John Frank acknowledged that "genetically engineered foods are a PR pro's potential nightmare," noting that industry got "a wake-up call" with the May 1999 release of a Cornell University study showing that pollen from Monsanto's Bt corn could drift onto milkweed plants and poison Monarch butterflies. The Monarch is "sort of the Bambi of the insect world," according to Marlin Rice, a professor of entomology at Iowa State University in Ames. "It's big and gawdy and gets a lot of good press. And you've got school kids all across the country raising them in jars." The Bt–Monarch controversy came on the heels of other recent studies showing that Bt crops kill nontarget beneficial insects such as lacewings and ladybugs, kill beneficial soil microorganisms, damage soil fertility, and may harm insect-eating birds.[67] However, it was the image problems associated with killing Bambi that sent industry spokespersons scurrying to counter the damage. Discoveries like this could end consumer complacency "in an instant," worried one source quoted in *PR Week.*

Perhaps the most interesting aspect of *PR Week*'s response to the Monarch butterfly study is the narrow range of options that it considered possible for the public relations industry. "Are we only limited to a defensive role in talking about GE foods?" it asked, answering that PR pros can also make a *positive* case for them by arguing that biotechnology is "needed to adequately feed a growing world population." The choice, in other words, was between playing defense or offense for the biotech team. The possibility that anyone might want to flack for the precautionary principle was not even considered. "The law of unintended consequences means studies like the butterfly study are likely to surface, focusing on something company researchers may never have considered," *PR Week* admitted, but rather than take such "unintended consequences" seriously, it advised PR pros to treat them as "brush fires" to be "quickly dealt with." This would entail setting up "early warning systems" to handle awkward scientific studies and activist groups; training seed company officials to deal with the popular press; getting seed companies to publicize their research; and roping in "third party spokespersons" to trumpet pro-biotech statements and opinions from government regulators. Farmers make especially good spokespersons, *PR Week* advised, because they "garner positive response from American consumers."[68]

The first line of attack against the Monarch butterfly study involved the usual nit-picking aimed at the scientific methodology used by Cornell's researchers. Why hadn't they measured the amount of Bt ingested by the dead butterflies? Why did they do their study in a laboratory instead of out in real farm fields?[69] (In fact, a separate study by scientists at Iowa State University *had* been conducted in real farm fields, with similar results.) The second line of attack involved rushing to sponsor a series of contrary studies. In November 1999—barely six months after the release of the Cornell study—the industry-funded Biotechnology Stewardship Research Group held a symposium to discuss the implications of its Monarch butterfly research, even though the research itself had barely begun. Prior to the meeting, the Biotechnology Industry Organization circulated a news release confidently predicting that "a panel of scientists is expected to conclude [that] genetically improved corn poses negligible harm to the Monarch butterfly population."[70]

The news release rather than the symposium itself served as the basis for most of the news coverage associated with the event. The *Chicago Tribune, Los Angeles Times, St. Louis Post-Dispatch,* and other papers published stories with headlines such as, "Scientists Discount Threat to Butterfly from Altered Corn."[71] This contrasted sharply with the observations of one of the few publications that actually sent a reporter to the meeting. "Luckily, Carol Yoon from the *New York Times* attended," recalls Rebecca Goldburg, a biologist with the Environmental Defense Fund who was also present. "During the afternoon, she stood up and said that she had just talked to her editors and that they had received a press release from industry stating that the meeting would conclude that Bt corn presented little risk to Monarchs. Carol asked if participants agreed with this conclusion. The answer was a clear 'No' from a number of researchers."[72]

"Far from culminating in a consensus," Yoon reported, "the day was marked by sometimes heated exchange and ended with some scientists concluding that the bioengineered corn was safer than had been feared while others said that it was premature to draw any such conclusion. . . . Many of the researchers emphasized that their results were preliminary, with many studies still far from complete. . . . Some researchers expressed concern that so many studies, still far from completion and none peer-reviewed or published, should be given such a public airing, in particular in a forum orchestrated by the industry whose product safety has been brought into question."[73]

In a follow-up story a week later, some of the scientists who partici-pated in the industry-funded event responded to these criticisms. "The sci-entists say part of the reason they chose to release preliminary data, some of the studies with as little as 10 percent of the work complete, was pres-sure from farmers seeking more information," the *Times* reported.[74]

This hasty approach to the airing of scientific results contrasts markedly with the treatment of "dear old Arpad Pusztai," whose 150 sec-onds on television brought immediate charges that he had violated an un-written scientific code by publicly discussing unpublished research. Pusztai's appearance prompted Monsanto's Colin Merritt to complain about the "unprofessional" way his findings had been made public. "You cannot go around releasing information of this kind unless it has been properly reviewed," Merritt complained.[75] In the months following Pusz-tai's suspension from the Rowett Research Institute, no fewer than four scientific panels were convened to attack his conclusions. Sir Robert May, the British government's chief scientist, described Pusztai's work as "garbage" and accused him of "violating every canon of scientific recti-tude." The critics were in no way appeased when Pusztai *did* publish his results in the *Lancet*.[76] Professor Ray Baker, head of the Biotechnology and Biological Sciences Research Council, immediately denounced the *Lancet* as "irresponsible" for publishing an "unworthy" paper, and the president of the British Royal Society attacked the journal for giving Pusztai's paper an "authenticity it does not deserve."[77] The editor of the *Lancet*, Richard Horton, even reported receiving a "very aggressive" phone call prior to publication from a senior member of the Royal Society, who called Hor-ton "immoral" and intimated that his job would be at risk if he published the paper.[78] These attacks on Pusztai's work were themselves broadcast through the news media rather than through the peer-reviewed journals where scientific debate is normally conducted.

Full-Court Press

In October 1999, to coincide with a two-day U.S. Senate Agriculture Committee hearing on ag biotech, the U.S. food industry launched the Alliance for Better Foods (ABF), its first public preemptive strike against an anti-GM consumer backlash. The alliance has its own website (www. betterfoods.org), which portrays genetic engineering as the key to a future cornucopia of nutritional abundance. ABF's members include the Grocery Manufacturers of America (GMA), the American Farm Bureau Federation, and 24 other trade associations representing virtually every segment of the food industry (except the organic foods sector).[79] It is run by the Washington office of BSMG Worldwide, a full-service PR firm whose clients include Monsanto, the Chemical Manufacturers Association, Procter & Gamble, Philip Morris, and numerous other large food, chemical and pharmaceutical corporations.[80]

The GMA is the driving force behind the Alliance for Better Foods, said GMA spokesperson Brian Sansoni.[81] The alliance doesn't include biotech companies or their trade association, the Biotechnology Industry Organization (BIO), he said, but was created to get the food industry "to speak from the same page" in support of the technology. "We didn't want the activists' misinformation and scare campaign to be the story—like what happened in Europe," he said.

Both critics and defenders of the technology now understand that the brewing public debate over transgenic food may involve even bigger stakes than they originally anticipated. The same vested interests that didn't trust the public enough to inform it that they were introducing genetically engineered food into the environment and grocery stores are now asking to be trusted as reliable experts on the question of whether this innovation is safe and good. Their fear—and the hope of activists on the other side of the issue—is that the debate on biotech foods could be the issue that awakens the public to the realization that government regulators are not presently functioning to safeguard the public's best interests.

Scientists like Arpad Pusztai, meanwhile, find themselves caught somewhere in the middle. Pusztai still believes in the potential promise of genetically modified foods, provided they are carefully tested before being marketed. "Everything in nature is a balance. Changes will bring good effects and bad effects, and you have to decide if it's worth it," he says. "In my opinion, in this case, it is not—certainly without testing first. We are

not talking about a delicate sort of issue where two scientists are dis-
agreeing. We are talking about our food."

Pusztai's own experience has left him doubtful that corporate and
government powers-that-be will do the right thing. "We are told there is
rigorous testing, but where is it? It is not published in any of the journals,"
he said.[82] "I have no regrets about speaking out. I did it for the simple reason that it would have taken me another two years at least to publish the
data. Meanwhile, all the stuff would have been on the supermarket
shelves. The politicians have been saying this bit of nonsense that GM
foods are the most rigorously tested food in the history of mankind. The
truth is different, however." He points to a June 2000 letter in *Science*
magazine by Spanish toxicologist Jose L. Domingo, who performed a computer search using the Medline and Toxline databases and could find only
eight published papers based on experiments related to health risks of
GM foods—and even two of those citations, Pusztai says, turned out to be
irrelevant.[83]

"You can count the number of relevant peer-reviewed papers on the
fingers of your hands," Pusztai says, "and that includes the two papers
from my laboratory that were published in the *Journal of Nutrition* in August 1999 and in the *Lancet* on October 13, 1999. I have a feeling that any
unbiased observer would say that this is a very poor record for an industry which is just about to save the world from famine and other calamities."

PART III THE EXPERTISE INDUSTRY

I n April 1999, the firm of Ernst & Young agreed to pay $185 million in one of the biggest out-of-court legal settlements ever paid by a financial consulting firm. According to the plaintiff, a bankrupt clothing retailer named Merry-Go-Round Enterprises Inc., Ernst & Young was guilty of "fraud, incompetence and crucial misrepresentations to the bankruptcy court." Brought in as a turnaround expert to help Merry-Go-Round stem its financial losses, Ernst & Young had actually helped push the company over the brink.[1]

"For years, we sold sleazy," explained Leonard Weinglass, the clothing chain's founder, describing the store's successful marketing mix of tank tops, slit miniskirts, and other risqué fashions for teenage girls. Somewhere down the line, however, Merry-Go-Round began to lose its way. Rapid expansion had left it overextended and losing money in droves. Its creditors and nearly everyone except Ernst & Young knew that the company would have to close down hundreds of its stores if it wanted to survive.

Instead of action, however, Ernst & Young frittered away months conducting studies, producing financial projections, and drafting proposals. Rather than closing stores, it recommended stocking up on merchandise and trying to increase sales. When Merry-Go-Round's chief executive disagreed, the law firm that had recommended Ernst & Young in the first place intervened to block his authority. By the time creditors finally pulled the plug, the company was more than $200 million in debt.

According to the *Wall Street Journal,* Ernst & Young's legal sin consisted of failing to disclose a hidden conflict of interest. "The law firm that recommended Ernst & Young and later intervened on its behalf had a business relationship with Ernst & Young—one that neither of them had disclosed to the bankruptcy court," the *Journal* reported. "Moreover, Ernst & Young had another business relationship, also undisclosed to the court, with the land-lord of some of the stores that could have been shuttered if there had been a quick round of closings." Rather than serve the needs of Merry-Go-Round, in other words, its advice had helped protect the interests of the landlords.[2]

When advising the business community, expert consultants like Ernst & Young have a legal and financial responsibility to inform their clients of any external entanglements that might influence their judgment and their ability to give unbiased, helpful advice. Failure to do so is a serious offense that carries dire penalties. Our society has evolved strong, detailed, and effective laws to protect the interests of businesses and their creditors. Failure to disclose a conflict of interest is only one of the requirements that can bring penalties down upon the head of a financial adviser. In fact, failure to disclose *any* risk factor that might influence the decision of a reasonable investor is regarded as fraud and can be punished not only with fines but with actual jail time.

No such standard applies, however, to the experts who inundate the general public with advice on other matters. Neither they nor the journalists who rely on their punditry feel much need to inquire into possible conflicts of interest, or to disclose them when they exist.

The experts who appear on the evening news and other public affairs programs come from prominent and not-so-prominent universities, think tanks with impressive-sounding names such as the Statistical Assessment Service or the National Center for Policy Analysis, "white hat" nonprofit organizations such as the American Cancer Society or the American Medical Association, and research journals such as the *New England Journal of Medicine*. Many experts are closely tied to powerful interest groups—typically government, industry, or professional bodies. These interest groups provide them with jobs, access to power and status, training, ability to publish their work in professional and academic journals, and other benefits. Affiliation with these organizations also serves to accredit the experts, enhancing their credibility in the eyes of the media and the public. Establishment experts also often have some degree of power to suppress the ideas of their critics in quiet, behind-the-scenes ways by preventing their work from being published in key journals or otherwise keeping their views from receiving prominent public airing.[3]

8

The Best Science
Money Can Buy

*Science has a face, a house, and a price; it is
important to ask who is doing science, in
what institutional context, and at what cost.
Understanding such things can give us
insight into why scientific tools are sharp for
certain types of problems and dull for others.*

—Robert Proctor, *Cancer Wars*[1]

According to historian Stephen Mason, science has its historical roots in two primary sources: "Firstly, the technical
tradition, in which practical experiences and skills were handed on and developed from one generation to another; and secondly, the spiritual tradition, in which human aspirations and ideas were passed on and
augmented." The technical tradition is the basis for the claim that science
provides useful ways of manipulating the material world. The spiritual
tradition is the basis for the claim that science can *explain* the world in
"objective," unbiased terms. Sometimes, however, these two traditions are
at odds.

Modern science considers itself "scientific" because it adheres to a
certain methodology. It uses quantitative methods and measurable phenomena; its data is empirically derived and verifiable by others through experiments that can be reproduced; and, finally, its practitioners are
impartial. Whereas ideological thinkers promulgate dogmas and defend
them in the face of evidence to the contrary, scientists work with "hy-
potheses" that they modify whenever the evidence dictates.

The standard description of the scientific method makes it sound like an almost machinelike process for sifting and separating truth from error. The method is typically described as involving the following steps:

1. Observe and describe some phenemenon.

2. Form a hypothesis to explain the phenemonon and its relationship to other known facts, usually through some kind of mathematical formula.

3. Use the hypothesis to make predictions.

4. Test those predictions by experiments or further observations to see if they are correct.

5. If not, reject or revise the hypothesis.

"Recognizing that personal and cultural beliefs influence both our perceptions and our interpretations of natural phenomena, we aim through the use of standard procedures and criteria to minimize those influences when developing a theory," explains University of Rochester physics professor Frank Wolfs. "The scientific method attempts to minimize the influence of bias or prejudice in the experimenter when testing a hypothesis or a theory." One way to minimize the influence of bias is to have several independent experimenters test the hypothesis. If it survives the hurdle of multiple experiments, it may rise to the level of an accepted theory, but the scientific method requires that the hypothesis be ruled out or modified if its predictions are incompatible with experimental tests. In science, Wolfs says, "experiment is supreme."[2]

Experience shows, however, that this commonly accepted description of the scientific method is often a myth. Not only is it a myth, it is a fairly recent myth, first elaborated in the late 1800s by statistician Karl Pearson.[3] Copernicus did not use the scientific method described above, nor did Sir Isaac Newton or Charles Darwin. The French philosopher and mathematician René Descartes is often credited with ushering in the age of scientific inquiry with his "Discourse on the Method of Rightly Conducting the Reason and Seeking the Truth in the Sciences," but the method of Descartes bears little relation to the steps described above. The molecular structure of benzene was first hypothesized not in a laboratory but in a dream. Many theories do not originate through some laborious process of formulating and modifying a hypothesis, but through sudden moments of inspiration. The actual thought processes of scientists are richer, more complex, and less machinelike in their inevitability than the standard model suggests. Science is a human endeavor, and real-world scientists approach their work with a combination of imagination, creativity, speculation, prior knowledge, library research, perseverance, and, in some cases, blind luck—the same combination of intellectual resources, in short, that scientists and nonscientists alike use in trying to solve problems.

The myth of a universal scientific method glosses over many far-from-pristine realities about the way scientists work in the real world. There is no mention, for example, of the time that a modern researcher spends writing grant proposals; coddling department heads, corporate donors, and government bureaucrats; or engaging in any of the other activities that are necessary to obtain research funding. Although the scientific method acknowledges the possibility of bias on the part of an *individual* scientist, it does not provide a way of countering the effects of *systemwide* bias. "In a field where there is active experimentation and open communication among members of the scientific community, the biases of individuals or groups may cancel out, because experimental tests are repeated by different scientists who may have different biases," Wolfs states. But what if different scientists share a *common* bias? Rather than canceling it out, they may actually reinforce it.

The standard description of the scientific method also tends to idealize the degree to which scientists are even capable of accurately observing and measuring the phenomena they study. "Anyone who has done much research knows only too well that he never seems to be able himself to reproduce the beautiful curves and straight lines that appear in published texts and papers," admits British biologist Gordon D. Hunter. "In fact, scientists who would be most insulted if I accused them of cheating usually select their best results only, not the typical ones, for publication; and some slightly less rigorous in their approach will find reasons for rejecting an inconvenient result. I well remember when my colleague David Vaird and I were working with a famous Nobel Prize winner (Sir Hans Krebs himself) on bovine ketosis. The results from four cows were perfect, but the fifth wretched cow behaved quite differently. Sir Hans shocked David by stating that there were clearly additional factors of which we were ignorant affecting the fifth cow, and it should be removed from the analysis. . . . Such subterfuges rarely do much harm, but it is an easy step to rejecting whole experiments or parts of experiments by convincing oneself that there were reasons that we can identify or guess at for it giving 'the wrong result.' "[4]

The idea that all scientific experiments are replicated to keep the process honest is also something of a myth. In reality, the number of findings from one scientist that get checked by others is quite small. Most scientists are too busy, research funds are too limited, and the pressure to produce new work is too great for this type of review to occur very often. What occurs instead is a system of "peer review," in which panels of experts are convened to pass judgment on the work of other researchers. Peer review is used mainly in two situations: during the grant approval process to decide which research should get funding, and after the research has been completed to determine whether the results should be accepted for publication in a scientific journal.

Like the myth of the scientific method, peer review is also a fairly new phenomenon. It began as an occasional, ad hoc practice during the middle of the nineteenth century but did not really become established until World War I, when the federal government began supporting scientists through the National Research Council. As government support for science increased, it became necessary to develop a formal system for deciding which projects should receive funding.

In some ways, the system of peer review functions like the antithesis of the scientific method described above. Whereas the scientific method assumes that "experiment is supreme" and purports to eliminate bias, peer review deliberately *imposes* the bias of peer reviewers on the scientific process, both before and after experiments are conducted. This does not necessarily mean that peer review is a bad thing. In some ways, it is a necessary response to the empiricist limitations of the scientific method as it is commonly defined. However, peer review can also institutionalize conflicts of interest and a certain amount of dogmatism. In 1994, the General Accounting Office of the U.S. Congress studied the use of peer review in government scientific grants and found that reviewers often know applicants and tend to give preferential treatment to the ones they know.[5] Women and minorities have charged that the system constitutes an "old boys' network" in science. The system also stacks the deck in favor of older, established scientists and against younger, more independent researchers. The process itself creates multiple opportunities for conflict of interest. Peer reviewers are often anonymous, which means that they do not have to face the researchers whose work they judge. Moreover, the realities of science in today's specialized world means that peer reviewers are often either colleagues or competitors of the scientist whose work they review. In fact, observes science historian Horace Freeland Judson, "the persons most qualified to judge the worth of a scientist's grant proposal or the merit of a submitted research paper are precisely those who are the scientist's closest competitors."[6]

"The problem with peer review is that we have good evidence on its deficiencies and poor evidence on its benefits," the *British Medical Journal* observed in 1997. "We know that it is expensive, slow, prone to bias, open to abuse, possibly anti-innovatory, and unable to detect fraud. We also know that the published papers that emerge from the process are often grossly deficient."[7]

In theory, the process of peer review offers protection against scientific errors and bias. In reality, it has proven incapable of filtering out the influence of government and corporate funders, whose biases often affect research outcomes.

Publication Bias

If you want to know just how craven some scientists can be, the archives of the tobacco industry offer a treasure trove of examples. Thanks to whistle-blowers and lawsuits, millions of pages of once-secret industry documents have become public and are freely available over the Internet. In 1998, for example, documents came to light regarding an industry-sponsored campaign in the early 1990s to plant sympathetic letters and articles in influential medical journals. Tobacco companies had secretly paid 13 scientists a total of $156,000 simply to write a few letters to influential medical journals. One biostatistician, Nathan Mantel of American University in Washington, received $10,000 for writing a single, eight-paragraph letter that was published in the *Journal of the American Medical Association*. Cancer researcher Gio Batta Gori received $20,137 for writing four letters and an opinion piece to the *Lancet*, the *Journal of the National Cancer Institute*, and the *Wall Street Journal*—nice work if you can get it, especially since the scientists didn't even have to write the letters themselves. Two tobacco-industry law firms were available to do the actual drafting and editing. All the scientists really had to do was sign their names at the bottom. "It's a systematic effort to pollute the scientific literature. It's not a legitimate scientific debate," observed Dr. Stanton

Glantz, a professor of medicine at the University of California–San Francisco and longtime tobacco industry critic. "Basically, the drill is that they hired people to write these letters, then they cited the letters as if they were independent, disinterested scientists writing."[8]

In some cases, scientists were paid to write not just letters but entire scientific articles. In at least one case, the going rate for this service was $25,000, which was paid to one scientist for writing an article for the publication *Risk Analysis*. The same fee went to former EPA official John Todhunter and tobacco consultant W. Gary Flamm for an article titled "EPA Process, Risk Assessment-Risk Management Issues," which they published in the *Journal of Regulatory Toxicology and Pharmacology*, where Flamm served as a member of the journal's editorial board. Not only did they fail to disclose that their article had been commissioned by the tobacco industry, journal editor C. Jelleff Carr says he "never asked that question, 'Were you paid to write that?' I think it would be almost improper for me to do it."[9]

The tobacco industry is hardly alone in attempting to influence the scientific publishing process. A similar example of industry influence came to light in 1999 regarding the diet–drug combo fen-phen (a combination of fenfluramine, dexfenfluramine, and phentermine), developed by Wyeth-Ayerst Laboratories. Wyeth-Ayerst had commissioned ghostwriters to write ten articles promoting fen-phen as a treatment for obesity. Two of the ten articles were actually published in peer-reviewed medical journals before studies linked fen-phen to heart valve damage and an often-fatal lung disease, forcing the company to pull the drugs from the market in September 1997. In lawsuits filed by injured fen-phen users, internal company documents were subpoenaed showing that Wyeth-Ayerst had also edited the draft articles to play down and occasionally delete descriptions of side effects associated with the drugs. The final articles were published under the names of prominent researchers, one of whom claimed later that he had no idea that Wyeth had commissioned the article on which his name appeared. "It's really deceptive," said Dr. Albert J. Stunkard of the University of Pennsylvania, whose article was published in the *American Journal of Medicine* in February 1996. "It sort of makes you uneasy."[10]

How did Stunkard's name end up on an article without his knowing who sponsored it? The process involved an intermediary hired by Wyeth-Ayerst called Excerpta Medica, Inc., which received $20,000 for each article. Excerpta's ghostwriters produced first-draft versions of the articles and then lined up well-known university researchers like Stunkard and paid them honoraria of $1,000 to $1,500 to edit the drafts and lend their names to the final work. Stunkard says Excerpta did not tell him that the honorarium originally came from Wyeth. One of the name-brand researchers even sent a letter back praising Excerpta's ghostwriting skills. "Let me congratulate you and your writer on an excellent and thorough review of the literature, clearly written," wrote Dr. Richard L. Atkinson, professor of medicine and nutritional science at the University of Wisconsin Medical School. "Perhaps I can get you to write all my papers for me! My only general comment is that this piece may make dexfenfluramine sound better than it really is."[11]

"The whole process strikes me as egregious," said Jerome P. Kassirer, then-editor of the *New England Journal of Medicine*—"the fact that Wyeth commissioned someone to write pieces that are favorable to them, the fact that they paid people to put their names on these things, the fact that people were willing to put their names on it, the fact that the journals published them without asking questions." Yet it would be a mistake to imagine that these failures of the scientific publishing system reflect greed or laziness on the part of the individuals involved. Naïveté might be a better word to describe the mind-set of the researchers who participate in this sort of arrangement. In any case, the Wyeth-Ayerst practice is not an isolated incident. "This is a common practice in the industry. It's not particular to us," said Wyeth spokesman Doug Petkus.

Medical editor Jenny Speicher agrees that the Wyeth-Ayerst case is not an aberration. "I used to work at *Medical Tribune*, a news publication for physicians," she said. "We had all these pharmaceutical and PR companies calling, asking what are the writing guidelines for articles, because they wanted to have their flack doctors write articles, or assign a freelance writer to write under a doctor's name. I've even been offered these writing jobs myself. We always told them that all of our articles had to have comments from independent researchers, so of course they weren't interested. But they kept on trying."

"Pharmaceutical companies hire PR firms to promote drugs," agrees science writer Norman Bauman. "Those promotions include hiring freelance writers to write articles for peer-reviewed journals, under the byline of doctors whom they also hire. This has been discussed extensively in the medical journals and also in the *Wall Street Journal,* and I personally know people who write these journal articles. The pay is OK—about $3,000 for a six- to ten-page journal article."

Even the *New England Journal of Medicine*—often described as the world's most prestigious medical journal—has been involved in controversies regarding hidden economic interests that shape its content and conclusions. In 1986, for example, *NEJM* published one study and rejected another that reached opposite conclusions about the antibiotic amoxicillin, even though both studies were based on the same data. Scientists involved with the first, favorable study had received $1.6 million in grants from the drug manufacturer, while the author of the critical study had refused corporate funding. *NEJM* proclaimed the pro-amoxicillin study the "authorized" version, and the author of the critical study underwent years of discipline and demotions from the academic bureaucracy at his university, which also took the side of the industry-funded scientist. Five years later, the dissenting scientist's critical study finally found publication in the *Journal of the American Medical Association,* and other large-scale testing of children showed that those who took amoxicillin actually experienced *lower* recovery rates than children who took no medicine at all.[12] In 1989, *NEJM* came under fire again when it published an article downplaying the dangers of exposure to asbestos while failing to disclose that the author had ties to the asbestos industry.[13] In 1996, a similar controversy emerged when the journal ran an editorial touting the benefits of diet drugs, again failing to note that the editorial's authors were paid consultants for companies that sell the drugs.[14]

In November 1997, questions of conflict of interest arose again when the *NEJM* published a scathing review of Sandra Steingraber's book *Living Downstream: An Ecologist Looks at Cancer and the Environment.* Authored by Jerry H. Berke, the review described Steingraber as "obsessed . . . with environmental pollution as the cause of cancer" and accused her of "oversights and simplifications . . . biased work . . . notoriously poor scholarship. . . . The focus on environmental pollution and agricultural chemicals to explain human cancer has simply not been fruitful nor given rise to useful preventive strategies. . . . *Living Downstream* frightens, at times misinforms, and then scorns genuine efforts at cancer prevention through lifestyle change. The objective of *Living Downstream* appears ultimately to be controversy."[15]

Berke was identified alongside the review as "Jerry H. Berke, MD, MPH." The *NEJM* failed to disclose, however, that Berke was director of toxicology for W. R. Grace, one of the world's largest chemical manufacturers and a notorious polluter. A leading manufacturer of asbestos-containing building products, W. R. Grace has been a defendant in several thousand asbestos-related cancer lawsuits and has paid millions of dollars in related court judgments. It is probably best known as the company that polluted the drinking water of the town of Woburn, Massachusetts, and later paid an $8 million out-of-court settlement to the families of seven Woburn children and one adult who contracted leukemia after drinking contaminated water. During the Woburn investigation, Grace was caught in two felony lies to the U.S. Environmental Protection Agency.

When questioned about its failure to identify Berke's affiliation, the *New England Journal of Medicine* offered contradictory and implausible explanations. First it attributed the omission to an "administrative oversight" and claimed that it didn't know about Berke's affiliation with W. R. Grace. Later, a journal representative admitted that they *did* know but said they thought Grace was a "hospital or research institute." If so, this ignorance would itself be remarkable, since the *NEJM* is located in Boston, and Grace had been the subject of more than a hundred news stories in the *Boston Globe* between 1994 and 1997. Moreover, *NEJM* editor Marcia Angell lives in Cambridge, Massachusetts, the world headquarters of W. R. Grace. Her home is only eight miles away from Woburn, whose leukemia lawsuit is also the central subject of *A Civil Action*, Jonathan Harr's best-selling book that was made into a movie starring John Travolta. During the months immediately preceding the publication of Berke's review, in fact, the film crew for *A Civil Action* was working in the Boston area and was itself the subject of numerous prominent news stories.[16]

In response to criticism of these lapses, *NEJM* editor Jerome P. Kassirer insisted that his journal's conflict-of-interest policy was "the tightest in the business."[17] The sad fact is that this boast is probably correct. In 1996, Sheldon Krimsky of Tufts University did a study of journal disclosures that dug into the industry connections of the authors of 789 scientific papers published by 1,105 researchers in 14 leading life science and biomedical journals. In 34 percent of the papers, at least one of the chief authors had an identifiable financial interest connected to the research, and Krimsky observed that the estimate of 34 percent was probably lower than the true level of financial conflict of interest, since he was unable to check if the researchers owned stock or had received consulting fees from the companies involved in commercial applications of their research.

None of these financial interests were disclosed in the journals, where readers could see them.[18] In 1999, a larger study by Krimsky examined 62,000 articles published in 210 different scientific journals and found that only one half of one percent of the articles included information about the authors' research-related financial ties. Although all of the journals had a formal requirement for disclosure of conflicts of interest, 142 of the journals had not published a single disclosure during 1997, the year under study.[19]

Corporate-sponsored scientific symposiums provide another means for manipulating the content of medical journals. In 1992, the *New England Journal of Medicine* itself published a survey of 625 such symposiums which found that 42 percent of them were sponsored by a single pharmaceutical sponsor. There was a correlation, moreover, between single-company sponsorship and practices that commercialize or corrupt the scientific review process, including symposiums with misleading titles designed to promote a specific brand-name product. "Industry-sponsored symposia are promotional in nature and . . . journals often abandon the peer-review process when they publish symposiums," the survey concluded.[20] Drummond Rennie, a deputy editor of the *Journal of the American Medical Association,* describes how the process works in plainer language:

> I'm the advertising guy for the drug. I tell a journal I will give them $100,000 to have a special issue on that drug. Plus I'll give the journal so much per reprint, and I'll order a lot of reprints. I'll select the editor and all the authors. I phone everyone who has written good things about that drug. I say, "I'll fly you and your wife first class to New Orleans for a symposium. I'll put your paper in the special issue of the journal, and you'll have an extra publication for your c.v." Then I'll put a reprint of that symposium on some doctor's desk and say, "Look at this marvelous drug."[21]

Does Money Matter?

As these examples illustrate, many of the factors that bias scientific results are considerably more subtle than outright bribery or fraud. "There is distortion that causes publication bias in little ways, and scientists just don't understand that they have been influenced," Rennie says. "There's influence everywhere, on people who would steadfastly deny it."[22] Scientists can be naive about politics and other external factors shaping their work and become indignant at the suggestion that their results are shaped by their funding. But science does not occur in a vacuum. In studying animal populations, biologists use the term "selection pressure" to describe the influence that environmental conditions exert upon the survival of certain genetic traits over others. Within the population of scientists, a similar type of selection pressure occurs as industry and government support, combined with the vicissitudes of political fashion, determine which careers flourish and which languish. As David Ozonoff of the Boston University School of Medicine has observed, "One can think of an idea almost as one thinks of a living organism. It has to be continually nourished with the resources that permit it to grow and reproduce. In a hostile environment that denies it the material necessities, scientific ideas tend to languish and die."[23]

Like other human institutions, the development of the scientific enterprise has seen both advances and reversals and is exquisitely sensitive to the larger social environment in which it exists. Germany, for example, was a world leader in science in the nineteenth and early twentieth centuries but went into scientific decline with the rise of fascism. Under the Nazis, scientists were seen as too "cosmopolitan," and the idea of a culturally rooted "German science" transformed applied scientists into "folk practitioners," elevated astrology at the expense of astronomy, and impoverished the country's previously renowned institutions for the study of theoretical physics. Something similar happened in Soviet Russia when previously accepted theories in astronomy, chemistry, medicine, psychology, and anthropology were criticized on the grounds that they conflicted with the principles of Marxist materialism. The most notorious example in the Soviet case was the rise of Lysenkoism, which rejected the theories of Mendelian genetics with catastrophic results for Russian agriculture. In the United States, political and social movements have also given rise to a number of dubious scientific trends, including the "creation science" of Christian fundamentalists as well as such movements as parapsychology and scientology.

The most dramatic trend influencing the direction of science during the past century, however, has been its increasing dependence on funding from government and industry. Unlike the "gentleman scientists" of the nineteenth century who enjoyed financial independence that allowed them to explore their personal scientific interests with considerable freedom, today's mainstream scientists are engaged in expensive research that requires the support of wealthy funders. A number of factors have contributed to this reality, from the rise of big government to the militarization of scientific research to the emergence of transnational corporations as important patrons of research.

The Second World War marked a watershed in the development of these trends, with the demands of wartime production, military intelligence, and political mobilization serving as precursors to the "military-industrial complex" that emerged during the Cold War in the 1950s. World War II also inaugurated the era of what has become known as "big science." Previously, scientists for the most part had been people who worked alone or with a handful of assistants, pursuing the inquiries that fit their interests and curiosity. It was a less rigorous approach to science than we expect today, but it also allowed more creativity and independence. Physicist Percy Bridgman, whose major work was done before the advent of "big science," recalled that in those days he "felt free to pursue other lines of interest, whether experiment, or theory, or fundamental criticism. . . . Another great advantage of working on a small scale is that one gives no hostage to one's own past. If I wake up in the morning with a new idea, the utilization of which involves scrapping elaborate preparations already made, I am free to scrap what I have done and start off on the new and better line. This would not be possible without crippling loss of morale if one were working on a large scale with a complex organization." When World War II made large-scale, applied research a priority, Bridgman said, "the older men, who had previously worked on their own problems in their own laboratories, put up with this as a patriotic necessity, to be tolerated only while they must, and to be escaped from as soon as decent. But the younger men . . . had never experienced independent work and did not know what it was like."[24]

The Manhattan Project took "big science" to unprecedented new levels. In the process it also radically transformed the assumptions and social practices of science itself, as military considerations forced scientists to work under conditions of strict censorship. "The Manhattan Project was secret," observe Stephen Hilgartner, Richard Bell, and Rory O'Conner in *Nukespeak*, their study of atomic-age thinking and rhetoric. "Its cities were built in secret, its research was done in secret, its scientists traveled under assumed names, its funds were concealed from Congress, and its

existence was systematically kept out of the media. . . . Compartmental-
ization, or the restriction of knowledge about various aspects of the project to the 'compartments' in which the knowledge was being developed,
was central to this strategy. . . . Press censorship complemented com-
partmentalization."[25] President Truman described the development of the
atom bomb as "the greatest achievement of organized science in history."
It was also the greatest *regimentation* of science in history, and spawned
the need for further regimentation and more secrecy.

Prior to the development of the atomic bomb, the scientific community believed with few exceptions that its work was beneficial to humanity. "Earlier uses of science for the development of new and deadlier
weapons had, upon occasion, brought forth critical comments by individual scientists; here and there, uncommonly reflective scientists had raised
some doubts about the generalized philosophy of progress shared by most
of the scientific community, but it was only in the aftermath of Hiroshima
that large numbers of scientists were moved to reflect in sustained ways
on the moral issues raised by their own activities," notes historian Lewis
Coser.[26]

Even before the bombing of Japan, a group of atomic scientists had
tried unsuccessfully to persuade the U.S. government against its use. In its
aftermath, they began to publish the *Bulletin of the Atomic Scientists,* which
campaigned for civilian control of atomic energy. Some of its members
called for scientists to abstain from military work altogether. In the 1950s,
however, the Red Scare and McCarthyism were brought to bear against scientists who raised these sorts of questions. "Furthermore, as more and
more scientific research began to be sponsored by the government, many
scientists considered it 'dangerous' to take stands on public issues," Coser
notes. By 1961, some 80 percent of all U.S. funds for research and development were being provided directly or indirectly by the military or by
two U.S. agencies with strong military connections, the Atomic Energy
Commission and the National Aeronautics and Space Administration.[27]

The terrifying potential of the new weaponry became a pretext for permanently institutionalizing the policy of secrecy and "need-to-know" classification of scientific information that had begun with the Manhattan
Project. In 1947, the Atomic Energy Commission expanded its policy of
secrecy beyond matters of direct military significance by imposing secrecy
in regard to public relations or "embarrassment" issues as well as issues of
legal liability. When a deputy medical director at the Manhattan Project

tried to declassify reports describing World War II experiments that involved injecting plutonium into human beings, AEC officials turned down the request, noting that "the coldly scientific manner in which the results are tabulated and discussed would have a very poor effect on the public."[28]

Alvin Weinberg, director of the Oak Ridge National Laboratory from 1955 to 1973, bluntly laid out the assumptions of atomic-age science. In order to avert catastrophe, he argued, society needed "a military priesthood which guards against inadvertent use of nuclear weapons, which maintains what a priori seems to be a precarious balance between readiness to go to war and vigilance against human errors that would precipitate war."[29] He did not mean the word "priesthood" lightly or loosely. "No government has lasted continuously for 1,000 years: only the Catholic Church has survived more or less continuously for 2,000 years or so," he said. "Our commitment to nuclear energy is assumed to last in perpetuity—can we think of a national entity that possesses the resiliency to remain alive for even a single half-life of plutonium-239? A permanent cadre of experts that will retain its continuity over immensely long times hardly seems feasible if the cadre is a national body. . . . The Catholic Church is the best example of what I have in mind: a central authority that proclaims and to a degree enforces doctrine, maintains its own long-term social stability, and has connections to every country's own Catholic Church."[30]

The idea of a "central authority" that "proclaims and enforces doctrine" runs contrary, of course, to the spirit of intellectual freedom and scientific inquiry that led Galileo to defy the Catholic Church in his defense of Copernican astronomy. Weinberg's comments show how much the practice and philosophy of science had changed under the pressures of government bureaucracy and military secrecy. Instead of a process for asking questions, it had become a dogma, a set of answers imposed by what was becoming a de facto state religion.

Nuts About Nukes

Just as Edward Bernays had used the theories of Sigmund Freud to develop a theory of public relations based on the belief that the public was irrational and pliable, the Atomic Energy Commission also turned to mental health experts in an effort to consign the public to the psychiatric couch. In 1948, AEC commissioner Sumner T. Pike appealed to the American Psychiatric Association to "cool off anyone who seems hysterical about atomic energy."[31] In 1957, the World Health Organization convened a Study Group on Mental Health Aspects of the Peaceful Uses of Atomic Energy, in the hope that "the behavioural sciences can make a valuable and concrete contribution to the adaptation of mankind to the advent of atomic power" by using expert knowledge of "personality dynamics" to build "positive morale."[32] The study group, composed of psychiatrists, professors, and representatives of the AEC and the European nuclear industry, began from the premise that the public's "irrational fears, irrational hopes, or irrational tendencies" were an "abnormal emotional response to atomic energy" which was "quite unjustified. . . . Even if all the objective evidence were interpreted in the most pessimistic way possible, the weight of evidence would not justify anxiety in the present, and only vaguely and remotely in the future. Yet anxiety exists and persists to a quite extraordinary degree. This can only be accounted for by looking into the psychological nature of man himself."[33]

What was it about our human nature that made us so irrational about nuclear power? The study group concluded that its very power made adults "regress to more infantile forms of behavior," so that they acted like "the very young child first experiencing the world." The split atom, they said, somehow evoked primal fears related to such "everyday childhood situations . . . as feeding and excretion." Thus, "of all the fears rising from radiation, whether it be from atomic bomb fall-out or from nuclear plant mishap, it is the danger to food which is generally the most disquieting." The same principle also applied to nuclear waste: "As with feeding, so with excretion. Public concern with atomic waste disposal is quite out of proportion to its importance, from which there must be a strong inference that some of the fear of 'fall-out' derives from a symbolic association between atomic waste and body waste."[34]

"This explanation is the most ludicrous kind of dime-store Freudianism; it trivializes people's concern about fallout and nuclear war," observe Hilgartner et al. "But the study group was deadly serious about the richness of insight which this crude, narrow-minded analysis provided."[35] Indeed, after an accidental radiation release at the Windscale nuclear reactor in England, the government was forced to confiscate and dump milk contaminated with radioiodine. A psychiatrist on the study group explained the negative newspaper headlines that accompanied the dumping by commenting, "Obviously all the editors were breast fed." It was, to him, a perfect example of "regression."[36]

These analyses share a retreat from the empiricist notion that experts should begin first with evidence and reason from it to their conclusions. For the experts in charge of nuclear planning, the political goals came first, the evidence second. Anyone who thought otherwise could simply be diagnosed as neurotic.

From Military Secrets to Trade Secrets

"The expansion of university research in the 1950s was largely the result of support from the military," wrote Dorothy Nelkin in her 1984 book *Science as Intellectual Property.* "In the context of the times, most university scientists supported collaboration with military objectives, a collaboration they deemed crucial to the development of the nation's scientific abilities. However, even during this period, university-military relations were a source of nagging concern. Doubts turned to disenchantment during the Vietnam War."[37]

At the Massachusetts Institute of Technology, Professor George Rathjens observed that "a very large fraction" of the school's students were destined to find careers dependent on the military:

They don't know, when they enter as freshmen, what they will be doing when they graduate, of course. But, on a probabilistic basis, it is reasonable for them to assume they are very likely to be working in defense programs. And they surely can't foresee how that work will affect mankind's welfare, when they can't possibly predict whether they will be working on a particular kind of bomber, against whom it might be used, or whether in an unjust or a just war. But, they have to make decisions about whether or not they want to get into a particular profession when they are about 18 years old, and for many, those decisions will be virtually irrevocable. It is hard to get out. I have talked to many people, scientists and engineers, who were working around Route 128, the high technology community around Boston, who were desperate during the Vietnamese War to get out of the defense business. They had no options. They really had nowhere else to go. They could go out and sell vacuum cleaners, perhaps, but if they wanted to use the skills that they spent a lifetime acquiring, they didn't have much choice. I have a friend, who was one of the principal weapon designers at Los Alamos for many years.

At age 50 or so, he decided he really didn't want to make bombs any-more. He had had enough. What does a person like that do? There just aren't very many options for a man like that, at that age.[38]

By the 1960s, military programs had come to employ nearly a third of the scientists and engineers in the United States. The militarization of science had become, and remains, a central organizing condition of U.S. government–funded science research. Even in 1998, nearly a decade after the end of the Cold War, military research and development represented 53 percent of the U.S. federal R & D budget.

Even outside the scope of military programs, a top-down, command-driven rhetoric of science has seeped into many aspects of national life. Billion-dollar foundations and massive government research contracts became commonplace. University professors mastered the intricate rules of grantsmanship and learned to walk the narrow path between consultation and conflict of interest. As federal tax policies underwrote and shaped private giving, the distinction between public and private grants began to blur. Lyndon Johnson brought the concept of policy-oriented social science to new levels in the pursuit of *two* wars—the Vietnam War and the War on Poverty. Presidential chronicler Theodore White described the Johnson years as the "Golden age of the action intellectual," as experts were brought in "to shape our defenses, guide our foreign policy, redesign our cities, eliminate poverty, reorganize our schools."[39] A few years later, President Nixon would invoke the military metaphor again when he declared "war on cancer" in his 1971 State of the Union speech. Each of these wars came with their concomitant experts, whose job was to reassure the public with confident promises that inevitable victory was near at hand, that there was "light at the end of the tunnel."

The last quarter of the twentieth century saw the commercialization of big science, as the rise of the so-called "knowledge-based" industries—computers, telecommunications, and biotechnology—prompted a wide variety of corporate research initiatives. In 1970, federal government funding for research and development totaled $14.9 billion, compared to $10.4 billion from industry. By 1997, government expenditures were $62.7 billion, compared to $133.3 billion from industry. After adjusting for inflation, government spending had barely risen, while business spending more than tripled.[40] Much of this increase, moreover, took place through corporate partnerships with universities and other academic institutions, blurring the traditional line between private and public research. In 1980, industrial funding made up only 3.8 percent of the total research budget for U.S. universities. "Seldom controversial, it provided contacts and financial benefits usually only to individual faculty members, and on the whole it did not divert them from university responsibilities," Nelkin noted. However, declining public funding in many areas of research "left many faculty and university administrators receptive to, indeed, eager for industrial support, and inevitably less critical of the implications for the ownership and control of research."

First reluctantly and then eagerly, universities began to collaborate with industry in fields such as biotechnology, agriculture, chemistry, mining, energy, and computer science. "It is now accepted practice for scientists and institutions to profit directly from the results of academic research through various types of commercial ventures," Nelkin observed in her 1984 book,[41] and what was a noteworthy trend back then has since become a defining characteristic of university research. Between 1981 and 1995, the proportion of U.S. industry–produced articles that were coauthored with at least one academic researcher roughly doubled, from 21.6 percent to 40.8 percent. The increase was even more dramatic in the field of biomedical research, where the number of coauthored articles quadrupled.[42] According to the Association of American Medical Colleges, corporate sponsorship of university medical research has grown from about 5 percent in the early 1980s to as much as 25 percent in some places today.[43]

In 1999, the Department of Plant and Microbial Biology at the University of California–Berkeley signed an unprecedented five-year, $25 million agreement with the Novartis biotech firm of Switzerland. In exchange for the funding, the university promised that Novartis would have first bid on a third of the research discoveries developed by the department. "The Berkeley agreement has inspired other major American research universities to seek similar agreements with industry," noted the National Center for Public Policy and Higher Education.[44] But although the deal was popular with the department that received the money, it drew a different reaction from many of the professors in other departments. A survey conducted by the chairman of the university's College of Natural Resources showed that two-thirds of the faculty in that college disagreed with the terms of the contract.

"We fear that in our public university, a professor's ability to attract private investment will be more important than academic qualifications, taking away the incentives for scientists to be socially responsible," stated professors Miguel Altieri and Andrew Paul Gutierrez in a letter to the university's alumni magazine. Altieri's academic career has been devoted to the study of "biological control"—the discipline of controlling agricultural pests through means other than pesticides. He noted bitterly that while money from Novartis was pouring in, university funding for biological control research had been eliminated. "For more than 40 years we trained leaders in the world about biological control . . . A whole theory was established here, because pesticides cause major environmental problems," Altieri said.[45] Another researcher, UC–Berkeley anthropologist Laura Nader, said the Novartis contract "sent a chill especially over younger, untenured faculty. Word gets around early . . . over the proper relationship between researchers and industry in a university setting. A siege mentality sets in, reminiscent of the McCarthy period and the so-called Red Scare, except then it was government which could be called to account and was, and now this is as yet unaccountable large companies."[46]

Just as military funding for research carried with it a set of obligations that had nothing to do with the pursuit of knowledge, corporate funding has transformed scientific and engineering knowledge into commodities in the new "information economy," giving rise to an elaborate web of interlocking directorates between corporate and academic boardrooms. By the end of the 1990s, the ivory tower of academia had become "Enterprise U," as schools sought to cash in with licensing and merchandising of school logos and an endless variety of university–industry partnerships and "technology transfers," from business-funded research parks to fee-for-service work such as drug trials carried out on university campuses. Professors, particularly in high-tech fields, were not only allowed but encouraged to moonlight as entrepreneurs in start-up businesses that attempted to convert their laboratory discoveries into commercial products. Just as science had earlier become a handmaiden to the military, now it was becoming a servant of Wall Street.

"We're adopting a business instead of an economic model," said chemist Brian M. Tissue of Virginia Polytechnic Institute and State University. "The rationale is collaborations are good because they bring in money. People say we can have better facilities and more students, and it's a win-win situation, but it's not. There *can* be benefits, but you're not training students anymore; you're bringing them in to work a contract. The emphasis shifts from what's good for the student to the bottom line."[47]

"More and more we see the career trajectories of scholars, especially of scientists, rise and fall not in relation to their intellectually-judged peer standing, but rather in relation to their skill at selling themselves to those, especially in the biomedical field, who have large sums of money to spend on a well-marketed promise of commercial viability," observed Martin Michaelson, an attorney who has represented Harvard University and a variety of other leading institutions of higher education. "It is a kind of gold rush," Michaelson said at a 1999 symposium sponsored by the American Association for the Advancement of Science. "More and more we see incentives to hoard, not disseminate, new knowledge; to suppress, not publish, research results; to titillate prospective buyers, rather than to make full disclosure to academic colleagues. And we see today, more than ever before, new science first—generally, very carefully, and thinly—described in the fine print of initial public offerings and SEC filings, rather than in the traditional, fuller loci of academic communication."[48]

Industry–academic entanglements can take many forms, some of which are not directly related to funding for specific research. Increasingly, scientists are being asked to sit on the boards of directors of for-profit companies, a service that requires relatively little time but can pay very well— often in excess of $50,000 per year. Other private-sector perks may include gifts to researchers of lab equipment or cash, or generous payment for speeches, travel, and consulting.

Corporate funding creates a culture of secrecy that can be as chilling to free academic inquiry as funding from the military. Instead of government censorship, we hear the language of commerce: nondisclosure agreements, patent rights, intellectual property rights, intellectual capital. Businesses frequently require scientists to keep "proprietary information" under wraps so that competitors can't horn in on their trade secrets. "If we could not maintain secrecy, research would be of little value," argued the late Arthur Bueche, vice president for research at General Electric. "Research properly leads to patents that protect ideas, but were it not for secrecy, it would be difficult to create a favorable patent position."[49]

In 1994 and 1995, researchers led by David Blumenthal at the Massachusetts General Hospital surveyed more than 3,000 academic researchers involved in the life sciences and found that 64 percent of their respondents reported having some sort of financial relationship with industry. They also found that scientists with industry relationships were more likely to delay or withhold publication of their data. Their study, published by the *Journal of the American Medical Association,* found that during the three years prior to the survey, 20 percent of researchers reported delaying publication of their research results for more than six months. The reasons cited for delaying publication included the desire to patent applications from their discovery and a desire by some researchers to "slow the dissemination of undesired results." The practice of withholding publication or refusing to share data with other scientists was particularly common among biotechnology researchers.[50]

"It used to be that if you published you could ask about results, reagents—now you have these confidentiality agreements," said Nobel Prize–winning biochemist Paul Berg, a professor of biochemistry at Stanford University. "Sometimes if you accept a grant from a company, you have to include a proviso that you won't distribute anything except with its okay. It has a negative impact on science."

In 1996, Steven Rosenberg, chief of surgery at the U.S. National Cancer Institute, observed that secrecy in research "is underappreciated, and it's holding back medical cancer research—it's holding back my research."

First, Do No Harmful Publicity

The problem of secrecy in science is particularly troubling when it involves conflicts of interest between a company's marketing objectives and the public's right to know. When research results are not to a sponsor's liking, the company may use heavy-handed tactics to suppress them—even if doing so comes at the expense of public health and the common good.

One such case came to light in 1997 regarding the work of Betty Dong, a researcher at the University of California. In the late 1980s, the Boots Pharmaceutical company took an interest in Dong's work after she published a limited study which suggested that Synthroid, a thyroid medication manufactured by Boots, was superior to drugs produced by the company's competitors. Boots offered $250,000 to finance a large-scale study that would confirm these preliminary findings. To the company's dismay, however, the larger study, which Dong completed in 1990, contradicted her earlier findings and showed that Synthroid was no more effective than the cheaper drugs made by Boots's competitors. What followed was a seven-year battle to discredit Dong and prevent publication of her work. The contract Dong and her university had signed with the company gave it exclusive access to the prepublished results of the study as well as final approval over whether it would ever be published. The study sat on the shelf for five years while Boots waged a campaign to discredit Dong and the study, bombarding the chancellor and other university officials with allegations of unethical conduct and quibbles over the study's method, even though the company itself had previously approved the method. In 1994, Dong submitted a paper based on her work to the *Journal of the American Medical Association.* It was accepted for publication and already set in type when the company invoked its veto right, forcing her to withdraw it.[51]

In 1995, Boots was purchased by Knoll Pharmaceutical, which continued to suppress Dong's conclusions. While she remained unable to publish her own results, Knoll published a reinterpretation of her data under the authorship of Gilbert Mayor, a doctor employed by the company. Mayor published his reanalysis of Dong's data without acknowledging her or her research associates, a practice that the *Journal of the American Medical Association* would later characterize as publishing "results hijacked from those who did the work."[52] After further legal battles and an exposé of Knoll's heavy-handed tactics in the *Wall Street Journal,* Dong was finally allowed to publish her own version of the study in *JAMA* in 1997—nearly seven years after its completion. During those seven years, Boots/Knoll had used Synthroid's claims of superiority to dominate the $600-million-per-year synthetic thyroid market. The publication of her work in *JAMA* prompted a class-action lawsuit on the part of Synthroid users who had been effectively duped into paying an estimated $365 million per year more than they needed for their medication. Knoll settled the lawsuit out of court for $98 million—a fraction of the extra profits it had made during the years it spent suppressing Dong's study.[53]

Another attempt to suppress research occurred in 1995, when liver specialist Nancy Olivieri at the University of Toronto wanted to warn patients about the toxic side effects of a drug she was testing. The Canadian drug giant Apotex, which was sponsoring the study in hopes of marketing the drug, told her to keep quiet, citing a nondisclosure agreement that she had signed. When Olivieri alerted her patients anyway and published her concerns in the *New England Journal of Medicine,* Apotex threatened her with legal action and she was fired from her hospital, a recipient of hundreds of thousands of dollars each year in research funding from Apotex.

In 1997, David Kern, an occupational health expert at Brown University, discovered eight cases of a new, deadly lung disease among workers at a Microfibres, Inc., a manufacturer of finely cut nylon flock based in Pawtucket, Rhode Island. Microfibres tried to suppress Kern's finding, citing a confidentiality agreement that he had signed at the time of an educational visit to the company more than a year before the start of his research. When Kern spoke out anyway, administrators at the hospital and university where he worked (a recipient of charitable contributions from Microfibres) insisted that he withdraw a previously submitted scientific communiqué about the disease outbreak and that he cease providing medical care to his patients who worked at the company. Kern's program—the state's only occupational health center—was subsequently closed, and his job was eliminated.[54] Even more disturbing was the response of many of his research colleagues. "There were courageous folks who stood up for me, but most looked the other way," he said. "I'm mightily discouraged by the failure of the community to do more."[55]

In 1999, *JAMA* editor Drummond Rennie complained that the influence of private funding on medical research has created "a race to the ethical bottom." Known cases of suppression may be only the tip of the iceberg. "The behavior of universities and scientists is sad, shocking, and frightening," Rennie said. "They are seduced by industry funding, and frightened that if they don't go along with these gag orders, the money will go to less rigorous institutions."[56]

Beyond the problem of outright fraud and suppression, moreover, there is a larger and more pervasive problem: the systemwide bias that industry funding creates among researchers in commercially profitable fields. "Virtually every academic in biotechnology is involved in exploiting it commercially," says Orville Chapman of the University of California at Los Angeles. "We've lost our credentials as unbiased on such subjects as cloning or the modification of living things, and we seem singularly reluctant to think it through."[57]

Predetermined Outcomes

A host of techniques exist for manipulating research protocols to produce studies whose conclusions fit their sponsor's predetermined interests.

These techniques include adjusting the time of a study (so that toxic effects do not have time to emerge), subtle manipulations of target and control groups or dosage levels, and subjective interpretations of complex data. Often such methods stop short of outright fraud, but lead to predictable results. "Usually associations that sponsor research have a fairly good idea what the outcome will be, or they won't fund it," says Joseph Hotchkiss of Cornell University. In *Tainted Truth: The Manipulation of Fact in America,* author Cynthia Crossen noted the striking correspondence between the results obtained through published research and the financial interests of its sponsors:

> The consistency of research support for the sponsor's desired outcome intrigued Richard Davidson, a general internist and associate professor of medicine at the University of Florida. "It struck me that every time I read an article about a drug company study, it never found the company's drug inferior to what it was being compared to," Davidson says. He decided to test that impression by reviewing 107 published studies comparing a new drug against a traditional therapy. Davidson confirmed what he had suspected—studies of new drugs sponsored by drug companies were more likely to favor those drugs than studies supported by noncommercial entities. In not a single case was a drug or treatment manufactured by the sponsoring company found inferior to another company's product.[58]

When other researchers have examined the link between funding sources and research outcomes, they have reached conclusions similar to Davidson's:

- In 1994, researchers in Boston studied the relationship between funding and reported drug performance in published trials of anti-inflammatory drugs used in the treatment of arthritis. They reviewed 56 drug trials and found that in every single case, the manufacturer-associated drug was reported as being equal or superior in efficacy and toxicity to the comparison drug. "These claims of superiority, especially in regard to side effects, are often not supported by the trial data," they added. "These data raise concerns about selective publication or biased interpretation of results in manufacturer-associated trials."[59]

- In 1996, researchers Mildred K. Cho and Lisa A. Bero compared studies of new drug therapies and found that 98 percent of the studies funded by a drug's maker reached favorable conclusions about its safety and efficacy, compared to 76 percent of studies funded by independent sources.[60]

- In 1998, the *New England Journal of Medicine* published a study that examined the relationship between drug-industry funding and research conclusions about calcium-channel blockers, a class of drugs used to treat high blood pressure. There are safety concerns about the use of calcium-channel blockers because of research showing that they present a higher risk of heart attacks than other older and cheaper forms of blood pressure medication such as diuretics and beta-blockers. The *NEJM* study examined 70 articles on channel blockers and classified them into three categories: favorable, neutral, and critical. It found that 96 percent of the authors of favorable articles had financial ties to manufacturers of calcium-channel blockers, compared with 60 percent of the neutral authors and 37 percent of the critical authors. Only two of the 70 articles disclosed the authors' corporate ties.[61]

- In October 1999, researchers at Northwestern University in Chicago studied the relationship between funding sources and conclusions reached by studies of new cancer drugs and found that studies sponsored by drug companies were nearly eight times less likely to report unfavorable conclusions than studies paid for by nonprofit organizations.[62]

Drug research is not the only field in which this pattern of funding-related bias can be detected. In 1996, journalists Dan Fagin and Marianne Lavelle reviewed recent studies published in major scientific journals regarding the safety of four chemicals: the herbicides alachlor and atrazine, formaldehyde, and perchloroethylene, the carcinogenic solvent used for dry-cleaning clothes. When non-industry scientists did the studies, 60 percent returned results *unfavorable* to the chemicals involved, whereas industry-funded scientists came back with *favorable* results 74 percent of the time. Fagin and Lavelle observed a particularly strong biasing influence with respect to agribusiness financing for research related to farm weed control. "Weed scientists—a close-knit fraternity of researchers in industry, academia, and government—like to call themselves 'nozzleheads' or 'spray and pray guys,' " they stated. "As the nicknames suggest, their focus is usually much narrower than weeds. As many of its leading practitioners admit, weed science almost always means herbicide science, and herbicide science almost always means herbicide-justification science. Using their clout as the most important source of research dollars, chemical companies have skillfully wielded weed scientists to ward off the EPA, organic farmers, and others who want to wean American farmers away from their dependence on atrazine, alachlor, and other chemical weedkillers."[63]

Sometimes industry-funded studies become so self-promotional that they seem almost like parodies. In May 1998, the prestigious Kinsey Institute for Research in Sex, Gender and Reproduction teamed with the psychology department of Indiana University to study the effect of odor on women's sexual arousal. "This is a complex area," explained research leader Cynthia Graham in describing her study, which was sponsored by the Olfactory Research Fund, an organization financed by the perfume and cologne industry. Described by the *Milwaukee Journal Sentinel* as a "rigorous experiment," the study asked 33 women to view an erotic movie or engage in sexual fantasy, while researchers measured physical changes to their genitals. To test the effect of fragrance on arousal, the experimenters had the women wear a necklace scented with either women's perfume, men's cologne, or water. "The strongest, scientifically significant finding from the study was that male cologne markedly increased sexual arousal among women in the two days after the end of a woman's menstrual period," the *Journal Sentinel* reported.[64]

The public today is bombarded with scientific information regarding the safety and efficacy of everything from drugs to seat belts to children's toys. Eating garlic bread brings families closer together, says research sponsored by Pepperidge Farms bakeries, which makes frozen garlic bread. Eating oat bran lowers cholesterol, according to research sponsored by Quaker Oats. Eating chocolate may *prevent* cavities, says the Princeton Dental Resource Center, which is financed by the M&M/Mars candy company and is not a part of Princeton University. A daily glass of red wine reduces your risk of heart disease, say the doctors hired by the liquor industry. Chromium picolinate taken as a dietary supplement will help you burn off fat, says the dietary supplement industry. Zinc lozenges might shorten the duration of the common cold, reports a researcher who happens to hold 9,000 shares of stock in a zinc lozenge company.

Much of this information is confusing and contradictory. Sometimes the contradictions reflect genuine disagreements, but often they simply mirror the opposing interests of different companies and industries. Wearing sunscreen at the beach is important to avoid skin cancer, say doctors affiliated with Partners for Sun Protection, an organization sponsored by Schering-Plough, the pharmaceutical company that makes Coppertone sun lotion. On the other hand, studies sponsored by the International Smart Tan Network, a trade group representing tanning salons, claim that "regular tanning sessions could prevent as many as 30,000 cancer deaths every year in the United States." According to the ISTN, "legitimate research" shows that "giant pharmaceutical firms" and "dermatology industry lobbyists" have fomented unwarranted "paranoia" about tanning-related skin cancers.

When covering these topics, journalists have a responsibility to do more than present a source simply as "a scientist from such-and-such university." The public needs to know the context with which to weigh the information it receives. Does the scientist or other expert receive any funding from companies with a stake in the topic? Are there other conflicts of interest? Is there a pattern to the expert's past pronouncements or affiliations that suggests a particular ideological bent? Do the expert's opinions match or contradict the opinions of the majority of other experts on the subject at hand? These questions deserve to be answered, but are rarely even asked.

9

The Junkyard Dogs

Unfortunately, and increasingly today, one can find examples of junk science that compromise the integrity of the field of science and, at the same time, create a scare environment where unnecessary regulations on industry in general, and on the consumer products industry in particular, are rammed through without respect to rhyme, reason, effect or cause.

—Michael A. Miles, former CEO of the Philip Morris tobacco company[1]

Given the prominent role that science plays in modern society, it is hardly surprising that debates should arise over its conclusions and methods. Some of the worst atrocities of the past century have been perpetrated in the name of science, including experiments with "scientific socialism," the racist science of eugenics, and the polluting depredations of modern industry. Major corporations and petty hustlers alike use the mantle of science to market all kinds of potions and remedies, many of which have no demonstrable efficacy and some of which are harmful. The history of psychiatry and the other social sciences is also riddled with scientific-sounding explanations for human behavior, on the basis of which innocent people have been sterilized, lobotomized, drugged against their will, or imprisoned.

The concept of "junk science," however, is a particular term coined by corporate attorneys, lobbyists, PR firms, and industry-funded think tanks. It has very little to do with the quality of the research in question. In the hotly contested terrain of regulatory and liability law, "junk science" is the term that corporate defenders apply to any research, no matter how rigorous, that justifies regulations to protect the environment and public health. The opposing term, "sound science," is used in reference to any research, no matter how flawed, that can be used to challenge, defeat, or reverse environmental and public health protections.

"Junk science" first emerged in the courtroom as a disparaging term for the paid expert witnesses that attorneys hire to testify on behalf of their clients. In many cases, of course, an expert witness is unnecessary. If one person shoots another in front of witnesses, you don't need a rocket scientist to know who is responsible. During the twentieth century, however, courts expanded the system of tort law under which personal-injury lawsuits are filed in order to cover cases in which proof of causation is somewhat more complicated. Many of these cases require a scientist's testimony particularly when the injury in question comes from environmental or toxic causes—for example, cancer in army veterans subjected to radiation from atomic bomb tests; asbestos-related mesothelioma; Reyes Syndrome caused by taking aspirin; or the link between swine flu vaccinations and Guillain-Barré Syndrome. By expanding the system of tort law, courts made it possible for people injured through these sorts of causes to collect damages from the companies responsible. Of course, the fact that these cases could have their day in court does not mean that the plaintiffs are guaranteed victory. In one of the "toxic tort" cases that has been frequently cited as an example of junk science in action, Merrell Dow pharmaceuticals successfully defended itself in court against 1,200 plaintiffs who charged that its morning-sickness drug, Bendectin, caused birth defects.

The idea that junk science was running amok in the courtroom received wide attention in the late 1980s with the publication of *Galileo's Revenge: Junk Science in the Courtroom*. Authored by engineer and attorney Peter Huber, *Galileo's Revenge* argued that money-grubbing lawyers are using spurious science to collect huge, undeserved injury settlements from innocent companies. The title of Huber's book reflects his contention that corporations today have become victims of Galileo's mythic status as a symbol of scientific integrity. Galileo may have been right, Huber said, when he stood alone against the repressive force of established convention, but scientists today who propose similarly heretical theories are mostly opportunists whose opinions merely contaminate the legal system by enabling frivolous lawsuits to proceed. "Maverick scientists shunned by their reputable colleagues have been embraced by lawyers," Huber wrote. "Almost any self-styled scientist, no matter how strange or iconoclastic his views, will be welcome to testify in court. . . . Junk science is impelled through our courts by a mix of opportunity and incentive. 'Let-it-all-in' legal theory creates the opportunity. The incentive is money."[2]

Junk scientists, Huber said, can be recognized because they "do not use regular channels of communication, such as journals, for reporting scientific information, but rely instead on the mass media and word of mouth."[3] Yet Huber's own book and his opinions about junk science reached the public through a massive publicity blitz, beginning with a 1986 forum on "the liability crisis" sponsored by the Manhattan Institute for Public Policy Research, where Huber holds the title of senior fellow. "Reporters from all the national papers and magazines were there and the event generated numerous news articles," stated the institute's internal report on the campaign. The forum then became the basis for a 24-page *Manhattan Report* that "was mailed to 25,000 carefully selected people in government, academia, business, media and the law. . . . We held two workshops, one in Washington, DC in June and one in New York in August. The first included thirty corporate government affairs officers while the second, a full-day seminar, brought together fifteen academic scholars from throughout the country. . . . With assistance from a number of our friends, we compiled a mailing list of over 400 journalists who have written about the liability crisis. . . . Our project director, Walter Olson, published numerous 'op eds' on the subject, including a major piece in the *Wall Street Journal*."[4]

Huber's own scholarship, moreover, is open to the same charges of "data dredging, wishful thinking, truculent dogmatism, and, now and again, outright fraud" that he attributes to junk science. In the *American University Law Review,* Kenneth Chesebro has pointed to numerous factual distortions in the legal case studies that Huber cites. Huber is also the source for a widely cited statistic which claims that liability lawsuits cost the American economy $300 billion per year. When University of Wisconsin law professor Marc Galanter examined that claim, however, he discovered that its sole basis in fact was a "single sentence spoken by corporate executive Robert Malott in a 1986 roundtable discussion of corporate liability." Malott had estimated that liability lawsuits cost corporations $80 billion per year—a number that Galanter notes is "far higher than the estimates in careful and systematic studies of these costs. Huber then multiplied Malott's surmise by 3.5, rounded it up to $300 billion, and called that the 'indirect cost' of the tort system."[5]

A court of law is not a laboratory, and good science does not prevail there any more often than justice itself does. Bad verdicts, like bad science, have been with us for a long time. For Huber, however, only certain offenses seemed to deserve the label "junk science." Although he made a few offhand references to smoking as "our most routine form of suicide," his anecdotal examples of junk science in action never mentioned the tobacco industry's hired use of scientific guns to defend itself in court. "Due in large part to the scientific testimony," boasted an R. J. Reynolds executive in a 1981 speech, "no plaintiff has ever collected a penny from any tobacco company in lawsuits claiming that smoking causes lung cancer or cardiovascular illness—even though 117 such cases have been brought since 1954."[6] This boast was still valid when *Galileo's Revenge* hit bookstore shelves, yet Huber never used the term "junk science" in reference to tobacco science—deference which may possibly reflect the fact that Huber's employer, the Manhattan Institute, is a conservative think tank that is significantly supported by tobacco money, along with other industries that have their own vested interests in limiting lawsuit-related corporate liability.[7]

By the 1990s, in fact, the tobacco industry itself was using the term "junk science" to assail its critics. Its behind-the-scenes sponsorship of organizations purporting to defend sound science constitutes one of the great underreported stories of the past decade. The *Lancet,* England's leading medical journal, published an account of this story for the first time on April 8, 2000. Written by University of California–San Francisco researchers Stanton Glantz and Elisa Ong, the *Lancet* story examined never-before-published internal documents from Philip Morris and R. J. Reynolds and discovered a covert campaign that was prodigiously expensive, international in scope, and capable of reaching even into the editorial offices of the *Lancet* itself.

The article by Glantz and Ong focused on the tobacco industry's activities in Europe, but that is only part of the tale. In the United States as well, the tobacco industry has successfully manipulated the rhetoric of "junk science." Even former U.S. Surgeon General C. Everett Koop, one of tobacco's most outspoken critics, has been unwittingly drafted into the campaign, his words twisted to make him sound like an industry ally.

Alar Mists

The concept of "junk science" broadened to arenas outside the courtroom in 1989 when pro-industry groups used the term to attack what has come to be known as "the great Alar scare." Alar was a chemical, first marketed in 1968, that apple growers sprayed on trees to make their apples ripen longer before falling off. In use, however, Alar breaks down to a by-product called "unsymmetrical dimethyl hydrazine," or UDMH. The first study showing that UDMH can cause cancer was published in 1973. Further studies published in 1977 and 1978 confirmed that Alar and UDMH caused tumors in laboratory animals. The U.S. Environmental Protection Agency opened an investigation of Alar's hazards in 1980, but shelved the investigation after a closed meeting with Alar's manufacturer, the Uniroyal Chemical Company. In 1984, the EPA reopened its investigation, concluding in 1985 that both Alar and UDMH were "probable human carcinogens." Under pressure from the manufacturer, however, the EPA allowed Alar to stay on the market. Its use continued, even after tests by the National Food Processors Association and Gerber Baby Foods repeatedly detected Alar in samples of applesauce and apple juice, including formulations for infants.

By 1989, the states of Massachusetts and New York had banned the chemical, and the American Academy of Pediatrics was urging a similar ban at the federal level. "Risk estimates based on the best available information at this time raise serious concern about the safety of continued, long-term exposure," stated an EPA letter to apple growers which estimated that 50 out of every million adults who ate apples on a regular basis would get cancer from long-term exposure to Alar—in other words, 50 times the human health hazard considered "acceptable" by EPA standards. The danger to children, the letter warned, was even greater. Aside from these urgings, however, federal agencies failed to take regulatory action.

On February 26, 1989, the public at large heard about Alar's dangers when CBS-TV's *60 Minutes* aired an exposé titled "A is for Apple," which became the opening salvo in a carefully planned publicity campaign developed for the Natural Resources Defense Council (NRDC). The NRDC is one of the handful of environmental groups that can afford to hire a public relations company, and it chose the firm of Fenton Communications, which developed and helped distribute public service announcements featuring actress Meryl Streep, who warned that Alar had been detected in apple juice bottled for children. An NRDC report, issued at the time of the *60 Minutes* broadcast, stressed that the cumulative risks to children were higher than those to adults, because children consume far more apple products per pound of body weight. The NRDC report itself focused on inconsistencies in government regulatory policies and the need for better policies to protect children. Nowhere did it suggest that eating a single apple or drinking a single glass of juice posed a significant risk. Nevertheless, the prominence of *60 Minutes* and Streep's movie-star status helped produce a dramatic public reaction, as some mothers poured apple juice down sink drains and school lunchrooms removed apples from their menus.

The apple industry, its back to the wall, hastily abandoned its use of Alar, and the market for apples quickly rebounded. Within five years, in fact, growers' profits were 50 percent higher than they had been at the time of the *60 Minutes* broadcast.[8] Apple growers in Washington State filed a libel lawsuit against CBS, NRDC, and Fenton Communications, claiming that the "scare" had cost them $100 million and sent orchards into bankruptcy, but their case was eventually dismissed. The judge who presided over the lawsuit pointed to failures in the federal government's food-safety policies and noted that "governmental methodology fails to take into consideration the distinct hazards faced by preschoolers. The government is in grievous error when allowable exposures are calculated . . . without regard for the age at which exposure occurs."[9] Notwithstanding years of industry efforts to disprove the merits of NRDC's warning, the National Academy of Sciences (NAS) in 1993 confirmed the central message of the Alar case, which is that infants and young children need greater protection from pesticides. The NAS called for an overhaul of regulatory procedures specifically to protect kids, finding that federal calculations for allowable levels of chemicals do not account for increased childhood consumption of fruit, for children's lower body weight, or for their heightened sensitivity to toxic exposures. "NRDC was absolutely on the right track when it excoriated the regulatory agencies for having allowed a toxic material to stay on the market for 25 years," stated Dr. Philip Landrigan, who chaired the NAS study committee. Subsequent reports by the World Health Organization's International Agency for Research on Cancer and the National Toxicology Program of the U.S. Public Health Service also concurred that Alar is carcinogenic.

In and of itself, the Alar saga is only one fairly minor skirmish in a decades-long struggle between industry and environmental groups. For industry's defenders, however, the "great Alar scare" has acquired an almost mythic status, thanks to a massive and still-continuing industry propaganda campaign that has successfully transformed Alar into a symbol of junk science and journalistic irresponsibility. The counterattack was led by Elizabeth Whelan, president of the American Council on Science and Health (ACSH), a self-proclaimed defender of sound science whose funding comes largely from the chemical, food, and pharmaceutical industries.

"It was the great Alar scare of 1989 that boosted Whelan into the media stratosphere," notes *Washington Post* media reporter Howard Kurtz.[10] ACSH and Whelan were fixtures on the anti-environmental scene long before the Alar issue emerged, downplaying risks from DDT, dioxin, asbestos, and a host of other polluting chemicals, but Whelan's prominent role in the Alar counterpublicity campaign helped make ACSH a common source for journalists seeking expert commentary on public health issues. "Television producers like Whelan because she's colorful and succinct," Kurtz says, "skewering her adversaries with such phrases as 'toxic terrorists' and referring to their research as 'voodoo statistics.' Newspaper reporters often dial her number because she is an easily accessible spokesperson for the 'other' side of many controversies."[11]

Between 1990 and 1995, ACSH held at least three press briefings on Alar at the National Press Club in Washington, D.C. In its version, Alar was a beneficial and safe chemical that had been forced off the market by a deliberate scare campaign. Other groups affiliated with the chemical and food industries joined in reinforcing this interpretation of the Alar controversy. The apple industry paid the Hill & Knowlton PR firm more than $1 million to produce and distribute advertisements claiming that children would have to eat "a boxcar load" of apples daily to be at risk. Hill & Knowlton widely circulated a statement by former U.S. Surgeon General C. Everett Koop proclaiming that apples were safe and that the scare was overblown. Porter/Novelli, a leading agribusiness PR firm, helped an industry group called the "Center for Produce Quality" distribute more than 20,000 "resource kits" to food retailers that scoffed at the scientific data presented on *60 Minutes*.[12] Industry-funded think tanks such as the Cato Institute, Heartland Institute, and the Competitive Enterprise Institute hammered home the argument that the "Alar scare" was an irrational episode of public hysteria produced by unscrupulous manipulators of media sensationalism.

Since 1989, this revisionist version of the Alar story has been repeated over and over again, distorting events and omitting facts to transform the story into a morality tale about the dangers of environmental fearmongering, government regulatory excess, and media irresponsibility. By 1991, an opinion poll by the Center for Produce Quality found that 68 percent of U.S. consumers believed the Alar crisis was overblown. This ACSH view of Alar has been picked up and repeated uncritically by countless pundits and journalists, many of whom are genuinely unaware of its ideologically driven distortions. A search of the NEXIS news database for the decade following the *60 Minutes* broadcast turned up nearly 5,000 references to the Alar affair. All but a handful treated the affair as a case of Chicken Little environmentalism, with headlines such as "Enviros Accused of Inciting Paranoia," "The Century of Science Scares," "Coalition Fights Restrictions of Food Police," "The *60 Minutes* Health Hoax," and "Pseudoscientific Hooey the Scare Tactic of Choice Nowadays." Among journalists, the word *Alar* has become a near-universal shorthand for an irrational health scare stemming from junk science.

Tobacco Science Meets Junk Science

For big tobacco, the industry campaign against "junk science" presented an interesting opportunity—a chance to reposition itself as something other than a pariah in the scientific community.

Just as every action in the physical world begets an equal and opposite reaction, every risk to public health seems to beget an equal and opposite effort at denial from the industry whose products are implicated. The tobacco industry, which U.S. Surgeons General have cited since the 1960s as "the greatest cause of illness, disability and premature deaths in this country,"[13] helped invent the strategy of using scientists as third-party advocates, and if Oscars were given for such campaigns, tobacco would certainly win a lifetime achievement award. Prior to the 1950s, tobacco companies routinely advertised tobacco's alleged health "benefits" with testimonials from doctors and celebrities. When the first scientific studies documenting tobacco's role in cancer and other fatal illnesses began to appear, the industry was thrown into a panic. A 1953 report by Dr. Ernst L. Wynder heralded to the scientific community a definitive link between cigarette smoking and cancer, creating what internal memos from the industry-funded Tobacco Institute refer to as the "1954 emergency." Fighting for its economic life, the tobacco industry launched what must be considered the costliest, longest-running, and most successful PR crisis-management campaign in history. In the words of the industry itself, the campaign was aimed at "promoting cigarettes and protecting them from these and other attacks," by "creating doubt about the health charge without actually denying it, and advocating the public's right to smoke, without actually urging them to take up the practice."[14]

For help, the tobacco industry turned in the 1950s to what was then the world's largest PR firm, Hill & Knowlton, which designed a brilliant and expensive campaign that was later described as follows in a 1993 lawsuit, *State of Mississippi vs. the Tobacco Cartel*:

> As a result of these efforts, the Tobacco Institute Research Committee (TIRC), an entity later known as The Council for Tobacco Research (CTR), was formed.
>
> The Tobacco Industry Research Committee immediately ran a full-page promotion in more than 400 newspapers aimed at an estimated 43 million Americans . . . entitled "A Frank Statement to Cigarette Smokers." . . . In this advertisement, the participating tobacco companies recognized their "special responsibility" to the public, and promised to learn the facts about smoking and health. The participating tobacco companies promised to sponsor independent research. . . . The participating tobacco companies also promised to cooperate closely with public health officials. . . .
>
> After thus beginning to lull the public into a false sense of security concerning smoking and health, the Tobacco Industry Research Committee continued to act as a front for tobacco industry interests. Despite the initial public statements and posturing, and the repeated assertions that they were committed to full disclosure and vitally concerned, the TIRC did not make the public health a primary concern. . . . In fact, there was a coordinated, industry-wide strategy designed actively to mislead and confuse the public about the true dangers associated with smoking cigarettes. Rather than work for the good of the public health as it had promised, and sponsor indepen-

dent research, the tobacco companies and consultants, acting through the tobacco trade association, refuted, undermined, and neutralized information coming from the scientific and medical community.[15]

To improve its credibility, the TIRC used the third party technique, hiring Dr. Clarence Little in June of 1954 to serve as its director. Previously, Little had served as managing director of the American Society for the Control of Cancer, the forerunner to today's American Cancer Society.[16] He promised that if research did discover a direct relationship between smoking and cancer, "the next job tackled will be to determine how to eliminate the danger from tobacco." This pretense of honest concern from a respected figure worked its expected magic. Opinion research by Hill & Knowlton showed that only 9 percent of newspapers expressing opinions on the TIRC were unfavorable, whereas 65 percent were favorable without reservation.[17]

There is no question that the tobacco industry knew what scientists were learning about tobacco. The TIRC maintained a library with cross-indexed medical and scientific papers from 2,500 medical journals, as well as press clippings, government reports, and other documents. TIRC employees culled this library in search of any and every scrap of scientific data with inconclusive or contrary results regarding tobacco and the harm to human health. These were compiled into a carefully selected 18-page booklet, titled "A Scientific Perspective on the Cigarette Controversy," which was published in 1954 and mailed to more than 200,000 people, including doctors, members of Congress, and the news media.

During the 1950s, tobacco companies more than doubled their advertising budgets, going from $76 million in 1953 to $122 million in 1957. The TIRC spent another $948,151 in 1954 alone, of which one-fourth went to Hill & Knowlton, another fourth went to pay for media ads, and most of the remainder went to administrative costs. Despite TIRC's promise to "sponsor independent research," only $80,000, or less than 10 percent of the total budget for the year, actually went to scientific projects.[18]

In 1963, the TIRC changed its name to the Council for Tobacco Research. In addition to this "scientific" council, Hill & Knowlton helped set up a separate PR and lobbying organization, the Tobacco Institute. Formed in 1958, the Tobacco Institute grew by 1990 into what the *Public Relations Journal* described as one of the "most formidable public relations/lobbying machines in history," spending an estimated $20 million a year and employing 120 PR professionals to fight the combined forces of the Surgeon General of the United States, the National Cancer Institute, the American Cancer Society, the American Heart Association, and the American Lung Association.[19]

Smoke-Filled Rooms

The tobacco industry's PR strategy has been described by the American Cancer Society as "a delaying action to mislead the public into believing that no change in smoking habits is indicated from existing statistical and pathological evidence."[20] Of course, no propaganda strategy can permanently mask the mountains of evidence that have accumulated regarding tobacco's deadly effects. By the 1980s, virtually no one believed the industry's attempts to deny that smoking causes cancer, heart disease, emphysema, and a long list of other diseases. Even the industry's own spokespersons could barely stand to repeat the same old lies. Philip Morris would not publicly admit that smoking causes cancer until the year 1999, but its attorneys and PR advisers were already planning a strategic retreat from this position as early as the 1970s. Rather than continue to defend a scientific position that everyone knew was bogus, they set out to build a scientific case against the mounting body of evidence showing that *non*smokers were also suffering adverse health effects from secondhand smoke inhaled in bars, restaurants, and other public places.

Secondhand smoke appears under a variety of names in the industry's internal memoranda, which refer to it variously as "indirect smoke," "passive smoke," "sidestream smoke," or "environmental tobacco smoke" (often abbreviated ETS). Industry executives realized early on that the issue of tobacco's indirect effects posed a potentially greater threat to business profits than the issue of its direct effects on smokers themselves. Once the public discovered that cigarettes were killing nonsmokers, anti-tobacco activists would press forward with increasing success in their campaigns to ban smoking in public places. "If smokers can't smoke on the way to work, at work, in stores, banks, restaurants, malls, and other public places, they are going to smoke less," complained Philip Morris political affairs director Ellen Merlo in a speech to tobacco vendors. "A large percentage of them are going to quit. In short, cigarette purchases will be drastically reduced and volume declines will accelerate."[21] A 1993 Philip Morris budget presentation complained that "smoking restrictions have been estimated, this year alone, to have decreased PM profits by $40 million."[22]

The campaign to cultivate pro-industry scientists on the issue of secondhand smoke was massive, multifaceted, and international. Some scientists were positioned as public voices in defense of tobacco, while others played behind-the-scenes roles, quietly cultivating allies or monitoring meetings and feeding back reports to the tobacco industry's legal and political strategists. A 1990 confidential memorandum by Covington & Burling, one of the main law firms representing Philip Morris, reported on efforts by industry consultants in Lisbon, Hanover, Budapest, Milan, Scotland, Copenhagen, Switzerland, Norway, Australia, Finland, and Asia. "Our European consultants have organized and will conduct a major scientific conference in Lisbon next month on indoor air quality in warm climates," it stated. "More than 100 scientists from throughout the world will attend. . . . The focus of the conference will not be tobacco; rather, the point of the conference is to show the insignificance of ETS by emphasizing the genuine problems of air quality in warm climates. Some degree of 'balance' in the presentation of the issues is of course necessary to achieve persuasiveness, but the overall results will be positive and important. . . . A major meeting of the Toxicology Forum will be held in Budapest in July, and will include a session on ETS delivered by one of our consultants. . . . We ask our consultants to cover all substantial scientific conferences where they can usefully influence scientific and public opinion. They also attend many other conferences on their own, as part of their ordinary scientific activities."[23]

In addition to scientific conferences, consultants were at work giving media briefings; trying to sway airline flight attendants in favor of in-flight smoking; producing and appearing in videos and op-ed pieces; and testifying in court proceedings regarding allegations of fraud in tobacco advertisements. "Our consultants have created the world's only learned scientific society addressing questions of indoor air quality," the report boasted. "It will soon have its own periodic newsletter, in which ETS and other [indoor air quality] issues will be discussed in a balanced fashion to an audience of regulators, scientists, building operators, etc. It will also have its own scientific journal, published by a major European publishing house, in which [indoor air quality] issues will again be addressed."[24]

Other consultants were writing books, one on environmental tobacco smoke and health, another "exposing the vagaries of medical truisms, including those relating to tobacco" as "a clever and entertaining way of suggesting that medical 'certainties' are frequently without genuine scientific basis." Other hired experts had publications pending in leading medical journals. "One of our consultants is awaiting the publication by a leading French medical journal of a major paper" that "very helpfully attacks the reliability of the evidence regarding ETS and lung cancer." Another had published a scientific paper showing that keeping pet birds was a bigger cancer risk than secondhand smoke. Yet another was an editor at the *Lancet* and "is continuing to publish numerous reviews, editorials and comments on ETS and other issues." In Scandinavia, a Philip Morris consultant was available to conduct research showing "how popular conceptions of health risks are often actually misconceptions, when compared to expert scientific evaluations."[25]

Straining at Gnats and Swallowing Camels

Organizations such as the American Heart Association, the American Lung Association, and the American Cancer Society estimate that direct smoking kills about 400,000 people per year in the United States—or, if you use the World Health Organization's estimate, about 3 million people per year worldwide. In 1986, U.S. Surgeon General C. Everett Koop released an analysis concluding that secondhand smoke was a significant health threat to nonsmokers, and a host of other studies by individual researchers and prominent health organizations have reached similar conclusions. The most common and serious consequences are asthma, emphysema, and heart disease. Estimates of the number of ETS-related deaths in the U.S. from heart disease alone have ranged from 37,000 to 62,000 per year. Children's lungs are still developing, and they are therefore considered especially sensitive to environmental tobacco smoke. According to one estimate by the state of California, ETS causes 2,700 cases per year of sudden infant death syndrome in the United States.

The U.S. Environmental Protection Agency's risk assessment of environmental tobacco smoke was published in 1993. It estimated that secondhand smoke causes some 150,000 to 300,000 cases per year of lower respiratory tract infections such as bronchitis and pneumonia in children up to 18 months of age, resulting in 7,500 to 15,000 hospitalizations, plus somewhere between 400,000 and a million cases of asthma. The EPA also decided, for the first time, that secondhand smoke should be classified as a "Class A carcinogen"—a government classificatory term which means that ETS is not merely suspected but *known* to cause lung cancer. The impact of secondhand smoke is small compared to the effect of direct smoking, but EPA estimated that some 3,000 lung cancer deaths per year among nonsmokers should be attributed to secondhand smoke.

Tobacco's defenders realized that challenging the entire body of evidence in EPA's risk assessment would be impossible. Its conclusion that secondhand smoke causes respiratory effects in children was widely shared and virtually undisputed. Its conclusion regarding the link between secondhand smoke and cancer was based on several different types of evidence, most of which are hard to dispute. First and most obviously, secondhand smoke contains essentially all of the same cancer-causing and toxic agents that people inhale when they smoke directly. Second, tests of humans exposed to secondhand smoke show that their bodies absorb and metabolize significant amounts of these toxins. Third, exposure to secondhand smoke has been shown to cause cancer in laboratory test animals, which suggests strongly that it does the same thing to humans. Fourth, EPA reviewed analyses of some 30 epidemiological studies from eight different countries and found that women who never smoked themselves but were exposed to their husband's smoke have a higher rate of lung cancer than women married to nonsmokers.

Taken together, these pieces of evidence make it difficult to avoid the conclusion that secondhand smoke causes lung cancer. However, EPA's estimate of the *number* of deaths was based solely on epidemiology, a branch of medical science that uses statistical analysis to study the distribution of disease in human populations. Epidemiology uses statistical correlations to draw conclusions about what causes disease, but it is a notoriously inexact science. In order to estimate someone's lifetime exposure to secondhand smoke, researchers must rely on that person's memories from years past, which may not be entirely accurate. Moreover, surveys cannot take into account all of the possible confounding factors that may bias a study's outcome. Were the people surveyed exposed to other lung carcinogens, such as asbestos or radon? Did they inhale more secondhand smoke than they remember, or maybe less? Owing to these and other uncertainties, the EPA's estimate of 3,000 deaths per year from ETS-related cancer is only a rough guess. It may be too high, or it may be too low. The tobacco industry's propagandists seized on this sliver of uncertainty. There is no particular logical reason, from a scientific or policy perspective, why anyone should focus on lung cancer. After all, it represents only a fraction of the total number of deaths attributed to secondhand smoke, and there is no particular reason to prefer death from emphysema or heart disease over death from lung cancer. The lung cancer estimate, however, was the part of the EPA risk assessment that was most open to debate on methodological grounds. By focusing on it, the tobacco industry hoped to distract attention from the report's irrefutable broader conclusions.

Professor Gary Huber (no relation to Peter Huber) was one of the industry-funded scientists who responded to the call. Huber had built a career for himself as a contrarian scientist who regularly disputed the growing body of scientific evidence about tobacco's deadly effects. Over the years, he received more than $7 million in tobacco industry research funding, and although his reputation as a "tobacco whore" cost him the respect of friends and academic colleagues, in industry circles he was something of a star, hobnobbing with top executives, fishing with senior attorneys, and participating in legal strategy sessions.[26] He worked first at Harvard until the university took away his laboratory. A stint at the University of Kentucky's pro-industry tobacco and health research institute ended when he was fired for alleged mismanagement, but he always landed on his feet, thanks to the tobacco money that followed him wherever he went.[27] After Kentucky, he landed at the University of Texas, where he ran a nutritional health center while simultaneously offering secret consulting services to Shook, Hardy and Bacon, a national law firm that represented both Philip Morris and R. J. Reynolds. During his time in Texas, industry lawyers paid him $1.7 million to collect and critique published scientific studies linking smoking to emphysema, asthma, and bronchitis. The tobacco attorneys went to extraordinary lengths to keep its payments to Huber a secret, routing the money through an outside account that bore a Greek code name to keep it off hospital books and make it difficult for an outsider to find.[28]

The purpose of the secrecy, apparently, was to preserve a veneer of third party independence so that Huber could appear credible when he spoke out publicly in defense of cigarettes. By the late 1980s, he had become one of the most vocal and visible scientific critics of studies probing the hazards of environmental tobacco smoke. In 1991, he authored an article for *Consumers Research* magazine, a *Consumer Reports* look-alike that is partially funded by the tobacco industry. The scientific studies linking secondhand smoke to cancer, he wrote, were "shoddy and poorly conceived." His article was repeatedly quoted by the tobacco industry's network of columnists and by opinion magazines opposed to government regulation of smoking. Michael Fumento (a graduate of the partly tobacco-funded National Journalism Center) wrote a piece for *Investor's Business Daily* that quoted Huber and several other tobacco-friendly researchers, calling them "scientists and policy analysts who say they couldn't care less about tobacco company profits" but "say the data the EPA cites do not bear out its conclusions." Huber's arguments were also repeated by Jacob Sullum, editor of the libertarian magazine *Reason* (which receives funding from Philip Morris), in an article that was then picked up by *Forbes Media Critic* magazine. Philip Morris and R. J. Reynolds liked the Sullum piece so much that in May 1994 the R. J. Reynolds company bought reprint rights to an editorial he had written for the *Wall Street Journal*. A few months later, Philip Morris paid Sullum $5,000 for the right to reprint one of his articles as a five-day series of full-page ads in newspapers through-out the country, including the *New York Times, Washington Post, Los Angeles Times, Chicago Tribune, Miami Herald, Boston Globe,* and *Baltimore Sun*. The ads appeared under the headline "If We Said It, You Might Not Believe It." The result, noted *Consumer Reports* magazine (no relation to *Consumers Research*), was that "Huber's argument has undoubtedly now been seen by millions more people than ever read the original EPA report, let alone any of the hundreds of scientific articles on the subject in medical journals."

Huber's vigilance on behalf of tobacco companies did not end there. In May 1993, he was intrigued to receive a letter from Garrey Carruthers, a former professor of agricultural economics and ex-governor of the state of New Mexico. "Dear Dr. Huber," the letter began, "I am creating a coalition of scientists, academicians, former public officials and representatives from business and industry, concerned about the advancement of sound science. The name of this coalition is The Advancement of Sound Science Coalition (TASSC), and its goal is to advance the principles of science used to formulate sound public policy." The letter asked Huber to lend his name to the coalition and to join Carruthers in "educating the public as to what constitutes the appropriate use of science in public policy."[29]

Huber looked over TASSC's materials and noticed that environmental tobacco smoke was included in its lengthy list of examples of "junk science." He drafted a letter to Anthony Andrade, one of his attorney handlers at Shook, Hardy and Bacon. "Dear Mr. Andrade," he wrote. "For your interest, I am enclosing some materials from a new group apparently dedicated to establishing sound science in public policy. . . . I call this to your attention because some of their membership has already identified environmental tobacco smoke as an issue where unsound science prevails, as you can see from the enclosed 'member survey' form. I am pursuing this matter and will keep you informed."[30]

If not for the tobacco industry's concerns about secrecy, they might have written back, telling Huber not to bother, because they were already on top of the matter. Philip Morris wasn't just working hand-in-hand with TASSC on the issue of environmental tobacco smoke. Actually, Philip Morris had *created* TASSC.

The Whitecoats Are Coming

One of the forerunners of TASSC at Philip Morris was a 1988 "Proposal for the Whitecoat Project," named after the white laboratory coats that scientists sometimes wear. The project had four goals: "Resist and roll back smoking restrictions. Restore smoker confidence. Reverse scientific and popular misconception that ETS is harmful. Restore social acceptability of smoking." To achieve these goals, the plan was to first "generate a body of scientific and technical knowledge" through research "undertaken by whitecoats, contract laboratories and commercial organizations"; then "disseminate and exploit such knowledge through specific communication programs." Covington & Burling, PM's law firm, would function as the executive arm of the Whitecoat Project, acting as a "legal buffer . . . the interface with the operating units (whitecoats, laboratories, etc.)."[31]

The effort to create a scientific defense for secondhand smoke was only one component in the tobacco industry's multimillion-dollar PR campaign. To defeat cigarette excise taxes, a Philip Morris strategy document outlined plans for "Co-op efforts with third party tax organizations"—libertarian anti-taxation think tanks, such as Americans for Tax Reform, Citizens for a Sound Economy, Citizens for Tax Justice, and the Tax Foundation.[32] Other third party allies included the National Journalism Center, the Heartland Institute, the Claremont Institute, and National Empowerment Television, a conservative TV network. In one memo to Philip Morris CEO Michael A. Miles, company vice president Craig L. Fuller noted that he was "working with many third party allies to develop position papers, op-eds and letters to the editor detailing how tobacco is already one of the most heavily regulated products in the marketplace, and derailing arguments against proposed bans on tobacco advertising."[33]

Through the Burson-Marsteller PR firm, Philip Morris also created the "National Smoker's Alliance," a supposedly independent organization of individual smokers which claimed that bans on smoking in public places infringed on basic American freedoms. The NSA was a "grassroots" version of the third party technique, designed to create the impression of a citizen groundswell against smoking restrictions. Burson-Marsteller spent millions of dollars of tobacco industry money to get the NSA up and running—buying full-page newspaper ads, hiring paid canvassers and tele-marketers, setting up a toll-free 800 number, and publishing newsletters and other folksy "grassroots" materials to mobilize the puffing masses. NSA's stated mission was to "empower" smokers to reclaim their rights—although, behind closed doors, industry executives fretted that they didn't want this rhetoric to go too far. They were well aware of opinion polls showing that 70 percent of all adult smokers wish they could kick the habit. "The issue of 'empowerment of smokers' was viewed as somewhat dangerous," stated a tobacco strategy document. "We don't want to 'em-power' them to the point that they'll quit."[34]

Owing to the publicity associated with Burson-Marsteller's role in setting up the NSA, Philip Morris executives felt that it was best to select some other PR firm to handle the launch of TASSC. They settled on APCO Associates, a subsidiary of the international advertising and PR firm of GCI/Grey Associates, which agreed to "organize coalition efforts to provide information with respect to the ETS issues to the media and to public officials" in exchange for a monthly retainer of $37,500 plus ex-penses.[35] The purpose of TASSC, as described in a memo from APCO's Tom Hockaday and Neal Cohen, was to "link the tobacco issue with other more 'politically correct' products"—in other words, to make the case that efforts to regulate tobacco were based on the same "junk science" as ef-forts to regulate Alar, food additives, automobile emissions, and other in-dustrial products that had not yet achieved tobacco's pariah status. "The credibility of EPA is defeatable, but not on the basis of ETS alone," stated a Philip Morris strategy document. "It must be part of a larger mosaic that concentrates all of the EPA's enemies against it at one time."[36]

Originally dubbed the "Restoring Integrity to Science Coalition," the Advancement of Sound Science Coalition was later renamed to resemble the venerable American Association for the Advancement of Science. After APCO's planners realized that the resulting acronym was not terribly flattering—ASSC, or worse, the ASS Coalition—they began putting a capitalized "the" at the beginning of the name, and TASSC was born, a "national coalition intended to educate the media, public officials and the public about the dangers of 'junk science.' "[37]

In September 1993, APCO president Margery Kraus sent a memo to Philip Morris communications director Vic Han, updating him on plans. "We look forward to the successful launching of TASSC this fall," she stated. "We believe the groundwork we conduct to complete the launch will enable TASSC to expand and assist Philip Morris in its efforts with issues in targeted states in 1994." APCO's work would focus on expanding TASSC's membership, finding outside money to help conceal the role of Philip Morris as its primary funder, compiling a litany of "additional examples of unsound science," and "coordinating and directing outreach to the scientific and academic communities." APCO would also direct and manage Garrey Carruthers, who had been hired as TASSC's public spokesman. "This includes developing and maintaining his schedule, prioritizing his time and energies, and briefing Carruthers and other appropriate TASSC representatives," Kraus wrote. She outlined a "comprehensive media relations strategy" designed to "maximize the use of TASSC and its members into Philip Morris's issues in targeted states. . . . This includes using TASSC as a tool in targeted legislative battles." Planned activities included publishing a monthly newsletter, issuing frequent news releases, drafting "boilerplate" speeches and op-ed pieces to be used by TASSC representatives, and placing articles in various trade publications to help recruit members from the agriculture, chemical, biotechnology, and food additive industries. In addition to APCO's monthly fee, $5,000 per month was budgeted "to compensate Garrey Carruthers."[38]

Considerable effort was expended to conceal the fact that TASSC was created and funded almost entirely by Philip Morris. APCO recommended that TASSC should first be introduced to the public through a "decentralized launch outside the large markets of Washington, DC and New York" in order to "avoid cynical reporters from major media." In smaller markets, APCO reasoned, there would be "less reviewing/challenging of TASSC messages." Also, a decentralized launch would "limit potential for counterattack. The opponents of TASSC tend to concentrate their efforts in top markets while skipping the secondary markets. This approach sends TASSC's message initially into these more receptive markets—and enables us to build upon early successes."[39]

The plan included a barnstorming media tour of cities in these secondary markets by Garrey Carruthers. "APCO will arrange on-the-ground visits with three to four reporters in each city. These interviews, using TASSC's trained spokespeople, third-party allies (e.g., authors of books on unsound science), members of the TASSC Science Board, and/or Governor Carruthers, will be scheduled for a one to two day media tour in each city." To set up the interviews, APCO used a list of sympathetic reporters provided by John Boltz, a manager of media affairs at Philip Morris. "We thought it best to remove any possible link to PM, thus Boltz is not making the calls," noted Philip Morris public affairs director Jack Lenzi. "With regard to media inquiries to PM about TASSC, I am putting together some Q and A. We will not deny being a corporate member/sponsor, will not specify dollars, and will refer them to the TASSC '800-' number, being manned by David Sheon (APCO)."[40] Other plans, developed later, included creation of a TASSC Internet page that could be used to "broadly distribute published studies/papers favorable to smoking/ETS debate" and "release PM authored papers . . . on ETS science and bad science/bad public policy."[41]

Carruthers began his media tour in December 1993, with stopovers in cities including San Diego, Dallas, and Denver. News releases sent out in advance of each stop described TASSC as a "grassroots-based, not-for-profit watchdog group of scientists and representatives from universities, independent organizations and industry, that advocates the use of sound science in the public policy arena." As examples of unsound science, it pointed to the "Alar scare," asbestos-abatement guidelines, the "dioxin scare" in Times Beach, Missouri, and "unprecedented regulations to limit radon levels in drinking water." In Texas, local TASSC recruits involved in the launch included Dr. Margaret Maxey and Floy Lilley, both of the University of Texas. "The Clean Air Act is a perfect example of laboratory science being superficially applied to reality," Lilley said. Carruthers took the opportunity to inveigh against politicized uses of science by the Environmental Protection Agency "to make science 'fit' with the political leanings of special interests." EPA's studies, he complained, "are frequently carried out without the benefit of peer review or quality assurance."[42] In Denver, Carruthers told a local radio station that the public has been "shafted by shoddy science, and it has cost consumers and government a good deal of money." When asked who was financing TASSC, Carruthers sidestepped the question. "We don't want to be caught being a crusader for a single industry," he said. "We're not out here defending the chemical industry; we're not out here defending the automobile industry, or the petroleum industry, or the tobacco industry; we're here just to ensure that sound science is used."[43]

Virtually every news release made some reference to the "Alar scare," usually invoking the name of former U.S. Surgeon General C. Everett Koop. In an "advertorial" titled "Science: A Tool, Not a Weapon," TASSC noted that "respected experts, including then–Surgeon General C. Everett Koop, said the scientific evidence showed no likelihood of harm from Alar. . . . This is not an isolated case of bad science being used by policy-makers," it added. "It's happened regarding asbestos, dioxin and toxic waste. . . . It's happening in the debate over environmental tobacco smoke, or second-hand smoke. The studies done so far on the topic do not demonstrate evidence that second-hand smoke causes cancer, even though that is the popular wisdom."[44] To the casual reader, it would almost appear as if the venerable Dr. Koop were a defender of environmental tobacco smoke, rather than one of its most prominent critics.[45]

EuroTASSC

By 1994, Philip Morris was budgeting $880,000 in funding for TASSC.[46] In consultation with APCO and Burson-Marsteller, the company began planning to establish a second, European sound science organization, tentatively named "Scientists for Sound Public Policy" (later renamed the European Science and Environment Forum). Like TASSC, the European organization would attempt to smuggle tobacco advocacy into a larger bundle of "sound science" issues, including the "ban on growth hormone for livestock; ban on [genetically engineered bovine growth hormone] to improve milk production; pesticide restrictions; ban on indoor smoking; restrictions on use of chlorine; ban on certain pharmaceutical products; restrictions on the use of biotechnology." The public and policymakers needed to be "educated," Burson-Marsteller explained, because "political decision-makers are vulnerable to activists' emotional appeals and press campaigns. . . . The precautionary principle is now the accepted guideline. Even if a hypothesis is not 100 percent scientifically proven, action should be taken, e.g. global warming." Companies that B-M thought could be recruited to support the European endeavor would include makers of "consumer products (food, beverages, tobacco), packaging industry, agrochemical industry, chemical industry, pharmaceutical industry, biotech industry, electric power industry, telecommunications."[47]

A turf war broke out between Burson-Marsteller and APCO over the question of which PR firm should handle the European campaign. Jim Lindheim of Burson-Marsteller laid claim to the account by stressing his firm's already-proven expertise at defending tobacco science in Europe. "We have the network, much of which is already sensitized to PM's special needs," he stated. We have a lot of experience in every country working with scientists. . . . We've got a large client base with 'scientific problems' whom we can tap for sponsorship."[48]

APCO's Margery Kraus responded by reminding Philip Morris regulatory affairs director Matthew Winokur that Burson-Marsteller's long history of tobacco industry work was public knowledge and therefore might taint the endeavor. "Given the sensitivities of other TASSC activities and a previous decision not to have TASSC work directly with Burson, due to these sensitivities in other TASSC work, I did not feel comfortable having Steig or anyone else from Burson assume primary responsibility for working with TASSC scientists," Kraus stated.[49] As for experience handling "scientific problems," she pointed to her parent company's work for "the following industries impacted by science and environmental policy decisions: chemical, pharmaceutical, nuclear, waste management and motor industries, power generation, biotech products, packaging and detergents, and paint. They have advised clients on a number of issues, including: agricultural manufacturing, animal testing, chlorine, dioxins, toxic waste, ozone/CFCs, power generation, coastal pollution, lead in gasoline, polyurethanes, lubricants."[50]

TASSC was intentionally designed to appear outwardly like a broad coalition of scientists from multiple disciplines. The other industries and interests—biotech, chemical, toxic waste, coastal pollution, lubricants— served as protective camouflage, concealing the tobacco money that was at the heart of the endeavor. TASSC signed up support from corporate executives at Santa Fe Pacific Gold Corporation, Procter & Gamble, the Louisiana Chemical Association, the National Pest Control Association, General Motors, Lawrence Livermore National Laboratory, Exxon, W. R. Grace & Co., Amoco, Occidental Petroleum, 3M, Chevron, and Dow

Chemical. Many of its numerous news releases attacking "junk science" made no mention of tobacco whatsoever. It objected to government guidelines for asbestos abatement; said the "dioxin scare" in Times Beach, Missouri, was a tempest in a teapot; scoffed at the need for an EPA Superfund cleanup in Aspen, Colorado; dismissed reports of health effects related to use of the Norplant contraceptive; denounced the Clean Water Act; and orchestrated a letter-writing campaign to oppose any government action aimed at limiting industrial activities linked to global warming.

ACSH TASSCwards

In many respects, TASSC was closely modeled after Elizabeth Whelan's American Council on Science and Health. Both organizations boasted a "board of scientific advisers" with several hundred members, many of whom worked for industry or served in university departments with corporate affiliations. Both relied heavily on corporate funding and shared pro-industry views on a wide range of issues.

Founded in 1978, ACSH is described in minutes from a meeting that year of the Manufacturing Chemists' Association (today known as the Chemical Manufacturers Association) as "a tax-exempt organization composed of scientists whose viewpoints are more similar to those of business than dissimilar." In recent years, ACSH has stopped publishing its complete list of corporate funders, but reports from prior years showed that as much as 76 percent of its budget came either directly from industry or from foundations that were closely linked to industry.[51]

The views of ACSH and Whelan have remained remarkably consistent over the years. Whelan describes herself as a lifelong conservative who is "more libertarian than Republican." Since the founding of ACSH, Whelan has attacked environmentalism and defended corporate polluters. In a 1981 article titled "Chemicals and Cancerphobia," she decried "the cancerphobia which now grips our nation and is dictating federal policy in a number of government agencies seems to be largely traceable to a fear of chemicals. . . . For businessmen, the implications are clear: more regulation, higher costs, fewer jobs, and limited production. For me as a scientist and consumer the implications are also clear: high prices, higher taxes, fewer products—a diminished standard of living. . . . [W]ith today's consumer advocates leading the show, we are heading toward not only zero risk, but zero food, zero jobs, zero energy, and zero growth. It may be that the prophets of doom, not the profits of industry, are the real hazards to our health."[52]

ACSH board chairman A. Alan Moghissi is a former Reagan-era EPA official with similar views. He characterizes environmentalism as a belief that "members of endangered species deserve protection and that, because there are billions of humans, humanity does not qualify for protection." The 17-member ACSH board of directors also includes representatives from two PR and advertising firms: Albert Nickel of Lyons Lavey Nickel Swift (their motto: "We change perceptions"), and Lorraine Thelian of Ketchum Communications. Thelian directs Ketchum's Washington, D.C., office, which handles the bulk of the firm's "environmental PR work" on behalf of clients including Dow Chemical, the Aspirin Foundation of America, Bristol-Myers Squibb, the American Automobile Manufacturers Association, the Consumer Aerosol Products Council, Genentech, the National Pharmaceutical Council, the North American Insulation Manufacturers Association, and the American Industrial Health Council, another industry-funded group that lobbies against what it considers "excessive" regulation of carcinogens. Ketchum boasts that its Washington office "has dealt with issues ranging from regulation of toxins, global climate change, electricity deregulation, nuclear energy, product and chemical contamination, and agricultural chemicals and Superfund sites, to name but a few."

ACSH calls the U.S. ban on DDT one of the 20 worst unfounded health scares of the twentieth century. It ridicules the risks that chemical endocrine disruptors pose to human health and fertility. In addition to pesticides and chemical food additives, it has defended asbestos, Agent Orange, and nuclear power. Whelan's nutritional advice has raised eyebrows among health experts, many of whom take exception to her claims that there is "no such thing as 'junk food,' " and that there is "insufficient evidence of a relationship between diet and any disease." ACSH periodically sends a "Media Update" out to its donors, demonstrating its success at influencing public opinion with examples of newspaper and magazine clippings in which the organization has been cited as an authoritative source. Among the actual newspaper headlines it boasts of generating, the following examples are typical:

- "A Global Scare: The Environmental Doomsday Machine Is in High Gear"[53]

- "Irradiation Only Sure Method to Protect U.S. Food Supply"[54]

- "Safe Meat: There Is a Better Way" (a *Wall Street Journal* editorial column in which Whelan criticizes the USDA for recalling *E. coli*–contaminated beef)[55]

- "Evidence Lacking that PCB Levels Harm Health"[56]

- "The Fuzzy Science Behind New Clean-Air Rules"[57]

- "Screaming About Breast Cancer"[58]

- "Environmental Alarmists Can't Explain Progress in Public Health"[59]

- "Eat Beef, America"[60] and "Salad Days Are Over"[61]

- "At Christmas Dinner, Let Us Be Thankful for Pesticides and Safe Food"[62]

With respect to the issue of tobacco, however, ACSH has taken a strong and consistently critical position in favor of public health. Whelan has authored numerous editorials and magazine articles about tobacco, along with books titled *A Smoking Gun: How the Tobacco Industry Gets Away with Murder* and *Cigarettes: What the Warning Label Doesn't Tell You.* She has testified as an expert witness for plaintiffs suing the tobacco industry and has even criticized her fellow conservatives for what she calls their "blurred vision" about tobacco. When presidential candidate Bob Dole opined that smoking was not addictive, Whelan publicly differed, as she has on other occasions. "Conservative politicians, their spokesmen and right-wing journalists almost uniformly condemned Clinton's 'war' against teen-age smoking," she complained in 1995. "Conservative pundits pounce on anti-smoking activists with gusto, questioning not just our methods, but our priorities. . . . Republicans, posturing themselves as friends of the tobacco industry, are doing themselves and America's youth a great disservice. As a public health professional and lifelong Republican I ask: Why?"

Despite some early feelers, Whelan's position on cigarettes effectively doomed the possibility of any direct collaboration between ACSH and the tobacco industry. Shortly after the organization's launch, ACSH director Frederick Stare sent an appeal for funds to Philip Morris vice president Ray Wakeham, but the appeal was unsuccessful. "Now that we are firmly established, and growing, we seek support from industry of all types," Stare wrote in December 1980, following up on a presentation he had recently given to a PM-supported corporate coalition called the Industrial Research Institute. "A few of the companies who are members of the Industrial Research Institute have provided us with limited financial assistance, but we now want very much for all of you to help, and generously," Stare stated. "We are a voice of scientific reason in a sea of pseudo-science, exaggeration, and misinformation. We believe it would be to your benefit to help ACSH. . . . Our basic corporate membership at present is $3,000, but we hope many of you will contribute a total of $10,000 or more."[63]

In an internal Philip Morris memorandum written two weeks later, Wakeham noted that he had read and agreed with a recent ACSH report downplaying the idea that there was a "cancer epidemic" in the United States. However, he added, "The little I know about Elizabeth Whelan, the executive director, would be enough to suggest that PM have nothing to do with the Council. Not only is she on record as being convinced that cigarette smoking is responsible for almost all it has been accused of but she has gone out of her way to accuse the cigarette industry of exerting pressure on magazines, particularly women's magazines, not to accept articles which have derogatory statements about the effect of smoking on women . . . I would not suggest that anyone in the cigarette industry support the American Council on Science and Health."[64]

In fact, ACSH frequently builds its defense of other polluting industries around the argument that tobacco deserves higher priority than the "hypothetical, miniscule" risks from environmental pollution. ACSH has its own magazine, *Priorities*, whose title and content derive from the notion that "unscientific" health advocates fail to prioritize real health risks while dwelling on risks that are "trivial at best, or, at worst, nonexistent."

If Whelan had been more agreeable on the tobacco issue, Philip Morris might never have felt a need to create TASSC. However, the company did not need to look far to find others who lacked her principles. Many of TASSC's closest supporters, in fact, were closely affiliated with the American Council on Science and Health. ACSH executive director Michael Fox was a member of TASSC's advisory board, as were ACSH chairman A. Alan Moghissi and board members Victor Herbert and F. J. Francis. Another 46 members of the ACSH advisory board also served on the advisory board of TASSC.

Trash Talk with the Junkman

In February 1994, APCO vice president Neal Cohen made the mistake of boasting candidly about some of the sneaky tactics that his company uses when setting up front groups. His remarks were made at a conference of the Public Affairs Council (PAC), an exclusive association of top-ranking corporate lobbyists and PR counselors. *New York Times* political reporter Jane Fritsch later used his remarks as the basis for a March 1996 article titled "Sometimes Lobbyists Strive to Keep Public in the Dark."[65]

Shortly after APCO suffered this embarrassment, the responsibility for managing TASSC was quietly transferred to the EOP Group, a well-connected, Washington-based lobby firm whose clients have included the American Crop Protection Association (the chief trade association of the pesticide industry), the American Petroleum Institute, AT&T, the Business Roundtable, the Chlorine Chemistry Council, Dow Chemical Company, Edison Electric Institute (nuclear power), Fort Howard Corp. (a paper manufacturer), International Food Additives Council, Monsanto Co., National Mining Association, and the Nuclear Energy Institute. In March 1997, EOP lobbyist Steven Milloy, described in a TASSC news release as "a nationally known expert and author on environmental risk and regulatory policy issues," was named TASSC's executive director.[66]

"Steven brings not only a deep and strong academic and professional background to TASSC, but he brings an equally deep, strong and passionate commitment to the principle of using sound science in making public policy decisions," said Garrey Carruthers. "The issue of junk science has become the topic of network news specials, major articles in newspapers, and a key topic in Congress and legislatures around the country. I look forward to working with Steven to continue to drive home the need for sound science in public policy making."[67]

Although the news release referred to Milloy's work "over the last six years" on "environmental and regulatory policy issues," it did not mention that he had worked specifically for the tobacco industry. During 1992 he worked for James Tozzi at Multinational Business Services. Tozzi, a former career bureaucrat at the U.S. Office of Management and Budget who had spearheaded the Reagan-era OMB campaign to gut environmental regulations, is described in internal Philip Morris documents as the company's "primary contact on the EPA/ETS risk assessment during the second half of 1992." During that period, it noted, "Tozzi has been invaluable in executing our Washington efforts including generating technical briefing papers, numerous letters to agencies and media interviews," a service for which Philip Morris paid an estimated $300,000 in consulting fees.[68] Philip Morris also paid Tozzi's company another $880,000 to establish a "nonprofit" think tank called the Institute for Regulatory Policy (IRP). On behalf of Philip Morris, the IRP put together "three different coalitions which support sound science—Coalition for Executive Order, Coalition for Moratorium on Risk Assessments, and Coalition of Cities and States on Environmental Mandates. . . . IRP could work with us as well as APCO in a coordinated manner," PM's Boland and Borelli had noted in February 1993.[69]

After leaving Tozzi's service, Milloy became president of his own organization called the Regulatory Impact Analysis Project, Inc., where he wrote a couple of reports arguing that "most environmental risks are so small or indistinguishable that their existence cannot be proven."[70] Shortly thereafter, he launched the "Junk Science Home Page" (www.junkscience.com). Calling himself "the Junkman," he offered daily attacks on environmentalists, public health and food safety regulators, anti-nuclear activists, animal rights activists, the EPA, and a wide range of other targets that he accused of using unsound science to advance various political agendas.

The tone of the Junk Science Home Page seemed calculated to lower rather than elevate scientific discourse. If his targets were not "psychologically challenged" or "bogus," they were fearmongering "blowhards," "turkeys," "wacko enviros," or members of the "food police." Using schoolyard taunts and accusations of "mindless anti-chemical hysteria," Milloy routinely attacked the world's most prestigious scientific journals, including *Science, Nature,* the *Lancet,* and the *Journal of the American Medical Association.* He dismissed reports of a thinning ozone layer as "nutty." He opposed automobile emissions testing as "just another clever ploy to separate you from your money." His website also featured an extended attack on *Our Stolen Future,* the book about endocrine disruptors by Theo Colborn, Dianne Dumanoski, and Peter Myers. Milloy's online parody, titled "Our Swollen Future," included a cartoon depiction of Colborn hauling a wheelbarrow of money to the bank (her implied motive for writing the book), and referred to Dianne Dumanoski as "Dianne Dumb-as-an-oxski." Nor was he above an occasional ethnic slur. "Tora, tora, tora," he wrote in response to reports that Japanese researchers were concerned about endocrine disruptors.

Milloy was also active in defense of the tobacco industry, particularly in regard to the issue of environmental tobacco smoke. He dismissed the EPA's 1993 report linking secondhand smoke to cancer as "a joke," and when the *British Medical Journal* published its own study with similar results in 1997, he scoffed that "it remains a joke today." After one researcher published a study linking secondhand smoke to cancer, Milloy wrote that she "must have pictures of journal editors in compromising positions with farm animals. How else can you explain her studies seeing the light of day?" In August 1997, the *New York Times* reported that Milloy was one of the paid speakers at a Miami briefing for foreign reporters sponsored by the British-American Tobacco Company, whose Brown & Williamson unit makes popular cigarettes like Kool, Carlton, and Lucky Strike. At the briefing, which was off-limits to U.S. journalists, the company flew in dozens of reporters from countries including Brazil, Argentina, Chile, and Peru and paid for their hotel rooms and expensive meals while the reporters sat through presentations that ridiculed "lawsuit-driven societies like the United States" for using "unsound science" to raise questions about "infinitesimal, if not hypothetical, risks" related to inhaling a "whiff" of tobacco smoke.[71]

The differences between ACSH and TASSC over the tobacco issue came to a head in June 1997, after Milloy attacked a Harvard University study published in the *New England Journal of Medicine* as an "abuse of statistics" and a case of "epidemiologists trying to pass off junk science as Nobel Prize work." This rhetoric became the basis for a story, titled "Smoke Rings," which appeared in a June 1997 issue of William F. Buckley, Jr.'s, conservative *National Review*. Elizabeth Whelan, who describes herself as "a longtime *National Review* fan," was so "disappointed" in the article that she wrote a letter to the editor warning that "*NR* should be wary of relying on a source that considers the *New England Journal of Medicine* a purveyor of junk science. In labeling the Harvard study 'junk science,' you may be inadvertently junking all science."

"We respect Dr. Whelan's work on many subjects, but when it comes to tobacco she loses her grip on reality," the *National Review* replied.[72] Even she, it seemed, could sometimes be a "wacko fearmonger."

Junk Bonds

Casual visitors to Milloy's Junk Science Home Page might be tempted to dismiss him as merely an obnoxious adolescent with a website. They would be surprised to discover that he is a well-connected fixture in conservative Washington policy circles. He currently holds the title of "adjunct scholar" at the libertarian Cato Institute, which was rated the fourth most influential think tank in Washington, D.C., in a 1999 survey of congressional staffers and journalists.[73]

Milloy's vitriolic style may seem strange to outsiders, but it generates and channels the anger that right-wing pseudopopulists have become adept at mobilizing against environmentalists. Milloy's website frequently provides phone and fax numbers that visitors can use to bombard news editors and politicians with correspondence. Using dittoheads to amplify his messages, he has claimed responsibility for engineering the 1999 firing of George Lundberg as editor of the *Journal of the American Medical Association,* and for the passage of legislation by Congress that substantially alters the rules regarding data disclosure by government-funded scientists.

In addition to the website, Milloy is a prolific author of eco-bashing articles that the Cato Institute helps circulate to newspapers and other publications. His diatribes against junk science have run in publications including the *New York Post,* the *Washington Times, Arizona Republic, Electricity Daily, San Francisco Examiner, Detroit Free Press, Investor's Business Daily, Cincinnati Enquirer, USA Today, New York Post,* London *Financial Times, San Francisco Examiner, Wall Street Journal, Chicago Tribune, Philadelphia Inquirer,* and *Chemical and Engineering News.* The *Chicago Sun-Times* has run "special reports" by Milloy that are offered as news stories rather than editorials, in which he downplays environmental concerns about issues such as biotech foods. He can rein in the rhetoric when he needs to, and some of his stories read like straight news. Perhaps the most disturbing thing about his writing for the *Chicago Sun-Times* is the newspaper's failure to provide its readers with any information about his background as an industry lobbyist. It describes him simply as "a Washington-based business writer specializing in science" who "holds advanced degrees in health sciences from Johns Hopkins University and a law degree from Georgetown University." (Milloy's "advanced degree" from Johns Hopkins is a master's degree in biostatistics.) Indeed, some of the publications that quote Milloy tend to inflate or distort his credentials. He has been described in various places as a "risk expert," an "economist," and a "statistician."

Like other corporate-funded front groups, the organizations that flack for sound science are sometimes fly-by-night organizations. Called into existence for a particular cause or legislative lobby campaign, they often dry up and blow away once the campaign is over. The tendency of groups to appear and disappear creates another form of camouflage, making it difficult for journalists and everyday citizens to sort out the bewildering proliferation of names and acronyms. This was indeed what happened with The Advancement of Sound Science Coalition, which was quietly retired in late 1998. Its legacy, however, continues. Milloy's Junk Science Home Page now claims to be sponsored by an organization called "Citizens for the Integrity of Science," about which no further information is publicly available. It is one of dozens, if not hundreds, of industry-funded organizations and conservative think tanks that continue to wave the sound science banner. Some are large and well-known, while others are small-scale operations, as the following examples illustrate:

- The *Washington Legal Foundation* continues to press the campaign against "junk science in the courtroom." It runs quarter-page advertisements in the *New York Times,* calling them "public service messages" by "free enterprise advocates with public interest know how." In a 1997 ad, headlined "Junk Science Makes Junk Law," the WLF recited the familiar litany—Alar, Bendectin, breast implants. "Just imagine the products Americans will never have because of junk science," it concluded.[74] Internal Philip Morris documents describe WLF as "a close ally of PM for many years. WLF has been involved in numerous aspects of the tobacco industry debate. They have filed amicus briefs against the EPA; they have written and promoted policy papers supporting our position on the advertising/First Amendment issue; and, most recently, they authored a major paper detailing why the tobacco industry is already one of the most highly regulated industries in America and does not need further regulatory control."[75]

- The *Hudson Institute,* a conservative think tank that spent the 1960s and 1970s envisioning nuclear war scenarios and defending the war in Vietnam, today employs "adjunct scholar" Dennis T. Avery as an in-house, anti-environmentalist expert on junk science. Avery is author of the tract *Saving the Planet with Pesticides and Plastic* and has championed the idea that organic food is more dangerous than foods grown using synthetic pesticides. In the fall of 1998, Avery began claiming that "people who eat organic and 'natural' foods are eight times as likely as the rest of the population to be attacked by a deadly new strain of *E. coli* bacteria (0157:H7)." This happens, he says, because organic food is grown in animal manure. He claims his data comes from the U.S. Centers for Disease Control (CDC), the federal agency that tracks outbreaks of foodborne illness. In reality, organic food is no more likely to be grown in animal manure than nonorganic food. The CDC vigorously denies Avery's claim and has even gone to the unusual step of issuing a news release disavowing it. Nevertheless, Avery's message has been repeated in media op-ed pieces written by Avery with titles such as "Organic Foods Can Make You Sick"[76] and in news stories by the *Wall Street Journal,* the Associated Press, and numerous other publications in the United States and Europe. In February 2000, Avery was the featured expert for an ABC *20/20* story by television reporter John Stossel which speculated that "buying organic could kill you." Stossel's piece made no mention of Avery's affiliation with the Hudson Institute, let alone any mention of the institute's corporate funding from agrichemical and agribusiness heavyweights, including Monsanto, DuPont, Dow-Elanco, Sandoz, Ciba-Geigy, ConAgra, Cargill, and Procter & Gamble. Stossel also claimed that *20/20*'s own laboratory tests had found as many pesticide residues on organic produce as on the conventionally grown variety—a claim the network would have to retract later when its researchers admitted that no such tests had been conducted.

- The *Competitive Enterprise Institute,* backed by major oil companies, claims that "thousands of scientists agree there's no solid evidence of a global-warming problem." It boasts of media hits in the *Wall Street Journal, Washington Post, USA Today, MacNeil/Lehrer News Hour, Good Morning America,* and *Larry King Live.* CEI's activities include a "Death by Regulation" project aimed at "shifting the policy debate" about environmental regulations by making the argument that "government intervention carries its own deadly consequences." It claims, for example, that automobile emissions standards drive consumers to buy smaller, flimsier automobiles, causing more deaths from car crashes. Similarly, it argues that there are "adverse public health effects of medical drug regulation and nutritional labeling." Drug regulations, it says, keep new medications off the market. As for nutritional labeling, it believes that wine makers should be able to advertise that wine consumption prevents heart attacks.[77] However, there should be no requirement for labeling of milk from rBGH-treated cows. During the peak of the PR campaign against EPA's secondhand smoke report, CEI cranked out opinion articles for major newspapers with titles such as "A Smoking Gun Firing Blanks," "EPA's Bad Science Mars ETS Report," and "Safety Is a Relative Thing for Cars; Why Not for Cigarettes?" CEI funders include the American Petroleum Institute, Amoco, ARCO Foundation, Armstrong Foundation, Burlington Northern Railroad Co., Carthage Foundation, Charles C. Koch Charitable Foundation, Claude R. Lambe Charitable Foundation, Coca-Cola, CSX Corp., David H. Koch Charitable Foundation, Detroit Farming Inc., Dow Chemical, EBCO Corp., Ford Motor Co., General Motors, IBM, JM Foundation, Lynde and Harry Bradley Foundation, Pfizer Inc., Philip Morris Companies, Phillip M. McKenna Foundation, Precision Valve Corp., Sarah Scaife Foundation, Smith Richardson Foundation, and Texaco Foundation.

- The Illinois-based *Heartland Institute* publishes anti-environmental books with titles like *Eco-Sanity* by institute president Joe Bast. It also has a "PolicyFax" system through which it makes position papers available on a wide range of issues, including reprints of essays by Jacob Sullum, ACSH, the Cato Institute, the National Smokers Alliance, Michael Fumento, and the Tobacco Institute. Although the PolicyFax database includes numerous reprints of articles by Elizabeth Whelan, her writings against the tobacco industry are *not* included. In addition to repeating the conservative line on everything from Alar to biotechnology to dioxin, Heartland enthusiastically reiterates the tobacco industry line on secondhand smoke. Its board of directors hails from General Motors, Amoco, Procter & Gamble, and Philip Morris, companies that are also among its principal contributors. An internal Philip Morris memo from March 1994 notes that Philip Morris "provided technical comments for the Heartland Institute's book on *Eco-Sanity*."[78]

- The *American Policy Center (APC)*, headed by longtime PR pro Thomas DeWeese, weighs in on what can safely be called the loony fringe of the sound science movement. One issue of the APC's newsletter attacks longtime environmentalist and author Jeremy Rifkin as "anti-industry, anti-civilization, anti-people" and accuses him of preaching "suicide, abortion, cannibalism and sodomy."[79] The APC is also the publisher of a report titled "Safeguarding the Future: Credible Science, Credible Decisions," which says EPA regulatory initiatives rest on "shaky scientific ground." It also publishes a newsletter called *EPA Watch,* edited by Bonner Cohen, which accuses the EPA of everything from destroying the U.S. economy to trying to stop people from taking showers. A Philip Morris strategy document describes *EPA Watch* as an "asset" created by PM funding allocated "to establish groups . . . that have a broader impact for PM." Another strategy memo discusses plans to promote "EPA Watch/Bonner Cohen as expert on EPA matters, i.e., regular syndicated radio features on EPA activities . . . news bureau function, speaking engagements, whatever can be done to increase his visibility and credibility on matters dealing with the EPA."[80]

- The *National Anxiety Center* calls itself "a think tank headquartered in Maplewood, New Jersey" whose mission is to dispel the "widespread, baseless fears" fostered by environmentalism regarding deforestation, pesticides, garbage, and endangered species. Its founder and sole proprietor is Alan Caruba, a longtime PR adviser to the pesticide industry and a personal friend of Steven Milloy. On his website (www.anxietycenter.com), Caruba attacks everyone from EPA director Carol Browner to now-deceased oceanologist Jacques Cousteau as co-conspirators in a "green genocide agenda" to "save the earth by killing humans." Caruba also contributes to the newsletter of the American Policy Center.

Experts at Being Experts

Since ideology, not science, unites industry's self-proclaimed debunkers of junk science, it is not surprising that many of industry's "experts" on scientific matters are themselves nonscientists. In July 1997, the Clearing-house on Environmental Advocacy and Research (CLEAR) issued an analysis of the "sound science" movement titled "Show Me the Science! Corporate Polluters and the 'Junk Science' Strategy." It examined the cre-dentials of many leading "science experts" in the *Directory of Environ-mental Scientists and Economists,* published in 1996 by the conservative National Center for Public Policy Research (NCPPR). Ostensibly, the di-rectory purported to identify experts in 27 policy fields, ranging alphabet-ically from agriculture to wildlife. "The environment is too important to leave in the hands of political activists," it stated in the introduction. "Yet, this is precisely where the United States has left most environmental de-cision making in recent years. Political activists—not authentic environ-mental scholars, scientists and economists—have come to dominate both the headlines and Washington's legislative agenda." Upon scrutinizing the directory, however, CLEAR found that fewer than half of the experts listed in NCPPR's directory were actual scientists, and in fact only 51 of the 141 individuals listed had a Ph.D. in any field whatsoever.

This does not mean that there are no reputable scientists who support the positions taken by groups like TASSC and ACSH. Norman Borlaug, a Nobel Prize recipient, has been involved with ACSH for many years and currently sits on the ACSH board of directors. Former U.S. Surgeon Gen-eral C. Everett Koop and former *JAMA* editor George Lundberg (whose firing Steven Milloy claims to have helped engineer) are also prominent ACSH supporters. For that matter, TASSC in its heyday was able to call on the support of Frederick J. Seitz, an eminent researcher in the field of solid-state physics, past president of the National Academy of Sciences, and retired president of Rockefeller University.

Even scientists are human beings. They may be brilliant in a partic-ular field of research but naive or uninformed about fields outside their specialty, and they are not immune from political ideologies or the lure of money. The conservative political views of Koop and Seitz are well-known. Although Koop certainly deserves credit for his principled stand regarding tobacco, since leaving public office he has participated in several ven-tures that call into question his objectivity and ability to avoid ethical con-flicts of interest. In April 1999, for example, he circulated a letter in Congress urging legislators to allow the Schering-Plough Corporation to extend the patent on its allergy drug Claritin. By keeping the drug under patent, the company would be able to prevent other companies from offering cheaper generic versions, thereby garnering an estimated $1 billion in additional profits. The following month, he met with members of Congress to defend the company's position on legislation involving another drug used to treat hepatitis C. Koop did not disclose that Schering-Plough had given a $1 million grant earlier that year to his nonprofit organization, the Koop Foundation.[81]

On another occasion, Koop testified in defense of latex gloves, which have been linked to life-threatening allergies. Latex allergies affect roughly 3 percent of the general population and upward of 10 percent of health care workers who are regularly exposed through the use of latex gloves and other medical supplies. An estimated 200,000 nurses have developed latex allergies, which can be disabling and even deadly. Alternatives to latex exist and are gradually being adopted by the health care industry, but Koop told Congress that latex glove concerns are "borderline hysteria." He also claimed—falsely, as he later discovered—that a study undercutting concerns about latex gloves had been conducted by the U.S. Centers for Disease Control and Prevention. In fact, the study he cited had been sponsored by a company that makes the gloves. And Koop had failed to disclose the fact that two years previously another maker of latex gloves had paid him a reported $656,250 in consulting fees to serve as a "spokesman for the company."[82]

"What this long admired and respected man has done in taking money from a glove manufacturer and then speaking out on its behalf is wrong," said Susan Wilburn, senior specialist in occupational safety and health for the American Nurses Association.[83] Another ANA representative, Michelle Nawar, noted that latex allergy "is a very serious disease" that "can be a debilitating, career-ending illness." In fact, five deaths have been reported from using latex gloves, four involving nurses.[84]

The conflicts of interest involving Frederick Seitz are even more telling. Shortly before his retirement from Rockefeller University in 1979, he went to work as a "permanent consultant" to the R. J. Reynolds tobacco company, a hiring that was deliberately not publicized.[85] The tobacco industry eagerly traded on Seitz's reputation, even though R. J. Reynolds CEO William Hobbs privately advised executives at Philip Morris in 1989 that Seitz was "quite elderly and not sufficiently rational to offer advice."[86] In June 1993, the CNN news network ran a report citing claims by Philip Morris that "prominent scientists privately agree" with its opinion of the EPA risk assessment of secondhand smoke. "We asked for specifics, promising anonymity if necessary," stated CNN correspondent Steve Young. "The only name Philip Morris provided was the former president of this prestigious institution, Rockefeller University, in New York." Although CNN never discovered Seitz's background as a tobacco industry consultant, he did not perform well in his role as third-party spokesperson. When Young called Seitz to ask directly if he had said that EPA's report was based on flawed science, Seitz responded, "No, I have not."

"You have not said that?" Young asked again.

"I have not said that, no," Seitz replied.

"Well, why not?"

"I haven't read it," Seitz replied.[87]

That same month, however, Multinational Business Services (Jim Tozzi's lobby shop and Steven Milloy's former employer) reported to Philip Morris that it had "initiated discussions with Dr. Seitz of Rockefeller University to support MBS findings on ETS."[88] The following year, a report appeared with Seitz listed as the author, concluding that "there is no good scientific evidence that moderate passive inhalation of tobacco smoke is truly dangerous under normal circumstances."[89]

The Legacy

Industry's campaign to stigmatize environmental and consumer health advocates has left its mark and continues to influence public and media attitudes. In 1999, University of Pennsylvania professor Edward S. Herman surveyed 258 articles in mainstream newspapers that used the term "junk science" during the years 1996 through 1998. Only 8 percent of the articles used the term in reference to corporate-manipulated science. By contrast, 62 percent used the term "junk science" in reference to scientific arguments used by environmentalists, other corporate critics, or personal-injury lawyers engaged in suing corporations.[90]

"What's starting to happen is that this term, 'junk science,' is being thrown around all the time," says Lucinda Finley, a law professor from the State University of New York at Buffalo who specializes in product liability and women's health. "People are calling scientists who disagree with them purveyors of 'junk.' But what we're really talking about is a very normal process of scientific disagreement and give-and-take. Calling someone a 'junk scientist' is just a way of shutting them up."[91]

Industry's campaign against junk science has also provided a pretext for growing infringements on such basic constitutional rights as freedom of speech. With the publication of *Galileo's Revenge*, Peter Huber took the concept of junk science out of the courtroom and introduced it to the mass media. Elizabeth Whelan's revisionist campaign to rehabilitate the image of Alar transformed Huber's concept into a weapon for *attacking* the media.

Huber charged that junk science was responsible for an avalanche of frivolous lawsuits, "The incentives for the lawyer today are simple and compelling," he wrote. "If the consensus in the scientific community is that a hazard is real and substantial, the trial bar will trumpet that consensus to support demands for compensation and punishment. If the consensus is that the hazard is imaginary or trivial, the bar will brush it aside, and dredge up experts from the fringe to swear otherwise. . . . Junk science, to put things bluntly, has become a very profitable business. . . . Costly towers of litigation are being erected on the soft, ever-shifting sands of junk science."[92]

Once junk science was redefined as a media problem, however, organizations like ACSH began to argue that what society needed was *more* lawsuits—lawsuits aimed not at corporations that make dangerous products, but at citizens who question their safety. Writer Tom Holt posed this argument directly in ACSH's quarterly magazine, *Priorities*. Holt's essay was titled "Could Lawsuits Be the Cure for Junk Science?" It began with a review of the Alar saga, complaining bitterly that existing libel law "has been a major stumbling block to the progress of a lawsuit brought by the Washington Apple Growers against the Natural Resources Defense Council, perpetrators of the Alar scare. The growers initially filed suit in Yakima County (WA) Superior Court; but . . . the growers lost their case." Fortunately, "agribusiness is now fighting back, shepherding what are known as 'agricultural product disparagement laws' through state legislatures."[93]

Agricultural product disparagement laws were designed to rewrite the rules of evidence so that future lawsuits against food industry critics would have a better chance of winning in court. In the years since Alar hit the headlines, cries of "never again" from the food industry prompted legislatures to pass product disparagement laws in 13 states—Alabama, Arizona, Colorado, Florida, Georgia, Idaho, Louisiana, Mississippi, North Dakota, Ohio, Oklahoma, South Dakota, and Texas. The new legislation was designed to protect industry profits by preventing people from expressing opinions that might discourage consumers from buying particular foods. "An anti-disparagement law is needed because of incidents such as the Alar scare several years ago. Apple producers suffered substantial financial losses when people stopped eating apples," argued the Ohio Farm Bureau in lobbying for the new law.[94] According to Holt, the new laws placed "the onus on the disparaging activist, rather than under liability law, which would place the onus on the grower or manufacturer of the disparaged product."[95] Shifting the onus meant that instead of corporations being forced to prove their critics were wrong, food safety critics could be judged guilty in court unless they could prove what they had said was *correct*.

In 1996, one of the new state laws was used for the first time when Texas cattle ranchers sued TV talk show host Oprah Winfrey over remarks that one of her guests made regarding the dangers of mad cow disease. The case finally went to trial in 1998, culminating in a victory for Winfrey, after which a second group of cattle ranchers stepped forward and filed a similar lawsuit in a separate jurisdiction. The second lawsuit was finally dismissed in early 2000. By then, Winfrey had spent millions of dollars in attorney fees to defend herself. In Ohio, a consumer group ran afoul of an anti-disparagement law when it discovered that a local egg producer was washing and repackaging old eggs for resale. "We interviewed over 40 employees who knew of the repackaging," says Mark Finnegan, an attorney for the group. "We had workers tell us they found maggots in the eggs." When the group went public with its finding, it got hit with a lawsuit and ran up large legal bills by the time the lawsuit was dropped.

Within the legal profession, this tactic of suing opponents into the ground is known as a "SLAPP suit"—a "strategic lawsuit against public participation." Often, an actual victory in court is not necessary in order to achieve victory. The real goal is to force the defendant to run up huge legal bills. For someone who lacks Oprah Winfrey's wealth, the costs of mounting a legal defense could literally mean financial bankruptcy, even if the case never goes to trial.

Friends and Enemies

Notwithstanding the differences between Steven Milloy and Elizabeth Whelan over the tobacco issue, they seem to have kissed and made up. An ACSH newsletter in early 2000 reported with satisfaction that ACSH had been mentioned favorably in several places on the Junk Science Home

Page. "The top story on Junkscience.com for December 24 was ACSH's 'Love Canal: Health Hype vs. Health Fact,' " it stated.[96]

ACSH returned the favor by helping disseminate a November 1999 "scientific study" in which Milloy claimed to find dioxin in Ben & Jerry's ice cream. By any reasonable standard of scientific inquiry, Milloy's study, coauthored with the Cato Institute's Michael Gough, would itself have to be condemned as junk science. Milloy has frequently attacked real scientists for using small sample sizes in their studies, but his own study relied on only a *single sample* of ice cream. He and Gough simply purchased a carton of Ben & Jerry's in a grocery store and took it to a laboratory for analysis. Their results, written in the style of a scientific research paper, were never published in a peer-reviewed scientific journal and would have a hard time finding a reputable publisher, given that their statement of methodology consisted in its entirety of a single sentence. As for the finding that Ben & Jerry's ice cream contains dioxin, this is hardly surprising, since dioxin accumulates in fatty tissues and is therefore common in dairy products. The real point of the study was to attack Ben & Jerry's for "hypocrisy," because the ice cream makers have been outspoken in calling for reforms that would reduce dioxin production and use a dioxin-free process to manufacture the cardboard cartons in which their product is packaged.

It would be more accurate to characterize the Milloy-Gough study as a publicity stunt than as scientific research. ACSH, however, loved it. "Ben & Jerry's might be described as a chemically holier-than-thou company," stated an editorial on the ACSH website. "So it was more than a bit ironic when two investigators . . . found that the product contained traces of dioxin. . . . Ben & Jerry's has been caught in its own game."[97] The ACSH newsletter boasted subsequently that "the ACSH editorial on Ben & Jerry's ice cream received more than 700 hits over a 36-hour period."[98]

The cozy relationship between ACSH and Milloy stands in marked contrast with their hostile relationship to other, reputable mainstream consumer and health groups such as the Center for Science in the Public Interest (CSPI). Milloy calls CSPI's *Nutrition Action Health Letter* a "rag" and accuses the organization of "doing its best to scare Americans about food." Whelan likewise calls CSPI "the nation's leading food terrorist group" for its warnings about excessive fat, sugar, and artificial additives in restaurant and snack foods. In one funding appeal to the Kellogg Company, she boasted of her organization's lengthy history of combat with

CSPI executive director Michael Jacobson over food issues. "We've been there to counter CSPI's claims as he has attacked virtually every aspect of modern-day food technology, whether it be caffeine, sugar, dietary fiber, the fat-replacer Olestra, dietary fat and cholesterol, moderate consumption of alcohol—or whatever other alleged carcinogen, toxin, or 'killer' ingredient his organization has singled out for indictment," she stated.

Whelan has long rankled at charges that ACSH is beholden to the corporations that pay its bills. "I've been called a paid liar for industry so many times, I've lost count," she complained in 1997. She frequently cites her stand on tobacco as evidence of her personal integrity and has responded to criticisms of her organization's reliance on industry funding by insinuating that prominent environmental and consumer groups are themselves beholden to tobacco money. "My counterparts, why aren't they quizzed as to funding?" she asked *Washington Post* reporter Howard Kurtz, adding that the Natural Resources Defense Council and CSPI receive "substantial funding from the cigarette families, including R. J. Reynolds family foundation. . . . Who knows where else they get their funding? They don't publish their funding list on a regular basis."

When Kurtz investigated these allegations, however, he found that unlike ACSH, the NRDC and CSPI *do* disclose their institutional funding sources. Whelan's claim that NRDC and CSPI take tobacco money is based on the fact that both organizations have received some funding from the Mary Reynolds Babcock Foundation, which is run by second- and third-generation heirs of tobacco money who choose to give their money to liberal causes.

But if CSPI's several-degrees-of-separation links to tobacco money are worth mentioning, it seems only fair to note that Whelan serves on the advisory council of Consumer Alert, a tobacco-financed front group for industry. Founded by former Bush administration chief of staff John Sununu, Consumer Alert is funded by Philip Morris along with the Coors Company, the Beer Institute, Monsanto, the Chemical Manufacturers Association, Chevron, Exxon, American Cyanamid, and a host of other usual corporate sponsors. In 1993, when the Clinton administration proposed raising cigarette taxes to fund its health plan, Consumer Alert worked closely with Philip Morris to attack the plan. "The antithesis of the Nader/Citizen Action brand of 'consumer defense,' Consumer Alert has worked with us in the promotion of the concept that the Clinton plan is anti-consumer," stated a Philip Morris strategy document. "Via continuation of their forums, position papers and op-eds, we are discussing a further media blitz for early Spring."[99]

In fact, ACSH has numerous ties, through its board of directors and advisory board, to many of the conservative, tobacco-funded organizations that Whelan accuses of "blurred vision" on tobacco. The ACSH advisory board includes representatives of the Hudson Institute, the Progress & Freedom Foundation and the Cato Institute, all of which receive funding from the tobacco industry and oppose efforts to regulate tobacco. *Priorities* magazine also repeatedly publishes articles from people affiliated with these and other pro-tobacco think tanks, including the Competitive Enterprise Institute and the Capital Research Center (which published two books in the 1990s denying that *direct* smoking causes cancer).[100] The 17-member ACSH board of directors includes Henry Miller, a former FDA official now at the Hoover Institution, who regularly grinds an ax against what he considers the FDA's "extraordinarily burdensome regulations" regarding genetically engineered foods and new drugs. In 1996, Miller also editorialized against the FDA's proposal to regulate tobacco. "The FDA's anti-tobacco initiative . . . has not been without its own costs to American consumers and taxpayers," he stated, describing FDA commissioner David Kessler as "personally consumed by this single issue."

Priorities has also published the work of Jacob Sullum, the *Reason* magazine editor whose vociferous defense of the tobacco industry appeared in full-page newspaper ads paid for by Philip Morris and R. J. Reynolds. Whelan is well aware of Sullum's track record as a tobacco defender, stating on one occasion that he "defies the now nearly unanimous view of scientists that ETS can be harmful."[101] In 1996, however, an essay by Sullum, titled "What the Doctor Orders," appeared as a *Priorities* cover story. In it, Sullum attacked government efforts to curb smoking, alcohol and drug abuse, along with handgun controls and motorcycle helmet and seat-belt laws, calling them examples of the "fundamentally collectivist . . . aims of the public health movement." In an accompanying letter, Whelan and ACSH Director of Public Health William London described Sullum's essay as "the most important critique of governmental public health activities we have seen," which "should be assigned reading in every school of public health." The same issue of *Priorities* offered commentaries on the Sullum article from eight other writers, who mingled similar words of praise with occasional criticisms. To finish off this "symposium," Sullum concluded with a final response in which he threw in an attack on Medicaid and Medicare for good measure.

What binds ACSH to thinkers like Milloy and Sullum is their common roots in a right-wing, "free market" ideology that overrides even Elizabeth Whelan's awareness of tobacco's dangers. These ideological underpinnings explain why Whelan blames the rest of the anti-tobacco movement for the failure of other conservatives to join them. "Discussions of tobacco and health policies are dominated almost exclusively by well-meaning social engineers and safety alarmists whose expansive agenda all but guarantees that many on the right reflexively gravitate to the opposite camp," she argues. "In this way, liberal anti-smoking enthusiasts have poisoned the waters for the political right."

The same ideology sometimes places Whelan at loggerheads with the opinions and strategies of the rest of the anti-tobacco movement. In May 1998, for example, ACSH and the pro-tobacco Competitive Enterprise Institute joined forces in a bizarre appeal for Congress to prove its "sincerity" by offering a tax rebate to adult smokers. Legislation then pending would have raised tobacco taxes (and thereby prices) in order to deter underage smoking. "If these taxes are truly aimed at reducing underage smoking, then Congress should give rebates of the tax to adult smokers," argued Whelan and CEI General Counsel Sam Kazman in a joint news release. "By rebating the revenues collected from adult smokers," they reasoned, "Congress could unequivocally demonstrate the purity of its motives—or it could drop the matter entirely."

Left unanswered was the question of how vendors were supposed to rebate the tax to adults without also rebating it to minors—who, after all, cannot legally buy their cigarettes directly, since sale of tobacco products to minors is already prohibited.

Defining Terms

One of the striking things about the concept of "junk science" has been the refusal of its theorists to offer a meaningful definition of the term. Huber defines junk science as "a hodgepodge of biased data, spurious inference and logical legerdemain, patched together by researchers whose enthusiasm for discovery and diagnosis far outstrips their skill." Milloy's website defines junk science as "bad science used by lawsuit-happy trial lawyers, the 'food police,' environmental Chicken Littles, power-drunk regulators, and unethical-to-dishonest scientists to fuel specious lawsuits, wacky social and political agendas, and the quest for personal fame and fortune." Neither of these definitions offers any way of distinguishing good from bad science. Instead, they consist of ad hominem attacks on the motives, morals, or competence of anyone who differs from the worldview of their authors.

The absence of real standards for distinguishing between junk science and sound science allows corporate apologists to use the term with confidence, while simultaneously managing to amicably disagree about an issue as fundamental and important as tobacco. The concept of junk science serves as a convenient way of reconciling their pro-corporate bias with pretensions of scientific superiority, while simultaneously glossing over ethical conflicts of interest.

Equally disturbing is the sheer amount of rhetorical venom and bile that the junkyard dogs of science have injected into public policy discussions, polarizing debates and lowering rather than elevating the tone of public scientific discourse. Some of the most respected voices in public life have been targeted for attack. Since its founding in 1936, Consumers Union and its monthly publication, *Consumer Reports*, have been icons of integrity, offering impartial scientific testing of consumer products and also serving as advocates for real consumer protection. None of this matters to "Junkman" Steven Milloy. In 1999 he launched a second website, called "Consumer Distorts" (www.consumerdistorts.com), which accuses *Consumer Reports* of socialism, sensationalism, and "scaring consumers away from products." ACSH has also gone to war repeatedly with Consumers Union, accusing it of "irresponsible fear-mongering" for its reports on health threats represented by pesticides and other chemicals found in foods and common household items.

The failure of the self-proclaimed "sound science" movement to provide a sound methodology is doubly disappointing because, in the end, the critics of junk science have a certain amount of truth on their side. There is indeed a great deal of bad science in the news media and in courtrooms, and not all of it comes from corporations. Over the years, both business marketers and advocacy groups have become highly skilled at inventing and exaggerating fears, dealing in dubious statistics and using emotional appeals to sell products or mobilize public support for causes. The time constraints and visual nature of television make simple messages stand out more easily than complex ones, and marketers have learned to exploit this reality of the modern mass media. In addition to the political goals that underlie these appeals, sometimes there are commercial motives as well. Great profits can be made by selling overhyped "natural" food supplements like shark cartilage and melatonin. ACSH has rightly criticized some of these marketing ploys as the scams that they are.

The problem is that neither Elizabeth Whelan nor Steven Milloy— nor, for that matter, any of the other attack dogs in the junk science war— seem capable of distinguishing between scam artists and reputable voices in today's debates over environmental safety and public health. The concept of junk science, as they have defined it, has proven itself unable to separate the wheat from the chaff. A movement that cannot tell whether tobacco science is junk science has little right to pose as society's scientific arbiter.

10

Global Warming
Is Good for You

*In the United States the mere threat of
impending climate change has impelled the
oil and coal industries to engineer a policy
of denial. While this campaign may seem at
this point no more sinister than any other
public relations program, it possesses a
subtle antidemocratic, even totalitarian
potential insofar as it curbs the free flow of
information, dominates the deliberations
of Congress, and obstructs all meaningful
international attempts to address the
gathering crisis.*

—Ross Gelbspan, *The Heat is On*[1]

With the exception of nuclear war, it is hard to imagine a
higher-stakes issue than global warming. The idea that
industrial emissions of carbon dioxide and other greenhouse gases might
lead to climate change has been seriously discussed among scientists
since 1957. It first became a topic of public debate during the brutally hot
summer of 1988, when Dr. James Hansen of NASA's Goddard Institute
for Space Studies warned a congressional panel that human industrial activities were already exerting a measurable and mounting impact on the
earth's climate. Hansen's testimony prompted *Time* magazine to editori-
alize that global warming's "possible consequences are so scary that it is
only prudent for governments to slow the buildup of carbon dioxide
through preventive measures."[2] As subsequent years saw a succession of
record global temperatures, climatologists became increasingly concerned

by what their computer models were telling them. The most authoritative statement of these concerns is a November 1995 report issued by the Intergovernmental Panel on Climate Change (IPCC), a group of some 2,500 climatologists from throughout the world that advises the United Nations. It predicted "widespread economic, social and environmental dislocation over the next century" if action is not taken soon to restrict greenhouse gas emissions. To avert catastrophe, the IPCC has called for policy measures to reduce emissions of greenhouse gases by 20 percent below 1990 levels initially and ultimately reduce those emissions by 70 percent.

Automobile exhausts, coal-burning power plants, factory smokestacks, and other vented wastes of the industrial age now pump six billion tons of carbon dioxide and other "greenhouse gases" into the earth's atmosphere each year. They are called greenhouse gases because they trap radiant energy from the sun that would otherwise be reflected back into space. The fact that a natural greenhouse effect occurs is well-known and is not debated. Without it, in fact, temperatures would drop so low that oceans would freeze and life as we know it would be impossible. What climatologists are concerned about, however, is that increased *levels* of greenhouse gases in the atmosphere are causing more heat to be trapped. Concentrations of greenhouse gases in the atmosphere are currently at their highest level in 420,000 years.[3]

"The basic science of global warming has not changed since the topic was raised earlier in this century," notes a December 1999 open letter by the directors of the U.S. National Oceanic and Atmospheric Administration and the British Meteorological Office. "Furthermore, the consensus of opinion has been growing, within both the scientific and the business communities. Our new data and understanding now point to the critical situation we face: to slow future change, we must start taking action soon. At the same time, because of our past and ongoing activities, we must start to learn to live with the likely consequences—more extreme weather, rising sea levels, changing precipitation patterns, ecological and agricultural dislocations, and the increased spread of human disease. . . . Ignoring climate change will surely be the most costly of all possible choices, for us and our children."[4]

"There is no debate among statured scientists of what is happening," says James McCarthy, who chairs the Advisory Committee on the Environment of the International Committee of Scientific Unions. "The only debate is the rate at which it's happening." Between 1987 and 1993, Mc-

Carthy oversaw the work of the leading climate scientists from 60 nations as they developed the IPCC's landmark 1995 report.

There are, of course, areas of considerable outstanding dispute and genuine scientific uncertainty. No one knows how rapid or drastic global warming will turn out to be, or how severely it will affect food production, ocean levels, or the spread of disease. There is also debate over the extent to which global warming has already contributed to droughts, intense hurricanes, and environmental degradation such as coral bleaching. Given these uncertainties, it is difficult to talk of a "worst-case scenario," but the scenarios that are plausible include many that are dire enough. A number of these possibilities are discussed in Ross Gelbspan's book *The Heat Is On*. Gelbspan quotes the late Dr. Henry Kendall, a Nobel Prize–winning physicist, who worried that climate change could disrupt farming at a time when earth's growing population is already creating unprecedented demands on agriculture. "The world's food supply," Kendall said in 1995, "must double within the next thirty years to feed the population, which will double within the next sixty years. Otherwise, before the middle of the next century—as many countries in the developing world run out of enough water to irrigate their crops—population will outrun its food supply, and you will see chaos. All we need is another hit from climate change a series of droughts or crop destroying rains and we're looking down the mouth of a cannon."[5]

Gelbspan worries that a global disaster of this magnitude would not only mean mass starvation but would threaten the survival of democratic institutions, particularly in developing nations. "In many of these countries, where democratic traditions are as fragile as the ecosystem, a reversion to dictatorship will require only a few ecological states of emergency," he warns. "Their governments will quickly find democracy to be too cumbersome for responding to disruptions in food supplies, water sources, and human health—as well as to a floodtide of environmental refugees from homelands that have become incapable of feeding and supporting them."[6] This vision of the future—a starving world under martial law—is by no means inevitable, but the groups pushing for strong measures to curb global warming believe that the nightmare scenarios are plausible enough to justify invoking the precautionary principle.

For the oil, coal, auto, and manufacturing industries, warnings of this sort involve another kind of high stakes. Any measures to control emissions of greenhouse gases threaten their long-standing habits of doing business.

They view scientists' conclusions about global warming with the same interest-driven hostility that the tobacco industry shows toward scientists who study lung cancer. Like the tobacco industry, they have pumped millions of dollars into efforts to debunk the science they hate. They have found little support, however, among the "statured scientists" to whom McCarthy refers—the people who are actually involved in relevant research and whose work has been published in peer-reviewed scientific journals. The global warming consensus among these scientists is so strong that the oil and auto industries have been forced far afield in their search for voices willing to join in their denial. What is remarkable, given this fact, is the extent to which industry PR has been successful in creating the illusion that global warming is some kind of controversial, hotly disputed theory.

Lobbying for Lethargy

In 1989, not long after James Hansen's highly publicized testimony before Congress and shortly after the first meeting of the UN's Intergovernmental Panel on Climate Change, the Burson-Marsteller PR firm created the Global Climate Coalition (GCC). Chaired by William O'Keefe, an executive for the American Petroleum Institute, the GCC operated until 1997 out of the offices of the National Association of Manufacturers. Its members have included the American Automobile Manufacturers Association, Amoco, the American Forest & Paper Association, American Petroleum Institute, Chevron, Chrysler, the U.S. Chamber of Commerce, Dow Chemical, Exxon, Ford, General Motors, Mobil, Shell, Texaco, Union Carbide, and more than 40 other corporations and trade associations. The GCC has also used "Junkman" Steven Milloy's former employer, the EOP Group, as well as the E. Bruce Harrison Company, a subsidiary of the giant Ruder Finn PR firm. Within the public relations industry, Harrison is an almost legendary figure who is ironically considered "the founder of green PR" because of his work for the pesticide industry in the 1960s, when he helped lead the attack on author Rachel Carson and her environmental classic *Silent Spring*.

GCC has been the most outspoken and confrontational industry group in the United States battling reductions in greenhouse gas emissions. Its activities have included publication of glossy reports, aggressive lobbying at international climate negotiation meetings, and raising concern about unemployment that it claims would result from emissions regulations. Since 1994 GCC alone has spent more than $63 million to combat any progress toward addressing the climate crisis. Its efforts are coordinated with separate campaigns by many of its members, such as the National Coal Association, which spent more than $700,000 on the global climate issue in 1992 and 1993, and the American Petroleum Institute, which paid the Burson-Marsteller PR firm $1.8 million in 1993 for a successful computer-driven "grassroots" letter and phone-in campaign to stop a proposed tax on fossil fuels.

These numbers may not seem huge compared to the billions that corporations spend on advertising. The Coca-Cola company alone, for example, spends nearly $300 million per year on soft drink advertisements. But the Global Climate Coalition is not advertising a product. Its propaganda budget serves solely to influence the news media and government policymakers on a single issue and comes on top of the marketing, lobbying, and campaign contributions that industry already spends in the regular course of doing business. In 1998, the oil and gas industries alone spent $58 million lobbying the U.S. Congress. For comparison's sake, environmental groups spent a relatively puny total of $4.7 million—on all issues combined, not just global warming.[7]

Industry's PR strategy with regard to the global warming issue is also eminently practical, with limited, realistic goals. Opinion polls for the past decade have consistently shown that the public would like to see something done about the global warming problem, along with many other environmental issues. Industry's PR strategy is not aimed at reversing the tide of public opinion, which may in any case be impossible. Its goal is simply to stop people from mobilizing to do anything about the problem, to create sufficient doubt in their minds about the seriousness of global warming that they will remain locked in debate and indecision. Friends of the Earth International describes this strategy as "lobbying for lethargy."

"People generally do not favor action on a non-alarming situation when arguments seem to be balanced on both sides and there is a clear doubt," explains Phil Lesly, author of *Lesly's Handbook of Public Relations and Communications*, a leading PR textbook. In order for the status quo to prevail, therefore, corporations have a simple task: "The weight of impressions on the public must be balanced so people will have doubts and lack motivation to take action. Accordingly, means are needed to get balancing information into the stream from sources that the public will find credible. There is no need for a clear-cut 'victory.' . . . Nurturing public doubts by demonstrating that this is not a clear-cut situation in support of the opponents usually is all that is necessary."[8]

In the Beginning There Was ICE

As political theorist Göran Therborn has observed, there are three basic ways to keep people apathetic about a problem: (1) argue that it doesn't exist; (2) argue that it's actually a good thing rather than a problem; or (3) argue that even if it is a problem, there's nothing they can do about it anyway. Industry's first propaganda responses to the problem of global warming focused on the first line of defense by attempting to deny that it was happening at all. In 1991, a corporate coalition composed of the National Coal Association, the Western Fuels Association, and Edison Electrical Institute created a PR front group called the "Information Council for the Environment" (ICE) and launched a $500,000 advertising and public relations campaign to, in ICE's own words, "reposition global warming as theory (not fact)."

To boost its credibility, ICE created a Scientific Advisory Panel that featured Patrick Michaels from the Department of Environmental Services at the University of Virginia; Robert Balling of Arizona State University; and Sherwood Idso of the U.S. Water Conservation Laboratory. ICE's plan called for placing these three scientists, along with fellow greenhouse skeptic S. Fred Singer, professor emeritus of environmental sciences at the University of Virginia, in broadcast appearances, op-ed pages, and newspaper interviews. Bracy Williams & Co., a Washington-based PR firm, did the advance publicity work for the interviews. Another company was contracted to conduct opinion polls, which identified "older, less-educated males from larger households who are not typically active information-seekers" and "younger, lower-income women" as "good targets for radio advertisements" that would "directly attack the proponents of global warming . . . through comparison of global warming to historical or mythical instances of gloom and doom."[9] One print advertisement prepared for the ICE campaign showed a sailing ship about to drop off the edge of a flat world into the jaws of a waiting dragon. The headline read: "Some say the earth is warming. Some also said the earth was flat." Another featured a cowering chicken under the headline "Who Told You the

Earth Was Warming . . . Chicken Little?" Another ad was targeted at Minneapolis readers and asked, "If the earth is getting warmer, why is Minneapolis getting colder?"[10]

"It will be interesting to see how the science approach sells," commented an internal memo by the Edison Electric Institute's William Brier. The campaign collapsed, however, after Brier's comments and other internal memoranda were leaked to the press. An embarrassed Michaels hastily disassociated himself from ICE, citing what he called its "blatant dishonesty."

Qualms notwithstanding, Michaels continues to benefit from his association with the fossil fuels industry. During an administrative hearing in Minnesota in May 1995, he testified that he had received $165,000 in funding during the previous five years from fuel companies, including $49,000 from the German Coal Association and funding from the Western Fuels company for a non-peer-reviewed journal that he edits called *World Climate Report*. Michaels has served as a paid expert witness for utilities in lawsuits involving the issue of global warming. He has written letters to the editor and op-ed pieces, appeared on television and radio, and testified before government bodies. He sits on the advisory boards of several industry-funded propaganda campaigns and is a "senior fellow" at the Cato Institute.

Other scientists who vocally defend the industry position have similar entanglements. Robert Balling is a geologist by training whose work prior to 1990 focused on desertification and soil-related issues. Beginning with his work for the ICE campaign, he has received nearly $300,000 in research funding from coal and oil interests, some of it in collaborations with Sherwood Idso. According to Peter Montague of the Environmental Research Foundation, S. Fred Singer "is now an 'independent' consultant" for companies including ARCO, Exxon Corporation, Shell Oil Company, Sun Oil Company, and Unocal Corporation. Rather than conducting research, Singer "spends his time writing letters to the editor and testifying before Congress."[11] Singer's Science and Environmental Policy Project (SEPP) was originally set up by the Rev. Sun Myung Moon's Unification Church, a frequent patron of conservative political causes. Although SEPP is no longer affiliated with Moon's cult, Singer's editorials frequently appear in the pages of the Unification Church–owned *Washington Times* newspaper.[12]

With all of these side deals and front groups in place, the collapse of ICE didn't even slow industry's propaganda effort. The scientists who participated in the ICE campaign—Michaels, Balling, Idso, and Singer—have simply been recycled into new organizations with new names. As Gelbspan observes, this "tiny group of dissenting scientists have been given prominent public visibility and congressional influence out of all proportion to their standing in the scientific community on the issue of global warming. They have used this platform to pound widely amplified drumbeats of doubt about climate change. These doubts are repeated in virtually every climate-related story in every newspaper and every TV and radio news outlet in the country. By keeping the discussion focused on whether there really *is* a problem, these dozen or so dissidents—contradicting the consensus view held by the world's top climate scientists—have until now prevented discussion about how to address the problem."[13]

Smoke and Mirrors

In addition to the Global Climate Coalition, a host of other industry-funded front groups have entered the fray. Although the GCC leads the campaign against climate change reform, it collaborates extensively with a network that includes industry trade associations, "property rights" groups affiliated with the anti-environmental Wise Use movement, and fringe groups such as Sovereignty International, which believes that global warming is a plot to enslave the world under a United Nations–led "world government."

Groups participating in industry's global warming campaign have included the American Energy Alliance (consisting of the National Association of Manufacturers, the American Petroleum Institute, and Edison Electric Institute), the Climate Council (run by Don Pearlman, a fixture at climate negotiations around the world and a member of the oil-client-heavy lobby firm of Patton Boggs), the International Climate Change Partnership (whose members include BP, Elf, and DuPont), the International Chamber of Commerce and Citizens for a Sound Economy (a Washington-based lobby group whose funders include BMW, Boeing, BP, Chevron, GM, Mobil, Toyota, and Unilever). In 1997, international global warming treaty negotiations were held in Kyoto, Japan, prompting a bevy of industry groups to mobilize. Some of the participating groups were the following:

- *The Global Climate Information Project (GCIP),* launched on September 9, 1997, by some of the nation's most powerful trade associations, spent more than $13 million in newspaper and television advertising. The ads were produced by Goddard*Claussen/First Tuesday, a California-based PR firm whose clients include the Chlorine Chemistry Council, the Chemical Manufacturers Association, DuPont Merck Pharmaceuticals, and the Vinyl Siding Institute. Goddard*Claussen is notorious for its "Harry and Louise" advertisement that helped derail President Clinton's 1993 health reform proposal. Its global warming ads used a similar fearmongering strategy by claiming that a Kyoto treaty would raise gasoline prices by 50 cents per gallon, leading to higher prices on everything from "heat to food to clothing." The GCIP was represented by Richard Pollock, former director of Ralph Nader's group, Critical Mass, who has switched sides and now works as a senior vice president for Shandwick Public Affairs, the second-largest PR firm in the United States. Recent Shandwick clients include Browning-Ferris Industries, Central Maine Power, Georgia-Pacific Corp., Monsanto Chemical Co., New York State Electric and Gas Co., Ciba-Geigy, Ford Motor Company, Hydro-Quebec, Pfizer, and Procter & Gamble.

- *The Coalition for Vehicle Choice (CVC),* a front group for automobile manufacturers, launched its own advertising campaign, including a three-page ad in the *Washington Post* that blasted the Kyoto climate talks as an assault on the U.S. economy. Sponsors for the ad included hundreds of oil and gas companies, auto dealers and parts stores, along with a number of far-right organizations such as the American Land Rights Association and Sovereignty International. CVC was originally founded in 1991 and has successfully prevented higher fuel-efficiency standards in U.S. autos and trucks. From the beginning, it has been represented by Ron DeFore, a former vice president of E. Bruce Harrison's PR firm. Its budget in 1993 was $2.2 million, all of which came from the big three automakers—Ford, GM, and Chrysler.

- *The National Center for Public Policy Research,* an industry-funded think tank, established a "Kyoto Earth Summit Information Center," issued an "Earth Summit Fact Sheet," and fed anti-treaty quotes to the media through a "free interview locator service" that offered "assistance to journalists seeking interviews with leading scientists, economists, and public policy experts on global warming."

- *The Advancement of Sound Science Coalition (TASSC)*, headed by "Junkman" Steven Milloy, attempted to stimulate anti-treaty e-mail to President Clinton by promising to enter writers' names in a $1,000 sweepstakes drawing. Milloy's website also heaps vitriol on the science of global warming, including attacks on the American Geophysical Union, the American Meteorological Society, and *Nature* magazine.

- The *American Policy Center (APC)* worked to mobilize a "Strike for Liberty," calling on truckers to pull over to the side of the road for an hour and for farmers to drive tractors into key cities to "shut down the nation" as a protest against any Kyoto treaty. Signing the treaty, APC warned, would mean that "with a single stroke of the pen, our nation as we built it, as we have known it and as we have loved it will begin to disappear." APC also appealed to anti-abortion activists with the claim that "Al Gore has said abortion should be used to reduce global warming."

Autograph Collections

Waving petitions from scientists seems to be a favorite PR strategy of greenhouse skeptics. The website of S. Fred Singer's Science and Environmental Policy Project lists no fewer than four petitions, including the 1992 "Statement by Atmospheric Scientists on Greenhouse Warming," the "Heidelberg Appeal" (also from 1992), Singer's own "Leipzig Declaration on Global Climate Change" (1997), and the "Oregon Petition," which was circulated in 1998 by physicist Frederick Seitz. Thanks to the echo chamber of numerous industry-funded think tanks, these petitions are widely cited by conservative voices in the "junk science" movement and given prominent play by reporters.

The Heidelberg Appeal was first circulated at the 1992 Earth Summit in Rio de Janeiro and has subsequently been endorsed by some 4,000 scientists, including 72 Nobel Prize winners. It has also been enthusiastically embraced by proponents of "sound science" such as Steven Milloy and Elizabeth Whelan and is frequently cited as proof that scientists reject not only the theory of global warming but also a host of other environmental health risks associated with everything from pesticides in food to antibiotic-resistant bacteria. The Heidelberg Appeal warns of the "emergence of an irrational ideology which is opposed to scientific and industrial progress and impedes economic and social development" and advises "the authorities in charge of our planet's destiny against decisions which are supported by pseudo-scientific arguments or false and non-relevant data. . . . The greatest evils which stalk our Earth are ignorance and oppression, and not Science, Technology and Industry."

The only problem is that the Heidelberg Appeal makes no mention whatsoever of global warming, or for that matter of pesticides or antibiotic-resistant bacteria. It is simply a brief statement supporting rationality and science. Based on the text alone, it is the sort of document that virtually any scientist in the world might feel comfortable signing.[14] Parts of the Heidelberg Appeal in fact appear to *endorse* environmental concerns, such as a sentence that states, "We fully subscribe to the objectives of a scientific ecology for a universe whose resources must be taken stock of, monitored and preserved." Its 72 Nobel laureates include 49 who also signed the "World Scientists' Warning to Humanity," which was circulated that same year by the liberal Union of Concerned Scientists (UCS) and attracted the majority of the world's living Nobel laureates in science along with some 1,700 other leading scientists.[15] In contrast with the vagueness of the Heidelberg Appeal, the "World Scientists' Warning" is a very explicit environmental manifesto, stating that "human beings and the natural world are on a collision course" and citing ozone depletion, global climate change, air pollution, groundwater depletion, deforestation, overfishing, and species extinction among the trends that threaten to "so alter the living world that it will be unable to sustain life in the manner that we know." More recently, 110 Nobel Prize–winning scientists signed another UCS petition, the 1997 "Call to Action," which called specifically on world leaders to sign an effective global warming treaty at Kyoto.[16]

Like the Heidelberg Appeal, the Leipzig Declaration is named after a German city, giving it a patina of gray eminence. Signed by 110 people, including many of the signers of the earlier "Statement by Atmospheric Scientists," it is widely cited by conservative voices in the "sound science" movement and is regarded in some circles as the gold standard of scientific expertise on the issue. It has been cited by Singer himself in editorial columns appearing in hundreds of conservative websites and major publications, including the *Wall Street Journal, Miami Herald, Detroit*

News, Chicago Tribune, Cleveland Plain Dealer, Memphis Commercial-Appeal, Seattle Times, and *Orange County Register.* Jeff Jacoby, a columnist with the *Boston Globe,* describes the signers of the Leipzig Declaration as "prominent scholars." The Heritage Foundation calls them "noted scientists," as do conservative think tanks such as Citizens for a Sound Economy, the Heartland Institute, and Australia's Institute for Public Affairs. Both the Leipzig Declaration and Seitz's Oregon Petition have been quoted as authoritative sources during deliberations in the U.S. Senate and House of Representatives.

When journalist David Olinger of the *St. Petersburg Times* investigated the Leipzig Declaration, however, he discovered that most of its signers have not dealt with climate issues at all and none of them is an acknowledged leading expert. Twenty-five of the signers were TV weathermen—a profession that requires no in-depth knowledge of climate research. Some did not even have a college degree, such as Dick Groeber of Dick's Weather Service in Springfield, Ohio. Did Groeber regard himself as a scientist? "I sort of consider myself so," he said when asked. "I had two or three years of college training in the scientific area, and 30 or 40 years of self-study."[17] Other signers included a dentist, a medical laboratory researcher, a civil engineer, and an amateur meteorologist. Some were not even found to reside at the addresses they had given.[18] A journalist with the Danish Broadcasting Company attempted to contact the declaration's 33 European signers and found that four of them could not be located, 12 denied ever having signed, and some had not even heard of the Leipzig Declaration. Those who did admit signing included a medical doctor, a nuclear scientist, and an expert on flying insects.[19] After discounting the signers whose credentials were inflated, irrelevant, false, or unverifiable, it turned out that only 20 of the names on the list had any scientific connection with the study of climate change, and some of those names were known to have obtained grants from the oil and fuel industry, including the German coal industry and the government of Kuwait (a major oil exporter).

Some Like It Hot

The Oregon Petition, sponsored by the Oregon Institute of Science and Medicine (OISM), was circulated in April 1998 in a bulk mailing to tens of thousands of U.S. scientists. In addition to the petition, the mailing included what appeared to be a reprint of a scientific paper. Authored by Arthur B. Robinson and three other people, the paper was titled "Environmental Effects of Atmospheric Carbon Dioxide" and was printed in the same typeface and format as the official Proceedings of the National Academy of Sciences (NAS). A cover note from Frederick Seitz, who had served as president of the NAS in the 1960s, added to the impression that Robinson's paper was an official publication of the academy's peer-reviewed journal.

Robinson's paper claimed to show that pumping carbon dioxide into the atmosphere is actually a *good* thing. "As atmospheric CO_2 increases," it stated, "plant growth rates increase. Also, leaves lose less water as CO_2 increases, so that plants are able to grow under drier conditions. Animal life, which depends upon plant life for food, increases proportionally." As a result, Robinson concluded, industrial activities can be counted on to encourage greater species biodiversity and a greener planet. "As coal, oil, and natural gas are used to feed and lift from poverty vast numbers of people across the globe, more CO_2 will be released into the atmosphere," the paper stated. "This will help to maintain and improve the health, longevity, prosperity, and productivity of all people. Human activities are believed to be responsible for the rise in CO_2 level of the atmosphere. Mankind is moving the carbon in coal, oil, and natural gas from below ground to the atmosphere and surface, where it is available for conversion into living things. We are living in an increasingly lush environment of plants and animals as a result of the CO_2 increase. Our children will enjoy an Earth with far more plant and animal life than that with which we now are blessed. This is a wonderful and unexpected gift from the Industrial Revolution."[20]

In reality, neither Robinson's paper nor OISM's petition drive had anything to do with the National Academy of Sciences, which first heard about the petition when its members began calling to ask if the NAS had taken a stand against the Kyoto treaty. The paper's author, Arthur Robinson, was not even a climate scientist. He was a biochemist with no published research in the field of climatology, and his paper had never been subjected to peer review by anyone with training in the field. In fact, the paper had never been accepted for publication *anywhere,* let alone in the NAS Proceedings. It was self-published by Robinson, who did the typesetting himself on his own computer under the auspices of the Oregon Institute of Science and Medicine, of which Robinson himself was the founder.

So what is the OISM, exactly? The bulk mailing that went out to scientists gave no further information, other than the address of a post office box. The OISM does have a website, however, where it describes itself as "a small research institute" in Cave Junction, Oregon, with a faculty of six people engaged in studying "biochemistry, diagnostic medicine, nutrition, preventive medicine and the molecular biology of aging."[21] The OISM also sells a book titled *Nuclear War Survival Skills* (foreword by H-bomb inventor Edward Teller), which argues that "the dangers from nuclear weapons have been distorted and exaggerated" into "demoralizing myths."[22] Like the Institute itself, Cave Junction (population 1,126) is a pretty obscure place. It is the sort of out-of-the-way location you might seek out if you were hoping to survive a nuclear war, but it is not known as a center for scientific and medical research.

"Robinson is hardly a reliable source," observes journalist Ross Gelbspan. "As late as 1994 he declared that ozone depletion is a 'hoax'—a position akin to defending the flat-earth theory. In his newsletter, he told readers it was safe to drink water irradiated by the Chernobyl nuclear plant, and he marketed a home-schooling kit for 'parents concerned about socialism in the public schools.' "[23]

None of the coauthors of "Environmental Effects of Atmospheric Carbon Dioxide" had any more standing than Robinson himself as a climate change researcher. They included Robinson's 22-year-old son, Zachary (home-schooled by his dad), along with astrophysicists Sallie Baliunas and Willie Soon. Both Baliunas and Soon worked with Frederick Seitz at the George C. Marshall Institute, a Washington, D.C., think tank where Seitz served as executive director.[24] Funded by a number of right-wing foundations, including Scaife and Bradley, the George C. Marshall Institute does not conduct any original research. It is a conservative think tank that was initially founded during the years of the Reagan administration to advocate funding for Reagan's Strategic Defense Initiative—the "Star Wars" weapons program.[25] Today, the Marshall Institute is still a big fan of high-tech weapons. In 1999, its website gave prominent placement to an essay by Col. Simon P. Worden titled "Why We Need the Air-Borne Laser," along with an essay titled "Missile Defense for Populations—What Does It Take? Why Are We Not Doing It?" Following the collapse of the Soviet Union, however, the Marshall Institute has adapted to the times by devoting much of its firepower to the war against environmentalism, and in particular against the "scaremongers" who raise warnings about global warming.

"The mailing is clearly designed to be deceptive by giving people the impression that the article, which is full of half-truths, is a reprint and has passed peer review," complained Raymond Pierrehumbert, an atmospheric chemist at the University of Chicago. NAS foreign secretary F. Sherwood Rowland, an atmospheric chemist, said researchers "are wondering if someone is trying to hoodwink them." NAS council member Ralph J. Cicerone, dean of the School of Physical Sciences at the University of California at Irvine, was particularly offended that Seitz described himself in the cover letter as a "past president" of the NAS. Although Seitz had indeed held that title in the 1960s, Cicerone hoped that scientists who received the petition mailing would not be misled into believing that he "still has a role in governing the organization."[26]

The NAS issued an unusually blunt formal response to the petition drive. "The NAS Council would like to make it clear that this petition has nothing to do with the National Academy of Sciences and that the manuscript was not published in the Proceedings of the National Academy of Sciences or in any other peer-reviewed journal," it stated in a news release. "The petition does not reflect the conclusions of expert reports of the Academy." In fact, it pointed out, its own prior published study had shown that "even given the considerable uncertainties in our knowledge of the relevant phenomena, greenhouse warming poses a potential threat sufficient to merit prompt responses. Investment in mitigation measures acts as insurance protection against the great uncertainties and the possibility of dramatic surprises."[27]

Notwithstanding this rebuke, the Oregon Petition managed to garner 15,000 signatures within a month's time. Fred Singer called the petition "the latest and largest effort by rank-and-file scientists to express their opposition to schemes that subvert science for the sake of a political agenda."[28]

Nebraska senator Chuck Hagel called it an "extraordinary response" and cited it as his basis for continuing to oppose a global warming treaty. "Nearly all of these 15,000 scientists have technical training suitable for evaluating climate research data," Hagel said.[29] Columns citing the Seitz petition and the Robinson paper as credible sources of opinion on the global warming issue have appeared in publications ranging from *Newsday*, the *Los Angeles Times,* and *Washington Post* to the *Austin-American States-man, Denver Post,* and *Wyoming Tribune-Eagle.*

In addition to the bulk mailing, OISM's website enables people to add their names to the petition over the Internet, and by June 2000 it claimed to have recruited more than 19,000 scientists. The institute is so lax about screening names, however, that virtually anyone can sign, including for example Al Caruba, the pesticide-industry PR man and conservative ideologue whose "National Anxiety Center" we describe briefly in chapter nine. Caruba has editorialized on his own website against the science of global warming, calling it the "biggest hoax of the decade," a "genocidal" campaign by environmentalists who believe that "humanity must be destroyed to 'Save the Earth.' . . . There is no global warming, but there is a global political agenda, comparable to the failed Soviet Union experiment with Communism, being orchestrated by the United Nations, supported by its many Green NGOs, to impose international treaties of every description that would turn the institution into a global government, superceding the sovereignty of every nation in the world."

When questioned in 1998, OISM's Arthur Robinson admitted that only 2,100 signers of the Oregon Petition had identified themselves as physicists, geophysicists, climatologists, or meteorologists, "and of those the greatest number are physicists."[30] The names of the signers are available on the OISM's website, but without listing any institutional affiliations or even city of residence, making it very difficult to determine their credentials or even whether they exist at all. When the Oregon Petition first circulated, in fact, environmental activists successfully added the names of several fictional characters and celebrities to the list, including John Grisham, Michael J. Fox, Drs. Frank Burns, B. J. Honeycutt, and Benjamin Pierce (from the TV show M*A*S*H), an individual by the name of "Dr. Red Wine," and Geraldine Halliwell, formerly known as pop singer Ginger Spice of the Spice Girls. Ginger's field of scientific specialization was listed as "biology."[31]

Casting Call

In April 1998, at about the same time that the OISM's petition first circulated, the *New York Times* reported on yet another propaganda scheme developed by the American Petroleum Institute. Joe Walker, a public relations representative of the API, had written an eight-page internal memorandum outlining the plan, which unfortunately for the plotters was leaked by a whistle-blower. Walker's memorandum called for recruiting scientists "who do not have a long history of visibility and/or participation in the climate change debate." Apparently, new faces were needed because the industry's long-standing scientific front men—Michaels, Balling, Idso, and Singer—had used up their credibility with journalists.[32]

Walker's plan called for spending $5 million over two years to "maximize the impact of scientific views consistent with ours on Congress, the media and other key audiences." To measure success, a media tracking service would be hired to tally the percentage of news articles that raise questions about climate science and the number of radio talk show appearances by scientists questioning the prevailing view. The budget included $600,000 to develop a cadre of 20 "respected climate scientists" and to "identify, recruit and train a team of five independent scientists to participate in media outreach." (Unanswered, of course, was the question of how anyone who has been recruited and trained by the petroleum industry can be honestly described as "independent.") Once trained, these scientific spokesmodels would be sent around to meet with science writers, newspaper editors, columnists, and television network correspondents, "thereby raising questions about and undercutting the 'prevailing scientific wisdom.' "[33]

"One of the creepiest revelations is that oil companies and their allies intend to recruit bona fide scientists to help muddy the waters about global warming," commented the *St. Louis Post-Dispatch,* seemingly unaware that this "third party" strategy had been part of the industry campaign from day one.[34]

Hot Talk, Slow Walk

During the 1990s, Clinton-bashing was a common theme in industry's appeals to conservatives, using the argument that the global warming issue was a liberal attempt to replace private property with "socialism," "bureaucracy," and "big government." Particularly strong criticisms were leveled at then-Vice President Al Gore, who has spoken with occasional eloquence about the greenhouse effect and wrote about it in his book *Earth in the Balance.* Ironically, industry's attacks on Clinton and Gore helped conceal the Clinton administration's own complicity in the effort to prevent any effective regulations on greenhouse emissions.

On the eve of Earth Day in April 1993, Clinton announced his intention to sign a treaty on global warming, only to spend the rest of his two terms in office waffling and backpedaling. His "Climate Change Action Plan" of October 1993 turned out to be a "voluntary effort," depending entirely on the goodwill of industry for implementation. By early 1996, he was forced to admit that the plan was off track and would not even come close to meeting its goal for greenhouse gas reductions by the year 2000.

In June 1997, Clinton addressed the United Nations Earth Summit and pledged a sustained U.S. commitment to stop global warming. Painting a near-apocalyptic picture of encroaching seas and killer heat, he acknowledged that America's record over the past five years was "not sufficient. . . . We must do better and we will." Four months later, however, he announced that realistic targets and timetables for cutting greenhouse gas emissions should be put off for 20 years, prompting Australian environmental writer Sharon Beder to comment that "champagne corks are popping in the boardrooms of BP, Shell, Esso, Mobil, Ford, General Motors, and the coal, steel and aluminum corporations of the US, Australia and Europe. . . . The new limits are so weak, compared with even the most pessimistic predictions of what the US would offer in the current negotiations, that two years of hard work by 150 countries towards reaching an agreement in December are now irrelevant."[35]

During negotiations in Kyoto, the United States lobbied heavily and successfully to weaken the treaty's actual provisions for limiting greenhouse gases. The resulting treaty proposed a reduction of only 7 percent in global greenhouse emissions by the year 2012, far below the 20 percent cut proposed by the IPCC and European nations or the 30 percent reduction demanded by low-lying island nations that fear massive flooding as melting polar ice leads to rising sea levels. The United States also successfully won a provision that will allow countries to exceed their emission targets by buying right-to-pollute credits from nations that achieve better-than-targeted reductions.

Greenpeace called the resulting Kyoto treaty "a tragedy and a farce." It was condemned as "too extreme" by U.S. industry, declared dead on arrival by Senate Republicans, and praised by some environmental groups; and it provided all the political wiggle room that the Clinton administration needed to have its cake and eat it too. Clinton embraced the agreement but simultaneously said he would not submit it to the Senate until impoverished Third World nations agreed to their own cutbacks in greenhouse gas emissions.

There is a method to this madness that is well understood in Washington lobbying circles, although it is rarely discussed in public. By talking tough about the environment while sitting on the Kyoto treaty, Clinton and Gore were able to preserve their "green credentials" for political purposes while blaming the treaty's demise on anti-environmental Republicans and an apathetic public. For Democrats, it was a "win-win situation." They could stay on the campaign-funding gravy train by doing what their corporate donors wanted, while giving lip service to solving the problem. The December 12, 1997 *New York Times* reported that Clinton was "in the risk-free position of being able to make a strong pro-environmental political pitch while not having to face a damaging vote in the Senate. . . . One senior White House official . . . said it was possible that the treaty would not be ready for submission . . . during the remainder of Mr. Clinton's term in office." And indeed, this prediction proved correct. Industry's "lobbyists for lethargy" had succeeded.

Stormy Weather

While Nero fiddles, the burning of Rome is proceeding and even appears to be occurring faster than some climatologists expected. The twelve warmest years in recorded history have all occurred since 1983. The U.S. National Oceanic and Atmospheric Administration (NOAA) and the World Meteorological Association concurred that 1997 was the hottest year ever, only to be surpassed by 1998, which was in turn surpassed by 1999. In January 2000, the National Research Council of the National Academy of Sciences—Fred Seitz's former stomping grounds—issued a major report concluding that global warming is an "undoubtedly real" problem and is in fact occurring 30 percent faster than the rate estimated just five years earlier by the IPCC.[36]

A series of extreme weather events also seemed to corroborate the IPCC's predictions. In 1998, a January ice storm caused widespread power outages in eastern Canada and the northeastern United States. In February, Florida was hit by the deadliest tornado outbreak in its history. April through June was the driest period in 104 years of record in Florida, Texas, Louisiana, and New Mexico, and May through June was the warmest period on record. Heat and dry weather caused devastating fires in central and eastern Russia, Indonesia, Brazil, Central America, and Florida. Massive floods hit Argentina, Peru, Bangladesh, India, and China, where the flooding of the Yangtze River killed more than 3,000 people and caused $30 billion in losses. Droughts plagued Guyana, Papua New Guinea, Pakistan, the Ukraine, Kazakhstan, and southern Russia. On October 4, 1998, Oklahoma was hit by 20 tornadoes, setting a national record for the most twisters ever during a single day. Three hurricanes and four tropical storms caused billions of dollars of damage to the United States. In late September, Hurricane Georges devastated the northern Caribbean, causing $4 billion in damages. A month later, Central America was devastated by Hurricane Mitch, Central America's worst natural disaster in 218 years, which killed more than 11,000 people and displaced another 2.4 million. In the Pacific, October's Supertyphoon Zeb inundated the northern Philippines, Taiwan, and Japan. Only eight days later, Supertyphoon Babs struck the Philippines, submerging parts of Manila.[37]

In 1999, farmers in the northeastern and mid-Atlantic regions of the United States suffered through a record drought. A prolonged heat wave killed 271 people in the Midwest and Northeast. Hurricane Floyd battered North Carolina, inflicting more than a billion dollars in damages, while Boston marked a record 304 consecutive days without snow. In India, a supercyclone killed some 10,000 people. Torrential rains and mudslides killed 15,000 in Venezuela. Hurricane-force windstorms destroyed trees, buildings, and monuments in France, leaving more than $4 billion in damages. The South Pacific islands of Tebua Tarawa and Abunuea in the nation of Vanuato disappeared beneath the ocean, the first victims of the global rise in sea levels. The wave of catastrophes continued in 2000, with a prolonged drought in Kenya while wet, warm weather spawned billions of crop-threatening locusts in Australia and drought-driven fires devastated Los Alamos. The melting and fissuring of Antarctica's ice shelf, which first became dramatically evident in 1995, led in May 2000 to the calving of three enormous icebergs with a combined surface area slightly smaller than the state of Connecticut.

It is impossible, of course, to prove that any of these individual events was caused by global warming, but cumulatively the evidence is becoming harder to deny. As the evidence continues to mount, even some members of the oil industry have begun to defect. In 1999, the oil companies BP Amoco and Royal Dutch/Shell, along with Dow Chemicals, left the

Global Climate Coalition and stated publicly that they now consider global warming a real, immediate problem. The following year saw similar moves from Ford, DaimlerChrysler, the Southern Company, Texaco, and General Motors.[38] The DuPont corporation claims it will voluntarily cut emissions of greenhouse gases to 35 percent of their 1990 level by the year 2010.

"You can't stop climate change given what we're doing right now," said Michael MacCracken in February 2000. MacCracken is director of the National Assessment Coordination Office of the U.S. Global Climate Change Research Program, which was launched by President Bush in 1989. It is already too late to stop global warming, he said, due to the accumulated carbon-dioxide emissions that have already entered the atmosphere. The best that can be hoped for is to minimize the problem and adapt to the changes. In the United States, necessary measures will include changing the way water supplies are managed in the western United States, beefing up public health programs, building higher bridges, and rethinking massive environmental restoration projects.[39]

For years, the PR apparatus of big coal and big oil persuaded many key decision-makers that global warming was a phantom—that it was not even happening. As the scientific data proving otherwise has accumulated, the contrarian line of argument has also shifted. Industry voices have begun to admit that the industrial greenhouse effect is real, and some are attempting to argue, like Arthur Robinson of the Oregon Institute of Science and Medicine, that it is actually a *good* thing—that it will enhance plant growth or that it will be of no consequence because the anticipated temperature changes will be relatively slight. Other voices are stepping forward with industry's standard lament, claiming that even if global warming is a bad thing, fixing the problem is impossible because it will cost trillions of dollars, ruin the economy, and eliminate jobs.

The Western Fuels Association (WFA), which provides coal to electrical utility companies, has been a major sponsor of efforts to respin the global warming debate. In the early 1990s, WFA backed the ICE campaign, which attempted to claim that the planet was actually cooling. Its more recent creations include the Greening Earth Society, which promotes that idea that increasing the amount of carbon dioxide in the atmosphere is "good for earth" because it will encourage greater plant growth. The Greening Earth Society has produced a video, titled "The Greening of the Planet Earth Continues," publishes a newsletter called the *World Climate Report*, and works closely with a group called the Center for the Study of Carbon Dioxide and Global Change. Each of these groups has its own separate website.[40]

Another web venture is a "grassroots mobilization effort" created for WFA by Bonner & Associates, a Washington, D.C., lobby firm that specializes in "grassroots public relations"—a PR subspecialty that uses telemarketing and computer databases to create the appearance of grassroots public support for a client's cause. The "Global Warming Cost" website[41] focuses on generating e-mail to elected officials. Between September 1997 and July 1998, WFA claims the site generated 20,000 e-mail messages to Congress opposing the Kyoto treaty. The way it works is simple. Visitors to the home page of the website are invited to click on an icon indicating whether they represent "business," "seniors," "farmers," "families," or "workers." This takes them to another Web page that requests their address and asks a handful of questions about the amount they spend on home heating, transportation, and other fuel costs. Based on this information, the website automatically generates a "customized" e-mail, directed to each senator and member of Congress in the visitor's voting area, asking them to "reject any effort to stiffen the United Nations Global Climate Change Treaty." It's all computerized, and the website makes no effort to verify that the resulting letter is accurate or even plausible.

Using the assumed name "George Jetson," for example, we plugged in an estimate that he currently spends $24,166,666 per year on gasoline, electricity, heating oil, and natural gas. (After all, it takes a lot of energy to propel those flying cars.)

The computer promptly generated messages to our elected officials. "I am proud to be a worker which you represent," Mr. Jetson stated. "Estimates suggest I will personally see my cost for electricity, for natural gas, and for gasoline go up by $24,239,987.52 a year!"

It's nice to know that the democratic system works. Thanks to the miracles of modern computer technology and sophisticated PR, even cartoon characters can do their part to save America from the eco-wackos and their newfangled scientific theories.

11

Questioning Authority

I know of no safe depository of the ultimate power of the society but the people themselves; and if we think them not enlightened enough to exercise their control with a wholesome discretion, the remedy is not to take it from them, but to inform their discretion.

—Thomas Jefferson[1]

When psychologists have explored the relationship between individuals and authority figures, they have found that it can be disturbingly easy for false experts to manipulate the thinking and behavior of others. One of the classic experiments in this regard was conducted in 1974 by Stanley Milgram, who tried to see how far people would go in following orders given by a seemingly authoritative scientist. The subjects of Milgram's research were taken into a modern laboratory and told that they would be helping conduct an experiment that involved administering electric shocks to see how punishment affected the learning process. The subjects were seated at a machine called a "shock generator," marked with a series of switches ranging from "slight shock" to "severe shock." Another person was designated as a "learner" and was hooked up to receive a jolt each time he gave the wrong answer on a test. A third individual, the "scientist," stood over the experiment giving instructions and supervision. Unbeknownst to the real subjects of the experiment, both the "learner" and the "scientist" were actors, and no actual electricity was used. As each fake shock was administered, the "learner" would cry out in pain. If the subject administering the shocks hesitated, the "scientist" would say something like, "Although the shocks may be painful, there is no permanent tissue damage, so please go on," or "It is absolutely essential that you continue." The result was that many subjects continued to administer shocks, even when the "learner" claimed heart trouble, cried out, or pleaded to be set free. "With numbing regularity," Milgram observed, "good people were seen to knuckle under the demands of authority and perform actions that were callous and severe. Men who are in everyday life responsible and decent were seduced by the trappings of authority, by the control of their perceptions, and by the uncritical acceptance of the experimenter's definition of the situation, into performing harsh acts."[2]

In another famous experiment, known as the "Doctor Fox Lecture," a distinguished-looking actor was hired to give a meaningless lecture, titled "Mathematical Game Theory as Applied to Physical Education." The talk, deliberately filled with "double talk, neologisms, non sequiturs, and contradictory statements," was delivered before three audiences composed of psychiatrists, social workers, psychologists, educators, and educational administrators, many of whom held advanced degrees. After each session, audiences received a questionnaire asking them to evaluate the speaker. None of the audience members saw through the lecture as a hoax, and most reported that they were favorably impressed with the speaker's expertise.[3]

The rich and powerful seem to be no better at seeing through bogus experts than anyone else. In September 1999, the *Wall Street Journal* announced the arrest of Martin A. Armstrong, charged with bilking Japanese investors out of $950 million. "For decades," the *Journal* reported, "Armstrong sold himself to investors as expert on anything of precious value, from coins minted by the Egyptian pharaohs to turn-of-the-century U.S. stamps, not to mention current-day markets for stocks, bonds, commodities and currencies. Now, Mr. Armstrong . . . stands accused in a federal indictment of using this market-wizard image to conduct one of the most common frauds in the history of finance: making big promises to investors that he couldn't deliver."

Armstrong's "self-confident forecasting style" had made him a hit at conferences in which he addressed hundreds of Japanese corporate chieftains. Even as his currency deals were losing hundreds of millions of their dollars, "Armstrong continued to confidently sell himself as a forecaster of market trends, often in language in which he mocks others' mistakes," the *Journal* noted. "Mr. Armstrong's reams of investing treatises, many posted on his website, range from the monetary history of Persia to the

'Panic cycle in global capital flows.' The historical data maintained by his Princeton Economic Institute has been used by many media outlets. The 'first and most important rule about investing is to "Know what you are buying and why!" ' he warned in a July 1997 report. . . . He wasn't shy about promotion, jumping at the chance to have his picture taken with heavyweights in any market in which he was playing. Princeton Economics' website, which is filled with Mr. Armstrong's essays on the market, shows a photo of Mr. Armstrong with former United Kingdom Prime Minister Margaret Thatcher at one of the firm's conferences in 1996."[4]

It is tempting to look at these examples and despair. If people are this easily duped, how can anyone hope to expert-proof themselves? The answer, of course, is that no one can, but there are some things we can all do to improve our chances.

Recognizing Propaganda

Between World Wars I and II, the rise of the public relations industry in the United States and the growing use of propaganda by fascist and communist governments prompted a group of social scientists and journalists to found a remarkable organization called the Institute for Propaganda Analysis. The IPA published a periodic newsletter that examined and exposed manipulative practices by advertisers, businesses, governments, and other organizations. Fearlessly eclectic, it hewed to no party lines and focused its energies on studying the ways that propaganda could be used to manipulate emotions. It is best known for identifying several basic types of rhetorical tricks used by propagandists:

1. *Name-calling.* This technique, in its crudest form, involves the use of insult words. Newt Gingrich, the former Speaker of the U.S. House of Representatives, is reported to have used this technique very deliberately, circulating a list of negative words and phrases that Republicans were instructed to use when speaking about their political opponents—words such as "betray," "corruption," "decay," "failure," "hypocrisy," "radical," "permissive," and "waste." The term "junk science," which we discussed in Chapter 9, is an obvious use of this same strategy. When name-calling is used, the IPA recommended that people should ask themselves the following questions: What does the name mean? Does the idea in question have a legit-

imate connection with the real meaning of the name? Is an idea that serves my best interests being dismissed through giving it a name I don't like?

2. *Glittering generalities.* This technique is a reverse form of name-calling. Instead of insults, it uses words that generate strong positive emotions—words like "democracy," "patriotism," "motherhood," "science," "progress," "prosperity." Politicians love to speak in these terms. Newt Gingrich advised Republicans to use words such as "caring," "children," "choice," "commitment," "common sense," "dream," "duty," "empowerment," "freedom," and "hard work" when talking about themselves and their own programs. Democrats, of course, use the same strategy. Think, for example, of President Clinton's talk of "the future," "growing the economy," or his campaign slogan: "I still believe in a place called Hope."

3. *Euphemisms* are another type of word game. Rather than attempt to associate positive or negative connotations, euphemisms merely try to obscure the meaning of what is being talked about by replacing plain English with deliberately vague jargon. Rutgers University professor William Lutz has written several books about this strategy, most recently *Doublespeak Defined.* Examples include the use of the term "strategic misrepresentations" as a euphemism for "lies," or the term "employee transition" as a substitute for "getting fired." Euphemisms have also transformed ordinary sewage sludge into "regulated organic nutrients" that don't stink but merely "exceed the odor threshold."

4. *Transfer* is described by the IPA as "a device by which the propagandist carries over the authority, sanction, and prestige of something we respect and revere to something he would have us accept. For example, most of us respect and revere our church and our nation. If the propagandist succeeds in getting church or nation to approve a campaign in behalf of some program, he thereby transfers its authority, sanction, and prestige to that program. Thus, we may accept something which otherwise we might reject." In 1998, the American Council on Science and Health convened what it called a "blue-ribbon committee" of scientists to issue a report on health risks associated with phthalates, a class of chemical additives used

in soft vinyl children's toys. People familiar with ACSH's record on other issues were not at all surprised when the blue-ribbon committee concluded that phthalates were safe. The committee's real purpose, after all, was to transfer the prestige of science onto the chemicals that ACSH was defending.

5. *Testimonial* is a specific type of transfer device in which admired individuals give their endorsement to an idea, product, or cause. Cereal companies put the pictures of famous athletes on their cereal boxes, politicians seek out the support of popular actors, and activist groups invite celebrities to speak at their rallies. Sometimes testimonials are transparently obvious. Whenever they are used, however, the IPA recommends asking questions such as the following: Why should we regard this person (or organization or publication) as a source of trustworthy information on the subject in question? What does the idea amount to on its own merits, without the benefit of the testimonial?

6. *Plain folks.* This device attempts to prove that the speaker is "of the people." Even a geeky multibillionaire like Bill Gates tries to convey the impression that he's just a regular guy who enjoys fast food and popular movies. Politicians also use the "plain folks" device to excess: George Bush insisting he eats pork rinds; Hillary Clinton slipping into a southern accent. Virtually every member of the U.S. Senate is a millionaire, but you wouldn't know it from the way they present themselves.

7. *Bandwagon.* This device attempts to persuade you that everyone else supports an idea, so you should support it too. Sometimes opinion polls are contrived for this very purpose, such as the so-called "Pepsi Challenge," which claimed that most people preferred the taste of Pepsi over Coca-Cola. "The propagandist hires a hall, rents radio stations, fills a great stadium, marches a million or at least a lot of men in a parade," the IPA observed. "He employs symbols, colors, music, movement, all the dramatic arts. He gets us to write letters, to send telegrams, to contribute to his cause. He appeals to the desire, common to most of us, to follow the crowd."

8. *Fear.* This device attempts to reach you at the level of one of your most primitive and compelling emotions. Politicians use it when

they talk about crime and claim to be advocates for law and order. Environmentalists use it when they talk about pollution-related cancer, and their opponents use fear when they claim that effective environmental regulations will destroy the economy and eliminate jobs. Fear can lead people to do things they would never otherwise consider. Few people believe that war is a good thing, for example, but most people can be convinced to support a *specific* war if they believe that they are fighting an enemy who is cruel, inhuman, and bent on destroying all that they hold dear.

The IPA disbanded at the beginning of World War II, and its analysis does not include some of the propaganda devices that came to light in later years, such as the "big lie," based on Nazi propaganda minister Joseph Goebbels's observation that "the bigger the lie, the more people will believe it." Another device, which the IPA did not mention but which is increasingly common today, is the tactic of "information glut"—jamming the public with so many statistics and other information that people simply give up in despair at the idea of trying to sort it all out.

To get an idea of how sophisticated modern propaganda has become, compare the IPA's list of propaganda techniques with another list—the 12 points that consultant Peter Sandman advises his clients to bear in mind when attempting to minimize public outrage over health risks. Like the IPA's list, Sandman is primarily interested in emotional factors that influence the public rather than what he and his clients consider the "rational, real" issues related to risk and public harm. His points, however, bear little surface similarity to the points on IPA's list:

1. *Voluntary vs. coerced.* Sandman observes that people are less likely to become outraged over risks that they voluntarily assume than over risks that are imposed upon them against their will. "Consider," he suggests, "the difference between getting pushed down a mountain on slippery sticks and deciding to go skiing."

2. *Natural vs. industrial.* People tend to trust what can be promoted as natural: organic food or natural means of pest control.

3. *Familiar vs. exotic.* "Exotic, high-tech facilities provoke more outrage than familiar risks (your home, your car, your jar of peanut butter)," Sandman observes.

4. *Not memorable vs. memorable.* If you want to minimize outrage, *not* memorable is preferable. "A memorable accident—Love Canal, Bhopal, Times Beach—makes the risk easier to imagine," Sandman explains. A memorable symbol or image can do the same thing. This is why evidence of genetically modified crops harming colorful Monarch butterflies prompted more concern than similar evidence of harm to other insects.

5. *Not dreaded vs. dreaded.* For example, diseases like cancer, AIDS, plague, and tuberculosis create a great deal more public concern than others, such as heart disease.

6. *Chronic vs. catastrophic.* Thousands of people are killed each year in highway accidents, but rarely in large groups. Plane accidents are much rarer and cause fewer deaths, but because they can cause large fatalities, air travel is much more widely feared than car travel.

7. *Knowable vs. unknowable.* People tend to be less apprehensive about risks that are known and measurable than about risks that cannot be measured. The unknowable aspects of some risks make them more upsetting.

8. *Individually controlled vs. controlled by others.* Individuals can decide whether they smoke cigarettes, exercise, or drive cars. They often can't decide whether a factory emits pollution in their community.

9. *Fair vs. unfair.* "People who must endure greater risks than their neighbors, without access to greater benefits, are naturally outraged," Sandman says, "especially if the rationale for so burdening them looks more like politics than science."

10. *Morally irrelevant vs. morally relevant.* Arguing that a risk is small will fall on deaf ears if creating the risk is morally wrong in the first place. "Imagine a police chief insisting that an occasional child molester is an 'acceptable risk,'" Sandman says.

11. *Trustworthy sources vs. untrustworthy sources.* The "third party technique," which we have discussed throughout this book, is a PR strategy built around the effort to put industry messages in the mouths of seemingly trustworthy sources.

12. *Responsive process vs. unresponsive process.* "Does the agency come across as trustworthy or dishonest, concerned or arrogant?" Sandman asks. "Does it tell the community what's going on before the real decisions are made? Does it listen and respond to community concerns?"

At his best, Sandman is advising companies to listen to the public and respond to its concerns. In practice, however, his advice often lends itself to manipulation. One way that industry and government bodies try to make it appear that their activities are being accepted "voluntarily" rather than "coerced," for example, is to create so-called community advisory panels (CAPs) to seek the advice of people who live where their facilities are located. One of Sandman's clients, the U.S. Department of Energy, used this tactic in trying to overcome the objections of Nevada residents over the DOE's efforts to establish a national dump site for high-level nuclear waste at Yucca Mountain, Nevada. "The Secretary of Energy announced that there would be a 'citizen advisory panel' to discuss the Yucca Mountain project," recall Judy Treichel and Steve Frishman, who have led the state's campaign to block the project. "However, the real purpose of the panel was to invite opponents of the site such as ourselves to draft standards that would make the Yucca Mountain program acceptable. We were also invited to workshops in which government, industry and public representatives were supposed to 'prioritize your values.' Then we were supposed to 'trade off' our values in order to reach an acceptable compromise. Our response was to 'just say no.' We were then told that we were being 'unreasonable.' "[5]

What both the IPA's list and Peter Sandman's 12 points have in common is that they focus on emotional issues rather than the public's rational concerns. This is indeed a pattern that is common to propagandists in general. The modern-day propagandists who work in advertising and public relations can tell you endless stories that "prove" how easily news and public opinion can be manipulated by irrational appeals. This is just the way people are, they say. This is how the media works. And indeed, only someone who is blind to history would deny that emotional and irrational appeals have frequently succeeded in manipulating the public. This, however, is only a partial truth about human nature. People are complicated creatures with multifaceted personalities. The poet Ezra Pound, for example, was simultaneously a sensitive artist and a vulgar, anti-Semitic shill for the Nazis. A lot of the way we behave depends upon which parts of our personality express themselves. If you appeal to someone's better nature, you will get a different result than if you appeal to the same person's worst impulses. In a world full of propaganda, it is hardly surprising that some of the worst appeals succeed. What propagandists can't tell you, however, is whether and to what degree the public's irrationality is a self-fulfilling prophecy of their own creation. That is a question that perhaps you can answer better than they can, by learning to tell the difference between communication strategies that treat you like a child and strategies that treat you like an adult.

Growing Up Guided

The difference between the world of a child and the world of an adult can largely be described in terms of control, competence, and responsibility. When you were a child, you had little control over decisions that affected you. You were expected to eat what you were given, go to school at the assigned time, go to sleep at a designated bedtime, and so forth. Adults made the decisions because it was assumed that you lacked the capacity to decide for yourself. Even the decisions you did make were not necessarily binding, and it was your parents, not you, who were responsible for the consequences of your mistakes.

As an adult, you are responsible for all these decisions and more. The responsibilities of adults in fact extend beyond their actual areas of competence, which explains a lot about the way the world works. If you want to build an addition to your home, you hire a contractor. To take care of your health, you hire a physician; for legal matters, an attorney. You buy shoes from a company with expertise in manufacturing footwear. In all of these situations, the fact that you yourself lack expertise is not much of a problem, because you know what you want, and the expert's job is simply to fulfill your wishes. In the words of the philosopher Georg Hegel, "We do not need to be shoemakers to know if the shoes fit, and just as little have we any need to be professional to acquire knowledge of matters of universal interest."

With regard to decisions about public issues, expertise in terms of skill, knowledge, or experience is often less important than basic questions of values. Is abortion wrong? Is it moral to deny medical care to a child whose parents have no health insurance? Should murderers be put to death? Is it acceptable to perform medical experiments on human beings without their consent? There are no scientific answers to these questions, or thousands more like them. They can only be answered by asking ourselves what we believe and what we value. In addressing these questions, finding knowledgeable experts is actually less important than finding experts who share our values. This doesn't mean that knowledge is unimportant. Knowledge matters, whether you are deciding about abortion or hiring someone to remodel your kitchen. But the contractors who remodel your kitchen don't get to tell you what color to paint the walls or whether you should have wood versus linoleum floors. Their advice is limited to letting you know how much each option will cost. In a democracy, that's the kind of deference we should expect from experts on public policy. And a contractor who spends a lot of time studying ways to minimize your outrage is probably not someone you really want to hire.

When hiring a contractor, you can turn to a state licensing board or the Better Business Bureau to see if someone has valid credentials and a reputation for doing honest work. There is no such system for accrediting public policy experts. However, if someone makes claims of a scientific nature you can ask what kind of education, licensing, and other credentials they possess in the field for which they are claiming expertise. It is also worth asking how experts rank among their peers, although you should bear in mind that every profession has its blind spots and tends to "circle the wagons" against outside criticisms. To judge from the literature of the American Medical Association, for example, you would think that malpractice lawsuits are a bigger problem than actual medical malpractice. As a rule of thumb, you should assume that specialists in any field are given to underestimating harm for which their own profession is responsible.

Expertise is justifiably linked in the public's mind to talent, skill, education, and experience. There are also a number of stereotypical attributes that are *unjustifiably* linked to expertise, and it is important to avoid relying on them. These stereotypes include age, wealth, maleness, whiteness, self-confidence, credentials, specialization, and techno-elitism. When evaluating a speaker's message, it is worth asking yourself if you are giving him extra points for having gray hair, a deep voice, an impressive-sounding degree, and a distinguished-looking business suit.

Scientific Uncertainties

Our society's esteem for science actually tends to encourage the very *un-scientific* notion that science is a source of infallible truths. In fact, all science is uncertain to some degree. Nature is complex, and research is difficult. The most that science can tell us about a given question is that there is a strong probability that such-and-such an answer is true. To understand scientific information, therefore, it helps to understand something about the statistical techniques that scientists use to quantify uncertainty. One of the classic journalistic textbooks on the subject is *News and Numbers: A Guide to Reporting Statistical Claims and Controversies in Health and Other Fields,* by the late Victor Cohn, a former science editor at the *Washington Post.*

Scientists live with uncertainty by measuring probability. An accepted numerical expression is the P value, a statistical calculation of the probability that a given result could have occurred just by chance. A P value of .05 or less—the conventionally accepted cutoff for "statistical significance"—means there are probably only five or fewer chances in 100 that a result reported in a scientific study could have happened by chance alone. When studying health risks, statistical significance is often impossible to achieve. If something kills one in 1,000 people, you would actually have to study several thousand people in order to achieve a P value of .05 or less, and even then the possibility of other confounding factors might call your result into question. "A condition that affects one person in hundreds of thousands may never be recognized or associated with a particular cause," Cohn says. "It is probable and perhaps inevitable that a large yet scattered number of environmentally or industrially caused illnesses remain forever undetected as environmental illnesses, because they remain only a fraction of the vastly greater normal case load."[6]

If you find any of these concepts difficult to grasp, you can take comfort in the fact that you are not alone. "Every major study of statistical presentations in the medical literature has found very high error rates, even among the best journals," says Thomas Lang, medical editing manager at the Cleveland Clinic Foundation and coauthor of *How to Report Statistics in Medicine: Annotated Guidelines for Authors, Editors, and Reviewers.* "Many of those errors were serious enough to call the authors' findings into question."

There are some specific guidelines to consider when evaluating scientific information. Cohn recommends that when someone tells you they've done a study you should ask, "What kind? How confident can you be in the results? Were there any possible flaws in the study?" The last question is particularly important, he says, because the answer may tell you whether you are dealing with an honest investigator or a salesperson who is trying to convince you of a particular point of view. "An honest researcher will almost always report flaws," Cohn says. "A dishonest one may claim perfection." Other questions to ask include:

- What kind of study protocol was used? Is enough information offered to satisfy you that the research method is sound in its design and that its conclusions are reliable?

- Why was the study performed?

- What is the study's statistical significance and margin for error?

- Was it submitted to independent peer review? Has it been published in a reputable scientific journal? (Bear in mind, however, that authors can pay to have scientific findings published, even in some peer-reviewed journals.)

- Are the results consistent with the results from other studies performed by other researchers?

- Is there a consensus among people in the same field?

- Who disagrees with you, and why?

Asking some of these questions may seem daunting. Scientific studies are laden with jargon of the trade that makes it difficult for outsiders to understand—words like "chi-square," "allele," "epizootic," and so forth. Don't let the language put you off. Often you can find a friendly scientist at your local university who is willing to translate things into plain English. University scientists are trained and paid to be educators, and many of them are happy to assist an intelligent, motivated person with questions. Above all, don't be afraid to ask, and don't let the incomprehensible stuff intimidate you. If someone wants you to believe something, the burden of proof should be on them to explain it to you in language that you can understand. If something is too complicated to explain, maybe it's also too complicated to be safe.

The Precautionary Principle

Given the uncertainties inherent to science (and to all human endeavors), we are strong believers in the importance of the precautionary principle, which we discussed in Chapter 6. Throughout this book, we have also stressed the importance of democracy in making decisions about technology and its impact upon people's lives. The reason that democracy matters in science and scientifically influenced policy is precisely that uncertainty exists and that different people reach different conclusions about important issues. Debate and compromise are the processes through which people resolve these differences. When a new technology is introduced, such as nuclear power or genetic engineering, some people will focus entirely on the potential benefits of the new technology while ignoring the dangers. Others will focus on the dangers and ignore the potential benefits, while other people fill in the continuum of opinion between these two poles. In an ideal decision-making process, the interplay of debate over differing views will hold the "reckless innovators" in check but enable beneficial innovations to move forward after the concerns of the "fearmongers" have been thoroughly vetted in scientific and public forums. This process may slow the pace of introduction of new technologies, which indeed is part of the point to having a democratic decision-making process.

By training and enculturation, most experts in the employ of government and industry are technophiles, skilled and enthusiastic about the deployment of technologies that possess increasingly awesome power. Like the Sorcerer's Apprentice, they are enchanted with the possibilities of this power, but often lack the wisdom necessary to perceive its dangers. It was a government expert, Atomic Energy Commission chairman Lewis L. Strauss, who promised the National Association of Science Writers in 1954 that atomic energy would bring "electrical energy too cheap to meter" within the space of a single generation.[7] Turn to the back issues of *Popular Science* magazine, and you will find other prophecies so bold, so optimistic, and so wrong that you would be better off turning for insight to the Psychic Friends Network. If these prophecies had been correct, we should by now be jet-packing to work, living in bubble-domed cities beneath the ocean, colonizing the moon and Mars. The cure to cancer, like prosperity, is always said to be just around the corner, yet somehow we never actually *turn* that corner. Predictions regarding computers are notorious for their rhetorical excess. "In from three to five years, we will have a machine with the general intelligence of an average human being," MIT computer scientist Marvin Minsky predicted in 1970. "I mean a machine that will be able to read Shakespeare, grease a car, play office politics, tell a joke, have a fight. At that point, the machine will begin to educate itself with fantastic speed. In a few months, it will be at a genius level, and a few months after that, its power will be incalculable."[8] Expert predictions of this sort have been appearing regularly ever since, although the day when computers will be able to grease your car (let alone read Shakespeare) keeps getting pushed back.

The views of these techno-optimists deserve to be part of the decision-making process, but they should not be allowed to crowd out the views and concerns of the skeptics—the people who are likely to experience the harmful effects of new technologies and who deserve to play a role in deciding when and how they should be introduced. Just as war is too important to leave to the generals, science and technology are too important to leave in the hands of the experts.

Opponents of the precautionary principle have caricatured it as a rule that "demands precautionary action even in the absence of evidence that a health or environmental hazard exists" and says "if we don't know something we mustn't wait for studies to give answers." This is not at all its intent. It is a guide for policy decisions in cases where knowledge is incomplete regarding risks that are serious or irreversible and that are unproven but plausible in the light of existing scientific knowledge. No one is suggesting that the precautionary principle should be invoked regarding purely fanciful risks. There are legitimate debates over whether a risk is plausible enough to warrant the precautionary principle. There are also reasonable debates over *how* to implement the precautionary principle. However, groups that seek to discredit the principle itself as "unscientific" are engaged in propaganda, not science.

Follow the Money

When you hire a contractor or an attorney, they work for you because you are the one who pays for their services. The PR experts who work behind the scenes and the visible experts who appear on the public stage to "educate" you about various issues are not working for you. They answer to a client whose interests and values may even run contrary to your own. Experts don't appear out of nowhere. They work for someone, and if they are trying to influence the outcome of issues that affect you, then you deserve to know who is paying their bills.

Not everyone agrees with this position. Jeff Stier is the associate director of the American Council on Science and Health (ACSH), which we described in Chapter 9. Stier goes so far as to claim that "today's conventional wisdom in favor of disclosing corporate funding of research is a 'new McCarthyism.'" Standards of public disclosure, he says, should mirror the standards followed in a court of law, where "evidence is admissible only if the probative value of that evidence exceeds its prejudicial effect." To disclose funding, he says, can have a "prejudicial effect" if it "unfairly taints studies that are scientifically solid." Rather than judging a study by its funding source, he says, you should simply ask whether its "hypothesis, methodology and conclusion" measure up to "rigorous scientific standards."[9] When we asked him for a list of ACSH's corporate and foundation donors, he used these arguments to justify his refusal. With all due respect, we think Stier's argument is an excuse to avoid scrutiny. Even in a court of law, expert witnesses are required to disclose what they are being paid for their testimony.

Some people, including the editors of leading scientific journals, raise more subtle questions about funding disclosure. The problem, they say, is knowing where to draw the line. If someone received a small grant 20 years ago from a pharmaceutical company to study a specific drug, should they have to disclose that fact whenever they comment about an entirely different drug manufactured by the same company? And what about *nonfinancial* factors that create bias? Nonprofit organizations also gain something by publishing their concerns. They may have an ideological ax to grind, and publicity may even bring indirect financial benefits by helping attract new members and contributions. Elizabeth Whelan of ACSH made these points during a letter exchange with Ned Groth of the Consumers Union. "You seem to believe that while commercial agendas are suspect, ideological agendas are not," Whelan complained. "This is a purely specious distinction. . . . A foundation's pursuit of an ideological agenda—perhaps one characterized by a desire for social change, redistribution of income, expanded regulatory control over the private sector, and general promotion of a coercive utopia—must be viewed with at least as much skepticism and suspicion as a corporation's pursuit of legitimate commercial interests."[10]

There is a certain amount of truth to Whelan's line of reasoning. Nevertheless, corporate funding is particularly important to track, for the following reasons:

- Corporations are consistently driven by a clear and self-evident bias—namely, the desire to maximize profits, whereas assessing "ideological bias" in nonprofit foundations is itself subjective and ideological.

- Even if money doesn't always *create* bias, it is a leading *indicator* of bias. Some nonprofit groups receive their money from the public at large or from a broad sector of the public. Consumers Union, for example, receives the majority of its funding from consumers who join in order to receive its publication, *Consumer Reports*. Groups such as ACSH receive a large percentage of their money from major corporations. Elizabeth Whelan may believe every word she says about the safety of pesticides, and perhaps she would have ended up believing the same things even if she had never received a dollar from the chemical and food industries. Nevertheless, the funding differences between Consumers Union and ACSH offer a fairly clear indication of whose interests are served by each organization.

- The money that corporations pour into influencing public policy is huge compared to the expenditures of nonprofit organizations. In 1998, for example, environmental organizations spent a total of $4.7 million on lobbying Congress. The sum total for all single-issue ideological groups combined—pro-choice advocates, anti-abortionists, human rights groups, feminists, consumer organizations, senior citizens, and a variety of other groups—was $76.2 million. By contrast, the agribusiness industry alone spent $119.3 million, and the lobbying expenditures of all industries combined added up to $1.2 *billion*. These numbers are just lobbying money and do not include campaign contributions, "soft money," or any of the other ways that corporations buy political influence. Of course, no one is truly immune from ideological bias. As a practical matter, however, the biases you need to worry about the most are the biases held by people who have the money and power to influence government policies that affect your life.[11]

The simplest way to find out who is funding an organization is simply to ask. Request an annual report or list of institutional donors. Don't just ask *who* is paying the bills. Ask *how much money* is involved. Spin doctors have mastered the art of the "nondenial denial." Remember the strategy that Philip Morris used to conceal its role as the creator and primary founder of The Advancement of Sound Science Coalition: "We will not deny being a corporate member/sponsor, will not specify dollars, and will refer them to the TASSC '800-' number."[12] The strategy of admitting to being a sponsor while refusing to specify dollar amounts was designed to deflect questions while avoiding outright lies that could embarrass the company if its funding role was later exposed.

Even if an organization itself doesn't disclose its funding, sometimes the information is available from other sources. Examine the interests and affiliations of the organization's board of directors. If the organization refuses to make any of this information publicly available or hedges its answers, that in itself is cause for suspicion.

The Devil in the Details

In addition to examining someone's funding sources, you can also learn a lot about them by asking what positions they have taken in the past on specific issues. Pay attention to nuances. Industry front groups like to portray themselves as moderate and representing the "middle ground." Watch for words like "sensible," "responsible," and "sound" in organization names. Just as the true mission of The Advancement of Sound Science Coalition was to stigmatize science that inconvenienced its sponsors, a group called "Citizens for Sound Environmental Policy" is likely to be in the business of trying to discredit genuine environmentalists. Industry-sponsored organizations frequently adopt misleading names. Examples have included the Foundation for Clean Air Progress, the National Environmental Policy Institute, the National Wilderness Institute, the Science and Environmental Policy Project, the Council for Solid Waste Solutions, Citizens for Sensible Control of Acid Rain, and the Alliance for Responsible CFC Policy.[13]

Be especially skeptical of "think tanks," which have proliferated in recent years as a way of generating self-serving scholarship to serve the advocacy goals of industry. Rather than centers for research and analysis, many of today's think tanks are little more than public relations fronts, usually headquartered in state or national seats of government. *Washington Post* columnist Joel Achenbach says, "We've got think tanks the way other towns have firehouses. This is a thoughtful town. A friend of mine worked at a think tank temporarily and the director told him when he entered, 'We are white men between the ages of 50 and 55, and we have no place else to go.'"[14]

Funded by big business and major foundations, think tanks devise and promote policies that shape the lives of everyday Americans: Social Security privatization, tax and investment laws, regulation of everything from oil to the Internet. They supply experts to testify on Capitol Hill, write articles for the op-ed pages of newspapers, and appear as TV commentators. They advise presidential aspirants and lead orientation seminars to train incoming members of Congress.

Think tanks have a decided political leaning. There are twice as many conservative think tanks as liberal ones, and the conservative ones generally have more money. This is no accident, as one of the important functions of think tanks is to provide a backdoor way for wealthy business interests to promote their ideas. "Modern think tanks are nonprofit, tax-exempt, political idea factories where donations can be as big as the donor's checkbook and are seldom publicized," notes Tom Brazaitis, writing for the *Cleveland Plain Dealer*. "Technology companies give to think tanks that promote open access to the internet. Wall Street firms donate to think tanks that espouse private investment of retirement funds." So much money now flows in, that the top 20 conservative think tanks now spend more money than all of the "soft money" contributions to the Republican party.[15]

A think tank's resident experts carry titles such as "senior fellow" or "adjunct scholar," but this does not necessarily mean that they even possess an academic degree in their area of claimed expertise. Elsewhere in this book we have criticized the ways that outside funding can corrupt the integrity of academic institutions. The same corrupting influences affect think tanks, only more so. Think tanks are like universities minus the students and minus the systems of peer review and other mechanisms that academia uses to promote diversity of thought. Real academics are expected to conduct their research first and draw their conclusions second, but this process is reversed at most policy-driven think tanks. As economist Jonathan Rowe has observed, the term "think" tanks is a misnomer.

His comment was directed at the conservative Heritage Foundation, but it applies equally well to many other think tanks, regardless of ideology: "They don't think; they justify."

Demand Accountability

One of the reasons that life in the information age has become such a welter of conflicting claims is that journalists have failed to live up to their responsibilities. Reporters are supposed to be one rung up from the average citizen on the information ladder, and they have a responsibility to verify the credentials and reliability of their sources. When they allow their reportage to be leavened with propaganda, they cheapen and degrade their product just as surely as a baker who adds sawdust to his flour. If you see a news story that fails to identify the background, credentials, and potential bias or conflicts of interest of a cited authority, complain. Send a letter, make a phone call.

The scientific press is expected to meet a higher standard of accountability than the general press. When it fails to meet this standard, the harm is multiplied, because general news reporters often repeat information that appears in scientific journals, using even less fact-checking than they would apply to information from other sources. In December 1999, for example, the *British Medical Journal* published a "study" claiming that shaken (not stirred) martinis have beneficial anti-oxidant properties. The so-called study was part of the *BMJ*'s annual joke issue. It accompanied other similarly humorous papers examining the effects of "too much sax" on jazz musicians, the frequency of swearing by surgeons, and the question of whether young women named Sharon are more likely to contract sexually transmitted diseases. To drive home the point that this was all tongue-in-cheek, the *BMJ*'s martini study made frequent pointed references to James Bond, commenting that "the well known fictional secret agent . . . not only is astute in matters of clandestine affairs at a personal and international level but may also possess insights of interest to medical science. . . . 007's profound state of health may be due, at least in part, to compliant bartenders." Notwithstanding these efforts to clue in the clueless, wire services including Reuters, Knight-Ridder, the Associated Press, UPI, and Scripps Howard all distributed stories on the martini's newfound power to ward off cancer and heart disease. Reports on the "antiaging oomph" of shaken martinis appeared as straight-faced news in more than 100 publications, including the *New York Times, Houston Chronicle, London Financial Times, Chicago Sun-Times, Milwaukee Journal Sentinel, Seattle Times, Forbes* magazine, and, of course, *Playboy*.[16]

Not only does the media fail to adequately investigate the information it reports, often it fails even to disclose information that is readily available. Take, for example, the thousands of video news releases (VNRs) that are incorporated into television news broadcasts. TV news directors certainly know who supplies their VNRs, and it would be very easy to place small subtitles at the bottom of the screen stating where they came from—for example, "Footage supplied by Pfizer Pharmaceutical." This is almost never done, mainly because the stations themselves realize that it would be embarrassing if people found out how much of their so-called news is actually canned material supplied by PR firms. It can only be hoped that as the public becomes better educated about the use of VNRs and other public relations tactics, pressure will be brought to bear upon the media to reform itself.

Inviting Public Participation

The slogan "question authority" first arose during the radical movements of the 1960s. It contains a great deal of wisdom, but it is inadequate. We *need* authorities in our lives—people we can trust to fix our cars and computers, to assist us when we become sick, to help us understand and better manage our world. The question really is what kind of relationship we should have with authorities. Should it be a relationship in which the experts regard the rest of us as "a herd to be led," in the words of Edward Bernays? Or should it be a relationship in which the experts regard themselves as servants of the public? The issue is not whether authorities should exist, but how to make them accountable.

One approach to addressing this problem has been developed by the Loka Institute, an organization based in Amherst, Massachusetts, that has been working since 1987 to promote ways that grassroots citizens and workers can become involved in the scientific process and technological decision-making. It has been studying a type of citizens' panel called a "consensus conference." Sometimes referred to as a "policy jury" or a "citizens' jury," a consensus conference is similar in some ways to the randomly selected juries used in U.S. courtrooms, except that instead of judging criminal cases, they attempt to reach verdicts on matters of public policy. To organize a consensus conference around a particular topic, advertisements are published seeking local "lay volunteer participants" who are chosen to reflect the demographic makeup of the community and who lack significant prior knowledge or involvement in the topic at hand. The final panel might consist of about 15 people, including homemakers, office and factory workers, and university-educated professionals. The participants engage in a process of study, discussion, and consultation with technical experts that culminates in a public forum and the production of a report summarizing the panel's conclusions about the topic at hand.

The use of consensus conferences was pioneered in Denmark and is now being widely adopted in Europe as a process for giving ordinary citizens a real chance to make their voices heard in debates on technology policy. "Not only are laypeople elevated to positions of preeminence, but a carefully planned program of reading and discussion culminating in a forum open to the public ensures that they become well-informed prior to rendering judgment," says Loka Institute director Richard Sclove. "Both the forum and the subsequent judgment, written up in a formal report, become a focus of intense national attention—usually at a time when the issue at hand is due to come before Parliament. Though consensus conferences are hardly meant to dictate public policy, they do give legislators some sense of where the people who elected them might stand on important questions. They can also help industry steer clear of new products or processes that are likely to spark public opposition."[17]

The Loka Institute also advocates increased funding for "community-based research" that is initiated and often carried out in collaboration with civic, grassroots, and workers groups. "This research differs from the bulk of the research and development conducted in the United States, most of which—at a cost of over $200 billion per year—is performed in response to business, military, or government needs or in pursuit of academic interests."[18] In 1994, Sclove notes, the Pepsi company announced plans to spend $50 million—approximately five times as much as the total annual U.S. investment in community-based research—to reinvent its Doritos-brand tortilla chips, intensifying the flavor on the outer surface, rounding the chip's corners, and redesigning the package. "A society that can afford $50 million to reinvent the Doritos chip can do better than $10 million for community-based research," he says.

If "community-based research" sounds like some pie-in-the-sky idea,

Sclove points out that it is already a common practice in Holland, where the Dutch have developed a network of "science shops" that respond to some 2,000 annual research requests. Other science shops have been established in Austria, the Czech Republic, Denmark, England, Germany, Malaysia, Northern Ireland, and Romania, as well as in the United States. In Highlander, Tennessee, for example, a local community group worked with university researchers to conduct health surveys and videotaped waste dumping by a local tanning company that was polluting the town's drinking water. In New York City, high school students collected and analyzed data on diesel exhaust exposure and lung function among their fellow students, coauthoring an article that was published in the July 1999 issue of the peer-reviewed *Journal of Public Health.*

These are only a couple of examples of how increased democracy and citizen participation could be brought to bear upon the scientific and policymaking process. The obstacles to doing this are not technical or economic; they are social and political. Society's failure to incorporate citizen participation into the scientific process reflects our assumption that scientific topics are too complex for the average citizen. In 1992, however, a study conducted by John Doble and Amy Richardson of the Public Agenda Foundation, a nonprofit organization founded by opinion pollster Daniel Yankelovich, found that even people who don't normally pay attention to scientific issues can do a good job of making science-related policy decisions. Doble and Richardson recruited a representative cross-section of 402 people from different parts of the United States to participate. They were given short, balanced presentations about two technically complex issues—global warming and solid waste disposal—and were then asked to discuss and decide what they thought would be the best policy solutions for dealing with those issues. Doble and Richardson also polled 418 leading U.S. scientists regarding the same issues. By and large, they found, the lay participants in the study made the same policy choices as the scientists. With regard to global warming, for example, both groups favored more spending on mass transit, higher fuel-efficiency standards for cars, tax incentives to encourage energy conservation, and programs to plant trees. "Our conclusion from this exercise is that the public as a whole—not just those who are attentive to science—can intelligently assess scientifically complex issues, even when experts are uncertain," Doble and Richardson stated.[19]

Even when the two groups made different policy choices, Doble added, the differences "seemed to stem not from different scientific understanding but from different value judgements." For example, scientists "understood very clearly that nuclear power does not contribute to the global warming problem, and felt that the country needs to build more nuclear power plants by a very large margin. Sixty-eight percent of the scientists said that." By contrast, only 36 percent of the nonscientists favored construction of nuclear power plants, but "in the discussion group, when people talked about the issue, it became clear that their concerns were not technical, they were managerial. . . . They didn't trust the energy companies, they didn't trust the utilities, they didn't trust the government regulators, they didn't trust the boards that oversee all this stuff, they didn't trust those groups to manage the technology safely." They understood the technical issues reasonably well, in other words, but for the public at large, those weren't the most important issues.[20]

Activate Yourself

In understanding the hold that experts have on our lives, we should consider the role that we ourselves play as consumers of information. Most propaganda is designed to influence people who are not very active or informed about the topic at hand. There is a reason for this strategy. Propagandists know that active, informed people are likely to already hold strong opinions that cannot be easily swayed. The people who are most easily manipulated are those who have not studied a subject much and are therefore susceptible to any argument that sounds plausible.

Of course, there is no way that anyone can be active and informed about every issue under the sun. The world is too complex for that, and our lives are too busy. However, each of us *can* choose those issues that move us most deeply and devote some time to them. Activism enriches our lives in multiple ways. It brings us into personal contact with other people who are informed, passionate, and altruistic in their commitment to help make the world a better place. These are good friends to have, and often they are better sources of information than the experts whose names appear in the newspapers or on television. Activism, in our opinion, is not just a civic duty. It is a path to enlightenment.

This book has largely been a catalogue of disturbing trends and failures to live up to the promise of an informed, democratic society. It is important to remember that these are not universal trends. We have described failures in the way the news media does its job, but there are also enterprising, committed journalists who take seriously their responsibility to serve as the public's eyes and ears. In addition to reporters, there are activist congressional aides, government whistle-blowers, public-interest groups, and even trial lawyers who actively investigate and challenge the official doctrines of government and industry. Maude De Victor, for example, was a 23-year counselor with the U.S. Veterans Authority when she noted a pattern of illness among army veterans who had been exposed to Agent Orange. She brought it to the attention of CBS news correspondent Bill Kurtis, whose resulting exposé earned him a coveted Peabody Award and three Emmys. De Victor herself was rewarded by being fired, blacklisted, and banned from full-time government work, but she is a heroine to people who long for government accountability and a world free of chemical toxins.

Activists and whistle-blowers come from all walks of life. Emelda West, a great-grandmother in her 70s, helped campaign against toxic releases in low-income communities in Louisiana. In Pensacola, Florida, Margaret Williams heads Citizens Against Toxic Exposure, a group formed in 1991 to battle the Environmental Protection Agency's digging on a toxic site near her home. When residents—most of them elderly and not well-off financially—began suffering eye and skin irritations and breathing problems, she quickly learned about the poisonous effects of dioxin. Although her group lost the battle to stop the digging, it recently persuaded the federal government to pay for the relocation of all 358 families.

Terri Swearingen had activism thrust upon her in 1982. "I was pregnant with our one and only child," she recalls. "That's when I first learned of plans to build one of the world's largest toxic waste incinerators in my community. When they began site preparation to begin building the incinerator in 1990, my life changed forever."[21]

The incinerator, owned by a company called Waste Technologies Industries (WTI), was sited in East Liverpool, Ohio, just across the border from her home in West Virginia. It was situated in a floodplain, with homes nearby and an elementary school just 400 yards away. Worse yet, it was located in a valley that experiences frequent air inversions, which trap the air and prevent the escape of pollution. In short, it is about the worst place you could imagine building a giant hazardous waste facility that emits dioxins, acid gases like hydrogen chloride, and heavy metals, including mercury, lead, and chromium.

"I'm a registered nurse," Swearingen says, "so I've actually seen the effects of lead poisoning in young children and the types of behavioral or developmental problems that it produces. One of the first things I learned about WTI was that the government was going to let them emit 4.7 tons of lead annually. I thought, how can the government do this? How can they let them emit lead? Lead never breaks down. It never degrades. It just accumulates. When you know a little bit about the effects of lead, the rest is just common sense. That's all you need to know to realize that they should never even consider building this thing next to a school."

When Swearingen first began trying to fight the incinerator, she says she was "at ground zero." She picked up *Rush to Burn,* a 1989 book about waste incineration by reporters at *Newsday* magazine. "I read the book twice and highlighted sections with the people involved. Then I just started calling them up and asking for help. They said, 'You're going to have to deal with this yourself.'"

She learned to tap the expertise of people such as Paul Connett, a professor of chemistry at St. Lawrence University whom Swearingen calls "our secret weapon." Connett helped translate complex scientific data into information that the community could understand. Other advice came from Herbert Needleman, the University of Pittsburgh researcher who has studied the neurotoxicology of lead in children, and David Ozonoff, chairman of Boston University's School of Public Health. To help challenge a risk assessment from the U.S. Environmental Protection Agency, she called on EPA whistle-blower Hugh Kaufman.

Swearingen herself led more than 20 civil disobedience protests against the incinerator and even testified before the U.S. Congress. She helped make the incinerator such a high-profile issue that in 1992 Al Gore, then a candidate for vice president, promised to stop the project if he were elected. "The very idea of putting WTI in a floodplain, you know it's just unbelievable to me," Gore said. "For the safety and health of local residents rightfully concerned about the impact of this incinerator on their families and their future, a thorough investigation is urgently needed."[22]

Like many politicians' promises, this one turned out to be worth less than the air in which it vibrated. Once in office, Gore backed down—not surprisingly, since Little Rock investment banker Jackson Stephens, the

Clinton-Gore campaign's biggest financial backer, was involved in financing the incinerator.

But even though the WTI incinerator was not stopped, it became a turning point against the construction of new incinerators. Swearingen's dogged protests—including her willingness to get arrested for the cause—gained enough attention to prompt Ohio Governor George Voinovich to halt future incinerator construction. The day after she was jailed for a demonstration in front of the White House, the Clinton administration declared a national moratorium on new incinerator construction and revised its rules to require stricter limits on the release of dioxin and heavy metals. In April 1997, she received the prestigious Goldman Environmental Prize in recognition of her leadership.

"I am not a scientist or a Ph.D," Swearingen said upon accepting the award. "I am a nurse and a housewife, but my most important credential is that I am a mother. . . . We know what is at stake. We have been forced to educate ourselves, and the final exam represents our children's future. . . . Because of this, we approach the problem with common sense and with passion. We don't buy into the notion that all it takes is better regulations and standards, better air pollution control devices and more bells and whistles. We don't believe that technology will solve all of our problems. We know that we must get to the front end of the problems, and that prevention is what is needed."[23]

She recalls talking about WTI recently with a 14-year-old girl. Upon learning that the incinerator was located next to a school, the girl blurted out, "But that wouldn't take *any* research to know it's wrong!" Swearingen marvels at a teenager's ability to grasp in a single sentence the point that eluded the EPA in its four-year, 4,000-page risk assessment.

"We have to reappraise what expertise is and who qualifies as an expert," Swearingen says. "There are the experts who are working in the corporate interest, who often serve to obscure the obvious and challenge common sense; and there are experts and non-experts who are working in the public interest. From my experience, I am distrusting more and more the professional experts, not because they are not clever, but because they do not ask the right questions. And that's the difference between being clever and being wise. Einstein said, 'A clever person solves a problem; a wise person avoids it.' . . . Citizens who are working in this arena—people who are battling to stop new dump sites or incinerator proposals, people who are risking their lives to prevent the destruction of rain forests or working to ban the industrial uses of chlorine and PVC plastics—are often labeled obstructionists and anti-progress. But we actually represent progress—not technological progress, but social progress. We have become the real experts, not because of our title or the university we attended, but because we have been threatened and we have a different way of seeing the world."[24]

Recommended Resources

Many of the books and other resources that we have used in researching this book are cited in the footnotes. The suggestions below indicate other resources that we have found particularly important and that we recommend for further reading.

There is one type of resource, however, that we endorse first and foremost: the public library. Librarians are a class of expert for which we have nothing but respect. They are trained not only in how to catalogue information but also in how to help patrons use a wide range of reference sources. Whether you are trying to understand the neurotoxicology of lead or investigate the funding of a Washington think tank, a few minutes spent talking to a librarian can often save hours of wasted time and yield remarkable discoveries. One of the trends during the past decade has been a retreat in public funding for libraries, as money has been shifted toward other information resources such as expensive computer systems. This is unfortunate, because often there is no substitute for talking to a human being with training in information sciences—especially in today's age of data glut. We might add that we have never met a mean librarian. Free public libraries have been and remain an important resource for the maintenance of an informed public and a democratic society. Use them, and support them!

BOOKS

Sharon Beder, *Global Spin: The Corporate Assault on Environmentalism* (White River Junction, VT: Chelsea Green Publishing Co., 1998). This book provides a comprehensive worldwide look at corporate anti-environmental PR campaigns, with chapters focusing on industry front groups, conservative think tanks, media strategies, efforts to tar-

get children, and the use of strategic lawsuits against public participation (SLAPP suits) to harass corporate critics.

Alex Carey, *Taking the Risk Out of Democracy: Corporate Propaganda versus Freedom and Liberty* (Chicago, IL: University of Illinois Press,
1997). This collection of essays by the late Australian academic Alex
Carey is both inspiring and disturbing. "The twentieth century," Carey
observed, "has been characterized by three developments of great political importance: the growth of democracy, the growth of corporate
power, and the growth of corporate propaganda as a means of protecting corporate power against democracy."

Robert A. Dahl, *Democracy and Its Critics* (New Haven, CT: Yale University Press, 1989). The concept of "democracy" is frequently invoked
but rarely examined in political discussions. Dahl's book provides
both a historic and a theoretical examination of democracy, beginning
with the city-states of ancient Greece and concluding with discussion
of the directions in which democracy must move if democratic societies are to exist in the future.

William Greider, *Who Will Tell the People: The Betrayal of American
Democracy* (New York, NY: Simon & Schuster, 1992). One of the
best books we have read on the ways that influence peddling operates
in Washington.

Theodore Roszak, *The Cult of Information: A Neo-Luddite Treatise on
High-Tech, Artificial Intelligence, and the True Art of Thinking* (Berkeley, CA: University of California Press, 1994). Although this book focuses in particular on debunking the overhyped claims of computer
scientists, it offers a wonderful, thoughtful, and in some places even
poetic critique of the notion that computers can think for us and that
"information" is equivalent to knowledge and wisdom.

John Stauber and Sheldon Rampton, *Toxic Sludge Is Good for You!: Lies,
Damn Lies and the Public Relations Industry* (Monroe, ME: Common
Courage Press, 1995). This was our first book together and provided
a detailed exposé of the techniques used by today's multibillion-dollar
PR industry, including a number of techniques that are not discussed
here, such as "grassroots PR," surveillance of activists, and corporate
"divide and conquer" strategies.

Washington Representatives (Washington, D.C.: Columbia Books). This annual directory is the best single reference work for tracking individuals and organizations with offices in Washington, D.C., working as lobbyists, foreign agents, legal advisers, industry front groups, and public relations representatives. It is superbly researched, cross-referenced, and an excellent first source for examining the backgrounds, interests, and interconnections of those influencing federal policy and the media in the nation's capital. Make sure your library carries it.

Derk Arend Wilcox (ed.), *The Right Guide* and *The Left Guide* (Ann Arbor, MI: Economics America, Inc.). These two directories, updated every couple of years, provide excellent brief summaries on organizations, their political and ideological leanings, funding, leadership, tax status, and mission. Make sure your library carries these important reference guides.

PERIODICALS

EXTRA! magazine is published by Fairness & Accuracy In Reporting (FAIR), a national media watchdog group that focuses awareness on the corporate allegiance of the media and its underrepresentation of points of view from women, minorities, and low-income groups. For information, contact FAIR, 130 W. 25th Street, New York, NY 10001; phone (212) 633-6700.

O'Dwyer's PR Services is a monthly trade publication of the public relations industry. Although unreservedly pro-PR, it offers honest reporting on the activities of PR firms and often better journalism than you'll find in the mainstream media. For subscription information, contact O'Dwyer's, 271 Madison Ave., New York, NY 10016; phone (212) 679-241.

PR Watch, published quarterly by our own Center for Media & Democracy, offers investigative reporting on manipulative and deceptive practices of the public relations industry. For a sample copy, contact the Center for Media & Democracy, 520 University Avenue, Suite 310, Madison, WI 53703; phone (608) 260-9713. Searchable back issues are available at www.prwatch.org.

Rachel's Environment and Health Weekly is a decade-old, two-page weekly newsletter on the cutting edge of environmental, health, and democracy issues. It is edited by Peter Montague and published by the non-profit Environmental Research Foundation, P.O. Box 5036, Annapolis, MD 21403. It is unabashedly activist and passionate, but very well written and documented, and it provides a good look at how good science can combine with a precautionary approach. The ERF is also happy to handle written and phone inquiries on issues of environmental and health expertise, referring citizens and reporters to solid sources from the academic and activist communities. Searchable back issues are available at www.rachel.org.

THE INTERNET

Given the speed with which websites come and go, we have elected not to provide a list of recommended sites in this book. However, we maintain a list of recommended links online at the website of the Center for Media and Democracy, at the following address: www.prwatch.org/links/index.html.

NOTES

PREFACE: THE SMELL TEST

1. Burson-Marsteller home page, <http://www.bm.com>, (September 27, 1999).
2. James Lindheim, "Restoring the Image of the Chemical Industry," *Chemistry and Industry,* no. 15, August 7, 1989, p. 491.

CHAPTER 1: THE THIRD MAN

1. Greg Miller and Leslie Helm, "Microsoft Tried to Grow 'Grass Roots,'" *Los Angeles Times,* April 10, 1998.
2. Ibid.
3. "An Open Letter to President Clinton from 240 Economists on Antitrust Protectionism," the Independent Institute, June 1999.
4. Robert MacMillan, "240 Economists Slam U.S. for Antitrust Actions," *Newsbytes,* June 2, 1999.
5. Joel Brinkley, "'Unbiased' Ads for Microsoft Came at a Price," *New York Times,* September 18, 1999, p. 1.
6. David J. Theroux, *"Winners, Losers and Microsoft* Strikes a Sensitive Nerve: Response to *New York Times* Article," Independent Institute news release, September 19, 1999, <http://independent.org/tii/news/990919Theroux.html>, (July 25, 2000).
7. David Callahan, "The Think Tank As Flack," *Washington Monthly,* vol. 31, no. 11 (November 1, 1999), p. 21.
8. Robert Dilenschneider, keynote speech at Media Relations '98, Marriott Marquis Hotel, New York, NY, April 27, 1998.
9. *Jack O'Dwyer's Newsletter,* vol. 31, no. 16 (April 22, 1998), p. 8.
10. Ben Wildavsky and Neil Munro, "Culture Clash," *National Journal,* vol. 30, no. 20 (May 16, 1998), p. 1102.
11. Mary Mosquera, "Spin Accelerates as Microsoft Trial Nears," *TechWeb News,* October 16, 1998.
12. Ted Bridis, Glenn Simpson, and Mylene Mangalindan, "When Microsoft's Spin Got Too Good, Oracle Hired Private Investigators," *Wall Street Journal,* June 29, 2000, p. 1.
13. Mary Jo Foley, "Microsoft Still Considering Image Makeover Plan," *PC Week Online,* April 13, 1998.

14. David Coursey, "Microsoft's PR Effort Is Just Part of the Game," *PC Magazine Online,* April 10, 1998, <http://www.zdnet.com/zdnn/content/zdnn/0410/306168.html>, (July 25, 2000).

15. Robert Cwiklik, "Ivory Tower Inc.: When Research and Lobbying Mix," *Wall Street Journal,* June 8, 1998.

16. Annabel Ferriman, "An End to Health Scares?" *British Medical Journal,* vol. 319, September 11, 1999, p. 716.

17. "State Ags Investigate Healthcare PR Alliances," *O'Dwyer's PR Services Report,* October 1999, p. 1.

18. Mark Megalli and Andy Friedman, *Masks of Deception. Corporate Front Groups in America* (Essential Information, 1991), p. 82.

19. Bob Burton, "Sometimes the Truth Leaks Out: Failed PR Campaigns 'Down Under,'" *PR Watch,* vol. 4, no. 4 (Fourth Quarter 1997).

20. Merrill Rose, "Activism in the 90s: Changing Roles for Public Relations," *Public Relations Quarterly,* vol. 36, no. 3 (1991), pp. 28–32.

21. Susan B. Trento, *The Power House: Robert Keith Gray and the Selling of Access and Influence in Washington* (New York: St. Martin's Press, 1992), p. 62.

22. Douglas Walton, *Appeal to Expert Opinion: Arguments from Authority* (University Park, PA: Pennsylvania State University Press, 1997), pp. 33–35.

23. Edward L. Bernays, *Public Relations* (Norman, OK: University of Oklahoma Press, 1952), pp. 163–164.

24. Jack O'Dwyer, "Hire a PR Firm to Get the Two 'I's'—Ink and Intelligence," *O'Dwyer's PR Services Report,* May 1997, p. 57.

25. Scott Cutlip, *The Unseen Power: Public Relations: A History* (Hillsdale, NJ: Lawrence Erlbaum Associates, Inc., 1994), p. 210.

26. Brian Tokar, "The Wise Use Backlash: Responding to Militant Anti-Environmentalism," *The Ecologist,* vol. 25, no. 4 (1995), p. 151.

27. *Jack O'Dwyer's Newsletter,* vol. 31, no. 36 (September 16, 1998), p. 8.

28. Neal Cohen, "Fine Tuning for Grassroots Effectiveness 1994," presentation to the Public Affairs Council National Grassroots Conference, February 1994.

29. Jennifer Sereno, talk to the Madison, Wisconsin chapter of the Public Relations Society of America, March 26, 1998.

30. Martin A. Lee and Norman Solomon, *Unreliable Sources: A Guide to Detecting Bias in the Media* (New York, NY: Carol Publishing, 1991), p. 66.

31. Trento, p. 233.

32. Kevin E. Foley, "Ethics and Sigma are in 'VNR Cartel,'" *O'Dwyer's PR Services Report,* April 1993, p. 13.

33. Debra Hauss, "Ways to Save Money on VNRs," *PR Week,* July 19, 1999, p. 24.

34. Darren Bosik, "TV Stations Desire Health, Medical VNRs the Most," *O'Dwyer's PR Services Report,* April 1991, p. 12.

35. Ted Anthony, "Film Review—Thirteenth Floor," Associated Press, May 27, 1999.

36. Walter Lippmann, *Public Opinion* (New York, NY: Free Press Paperbacks, 1997), pp. 27–28.

37. Ibid., p. 10.

38. Ibid., pp. 41–42.

39. Ibid., pp. 19–20.

40. Ibid., p. 241.

41. Ibid., p. 244.

42. Ibid., p. 251.

43. Ibid., p. 158.

44. "O'Dwyer's 1999 PR Buyer's Guide: Celebrities," *O'Dwyer's PR Services Report,* January 1999, p. 42.

45. Gerard F. Anderson and Jean-Pierre Poullier, "Health Spending, Access, and Outcomes: Trends in Industrialized Countries," *Health Affairs,* Vol. 18, No. 3 (May–June 1999), pp. 178–192.

46. "PR Pros Are Among Least Believable Public Figures," *O'Dwyer's PR Services Report,* August 1999, p. 1.

47. Ibid.

48. Randall Rothenberg, "The Age of Spin," *Esquire,* December 1996, p. 71.

CHAPTER 2: THE BIRTH OF SPIN

1. Thomas L. Haskell, "Power to the Experts" (review of Burton J. Bledstein's *The Culture of Professionalism*), *New York Review of Books,* October 13, 1977.

2. *Chicago Times-Herald,* October 22, 1897; University of Chicago, *University Record,* II (October 22, 1897), pp. 246–249.

3. Howard S. Miller *Dollars for Research: Science and Its Patrons in Nineteenth-Century America,* (Seattle, WA: University of Washington Press, 1970), p. 184.

4. Stephen F. Mason, *A History of the Sciences* (New York, NY: Macmillan, 1962), p. 591.

5. Ibid., p. 142.

6. Quoted in David F. Noble, *The Religion of Technology* (New York, NY: Penguin Books, 1997), p. 204.

7. Quoted in Lewis A. Coser, *Men of Ideas: A Sociologist's View* (New York, NY: Free Press, 1970), pp. 28–29.

8. Frank Fischer, *Technocracy and the Politics of Expertise* (Newbury Park, CA: Sage Publications, Inc., 1990), pp. 67–68.

9. Coser, pp. 150–152.

10. E. H. Carr, *Studies in Revolution* (New York: Grossett and Dunlap, 1964), p. 2. Cited in Fischer, p. 69.

11. Howard P. Segal, *Technological Utopianism in American Culture* (Chicago: University of Chicago Press, 1985), pp. 62–63. Cited in Fischer, p. 69.

12. Fischer, p. 69.

13. Ibid., pp. 74–75.

14. H. H. Gerth and C. W. Mills, trans. and eds., *From Max Weber, Essays in Sociology* (New York: Oxford University Press, Inc., 1947), pp. 232–233. In Coser, p. 174.

15. V. I. Lenin, "The Immediate Tasks of the Soviet Government," in *Lenin: Selected Works* (New York: International Publishers, 1971), p. 417. In Fischer, p. 303.

16. Fischer, pp. 125, 306, 335.

17. Ibid., p. 132.

18. Ibid., p. 84.

19. Quoted from Ralph Chaplin in Howard Scott, *Science Versus Chaos* (New York: Technocracy, Inc., 1933), foreword. In Fischer, p. 85.

20. Fischer, p. 86.

21. Frederick Lewis Allen, *Only Yesterday* (New York, NY: Bantam Books, 1959), pp. 69, 140.

22. Scott Cutlip, *The Unseen Power: Public Relations: A History* (Hillsdale, NJ: Lawrence Erlbaum Associates, Inc., 1994), pp. 170–176.

23. Irwin Ross, *The Image Merchants: The Fabulous World of Public Relations* (Garden City, NY: Doubleday & Co., Inc., 1959), pp. 51–52.

24. Ibid., p. 61.

25. Ibid., p. 52.

26. Edward L. Bernays, *Propaganda* (New York: 1928), p. 9.

27. Richard Swift, "One-Trick Pony" (interview with Stuart Ewen), *New Internationalist* 314 (July 1999), pp. 16–17.

28. Stuart Ewen, *PR! A Social History of Spin* (New York, NY: HarperCollins, 1996), pp. 9–10.

29. Bernays, *Crystallizing Public Opinion* (New York, NY: 1923), pp. 109, 122.

30. Ibid., p. 109.

31. Bernays, *Propaganda*, pp. 47–48.

32. Bernays, *Crystallizing Public Opinion,* p. 217.

33. Ibid., p. 122.

34. Cutlip, pp. 162–163.

35. Ibid., pp. 196–197.

36. "The Public Relations Counsel and Propaganda," *Propaganda Analysis* (Institute for Propaganda Analysis), August 1938, p. 62.

37. Cutlip, pp. 208–209.

38. Edward L. Bernays, *Biography of an Idea* (New York, NY: Simon and Schuster, 1965), p. 445.

39. Cutlip, p. 185.

40. Bernays, *Biography of an Idea*, p. 445.

41. Ibid., p. 446.

42. Ibid., p. 449.

43. Ibid., pp. 458–459.

44. Neil Baldwin, *Edison: Inventing the Century* (New York, NY: Hyperion, 1995), p. 396.

45. Cutlip, p. 207.

46. Bernays, *Biography of an Idea*, pp. 456–457.

47. Ibid., pp. 466, 468–472.

48. Ibid., p. 645.

CHAPTER 3: DECIDING WHAT YOU'LL SWALLOW

1. International Food Information Council, "How Americans Relate to Genetically Engineered Foods" (research report), September 14, 1992, pp. 1, 2.

2. Ibid., pp. 1, 4–5.

3. Ibid., p. 6.

4. Ibid., p. 13.

5. Ibid., p. 31, 32.

6. Libby Mikesell and Tom Stenzel, "Re: Refining the Dictionary" (memo to Biotech Research Core Team), International Food Information Council, October 28, 1992.

7. Robert Youngson, *Scientific Blunders: A Brief History of How Wrong Scientists Can Sometimes Be* (New York, NY: Carroll & Graf Publishers, Inc., 1998), p. 301.

8. Ibid., pp. 225–226. Isaac Asimov reached similar conclusions in his encyclopedic *New Guide to Science* (New York, NY: Basic Books, 1985), p. 845: "Psychoanalysis still remains an art rather than a science. Rigorously controlled experiments such as those conducted in physics and the other 'hard' sciences are, of course, exceedingly difficult in psychiatry. The practitioners must base their conclusions largely on intuition or subjective judgment. . . . Nor has it developed any all-embracing and generally accepted theory, comparable to the germ theory of infectious disease. In fact, there are almost as many schools of psychiatry as there are psychiatrists."

9. "Television Show Spotlights Major PR Controversies," *O'Dwyer's PR Services Report*, April 1991, p. 62.

10. Ibid.

11. Randall Rothenberg, "The Age of Spin," *Esquire*, December 1996, p. 71.

12. Jack O'Dwyer, "Marketing is Perception—Not Truth," *Jack O'Dwyer's Newsletter*, vol. 25, no. 8 (February 19, 1992), p. 7.

13. Rothenberg, p. 71.

14. "Cutlip Tells of Heroes and Goals Encountered in 55-Year PR Career," *O'Dwyer's PR Services Report,* May 1991, p. 12.

15. Rothenberg, p. 76.

16. William Greider, *Who Will Tell the People: The Betrayal of American Democracy* (New York, NY: Touchstone Books, 1992), p. 54.

17. James E. Lukaszewski, "When the Press Attacks: Should You Stonewall or Cooperate?" presentation at Media Relations '98, Marriott Marquis Hotel, New York, NY, April 27, 1998.

18. James E. Lukaszewski, "Face the Press: Media Training for Public Relations Professionals," presentation at Media Relations '98, Marriott Marquis Hotel, New York, NY, April 28, 1998.

19. Lukaszewski, "When the Press Attacks."

20. Lukaszewski, "Face the Press."

21. Ibid.

22. A news release based on the study is available at CSPI's website: <http://www.cspinet.org/nah/octfern.html>, (July 25, 2000).

23. PR Newswire, "Much Ado About Nothing—Sound Science Group Responds to the Latest CSPI Scare" (news release from The Advancement of Sound Science Coalition), February 21, 1996.

24. Ibid.

25. Bob Condor, "Dr. Robert Kushner" (interview), *Chicago Tribune,* July 18, 1999, p. 3.

PART TWO—RISKY BUSINESS (PREFACE)

1. Peter Bernstein, *Against the Gods: The Remarkable Story of Risk* (New York, NY: John Wiley & Sons, 1998).

2. Matthew White, Atlas—Wars and Democide of the Twentieth Century, <http://users.erols.com/mwhite28/war-1900.htm>, (July 25, 2000).

CHAPTER 4: DYING FOR A LIVING

1. Rachel Scott, *Muscle and Blood* (New York, NY: E. P. Dutton & Co., 1974), p. 293.

2. David Rosner and Gerald Markowitz, "Workers' Health and Safety—Some Historical Notes," in Rosner and Markowitz (eds.), *Dying for Work: Workers' Safety and Health in Twentieth-Century America* (Bloomington, IN: Indiana University Press, 1987), p. xvii.

3. Marie H. Bias-Jones, "For Survivors of the Hawk's Nest Tunnel, It Was Just a Job," *Charleston Gazette,* August 7, 1996, p. 4.

4. Scott, p. 175.

5. Rosner and Markowitz, p. xvii.

6. Abid Aslam, "Environment: New Book Records Neglect by Union Carbide," Inter Press Service, May 2, 1990.

7. Robert D. Bullard, *Unequal Protection* (San Francisco, CA: Sierra Club Books, 1994). Quoted in Craig Fluorney, "In the War for Justice, There's No Shortage of Environmental Fights," *Dallas Morning News,* July 3, 1994, p. 8J.

8. James L. Weeks, "Deadly Dust" (book review), *Science,* vol. 256, no. 5053 (April 3, 1992), p. 116.

9. Scott, p. 175.

10. Ibid.

11. Ibid., p. 179.

12. Gerald Markowitz and David Rosner, "The Reawakening of National Concern About Silicosis," *Public Health Reports,* vol. 113, no. 4 (July 17, 1998), p. 302.

13. "Preventing Silicosis and Death in Construction Workers," Centers for Disease Control and Prevention. Cited in James E. Roughton and John C. Pierdomenico, "Crystalline Silica: The New Asbestos," *Professional Safety,* vol. 43, no. 5 (May 1998), pp. 12–13.

14. Gardiner Harris, "Dust, Deception and Death," *Courier-Journal* (Louisville, KY), April 19, 1998, p. 01K.

15. Jim Morris, "Silicosis: A Slow Death," *Houston Chronicle,* August 9, 1992, p. A1.

16. Ibid.

17. Quoted in Markowitz and Rosner, "The Reawakening of National Concern About Silicosis," p. 302.

18. David Rosner and Gerald Markowitz, *Deadly Dust: Silicosis and the Politics of Occupational Disease in Twentieth Century America* (Princeton, NJ: Princeton University Press, 1991), p. 186.

19. Mark Savit, "Will Crystalline Silica Become the Next Asbestos?" *Aggman Online,* March and April 1997, <http://www.aggman.com/Pages/Agg397/Regulations397.html> and <http://www.aggman.com/Pages/Agg497/Opinion497.html>, (July 25, 2000).

20. Gerald Markowitz and David Rosner, "The Reawakening of National Concern About Silicosis," p. 302.

21. J. Paul Leigh, et al., "Occupational Injury and Illness in the United States: Estimates of Costs, Morbidity and Mortality," *Archives of Internal Medicine,* July 28, 1997, pp. 1357–1368.

22. William Serrin, "The Wages of Work," *The Nation,* vol. 252, no. 3 (January 28, 1991), p. 80.

23. David Kotelchuck, "Asbestosis—Science for Sale," *Science for the People,* v. 7, no. 5 (September 1995), p. 10.

24. Jim Morris, "Worked to Death," *Houston Chronicle,* October 9, 1994, p. A1.

25. Scott, p. 199.

26. David F. Noble, "The Chemistry of Risk," *Seven Days*, vol. 3, no. 7 (June 5, 1979), p. 24.

27. Ibid., p. 25.

28. Quoted in Scott, p. 40.

29. Scott, p. 41.

30. Serrin, p. 80.

31. William Graebner, "Hegemony Through Science: Information Engineering and Lead Toxicology, 1925–1965," in Rosner and Markowitz (eds.), *Dying for Work: Workers' Safety and Health in Twentieth-Century America* (Bloomington, IN: Indiana University Press, 1987), p. 143.

32. David Rosner and Gerald Markowitz, " 'A Gift of God'? The Public Health Controversy Over Leaded Gasoline in the 1920s," in Rosner and Markowitz, *Dying for Work*, p. 125.

33. Ibid., p. 128.

34. Ibid., p. 125.

35. Ibid., pp. 123–130.

36. Quoted in *Rachel's Environment & Health Weekly*, no. 539 (March 27, 1997).

37. Rosner and Markowitz, " 'A Gift of God'?" p. 131.

38. Ellen Ruppel Shell, "An Element of Doubt: Disinterested Research Casts Doubt on Claims that Lead Poisoning from Paint is Widespread Among American Children," *Atlantic Monthly*, vol. 276, no. 6 (Dec. 1995), p. 24.

39. Deborah Baldwin, "Heavy Metal," *Common Cause Magazine*, Summer 1992.

40. William Graebner, "Hegemony Through Science: Information Engineering and Lead Toxicology, 1925–1965," in Rosner and Markowitz, *Dying for Work*, p. 147.

41. Baldwin.

42. Ellen M. Perlmutter, "Pitt Scientist Prevails Over Lead, Critics, Wins $250,000 Heinz Award," *Pittsburgh Post-Gazette*, 12/1/95, p. A1.

43. Baldwin.

44. Ibid.

CHAPTER 5: PACKAGING THE BEAST

1. Karwoski and Courage Public Relations, "Karwoski & Courage—A Fable," <http://www.creativepr.com/fable.html>, (July 25, 2000).

2. Karen Silkwood was a chemical technician at the Kerr-McGee company's plutonium fuels production plant in Crescent, Oklahoma. An activist who was critical of plant safety, she died under suspicious circumstances. During the week prior to her death, she was reportedly gathering evidence to support her claim that the company was negligent in maintaining plant safety, and at the same time she was involved in a number of unexplained exposures to plutonium. On November 13, 1974, she was killed when

her car crashed into a concrete embankment en route to a meeting with a *New York Times* reporter to deliver documents proving her allegations about plant safety. Her files were never recovered from the wreck. Many people believe that her car was forced off the road, causing her death.

3. In 1990, local communities began organizing, and Ken Saro-Wiwa was chosen to head a new activist organization, MOSOP. After an angry mob killed four Ogoni opponents of MOSOP, the government arrested Ken Saro-Wiwa and the eight others, subjecting them to nine months of torture before convicting them of "inciting" the murders in a special military trial that was condemned as "fundamentally flawed and unfair" by international legal observers.

4. "Clear Thinking in Troubled Times" (Shell newspaper ad), quoted in "Clear Thinking," *Moneyclips,* November 21, 1995.

5. Andy Rowell, "Shell Shocked: Did the Shell Petroleum Company Silence Nigerian Environmentalist Ken Saro-Wiwa?" *The Village Voice,* November 21, 1995, p. 21.

6. Polly Ghazi, "Shell Refused to Help Saro-Wiwa Unless Protest Called Off," *The Observer* (London), November 19, 1995, p. 1.

7. Thomas Buckmaster, "Defusing Sensitive Issues Through Risk Communication," presentation at the Public Affairs Council's National Grassroots Conference for Corporate and Association Professionals, Key West, Florida, February 9–13, 1997. Quoted in *PR Watch,* vol. 4, no. 1 (first quarter 1997).

8. Daniel E. Geer, "Risk Management Is Where the Money Is," presentation to the Digital Commerce Society of Boston, November 3, 1998.

9. Ian Stewart, "Playing with Numbers," *Guardian* (London), March 28, 1996.

10. C. R. Cothern, W. A. Coniglio and W. L. Marcus, "Estimating Risk to Human Health," *Environmental Science and Technology,* vol. 20 (February 1986), p. 111.

11. Peter Montague, "The Waning Days of Risk Assessment," *Rachel's Environment and Health Weekly,* no. 652 (May 27, 1999).

12. David F. Noble, "Cost-Benefit Analysis," *Health/PAC Bulletin,* vol. 11, no. 6 (July/August 1980), p. 27.

13. Ibid., p. 30.

14. H.W. Lewis, *Technological Risk* (New York, NY: W.W. Norton & Co., 1990), pp. 43–45.

15. Ibid., pp. 45, 41.

16. Ibid., pp. 26, 48.

17. Steven Fink, *Crisis Management* (New York: American Management Association, 1986), pp. 169–170. An exact figure for the dead and injured does not exist. Estimates of the number of dead range from a low of 1,700 to a high of 4,500. The figure of 200,000 injured has been widely cited and is generally considered a conservative estimate.

18. Peter Sandman, "Speak Out: When Outrage Is a Hazard," essay on the Qest Consult-

ing Group website, <http://www.qest.com.au/downloads/speakout.doc>, (July 25, 2000).

19. Suketu Mehta, "After Bhopal: What Does It Mean to Take 'Moral Responsibility' for a Disaster?" *Village Voice,* December 10, 1996, p. 54. See also Wilbert Lepkowski, "Ten Years Later: Bhopal," *Chemical & Engineering News,* December 19, 1994, pp. 8–18.

20. Fink, pp. 169–170.

21. Geoffrey Bennet, *By Human Error: Disaster of a Century* (London: Seelcy, Service, 1961), p. 144.

22. Carl Sagan, "Galileo: To Launch or Not to Launch," October 9, 1989, <http://www.jpl.nasa.gov/cassini/rtg/sagan.htm>, (July 25, 2000).

23. Mark Carreau, "10 Years After Challenger, NASA Feels Shuttle Safety Never Better," *Houston Chronicle,* January 19, 1996, p. 1, <http://www.chron.com/content/chronicle/page1/96/01/21/shuttle.html>, (July 25, 2000).

24. "Crisis Busters," *PR Week,* May 17, 1999, p. 16.

25. Ibid., p. 17.

26. Gary Lewi, "How to Polish a Tarnished Reputation," presentation at Media Relations '98, Marriott Marquis Hotel, New York, NY, April 27, 1998.

27. Steve Crescenzo, "Fighting a Blitzkrieg: PR Firms Representing Swiss Authorities Find Themselves in a Foxhole," *Public Relations Tactics,* vol. 4, no. 7 (July 1997), pp. 1, 12.

28. *Public Relations Tactics,* November 1995.

29. Kathleen Fearn-Banks, *Crisis Communications: A Casebook Approach* (Mahwah, NJ: Lawrence Erlbaum Associates, 1996), pp. 149–150.

30. Larry Dobrow, "Got a Plan? H&K CD-ROM Simulates Crisis Exercise," *PR Week,* April 12, 1999, p. 5.

31. Larry Kamer, "Crisis Drill: Testing Your Company Before Disaster Strikes," presentation at Media Relations '98, Marriott Marquis Hotel, New York, NY, April 27, 1998.

32. Paul Holmes, "This Is a Drill," *Reputation Management,* May/June 1997, pp. 17–28.

33. Ibid., p. 27.

CHAPTER 6: PREVENTING PRECAUTION

1. Crisis Management Plan for the Clorox Company, 1991 Draft Prepared by Ketchum Public Relations. For further excerpts, see the appendix to our previous book, *Toxic Sludge Is Good for You!: Lies, Damn Lies and the Public Relations Industry* (Monroe, ME: Common Courage Press, 1995).

2. Charles Campbell, "Crisis Plan's Leak Smudges Clorox," *Los Angeles Times,* May 14, 1991, p. 9D.

3. Hank Baughman and Patty Tascarella, "Ketchum—Winning in the Age of Zapping," *Executive Report,* vol. 10, no. 5 (January 1992), sec. 1, p. 16.

4. Greenpeace scientist Pat Costner notes that sodium hypochlorite is problematic in two ways: "First, its production and use requires the continued production of elemental chlorine, the root source of effectively all anthropogenic dioxins as well as a known dioxin source in its own right. Secondly, some sodium hypochlorite has been found to be contaminated with dioxins," she says. However, notes former Greenpeace organizer Charlie Cray, "sodium hypochlorite is probably low down on the list of priorities for phasing out the various uses of chlorine, since other uses of chlorine are far greater in terms of their quantity, and since it is not as toxic, persistent and bioaccumulative in the environment." Quoted in Margo Robb, "Fwd: Re: chlorine," July 3, 2000, personal e-mail to Sheldon Rampton.

5. Carolyn Raffensperger and Joel Tickner, eds., *Protecting Public Health and the Environment: Implementing the Precautionary Principle* (Washington, D.C.: Island Press, 1999), p. 1.

6. Jean Halloran, "Re: Beef Hormones," May 27, 1999, personal e-mail to John Stauber.

7. Frederick Kirschenmann, "The Organic Rule: Risk Assessment vs. the Precautionary Principle," February 10, 1998, <http://www.pmac.net/nosfk5.htm>, (July 25, 2000).

8. Ibid.

9. Gregory Bond, Ph.D., M.P.H., "In Search of Balance Between Science and Societal Concerns in Shaping Environmental Health Policy," a presentation at the First Annual Isadore Bernstein Symposium, "Environmental Health Policy: Whither the Science?" March 12, 1999, University of Michigan School of Public Health, Ann Arbor, MI.

10. John O. Mongoven, "The Precautionary Principle," *eco.logic*, March 1995, pp. 14–16. *eco.logic* is a publication of the Environmental Conservation Organization, Hollow Rock, TN.

11. Ibid.

12. "MBD Profile," Mongoven, Biscoe & Duchin (undated).

13. "MBD—A Brief Description," Mongoven, Biscoe & Duchin (undated).

14. "Core Issues Monitored by MBD," Mongoven, Biscoe & Duchin (undated).

15. "MBD—A Brief Description."

16. "Table of Contents of Each Organizational Profile," Mongoven, Biscoe & Duchin (undated).

17. For examples of deceptive efforts by MBD and other PR firms to infiltrate and interrogate various activist groups, see Chapter 5, "Spies for Hire," in our previous book, *Toxic Sludge Is Good for You!: Lies, Damn Lies and the Public Relations Industry* (Monroe, ME: Common Courage Press, 1995), pp. 47–64.

18. Bartholomew Mongoven, Letter to the Wilderness Society, Sydney, Australia, January 25, 1995.

19. Samantha Sparks, "South Africa: U.S. Clergy Group Linked to Shell Oil," Inter Press

Service, October 7, 1987. See also "Ex-Nestlé Firm Goes Bankrupt," *O'Dwyer's PR Services,* November 1990, p. 1.

20. Alan Guebert, "Pork Battles: Pork Groups Pays Firm to 'Monitor' Other Ag Groups Using Checkoff Money," *The Pantagraph* (Bloomington, IL), February 9, 1997, p. E4.

21. "MBD Update and Analysis: Confidential For: Chlorine Chemistry Council," Mongoven, Biscoe & Duchin, May 18, 1994, p. 2.

22. "MBD Issue Research and Analysis: Activists and Chlorine in August," Mongoven, Biscoe & Duchin, 1994, pp. 1–2.

23. Ibid., pp. 1–4.

24. Ibid., pp. 5–6.

25. There are some 75 different types of dioxin, however, with varying levels of toxicity.

26. Leslie Roberts, "Flap Erupts Over Dioxin Meeting," *Science,* vol. 251, no. 4996 (February 22, 1991), p. 866.

27. "MBD Update and Analysis," p. 6.

28   Gordon Graff, "The Chlorine Controversy," *Technology Review,* vol. 98, no. 1 (January 1995), p. 54.

29. American Public Health Association, Policy Statement 9304, "Recognizing and Addressing the Environmental and Occupational Health Problems Posed by Chlorinated Organic Chemicals," *American Journal of Public Health,* vol. 84, no. 3 (March 1994), pp. 514–515. Quoted in *Rachel's Environment & Health Weekly,* no. 495, May 23, 1996.

30. Theo Colborn, Dianne Dumanoski, and John Peterson Myers, *Our Stolen Future: Are We Threatening Our Fertility, Intelligence, and Survival?—A Scientific Detective Story* (New York, NY: Dutton Books, 1996), pp. 185, 210.

31. Ibid., p. 218.

32. "Exposure to Environmental Chemicals: PR Hype or Public Health Concern," debate between Elizabeth Whelan, Peter Myers, and Theo Colborn, sponsored by Environmental Media Services, June 12, 1996.

33. Jack Mongoven, "Re: MBD Activist Report for August," memorandum to Clyde Greenert and Brad Lienhart, September 7, 1994.

34. "Summary of MBD Recommendations to CCC, August 1994," Mongoven, Biscoe & Duchin, p. 2.

35. Devra Lee Davis et al., "International Trends in Cancer Mortality in France, West Germany, Italy, Japan, England and Wales, and the USA," *Lancet,* vol. 336, no. 8713 (August 25, 1990), pp. 474–481.

36. Devra Lee Davis, Capitol Hill Hearing Testimony on Use of Estrogenic Pesticides and Breast Cancer, U.S. Congress Subcommittee on Health and the Environment, October 21, 1993.

37. Karen Wright, "Going by the Numbers," *New York Times,* December 15, 1991, section 6, p. 59.

38. Devra Lee Davis et al., "Medical Hypothesis: Xenoestrogens as Preventable Causes of Breast Cancer," *Environmental Health Perspectives,* vol. 101, no. 3 (October 1993), pp. 372–377.

39. Gayle Greene and Vicki Ratner, "A Toxic Link to Breast Cancer?" *The Nation,* vol. 258, no. 24 (June 20, 1994), p. 866.

40. Michael Castleman, "Despite Mounting Evidence," *Mother Jones,* no. 3, vol. 19 (May 1994), p. 33.

41. Mary S. Wolff et al., "Blood Levels of Organochlorine Residues and Risk of Breast Cancer," *Journal of the National Cancer Institute,* vol. 85, no. 8 (April 21, 1993), pp. 648–652.

42. F. Laden and D. J. Hunter, "Environmental Risk Factors and Female Breast Cancer," *Annual Review of Public Health,* vol. 19 (1998), pp. 101–123. See also N. Krieger et al., "Breast Cancer and Serum Organochlorines: A Prospective Study Among White, Black, and Asian Women," *Journal of the National Cancer Institute,* vol. 86, no. 8 (April 20, 1994), pp. 589–599.

43. E. J. Feuer et al., "The Lifetime Risk of Developing Breast Cancer," *Journal of the National Cancer Institute,* vol. 85, no. 11 (June 2, 1993), pp. 892–897. Lezak Shallat, "Up in Arms Over Breast Cancer," *Women's Health Journal,* January 1995, p. 31.

44. Davis, Capitol Hill Hearing Testimony.

45. Ibid.

46. Michele Landsberg, "Breast Cancer Battle Now Focuses on Deadly Chemicals," *Toronto Star,* July 20, 1997, p. A2.

47. Wright, "Going by the Numbers."

48. Michelle Slatalla, "The Lagging War on Breast Cancer," *Newsday,* October 3, 1993, p. 4.

49. Peter H. Stone, "From the K Street Corridor," *National Journal,* vol. 26, no. 51–52 (December 17, 1994), p. 2975.

50. Peter H. Stone, "Back Off!" *National Journal,* vol. 26, no. 45 (December 3, 1994), p. 2840.

51. Allison Lucas, "Health Studies Raise More Questions in Chlorine Dispute," *Chemical Week,* December 21, 1994, p. 26.

52. Joseph Walker, "Gender-Bending Chemicals," *Quill,* October 1996, FACSNET, <http://www.facsnet.org/tools/nbgs/a__thru__h/g/genderben.php3>, (July 25, 2000).

53. "MBD Update and Analysis," p. 10.

54. "Summary of MBD Recommendations to CCC," p. 3.

55. "Koch Hit With Record Fine for Pipeline Spills in Six States," *Octane Week,* January 24, 2000.

56. *ex femina, The Newsletter of the Independent Women's Forum,* special edition (May 1999), Washington, DC.

CHAPTER 7: ATTACK OF THE KILLER POTATOES

1. Alastair Thompson, "A Conversation with Robert Shapiro," State of the World Forum, October 28, 1998, <http://www.worldforum98.org/technology/article__shapiro2.html>, (October 30, 1998).

2. Pennie Taylor, "Smear Campaign Fails to Silence Scientist Who Spilled GM Beans," *Sunday Herald* (Scotland), May 23, 1999, p. 7.

3. B. G. Hammond, J. L. Vicini, G. F. Hartnell, et al., "The Feeding Value of Soybeans Fed to Rats, Chickens, Catfish and Dairy Cattle Is Not Altered by Genetic Incorporation of Glycophosphate-Tolerance," *Journal of Nutrition,* no. 126 (1996), pp. 717–727.

4. Arpad Pusztai, "SOAEFD Flexible Fund Project RO 818: Report of the Project Coordinator on Data Produced at the Rowett Research Institute (RRI), October 22, 1998, <http://www.rri.sari.ac.uk/gmo/ajp.htm>, (July 25, 2000).

5. Liane Clorfene-Casten, "FrankenFoods: Monsanto Engineers the Farming Biz," *Conscious Choice: The Journal of Ecology and Natural Living,* vol. 12, no. 5 (May 31, 1999), pp. 48–49.

6. Alan Rimmer, "I Have Been Crucified, Says Dr. Arpad Pusztai," *Sunday Mirror,* February 21, 1999, p. 7.

7. Ibid.

8. Arpad Pusztai, "Reply," December 9, 1999, personal e-mail to Sheldon Rampton.

9. Nigel Hawkes, "Scientist's Potato Alert Was False, Laboratory Admits," *The Times* (London), August 13, 1998.

10. Arpad Pusztai, "Your Book," November 23, 1999, personal e-mail to Sheldon Rampton.

11. Euan McColm, "Doctor's Monster Mistake," *Scottish Daily Record & Sunday Mail,* October 13, 1998, p. 6.

12. Charles Arthur, "The Strange Case of the Rats, the 'Cover-up' and a Political Hot Potato," *The Independent* (London), February 16, 1999, p. 3.

13. Charles Clover and Aisling Irwin, "Heartfelt Fears of the Whistleblower Who Spilled the Beans over GM," *The Daily Telegraph* (London), June 10, 1999, p. 4.

14. Christopher Leake and Lorraine Fraser, "Scientist in Frankenstein Food Alert Is Proved Right," *Mail on Sunday,* January 31, 1999, p. 20. Euan McColm, "Doctor's Monster Mistake," *Scottish Daily Record & Sunday Mail,* October 13,1998, p. 6.

15. Pennie Taylor, "GM Food Feud Comes to the Boil," *Sunday Herald* (Scotland), March 14, 1999, p. 3.

16. Ibid., and Charles Clover and Aisling Irwin, "Heartfelt Fears of the Whistleblower Who Spilled the Beans over GM," *The Daily Telegraph* (London), June 10, 1999, p. 4.

17. Geoffrey Lean, "How I Told the Truth and Was Sacked," *The Independent* (London), March 7, 1999, p. 11.

18. Christopher Leake, "Minister Blackened My Name Says Doctor," *Mail on Sunday* (London), February 14, 1999, p. 5.

19. Taylor, "Smear Campaign."

20. Stuart E. Eizenstat, testimony before the U.S. Senate Committee on Finance during hearings on his nomination to be Deputy Secretary of the Treasury, June 29, 1999.

21. For a review of the history and scientific issues pertaining to mad cow disease, see our previous book, *Mad Cow U.S.A.: Could the Nightmare Happen Here?* (Monroe, ME: Common Courage Press, 1997). For a specific discussion of the impact of the mad cow scandal on European opinions about biotech foods, see Frank Mitsch, *Ag Biotech: Thanks, But No Thanks?* Deutsche Banc, July 12, 1999, p. 6.

22. Sarah Ryle, "Food Furor: The Man With the Worst Job in Britain," *The Observer* (London), February 21, 1999, p. 13.

23. Howard J. Lewis, "Science Journalism Around the World: Vive la Difference!" *ScienceWriters* (newsletter of the National Association of Science Writers), vol. 48, no. 2 (Summer 1999), p. 12.

24. Ziauddin Sardar, "Loss of Innocence. Genetically Modified Foods," *New Statesman* (UK), No. 4425, vol. 129 (February 26, 1999), p. 47.

25. Tom Rhodes, "Bitter Harvest," *Sunday Times* (London), August 22, 1999.

26. Marian Burros, "Additives in Advice on Foods?" *New York Times,* November 15, 1995, p. C1.

27. James C. Barr and E. Linwood Tipton, letter to Mary Jane Wilkinson, February 8, 1996.

28. Dairy Coalition, "Dairy Coalition Has Meeting, Heated at Times, with *USA Today*" (memorandum), February 9, 1996.

29. Dairy Coalition, "Making Headway with the Media" (memorandum), February 23, 1996.

30. Ibid.

31. For further documentation of this point, see Larry Lebowitz, "Hormone-Free Milk? There's No Guarantee," *Fort Lauderdale Sun-Sentinel,* April 4, 1998, p. 1A.

32. Jennifer Nix, "Hard-Hitting TV News Hard to Get on Air," *Variety,* April 20–26, 1998, p. 5.

33. "Improving on Mother Nature?" *Consumer Reports,* vol. 60, no. 7 (July 1995), p. 480.

34. Michael Pollan, "Playing God in the Garden," *The New York Times Magazine,* October 25, 1998.

35. Phil Bereano and Florian Kraus, "The Politics of Genetically Engineered Foods: The United States Versus Europe," *Loka Alert* vol. 6, no. 7 (November 22, 1999), Loka Institute, Amherst, MA.

36. Clive James, "ISAA Briefs: Global Review of Commercialized Transgenic Crops," 1998, Ag Biotech InfoNet, <http://www.biotech-info.net/isaaa__briefs.html>, (July 25, 2000). See also Paul Jacobs, "Protest May Mow Down Trend to Alter Crops: Public Outcry Over Genetically Modified Foods Has the U.S. Agriculture Industry Backpedaling," *Los Angeles Times*, October 5, 1999; and Frank Mitsch, *Ag Biotech: Thanks, But No Thanks?* Deutsche Banc, July 12, 1999, p. 20.

37. "Greenwar" (editorial), *Wall Street Journal*, August 11, 1999.

38. John Vidal and David Hencke, "Genetic Food Facing Crisis," *The Guardian* (London), November 18, 1998.

39. Geoffrey Lean, "GM Foods—Victory for Grassroots Action," *The Independent* (London), May 3, 1999.

40. Quoted in Bereano and Kraus, "The Politics of Genetically Engineered Foods: The United States Versus Europe."

41. "Let the Harvest Begin" (attachment to a letter from Donald B. Easum of Global Business Access Ltd. on behalf of Monsanto), May 1998.

42. Claudia Parson, "Aid Agencies Say Biotechnology Won't End Hunger," Reuters, September 1998.

43. Charles Benbrook, "Evidence of the Magnitude and Consequences of the Roundup Ready Soybean Yield Drag from University-Based Varietal Trials in 1998," Ag BioTech InfoNet Technical Paper Number 1, July 13, 1999, <http://www.biotech-info.net/RR__yield__drag__98.pdf>, (July 25, 2000).

44. "Playing God in the Garden," *New York Times*, October 25, 1998.

45. "Allergies to Transgenic Foods" (editorial), *New England Journal of Medicine*, vol. 334, no. 11 (March 14, 1996), p. 726.

46. "Playing God in the Garden," *New York Times*, October 25, 1998.

47. Mary Challender, "Sufferers Hope to Get Word Out on L-Tryptophan Illness," *Des Moines Register*, October 12, 1993.

48. Ibid.

49. Arthur N. Mayeno et al., "Characterization of 'Peak E,' a Novel Amino Acid Associated with Eosinophilia-Myalgia Syndrome," *Science*, vol. 250, no. 4988 (December 21, 1990), pp. 1707–1708.

50. EMS was first identified as a disease syndrome in October 1989. FDA advisories and product recalls for L-tryptophan began in November 1989, with a more comprehensive recall issued in March 1990. For a brief synopsis of the process by which the disease was discovered and the FDA-initiated regulatory measures, see Stephen A. Gold et al., "The Clinical Impact of Adverse Event Reporting," in *Medscape Clinician Reviews*, vol. 7, no. 7 (1997).

51. For an attempt to ascertain what caused the disease, see Arthur N. Mayeno and Ger-

ald J. Gleich, "Eosinophilia-myalgia Syndrome and Tryptophan Production: A Cautionary Tale," *Trends in Biotechnology,* vol. 12, no. 9 (September 1994), pp. 346–352. Also see Hertzman, P.A., "L-tryptophan Related Eosinophilia-myalgia Syndrome," in *Drug and Device Induced Disease: Developing a Blueprint for the Future,* Proceedings of a MEDWATCH Conference, January 21–22, 1994, Rockville, MD, Food and Drug Administration.

52. Verlyn Klinkenborg, "Biotechnology and the Future of Agriculture," *New York Times,* December 8, 1997.

53. Statement delivered by Julian Edwards, Director General, Consumers International, before the Codex Committee on Food Labeling, 26th Session, Ottawa, Canada, May 26–29, 1998.

54. Karen Charman, "America for Sale: Destruction of the Heartland," unpublished master's thesis, 1994 (updated).

55. "New Study Backs Up Biotech Fears," Inter Press Service, September 4, 1998.

56. Carol Kaesuk Yoon, "Squash with Altered Genes Raises Fears of 'Superweeds,'" *New York Times,* November 3, 1999.

57. Terence Corcoran, "Attack of the Tomato Killers," *Financial Post* (Canada), May 8, 1999, p. C7.

58. David Barboza, "Biotech Companies Take On Critics of Gene-Altered Food," *New York Times,* November 12, 1999, p. 1.

59. "Greenwar" (editorial), *Wall Street Journal,* August 11, 1999.

60. Andy Coghlan and Kurt Kleiner, "Spud U Dislike," *New Scientist,* September 15, 1998, <http://www.newscientist.com/ns/980815/nspuds.html>, (July 25, 2000).

61. "Monster Mash," *New Scientist,* February 20, 1999, <http://www.newscientist.com/nsplus/insight/gmworld/gmfood/gmnews62.html>, (July 25, 2000).

62. Scott Kilman, "Food Fright: Biotech Scare Sweeps Europe, and Companies Wonder if U.S. Is Next," *Wall Street Journal,* October 7, 1999, p. A1.

63. "Biotech Crops Gain Favor on the Farm: Controversy Abroad Hasn't Slowed Planting," *St. Louis Post-Dispatch,* May 23, 1999. "U.S. Agriculture Loses Huge Markets Thanks to GMOs," *Reuters,* March 3, 1999.

64. Rick Weiss, "Food War Claims Its Casualties," *Washington Post,* September 12, 1999, p. A1.

65. Testimony of Tim Hume, board member of the National Corn Growers Association, before the Senate Agriculture Committee, October 7, 1999.

66. Jim Ostroff, "Genetically Modified Foods: Peril or Promise? U.S. Fight Over Bioengineering Starting to Take Shape—in Congress, in Stores, and in the Minds of Consumers," *Supermarket News,* October 25, 1999.

67. A. Birch et al., "Interactions Between Plant Resistance Genes, Pest Aphid Populations

and Beneficial Aphid Predators," 1996/1997 Scottish Crop Res. Inst. Annual Report, Dundee, pp. 68–72; A. Hilbeck et al., "Effects of Transgenic *Bacillus thuringiensis* Corn-Fed Prey on Mortality and Development Time of Immature *Chrysoperla carnea* (Neuroptera: Chrysopidae)," *Environmental Entomology* no. 27 (1998), pp. 480–487. Deepak Saxena, Saul Flores, and G. Stotzky, "Transgenic Plants: Insecticidal Toxin in Root Exudates from Bt Corn," *Nature,* no. 402 (December 2, 1999), p. 480.

68. John Frank, "Field of Bad Dreams," *PR Week,* July 5, 1999, p. 17.

69. "Butterflies and Bt Corn Pollen: Lab Research and Field Realities," Monsanto position paper, February 15, 2000.

70. Biotechnology Industry Organization, "Scientific Symposium to Show No Harm to Monarch Butterfly" (news release), November 2, 1999.

71. Robert Steyer, "Scientists Discount Threat to Butterflies from Altered Corn," *St. Louis Post-Dispatch,* November 2, 1999, p. A5.

72. Rebecca Goldburg, "Industry Manipulation of Research Results on Bt Corn and Monarchs," November 4, 1999, e-mail to distribution list.

73. Carol Kaesuk Yoon, "No Consensus on the Effects of Engineering on Corn Crops," *New York Times,* November 4, 1999.

74. David Barboza, "Biotech Companies Take on Critics of Gene-Altered Foods," *New York Times,* November 12, 1999, p. 1.

75. Camillo Fracassini, "Food Row: Scientist 'Sacked' Over Data Mistake," *The Scotsman,* August 13, 1998, p. 1.

76. S. W. B. Ewen and Arpad Pusztai, "Effects of Diets Containing Genetically Modified Potatoes Expressing Galanthus Nivalis Lectin on Rat Small Intestines," *The Lancet,* no. 354 (1999), pp. 1353–1354. Not all of Pusztai's research points to problems with GM foods. In 1999 he published a study in the *Journal of Nutrition* which examined the effect of a different lectin transgene inserted into peas and found no adverse affects. See Arpad Pusztai, G. Grant, S. Bardocz, R. Alonso, M. J. Chrispeels, H. E. Schroeder, L. M. Tabe and T. J. V. Higgins, "Expression of the Insecticidal Bean Alpha-amylase Inhibitor Transgene Has Minimal Detrimental Effect on the Nutritional Value of Peas Fed to Rats at 30% of the Diet," *Journal of Nutrition,* no. 129 (1999), pp. 1597–1603.

77. Robin McKie, "Why Britain's Scientific Establishment Got So Ratty with This Gentle Boffin," *The Observer,* October 17, 1999, p. 10.

78. Laurie Flynn and Michael Sean Gillard, "Pro-GM Food Scientist 'Threatened Editor,' " *The Guardian* (London), November 1, 1999.

79. "BetterFoods.org—Who We Are," <http://betterfoods.org/memlist.htm>, (July 25, 2000).

80. *1999 O'Dwyer's Directory of Public Relations Firms* (New York, NY: J. R. O'Dwyer Co.,

Inc., 1999) lists all clients but Philip Morris, who is listed in *1999 Washington Representatives* (New York, NY: Columbia Books, Inc., 1999).

81. Telephone interview by Karen Charman with Brian Sansoni, October 27, 1999.

82. Stephen Rouse, "GM Scientist Defends Himself on Internet," *Aberdeen Press and Journal,* June 14, 1999, p. 2.

83. Jose L. Domingo, "Health Risks of GM Foods: Many Opinions but Few Data," *Science,* vol. 288 (June 9, 2000), pp. 1748–1749.

PART THREE—THE EXPERTISE INDUSTRY (PREFACE)

1. Elizabeth MacDonald and Scot J. Paltrow, "Merry-Go-Round: Ernst & Young Advised the Client, but Not About Everything," *Wall Street Journal,* August 10, 1999, p. A1.

2. Ibid.

3. See Brian Martin, *Confronting the Experts* (Albany, NY: State University of New York Press, 1996), pp. 5, 175–176.

CHAPTER 8: THE BEST SCIENCE MONEY CAN BUY

1. Robert N. Proctor, *Cancer Wars: How Politics Shapes What We Know and Don't Know About Cancer* (New York, NY: Basic Books, 1995), p. 9,

2. Frank Wolfs, "Appendix E: Introduction to the Scientific Method," <http://teacher.nsrl.rochester.edu/phy__labs/AppendixE/AppendixE.html>, (July 25, 2000).

3. Karl Pearson, *The Grammar of Science* (London: MacMillan, 1896). A statistician, Pearson invented the chi-square test of statistical significance. "The scientific method," he wrote, "consists in the careful and often laborious classification of facts, the comparison of their relationships and sequences, and finally in the discovery by aid of the disciplined imagination of a brief statement or formula, which in a few words resumes a wide range of facts. Such a formula is called a scientific law" (*The Grammar of Science,* p. 77). "The man who classifies facts of any kind whatever, who sees their mutual relation and describes their sequences, is applying the scientific method and is a man of science," he stated. "The facts may belong to the past history of mankind, to the social statistics of our great cities, to the atmosphere of the most distant stars, to the digestive organs of a worm or to the life of a scarcely visible bacillus. It is not the facts themselves which make science, but the method by which they are dealt with" (*The Grammar of Science,* Part 1, 12). His preoccupation with statistical correlations made him a prominent exponent of the "biometrical movement," which sought to measure traits within populations, and also a leading figure in developing the racist pseudoscience of eugenics. "History shows me one way, and one way only, in which a high state of civilization has been produced," he stated, "namely the struggle of race with

race, and the survival of the physically and mentally fitter race. . . . My view—and I think it may be called the scientific view of a nation—is that of an organized whole, kept up to a high pitch of internal efficiency by insuring that its numbers are substantially recruited from the better stocks, and kept up to a high pitch of external efficiency by contest, chiefly by way of war with inferior races" (Karl Pearson, *National Life from the Standpoint of Science,* 2nd Edition, Cambridge: Cambridge University Press, 1919).

4. Gordon D. Hunter, *Scrapie and Mad Cow Disease* (New York: Vantage Press, 1993), pp. 25–26.

5. "Peer Review: Reforms Needed to Ensure Fairness in Federal Agency Grant Selection," General Accounting Office, June 24, 1994, GAO/PEMD-94-1.

6. Horace Freeland Judson, "Structural Transformations of the Sciences and the End of Peer Review," *Journal of the American Medical Association,* no. 272 (July 13, 1994), pp. 92–94.

7. Richard Smith, "Peer Review: Reform or Revolution?" *British Medical Journal,* no. 315 (1997), pp. 759–760.

8. David Hanners, "Scientists Were Paid to Write Letters: Tobacco Industry Sought to Discredit EPA Report," *St. Louis Pioneer Dispatch,* August 4, 1998.

9. Ibid.

10. Charles Ornstein, "Fen-phen Maker Accused of Funding Journal Articles," *Dallas Morning News,* May 23, 1999, p. 1A.

11. Ibid.

12. Robert Bell, *Impure Science: Fraud, Compromise and Political Influence in Scientific Research* (New York, NY: John Wiley & Sons, Inc., 1992), pp. 190–219.

13. Brooke T. Mossman and J. Bernard L. Gee, "Asbestos-related Diseases," *New England Journal of Medicine,* vol. 320, no. 26 (June 29, 1989), pp. 1721–1730. For a detailed critique of this incident, see Paul Brodeur and Bill Ravanesi, "Old Tricks," *The Networker* (newsletter of the Science and Environmental Health Network), June 1998.

14. For *NEJM*'s response to the controversy over this incident, see Marcia Angell and Jerome P. Kassirer, "Editorials and Conflicts of Interest," *New England Journal of Medicine,* no. 335 (1996), pp. 1055–1056. For the researchers' side, see JoAnn E. Mason, "Adventures in Scientific Discourse," *Epidemiology,* vol. 8, no. 3 (May 1997).

15. Jerry H. Berke, "Living Downstream" (book review), *New England Journal of Medicine,* no. 337 (1997), p. 1562.

16. Nate Blakeslee, "Carcinogenic Cornucopia," *Texas Observer,* January 30, 1998.

17. "Medical Journal Apologizes for Ethics Blunder," *Washington Post,* December 28, 1997.

18. Sheldon Krimsky et al., "Scientific Journals and Their Authors' Financial Interests: A Pilot Study," *Psychother Psychosom,* vol. 67, nos. 4–5 (July–October 1998), pp. 194–201.

19. Reported in Ralph T. King, "Medical Journals Rarely Disclose Researchers' Ties, Draw-

ing Ire," *Wall Street Journal,* February 2, 1999. See also Sheldon Krimsky, "Will Disclosure of Financial Interests Brighten the Image of Entrepreneurial Science?" (Abstract A-29), in *1999 AAAS Annual Meeting and Science Innovation Exposition: Challenges for a New Century,* C. J. Boyd, ed., American Association for the Advancement of Science.

20. Lisa A. Bero, Alison Galbraith, and Drummond Rennie, "The Publication of Sponsored Symposiums in Medical Journals," *New England Journal of Medicine,* vol. 327, no. 16 (October 15, 1992), pp. 1135–1140.

21. Cynthia Crossen, *Tainted Truth: The Manipulation of Fact in America* (New York: Simon & Schuster, 1994), pp. 183–184.

22. David Shenk, "Money + Science = Ethics Problems On Campus," *The Nation,* March 22, 1999, p. 14.

23. David Ozonoff, "The Political Economy of Cancer Research," *Science and Nature,* no. 2 (1979), p. 15.

24. Percy W. Bridgman, *Reflections of a Physicist* (New York: Philosophical Library, Inc., 1950), pp. 294–296, 299–300. Quoted in Lewis A. Coser, *Men of Ideas: A Sociologist's View* (New York, NY: Free Press, 1970), pp. 300–301.

25. Stephen Hilgartner, Richard C. Bell, and Rory O'Connor, *Nukespeak: The Selling of Nuclear Technology in America* (New York, NY: Penguin Books, 1983), pp. 25–35.

26. Coser, p. 306.

27. Ibid., p. 308.

28. Quoted in Susan Lederer, remarks at AAAS symposium on Secrecy in Science, MIT, Cambridge, MA, March 29, 1999.

29. Alvin M. Weinberg, "Social Institutions and Nuclear Energy," *Science,* vol. 177, no. 4043, July 7, 1972, p. 34. Quoted in Hilgartner, p. 58.

30. J. Gustave Speth, Arthur R. Tamplin, and Thomas B. Cochran, "Plutonium Recycle: The Fateful Step," *Bulletin of the Atomic Scientists,* vol. XXX, no. 9, November 1974, p. 20. Quoted in Hilgartner, p. 58. The half-life of plutonium, by the way, is 24,400 years.

31. *New York Times,* May 20, 1948, p. 2. Cited in Hilgartner, p. 101.

32. World Health Organization (WHO), *Mental Health Aspects of the Peaceful Uses of Atomic Energy,* Report of a Study Group, Technical Report Series no. 151, Geneva, 1958, p. 6. Also annex 1, "Statement of the Sub-committee on the Peaceful Uses of Atomic Energy of the World Federation for Mental Health, approved by the 25th Meeting of the Executive Board of the WFMH, London, 8–12 February 1957," pp. 47–48. Quoted in Hilgartner et al., p. 102.

33. Ibid., p. 31.

34. Ibid., pp. 31, 33.

35. Hilgartner, p. 103.

36. Ritchie Calder, *Living With the Atom* (Chicago: The University of Chicago Press, 1962), pp. 24–25. Quoted in Hilgartner et al., p. 103.

37. Dorothy Nelkin, *Science As Intellectual Property: Who Controls Scientific Research?* (New York, NY: Macmillan Publishing Co., 1984), pp. 85–86.

38. George Rathjens, "The Role of the Scientist in Military Preparedness," from Warfare in the 1990s (conference proceedings), October 1981, <http://itest.slu.edu/dloads/80s/warfare.txt>, (July 25, 2000).

39. Theodore H. White, "The Action Intellectuals," *Life,* June 9, June 16, June 23, 1967. Cited in Frank Fischer, *Technocracy and the Politics of Expertise* (Newbury Park, CA: Sage Publications, Inc., 1990), p. 152.

40. "U.S. Expenditures for Research and Development by Source of Funds and Performer," *Wall Street Journal Almanac 1999* (New York, NY: Ballantine Books, 1998), p. 363.

41. Dorothy Nelkin, *Science As Intellectual Property: Who Controls Scientific Research?* (New York, NY: Macmillan Publishing Co., 1984), pp. 18–21.

42. "Industry Trends in Research Support and Links to Public Research," National Science Board, 1998, <http://www.nsf.gov/pubs/1998/nsb9899/nsb9899.htm>, (July 25, 2000).

43. Melissa B. Robinson, "Medical School Faculty Say Budget Cuts Are Hurting Teaching," Associated Press, May 19, 1999.

44. Carl Irving, "UC Berkeley's Experiment in Research Funding," *National Crosstalk,* Fall 1999, <http://www.highereducation.org/crosstalk/ct1099/news1099-berkeley.html>, (July 25, 2000).

45. Ibid.

46. Remarks by Laura Nader, delivered at AAAS symposium on Secrecy in Science, MIT, Cambridge, MA, March 29, 1999, <http://www.aaas.org/spp/secrecy/Presents/nader.htm>, (July 25, 2000).

47. "Special Report: What Happens When Universities Become Businesses?" (Research Corporation Annual Report, 1997), p. 6.

48. Remarks by Martin Michaelson, delivered at AAAS symposium on Secrecy in Science, MIT, Cambridge, MA, March 29, 1999 <http://www.aaas.org/spp/secrecy/Presents/michael.htm>, (July 25, 2000).

49. Letter from Arthur Bueche to S. Dedijer, quoted in S. Dedijer, "Management Intelligence and Secrecy Management," in Manfred Schmutzer, *Technische Innovation* (Wien: Interdisziplinares Forschungszentrum, 1979), p. 119.

50. David Blumenthal et al., "Withholding Research Results in Academic Life Science," *Journal of the American Medical Association,* vol. 277, no. 15 (April 16, 1997).

51. Drummond Rennie, "Thyroid Storm" (editorial), *Journal of the American Medical Association,* vol. 277, no. 15 (April 16, 1997), p. 1242.

52. Ibid.

53. Shenk, pp. 11–12.

54. Robert Lee Hotz, "Secrecy Is Often the Price of Medical Research Funding," *Los Angeles Times,* May 18, 1999, p. A-1.

55. Richard A. Knox, "Disclosure Fight May Push Doctor Out of Occupational Health Field," *Boston Globe,* May 22, 1999, p. B5.

56. Richard A. Knox, "Science and Secrecy," *Boston Globe,* March 30, 1999, p. A3.

57. "Special Report: What Happens When Universities Become Businesses?" (Research Corporation Annual Report, 1997), p. 9.

58. Richard A. Davidson, "Source of Funding and Outcome of Clinical Trials," *Journal of General Internal Medicine,* vol. 12, no. 3 (May–June 1986), pp. 155–158. Quoted in Crossen, p. 169.

59. P. A. Rochon, J. H. Gurwitz, R. W. Simms, P. R. Fortin, D. T. Felson, K. L. Minaker, et al., "A Study of Manufacturer-Supported Trials of Nonsteroidal Anti-inflammatory Drugs in the Treatment of Arthritis," *Archives of Internal Medicine,* vol. 154, no. 2 (January 24, 1994), pp. 157–163.

60. Mildred K. Cho and Lisa A. Bero, "The Quality of Drug Studies Published in Symposium Proceedings," *Annals of Internal Medicine,* vol. 124, no. 5 (3/1/96), pp. 485–489.

61. Henry Thomas Stelfox et al., "Conflict of Interest in the Debate over Calcium-Channel Antagonists," *New England Journal of Medicine,* vol. 338, no. 2 (January 8, 1998), pp. 101–106.

62. M. Friedberg, B. Saffran, T. J. Stinson, W. Nelson, and C. L. Bennett, "Evaluation of Conflict of Interest in Economic Analyses of New Drugs Used in Oncology," *Journal of the American Medical Association,* vol. 282, no. 15 (October 20, 1999), pp. 1453–1457.

63. Dan Fagin and Marianne Lavelle, *Toxic Deception* (Secaucus, NJ: Birch Lane Press, 1996), pp. 51–52.

64. Neil D. Rosenberg, "Love Makes the World Go 'Round, and Cologne May Offer Some Help," *Milwaukee Journal Sentinel,* May 11, 1998, p. 1.

CHAPTER 9: THE JUNKYARD DOGS

Many of the documents cited in this chapter have been released into the public domain as a result of the legal settlement between the tobacco industry and U.S. state attorney generals. Each page of those documents has been assigned a unique "Bates number." They can be accessed from the documents websites of Philip Morris (www.pmdocs. com) and R. J. Reynolds (www.rjrt.com).

1. Michael A. Miles, Speech to the Economic Club of Chicago, February 9, 1993, Bates nos. 2501187852–2501187863.

2. Peter Huber, *Galileo's Revenge: Junk Science in the Courtroom* (New York, NY: Basic Books, 1991), pp. 2, 3.

3. Ibid., p. 33.

4. Memorandum from William M. H. Hammett, President, Manhattan Institute for Policy Research, to All Civil Justice Contacts, January 7, 1987. Quoted in Kenneth J. Chesebro, "Galileo's Retort: Peter Huber's Junk Scholarship," *The American University Law Review,* vol. 42, no. 4 (Summer 1993).

5. Marc Galanter, "Pick a Number, Any Number," *Am. Law,* April 1992, p. 84. Quoted in Chesebro, p. 1655.

6. Colin Stokes, "RJR's Support of Biomedical Research," 1981, Bates nos. 503082904–503082915.

7. Memorandum from William M. H. Hammett, quoted in Chesebro. Chesebro notes that funding for Huber's project at the Manhattan Institute comes from 14 of the nation's largest insurance companies, 16 of the biggest chemical and pharmaceutical manufacturers, and 21 of the largest industrial manufacturers. It is work that pays well. In 1993, Chesebro points out, Huber and two other employees at the Manhattan Institute's Judicial Studies Program were "slated to split $500,000 this year in salaries and benefits."

8. Peter Montague, "How They Lie, Pt. 3: The Alar Story," *Rachel's Environment & Health Weekly,* nos. 530–534 (January 23–February 20, 1997).

9. Ibid.

10. Howard Kurtz, "Dr. Whelan's Media Operation," *Columbia Journalism Review,* March/April 1990.

11. Ibid.

12. Janet Key, "Seeds of Debate Over Food Safety," *Chicago Tribune,* March 19, 1989.

13. H. S. Diehl, *Tobacco and Your Health: The Smoking Controversy* (1969), p. 1.

14. Memo from Tobacco Institute vice president Fred Panzer to president Horace Kornegay, May 1, 1972. Cited in Richard W. Pollay, "Propaganda, Puffing and the Public Interest," *Public Relations Review,* vol. XVI, no. 3, Fall 1990, p. 50.

15. Mike Moore, Attorney General, State of Mississippi in lawsuit filed on May 23, 1994.

16. Scott M. Cutlip, "The Tobacco Wars: A Matter of Public Relations Ethics," *Journal of Corporate Public Relations,* vol. 3 (1992–1993), p. 28.

17. Scott M. Cutlip, *The Unseen Power: Public Relations: A History* (Hillsdale, NJ: Lawrence Erlbaum Associates, 1994), p. 488.

18. Pollay, pp. 45–49.

19. Cutlip, *The Unseen Power,* p. 501.

20. Ibid.

21. Speech by Ellen Merlo to the Philip Morris USA vendor conference, January 25, 1994, Bates nos. 2024007050–2024007066.

22. Corporate Affairs 1994 Budget Presentation, October 21, 1993 (overhead slides), Bates nos. 2046847121–2046847137.

23. Covington and Burling (London), Report on the European Consultancy Program, March 1990, Bates nos. 2500048956–2500048969.

24. Ibid.

25. Ibid.

26. Huber eventually switched sides, agreeing in 1998 to testify in court for plaintiffs against the tobacco industry. His motives for switching, he said, included the death of his father from a smoking-related lung disease. "My daughter came to me and said, 'Dad, you've got to be careful. These guys are pimping you,' " he told *NBC Nightly News* reporter Bob Kur on March 4, 1998. For further details about Huber's defection, see Lee Hancock and Mark Curriden, "Researcher's Defection Sets Stage for Court Showdown With Tobacco Industry," *Buffalo News,* January 4, 1998, p. 11A.

27. For information about the institute's pro-tobacco bias, see R. G. Dunlop, "Lawmakers Refuse Close Look at Institute," *Courier-Journal* (Louisville, KY), July 31, 1996, p. 4A.

28. "Study's Tobacco Funding Hidden by School," *Austin American-Statesman,* November 16, 1997, p. B5.

29. Letter from Carrey Carruthers to Gary L. Huber, May 21, 1993, Bates nos. 2024233657–2024233658.

30. Letter from Gary L. Huber to Anthony J. Andrade, September 27, 1993, Bates no. 2024233656.

31. Proposal for the Organization of the Whitecoat Project, 1988, Bates nos. 2501474262–2501474265.

32. Corporate Affairs 1994 Budget Presentation, October 21, 1993, Bates nos. 2045521070–2045521111.

33. Craig L. Fuller, February Monthly Report to Michael A. Miles (Philip Morris Interoffice Correspondence), March 17, 1994, Bates nos. 2041424310–2041424316.

34. Task Force Review of Y&R ETS Materials, p. 1, Bates no. 2025835738.

35. Ellen Merlo, letter and contract to Margery Kraus, March 3, 1993, Bates nos. 2045930469–2045930472.

36. Victor Han, "Re: Burson/ETS," memo to Ellen Merlo, February 22, 1993, Bates nos. 2023920035–2023920040.

37. Ellen Merlo, Philip Morris Interoffice Correspondence, February 19, 1993, Bates nos. 2021252097–2021252110.

38. Letter from Margery Kraus to Vic Han, September 23, 1993, Bates nos. 2024233677–2024233682.

39. APCO Associates, "Revised Plan for the Public Launching of TASSC (Through 1993)," October 15, 1993, Bates nos. 2045930493–2045930504.

40. Jack Lenzi, "Re: TASSC Update," note to Ellen Merlo, November 15, 1993, Bates no. 2024233664.

41. Consumer Issues Program, Draft I., Bates nos. 2046039179–2046039194.

42. "National Watchdog Organization Launched to Fight Unsound Science Comes to Texas" (news release), December 3, 1993, Bates nos. 2046988980–2046988982.

43. Garry Carruthers and Donald Stedman, interview with KWMX 107.8-FM, "Mile High Magazine," Denver, CO, November 21, 1993, Bates nos. 2046988927–2046988943.

44. "Science: A Tool, Not a Weapon," Draft Advertorial #1, 1993, Bates nos. 2023332314–2023332316.

45. See, for example, "A Symposium: Doctors and Smoking: The Cigarette Century," *New York Times,* April 10, 1986, in which Koop stated, "For most of the past 20 or 30 years, we've been focusing our attention primarily on the smoker. But cigarette smoking is a cloud that has no silver lining. Smokers engage in mainstream smoking; the sidestream smoker involuntarily inhales smoke in the ambient air. . . . Both the sidestream smoker and the mainstream smoker are breathing in the same 4,000 or so constituents of cigarette smoke. . . . This ought to be alarming news for the two-thirds of the American adult population who do not smoke—or who think they do not smoke. They may have saved themselves from the stink and the mess of smoking, but they have not completely protected themselves from all of the health hazards. And that is at the heart of the movement by nonsmokers to ban smoking in virtually every public space."

46. 1994 Communications Plan, Bates nos. 2023918833–2023918852. See also Ellen Merlo, "Re: TASSC," memo to Matthew Winokur, April 29, 1994, Bates no. 2024233594.

47. Scientists for Sound Public Policy: Assessment Project and Symposium (slide presentation), Burson-Marsteller, Bates nos. 2028363773–2028363791.

48. Jim Lindheim, "Scientist Group in Europe," memorandum to David Greenberg and Matt Winokur, April 18, 1994, Bates nos. 2025493128–2025493129.

49. Margery Kraus, "Re: Sound Science/Lindheim Meeting/Next Steps," memorandum to David Greenberg and Matt Winoker, April 26, 1994, Bates nos. 2025493192–2025493194.

50. Tom Hockaday and Neal Cohen, "Re: Thoughts on TASSC Europe," memorandum to Matthew Winokur, March 25, 1994, Bates nos. 2024233595–2024233602.

51. Known corporate funders of ACSH have included American Cyanamid, American Meat Institute, Amoco, Anheuser-Busch, Archer Daniels Midland, Ashland Oil Foundation, Boise Cascade, Bristol-Myers Squibb, Burger King, Chevron, Ciba-Geigy, Coca-Cola, Consolidated Edison, Coors, Dow Chemical, DuPont, Exxon, Ford Motor Co., Frito-Lay, General Electric, General Mills, General Motors, Hershey Foods, Johnson & Johnson, Joseph E. Seagrams & Sons, the Kellogg Co., Kraft Foundation, Kraft General Foods, Merck Pharmaceuticals, Mobil, Monsanto, National Agricultural Chemicals Association, National Dairy Council, National Soft Drink Association, National Starch

and Chemical Foundation, Nestlé, NutraSweet Co. (owned by Monsanto), Oscar Mayer Foods, Pepsi-Cola, Pfizer, Procter & Gamble, Shell Oil, Sugar Association, Union Carbide Corp., Uniroyal Chemical Co., USX Corp., and Wine Growers of California.

52. Elizabeth M. Whelan, "Chemicals and Cancerphobia," *Society,* March/April 1981, p. 7. Cited in Stephen Hilgartner, "The Political Language of Risk: Defining Occupational Health," in Dorothy Nelkin, ed., *The Language of Risk: Conflicting Perspectives on Occupational Health* (Beverly Hills, CA: Sage), pp. 25–65.

53. *Daily Messenger,* Canandauigua, NY, December 8, 1997.

54. *Scranton Times,* Scranton, PA, September 12, 1997.

55. *Wall Street Journal,* August 26, 1997.

56. *Record,* Troy, NY, September 13, 1997.

57. *Orange County Register,* July 14, 1997.

58. *Washington Times,* June 18, 1997.

59. *Intelligencer,* Wheeling, WV, January 16, 1998.

60. *Agri-News,* Billings, MT, January 2, 1998.

61. *San Mateo County Times,* San Mateo, CA, August 1, 1997.

62. *Houston Chronicle,* Houston, TX, December 14, 1997.

63. Frederick Stare, letter to H. R. R. Wakeham, December 5, 1980, Bates nos. 1000283163–1000283164.

64. R. H. H. Wakeham, memorandum, January 5, 1981, Bates nos. 1000283166–1000283167.

65. Jane Fritsch, "Sometimes Lobbyists Strive to Keep Public in the Dark," *New York Times,* March 19, 1996.

66. Milloy claims that he has never personally engaged in lobbying. When pressed, he characterizes the EOP Group as a "regulatory consulting group" where all employees were registered as lobbyists "as a matter of course" in order to ensure compliance with federal law. According to the *Legal Times,* however, the EOP Group received $1,380,000 in lobby fees in 1997 alone. The *Political Finance & Lobby Reporter* gives some specific examples: "hired by Dow Elanco, Indianapolis, to lobby on legislation and regulations affecting the registration of pesticides; by the American Automobile Manufacturers Association, Washington, D.C., to lobby on global warming legislation; and by OHM Remediation Services Corp., Findlay, Ohio, to lobby with regard to a contract for toxic waste cleanup services." The EOP Group's methods of "regulatory consulting" featured prominently during the bribery and influence-peddling trial of former Clinton administration agriculture secretary Mike Espy, where it was disclosed that the EOP had hired Espy's girlfriend at a salary of $35,000 per year, even though her performance was, in the company's own estimation, "sporadic at best." While lobbying for forgiveness of a $286 million penalty owed by one of its clients in 1994, the EOP Group paid

a ticket scalper $6,600 so it could take Espy to the Super Bowl—a violation of federal ethics laws for which the client eventually paid a fine of $1 million. (Espy himself eventually beat the rap.)

67. "TASSC Names Executive Director" (news release), *PR Newswire,* March 3, 1997.

68. New Project (1993), Bates nos. 2046662829–2046662837.

69. J. Boland and T. Borelli, "Monthly Budget Supplement Re: ETS/OSHA Federal Activities" (Philip Morris Interoffice Correspondence, February 17, 1993, Bates nos. 2046597149–2046597150.

70. One of those reports, titled "Choices in Risk Assessment, the Role of Science Policy in the Environmental Risk Management Process," was prepared for Sandia National Laboratories. University of California–San Francisco professor Stanton Glantz, a prominent critic of the tobacco industry, scrutinized the report in 1996, noting that it was "mentioned many times" by tobacco industry witnesses in government hearings. "The organizations used to provide information for the report," he observed, "are dominated by industry associations which represent polluters (including the American Automobile Manufacturers Association, the American Petroleum Institute, the Chemical Manufacturers Association, the Halogenated Solvents Industry Association, the National Agricultural Chemicals Association, and many others). . . . Even though 'Choices' deals extensively with tobacco smoke as a science policy issue, they did not contact recognized governmental or previewed authorities in the preparation of the report (such as the Centers for Disease Control Office on Smoking and Health or various health groups such as the American Cancer Society)." Instead, "The authors of 'Choices' relied on several sources closely allied with the tobacco industry, including Philip Morris Companies, the Health Policy Institute, and ENVIRON Corporation." Stanton Glantz, Post-OSHA Hearings Comments, 1996 <http://www.tobacco.org/Misc/osha-post.html>, (July 25, 2000).

71. Barry Meier, "Tobacco Industry, Conciliatory in U.S., Goes on the Attack in the Third World," *New York Times,* January 18, 1998, section 1, p. 14.

72. Elizabeth Whelan, "Secondhand Facts?" (letter to the editor), *National Review,* July 28, 1997.

73. "Heritage, Brookings Get Top Rankings," *O'Dwyer's Washington Report,* vol. 9, no. 17, August 23, 1999, p. 4.

74. "Junk Science Makes Junk Law" (*New York Times* advertisement), Washington Legal Foundation, February 10, 1997.

75. "Tobacco Strategy," Bates nos. 2022887066–2022887072.

76. Neal Smith, "Organic Foods Can Make You Sick," *Des Moines Register,* March 12, 1999.

77. The Human Cost of Regulation: Reframing the Debate on Risk Management, Competitive Enterprise Institute, 1994, Bates nos. 2047099454–2047099464.

78. Thomas Borelli, "February Activity Report," Philip Morris Interoffice Correspondence to Jim Botticelli, February 1, 1994, Bates nos. 2046585282–2046585283.

79. Karen Anderson, "One Man's Demented Vision Becomes a Nation's Nightmare," *The DeWeese Report,* vol. 3, no. 12 (December 1997), p. 1.

80. Ellen Merlo, "Burson/ETS," memo to Victor Han, February 22, 1993, Bates nos. 2023920035–2023920040.

81. Holcomb B. Noble, "Hailed as a Surgeon General, Koop Criticized on Web Ethics," *New York Times,* September 4, 1999.

82. Holcomb B. Noble, "Koop Criticized for Role in Warning on Hospital Gloves," *New York Times,* October 29, 1999.

83. Ibid.

84. Marcy Gordon, "Koop Criticized for Contract," *AP Online,* October 29, 1999.

85. See, for example, a September 13, 1978, letter from R. J. Reynolds to William Shinn at the tobacco law firm of Shook, Hardy and Bacon, informing Shinn that Seitz had been invited to attend an informational presentation at the Tobacco Institute. "Dr. Seitz is doing some consulting work for us, and I thought the presentation would be of interest to him," the letter noted. "The fact that he is assisting us has not been publicly announced, so I do not wish to emphasize the fact at the meeting." (From the RJR documents website, Bates no. 503648881.) The articles of incorporation of the R. J. Reynolds Industries Foundation for Bio-medical Research, its research arm, list Seitz as a member of the founding board of directors. (Bates nos. 504480764–504480767.)

86. Alexander Holtzman, "Fred Seitz," Philip Morris Interoffice Correspondence to Bill Murray, August 31, 1989, Bates no. 2023266534.

87. Steve Young, "Tobacco Giant Questions EPA Study on Secondhand Smoke," CNN's *Moneyline* (transcript #930-3), June 24, 1993.

88. Multinational Business Services, Inc., Invoice #SPPM-0693 to Steven Parrish, Vice President and General Counsel of Philip Morris USA, June 1993, Bates nos. 2023593676–2023593679.

89. Craig L. Fuller, February Monthly Report to Michael A. Miles (Philip Morris Interoffice Correspondence), March 17, 1994, Bates nos. 2041424310–2041424316.

90. Edward S. Herman, *The Myth of the Liberal Media: An Edward Herman Reader* (New York: Peter Lang Publishing Inc., 2000), p. 235.

91. Ruth Conniff, "Warning: Feminism Is Hazardous to Your Health," *The Progressive,* vol. 61, no. 4 (April 1997), p. 33.

92. Huber, pp. 175, 187, 213.

93. Tom Holt, "Could Lawsuits be the Cure for Junk Science?" *Priorities* (American Council on Science and Health), vol. 7, no. 2 (1995).

94. Flier circulated by Ohio Farm Bureau during 1996 lobbying for Ohio's agricultural product disparagement law.

95. Holt, "Could Lawsuits Be the Cure for Junk Science?"

96. "ACSH Web Briefs," *News from ACSH,* vol. 8, no. 1 (2000), p. 7.

97. Francis Koschier, "Humpty Dumpty Sat on a Wall" (ACSH editorial), <http://www.acsh.org/press/editorials/ice__cream111099.html>, (July 25, 2000).

98. "ACSH Web Briefs."

99. Tobacco Strategy, March 1994, Bates nos. 2022887066–2022887072.

100. Dave Zweifel, "Media Snookered by Prof's Cancer Report," *Capital Times* (Madison, WI), June 8, 1992, p. 6A.

101. Elizabeth Whelan, "Cigarettes and Blurred Vision Among 'Right' Minded People," *Priorities* (American Council on Science and Health), vol. 6, no. 3, 1994.

CHAPTER 10: GLOBAL WARMING IS GOOD FOR YOU

1. Ross Gelbspan, *The Heat Is On: The Climate Crisis, the Coverup, the Prescription* (Cambridge, MA: Perseus Books, 1998), p. 154.

2. Quoted in Joseph L. Bast, Peter J. Hill, and Richard C. Rue, *Eco-Sanity: A Common-Sense Guide to Environmentalism* (Lanham, MD: Madison Books, 1994), p. 53.

3. Bernhard Stauffer, "Climate Change: Cornucopia of Ice Core Results," *Nature* 399:6735 (June 3, 1999), p. 412. See also Rick Callahan, "Humans Changing Climate," *Associated Press,* June 7, 1999.

4. Peter D. Ewins and D. James Baker, Open Letter, December 22, 1999.

5. Ross Gelbspan, *The Heat Is On: The High Stakes Battle Over Earth's Threatened Climate* (Reading, MA: Addison-Wesley Publishing Co., Inc., 1997), p. 155.

6. Ibid., pp. 154–155.

7. Lobbying Spending By Industry, 1998 data, Center for Responsive Politics <http://www.opensecrets.org/lobbyists/98industry.htm>, (July 25, 2000).

8. Philip Lesly, "Coping with Opposition Groups," *Public Relations Review,* vol. 18, no. 4 (1992), pp. 325–334.

9. Mary O'Driscoll, "Greenhouse Ads Target 'Low-income' Women, 'Less-educated' Men," *The Energy Daily,* vol. 19, no. 120, June 24, 1991, p. 1. Some journalistic accounts have alleged that Bracy Williams "ran" the ICE campaign, and indeed the PR firm played a prominent role. In 1998, Michael Bracy attempted to minimize this. "In the early 1990's, Bracy Williams and Company did a limited amount of work for one of the companies involved with ICE, but by no means did we form or 'run' the group," he stated. (Michael Bracy, personal e-mail correspondence with Tom Wheeler, July 23, 1998.)

10. "Inside Track: Sowing Seeds of Doubt in the Greenhouse," *Greenwire,* June 20, 1991. Also, Sheila Kaplan, "Cold Facts," *Legal Times,* July 1, 1991, p. 5.

11. Peter Montague, "Ignorance is Strength," *Rachel's Environment and Health Weekly,* no. 467, November 9, 1995.

12. Sharon Beder, *Global Spin: The Corporate Assault on Environmentalism* (White River Junction, VT: Chelsea Green Publishing Co., 1997), p. 94.

13. Gelbspan, p. 40.

14. The late Linus Pauling was one of the signers of the Heidelberg Appeal. The recipient of two Nobel Prizes (for chemistry and for peace), Pauling became associated in his later years with a controversial nutritional theory that advocated massive daily consumption of vitamin C. Although Pauling's earlier work is widely praised, his theories regarding vitamin C have been almost universally dismissed as pseudoscience. It appears, therefore, that (1) even Nobel laureates sometimes practice pseudoscience, and (2) even the practitioners of pseudoscience believe they are against it.

15. The Nobel Prize winners who have endorsed both the Heidelberg Appeal and the "World Scientists' Warning" are: Philip W. Anderson, Julius Axelrod, Baruj Benacerraf, Hans A. Bethe, James W. Black, Nicolaas Bloembergen, Thomas R. Cech, Stanley Cohen, John W. Cornforth, Jean Dausset, Johann Deisenhofer, Christian R. de Duve, Manfred Eigen, Richard R. Ernst, Donald A. Glaser, Herbert A. Hauptman, Dudley Herschbach, Antony Hewish, Roald Hoffmann, Robert Huber, Jerome Karle, John Kendrew, Klaus von Klitzing, Aaron Klug, Edwin G. Krebs, Leon M. Lederman, Yuan T. Lee, Jean-Marie Lehn, Wassily Leontief, Rita Levi-Montalcini, William N. Lipscomb, Simon van der Meer, Cesar Milstein, Joseph E. Murray, Daniel Nathans, Louis Neel, Erwin Neher, Marshall W. Nirenberg, George E. Palade, Max F. Perutz, John Polanyi, Ilya Prigogine, Heinrich Rohrer, Arthur L. Schawlow, Charles H. Townes, John Vane, Thomas H. Weller, Torsten N. Wiesel, and Robert W. Wilson.

16. World Scientists' Call for Action at the Kyoto Climate Summit, 1997.

17. David Olinger, "Cool to the Warnings of Global Warming's Dangers," *St. Petersburg Times,* July 29, 1996.

18. Hans Bulow and Poul-Eric Heilburth, "The Energy Conspiracy" (video documentary), Filmakers Library, 124 East 40th Street, New York, NY 10016.

19. Danish Broadcasting Corporation (DR1) report, cited in Christian Jensen, "Re: Fred Singer's Comment on Trenberth's Article," *naturalSCIENCE,* February 11, 1998, <http://naturalscience.com/ns/letters/ns__let08.html>.

20. Arthur B. Robinson, Sallie L. Baliunas, Willie Soon, and Zachary W. Robinson, "Environmental Effects of Increased Atmospheric Carbon Dioxide," George C. Marshall Institute, April 1998.

21. "Overview—Oregon Institute of Science and Medicine," <http://www.oism.org/>, (June 15, 1998).

22. Cresson Kearny, *Nuclear War Survival Skills,* Chapter 1, <http://www.oism.org/nwss/s73p912.htm>, (June 15, 1998).

23. Ross Gelbspan, "Putting the Globe at Risk," *The Nation,* November 30, 1998, p. 20.

24. David Malakoff, "Advocacy Mailing Draws Fire," *Science,* April 10, 1998, p. 195.

25. David Helvarg, "The Greenhouse Spin," *The Nation,* December 16, 1996, p. 21.

26. Malakoff, *Science,* April 10, 1998, p. 195.

27. "Top Scientist Denies Threat of Global Warming," *Vancouver Sun,* June 3, 1998, p. B2.

28. "Climate Change III· Academy Slams Skeptics' Petition," *National Journal's Daily Energy Briefing,* April 22, 1998.

29. Al Kamen, "A Chair for the Fallen," *Washington Post,* May 1, 1998, p. A13.

30. William K. Stevens, "Science Academy Disputes Attack on Global Warming," *New York Times,* p. A20.

31. Jake Thompson, "Spice Girl on Petition Hagel Touted," *Omaha World-Herald,* May 1, 1998, p. 12.

32. Ross Gelbspan, "Putting the Globe at Risk," *The Nation,* November 30, 1998, p. 20.

33. John H. Cushman, Jr., "Industrial Group Plans to Battle Climate Treaty," *New York Times,* April 26, 1998, p. 1.

34. "A Misinformation Campaign," *St. Louis Post-Dispatch,* April 23, 1998, p. B6.

35. Sharon Beder, Paul Brown and John Vidal, "Environment: Who Killed Kyoto?" *The Guardian* (London), October 29, 1997, p. 4.

36. "Panel Says Global Warming Is 'Real,'" *Business Wire,* June 13, 2000. See also Patrick Connole, "Global Warming Real and Worsening," *Reuters Online Service,* January 13, 2000.

37. National Oceanic and Atmospheric Administration, "1998 Warmest Year on Record, NOAA Announces," <http://www.publicaffairs.noaa.gov/releases99/jan99/noaa99-1.html>, (July 25, 2000).

38. As a result of these departures, GCC was forced to reorganize itself as an umbrella group of trade associations rather than of individual companies. By 1999, the science of global warming had become so robust that many companies saw their affiliation with the GCC as a public relations liability. However, it is likely that many will continue to undermine efforts to address the climate crisis through their various trade associations—for example, the American Petroleum Institute, the American Association of Automobile Manufacturers, the National Coal Foundation, and so on.

39. Seth Borenstein, "Experts Give Dire Warning About Changing Climate," Knight Ridder Newspapers, February 21, 2000.

40. The URLs are: www.greeningearthsociety.org, www.nhes.org, and www.co2science.org.

41. The URL is: www.globalwarmingcost.org.

CHAPTER 11: QUESTIONING AUTHORITY

1. Thomas Jefferson, *Writings* (New York, NY: Library of America, 1984), p. 493.

2. Stanley Milgram, *Obedience to Authority* (New York: Harper & Row, 1974), p. 20.

3. Donald Naftulin, John E. Ware, Jr., and Frank A. Donnelly, "The Doctor Fox Lecture: A Paradigm of Education Seduction," *Journal of Medical Education* 48 (1973): 630–636, p. 631.

4. Jathon Sapsford, Peter A. McKay, Mitchell Pacelle, and Bill Spindle, "Armstrong's Visions of Business Glory Collapse in Securities-Fraud Indictment," *Wall Street Journal*, September 15, 1999, pp. C1, C11.

5. Judy Treichel and Steve Frishman, "Sandman's Cagey Tactics," *PR Watch*, vol. 6, no. 2 (second quarter 1999).

6. Take, for example, the case of Milorganite, a fertilizer made from the city of Milwaukee's heat-dried sewage sludge. In 1987, researchers encountered a cluster of Lou Gehrig's disease among people who had been exposed to Milorganite. Lou Gehrig's disease normally kills 1.23 out of every 100,000 Americans, yet it hit three former members of the 1964 squad of the San Francisco 49ers football team, whose practice field had been fertilized with Milorganite. Subsequent investigations by the *Milwaukee Sentinel* found that 2 of 155 deaths among people who had worked at the city's Milorganite plant resulted from Lou Gehrig's disease. The *Sentinel* also turned up 25 other cases of the disease in Wisconsin residents who said they had been exposed to the fertilizer. But did these cases prove that Milorganite caused the disease, or were they merely an odd coincidence? The city brought in epidemiologists from Milwaukee's Medical College of Wisconsin and the U.S. Environmental Protection Agency. They reviewed death certificates for Wisconsin and found that the statewide rate of Lou Gehrig's disease was 1.90 per 100,000—slightly higher than the national average, but not enough of an increase to meet the standard of statistical significance. The epidemiologists gave Milorganite a clean bill of health, which is the scientifically correct conclusion. Does this mean that there is no link at all between Milorganite and Lou Gehrig's disease? Science simply has no way of answering that question. All it can say is that if there is a link, the risk appears to be low.

7. U.S. Atomic Energy Commission press release, remarks prepared for delivery at Founders' Day Dinner, National Association of Science Writers, September 16, 1954, p. 9. Cited in Stephen Hilgartner, Richard C. Bell, and Rory O'Connor, *Nukespeak: The Selling of Nuclear Technology in America* (New York, NY: Penguin Books, 1983), p. 44.

8. *Life,* November 20, 1970, p. 586, quoted in Theodor Roszak, *The Cult of Information: A Neo-Luddite Treatise on High-Tech, Artificial Intelligence, and the True Art of Thinking* (Berkeley, CA: University of California Press, 1994), p. 122.

9. Jeff Stier, " 'Flagging for Bias' Can Unfairly Taint Studies," *Wall Street Journal,* February 17, 1999.

10. Elizabeth Whelan, open letter to Ned Groth, August 16, 1999, <http://www.acsh.org/press/editorials/reply081699.html>, (July 25, 2000).

11. "Lobbyist Spending by Industry" (1998), Center for Responsive Politics, <http://www.opensecrets.org/lobbyists/98industry.htm>, (July 25, 2000).

12. Consumer Issues Program, Draft I. Bates nos. 2046039179–2046039194.

13. For details and further examples, see Carl Pope, "Going to Extremes: Anti-environmental Groups Hide Their Extremism," *Sierra,* vol. 80, no. 5 (1995), p. 14.

14. Joel Achenbach, "Putting All the X in One Basket," *Washington Post,* April 27, 1994, p. B1.

15. Tom Brazaitis, "Big Think Tanks Lead the Charge in Washington," *The Plain Dealer* (Cleveland), December 19, 1999, p. 1A. See also David Callahan, "$1 Billion for Ideas: Conservative Think Tanks in the 1990s," National Committee for Responsive Philanthropy, March 1999.

16. See, for example, Eric Nagourney, "Recipe for Health: Shaken, Not Stirred," *New York Times,* December 21, 1999, p. F8; and Lee Bowman, "Martini Recipe for Good Health?" *Houston Chronicle,* December 17, 1999, p. 32.

17. Richard E. Sclove, "Town Meetings on Technology," *Technology Review,* July 1996. Australian professor Brian Martin has also studied the use of citizen juries. He uses the term "demarchy" to contrast this decision-making process with the conventional methods of traditional representative democracy. For further information about his views on the subject, visit Martin's website at <http://www.uow.edu.au/arts/sts/bmartin/>, (July 25, 2000).

18. Richard E. Sclove and Madeleine L. Scammell, "Community-based Research in the United States" (summary), *Loka Alert* vol. 5, no. 4 (August 2, 1998).

19. John Doble and Amy Richardson, "You Don't Have to be a Rocket Scientist," *Technology Review,* vol. 95, no. 1 (January 1992), p. 51.

20. "Tackling the Question of Science Literacy," Education Report, Australian Broadcasting Corporation, April 17, 1996.

21. Terri Swearingen, speech upon acceptance of the Goldman Environmental Prize, San Francisco, CA, April 14, 1997.

22. Jake Tapper, "The Town that Haunts Al Gore," *Salon,* April 26, 2000.

23. Terri Swearingen, Goldman Environmental Prize speech.

24. Ibid.

INDEX

CENTER FOR MEDIA AND DEMOCRACY

This book is a project of the nonprofit Center for Media and Democracy, a public interest organization dedicated to investigative reporting on the hidden PR manipulations of government and industry. The Center publishes a quarterly journal, *PR Watch,* whose past issues are on web at www.prwatch.org.

The Center is an information resource for citizens, journalists, academics, and researchers. Funding comes from individuals and other nonprofit organizations; no business or government grants are accepted. If you are interested in subscribing to *PR Watch* or for more information contact:

Center for Media and Democracy
520 University Avenue, Suite #310
Madison, WI 53703
Phone (608) 260-9713
www.prwatch.org